Reading Alice Munro's Breakthrough Books

READING ALICE MUNRO'S BREAKTHROUGH BOOKS
A Suite in Four Voices

J.R. (Tim) Struthers
Ailsa Cox
Corinne Bigot
Catherine Sheldrick Ross

Edinburgh University Press is one of the leading university presses in the UK. We publish academic books and journals in our selected subject areas across the humanities and social sciences, combining cutting-edge scholarship with high editorial and production values to produce academic works of lasting importance. For more information visit our website: edinburghuniversitypress.com

© J.R. (Tim) Struthers, Ailsa Cox, Corinne Bigot, Catherine Sheldrick Ross, 2024
Introduction © Robert Thacker, 2024

Edinburgh University Press Ltd
13 Infirmary Street
Edinburgh EH1 1LT

Typeset in 10/12 Adobe Sabon by
Cheshire Typesetting Ltd, Cuddington, Cheshire, and
printed and bound in Great Britain

A CIP record for this book is available from the British Library

ISBN 978 1 3995 3452 9 (hardback)
ISBN 978 1 3995 3454 3 (webready PDF)
ISBN 978 1 3995 3455 0 (epub)

The right of J.R. (Tim) Struthers, Ailsa Cox, Corinne Bigot, Catherine Sheldrick Ross to be identified as Author of this work has been asserted in accordance with the Copyright, Designs and Patent Act 1988, and the Copyright and Related Rights Regulations 2003 (SI No. 2498)

Contents

Contributor Biographies　　　　　　　　　　　　　　　　　　　　vii
Acknowledgements　　　　　　　　　　　　　　　　　　　　　　　x

Introduction: Catch and Release – Alice Munro and 'the human palimpsest'　　1
Robert Thacker

Seeing in Circles: The Fierce Originality of *The Progress of Love* (1986)　　6
J.R. (Tim) Struthers
　1. Welcome to My House!　　　　　　　　　　　　　　　　　　　6
　2. Epic Inclusiveness in 'The Progress of Love'　　　　　　　　　　9
　3. Verbal Play in 'Lichen'　　　　　　　　　　　　　　　　　　23
　4. Ways of Knowing and Ways of Being in 'Monsieur les Deux
　　　Chapeaux'　　　　　　　　　　　　　　　　　　　　　　　34
　5. Did You Enjoy Your Visit?　　　　　　　　　　　　　　　　46

'The Old Order Changeth': Change, Renovation and Modernity in
Friend of My Youth (1990)　　　　　　　　　　　　　　　　　　51
Ailsa Cox
　1. Looking Through Binoculars: The Short Story Genre and Moments
　　　of Change　　　　　　　　　　　　　　　　　　　　　　　51
　2. Textual Instability in 'Differently'　　　　　　　　　　　　　55
　3. Approaching the First Three Stories　　　　　　　　　　　　61
　4. The Coda: 'Wigtime'　　　　　　　　　　　　　　　　　　77
　5. Reading Across a Short Story Collection　　　　　　　　　　81

The Art of Misreading; or, The Driving Force of Misunderstanding:
Open Secrets (1994)　　　　　　　　　　　　　　　　　　　　88
Corinne Bigot
　1. Introducing a Dark Collection　　　　　　　　　　　　　　88
　2. 'Open Secrets': Death by Landscape　　　　　　　　　　　　95
　3. Approaching the First Three Stories　　　　　　　　　　　　99
　4. 'Vandals' as Coda: On (Not) Reading Signs　　　　　　　　113
　5. The Art of Misreading　　　　　　　　　　　　　　　　　118

Rereading *The Love of a Good Woman* (1998) 127
Catherine Sheldrick Ross
   1. Introduction: 'An Extra Dimension to Life' 127
   2. 'The Love of a Good Woman': 'The Book Had Just Shifted This Much' 132
   3. 'Jakarta': 'A Place of Their Own' 147
   4. 'Cortes Island': Sources and Transformations 155
   5. What Ordinary Readers Say about Reading *The Love of a Good Woman* 164

Works Consulted 166
Index of Stories and Story Collections 186
General Index 189

Contributor Biographies

Ron Shuebrook is a Canadian artist who is Professor Emeritus at OCAD University in Toronto where he served as President from 2000 to 2005 and as Vice-President, Academic from 1998 to 2002. He has taught and been an administrator at six other Canadian universities and art schools and is a former President of the Royal Canadian Academy of Arts and a former President of the Universities Art Association of Canada. He received an honorary doctorate from OCAD University in 2005 as well as a Queen Elizabeth II Diamond Jubilee Medal in 2012. Shuebrook exhibits nationally and internationally and is represented by Olga Korper Gallery as well as other galleries. His work is in more than sixty public and corporate collections, including the National Gallery of Canada and the Art Gallery of Ontario, and in numerous private collections. An image of an untitled painting of his from 1989 (in the Art Gallery of Guelph collection) is reproduced in *Abstract Painting in Canada* by Roald Nasgaard. A pair of drawings by him from 2013 were used as the cover art for Guernica Editions' companion volumes *Clark Blaise: Essays on His Works* and *Clark Blaise: The Interviews* (2016). And a pair of paintings by him from 2017 were used as the cover art for Guernica Editions' companion volumes *Alice Munro Country* and *Alice Munro Everlasting* (2020). He lives in Guelph, Ontario and Blandford, Nova Scotia.

Robert Thacker is Charles A. Dana Professor of Canadian Studies and English Emeritus at St Lawrence University in Canton, New York. The author of over seventy-five academic articles on Alice Munro, Willa Cather, the North American West and Canadian Literature in English, his books include *The Great Prairie Fact and Literary Imagination* (1989), *Alice Munro: Writing Her Lives: A Biography* (2005; updated ed., 2011), *Reading Alice Munro, 1973–2013* (2016) and *Alice Munro's Late Style: "Writing is the Final Thing"* (2023). His Munro biography was completed with Ms Munro's co-operation and, at her request, he wrote the short Munro biography available on the Nobel Foundation website.

Beyond his own writing, Thacker has been widely active. He was the Editor of the *American Review of Canadian Studies* (1994–2002), edited two volumes of critical essays on Munro (*The Rest of the Story* [1999], *Alice Munro* [2016]), co-edited two volumes comparing the Canadian and the US West and co-edited three volumes of *Cather Studies*. He edited a volume of Cather's poems in the Alfred A. Knopf Everyman series (2013) and is one of three editors of the *Willa Cather Review*.

Largely because of his Munro work, in November 2023 Thacker was awarded the Donner Medal in Canadian Studies by the Association for Canadian Studies in the United States. He now lives in Fort Collins, Colorado.

J.R. (Tim) Struthers is highly respected throughout Canada and internationally by scholars and creative writers for his work as a bibliographer, an interviewer, a literary critic, an editor and publisher of Red Kite Press. To date he has edited some thirty volumes of theory, criticism, autobiography, short stories and poetry over a period, it amuses him to say, of six different decades. Among these titles are his important pair of edited collections published in 2020, *Alice Munro Country* and *Alice Munro Everlasting*. Tim has been publishing on Canadian literature for some fifty years, beginning, in 1975, with the first two scholarly articles worldwide on Alice Munro and including, in the past decade, ten more articles on Munro. He has conducted some forty interviews with Canadian writers, including two published interviews with Munro, and has been described by W.J. Keith, FRSC, as 'probably the best literary interviewer in Canada'.

Recognised for the delight he has taken in all of his publishing activities, and for the enthusiasm he has imparted as a university teacher, Tim also organised and hosted the largest celebration in history of Canadian literature and culture: the epic five-and-a-half-day and five-evening 'A Visionary Tradition' conference held in Guelph from 10 to 15 November 1999. He brought to a close on 31 August 2022 a fifty-year university teaching career, including some thirty-seven years full-time at the University of Guelph commencing appropriately for a Canadianist on Canada Day, 1 July 1985. Tim lives with the love of his life, short story writer and poet and Early Modern Literature scholar Marianne Micros, in Guelph, Ontario, Canada.

Ailsa Cox is Emerita Professor of Short Fiction at Edge Hill University in the United Kingdom. She is the author of *Alice Munro* (2004), *Writing Short Stories* (2005; 2nd ed., 2016) and, with Christine Lorre-Johnston, *The Mind's Eye: Alice Munro's Dance of the Happy Shades* (2015). In the past decade, she has published chapters on Munro in seven collections edited by short story specialists in Europe, Canada and the United States, including volumes edited by Maggie Awadalla and Paul March-Russell (2013), Charles E. May (2013), Jochen Achilles and Ina Bergmann (2015), Robert Thacker (2016), Janice Fiamengo and Gerald Lynch (2017), Christine Lorre-Johnston and Eleanora Rao (2018) and J.R. (Tim) Struthers (2020). Ailsa has also contributed essays to both *The Cambridge History of the English Short Story* (2016) and *The Edinburgh Companion to the Short Story in English* (2018). Along with her essay on 'Katherine Mansfield and the Short Story' in *The Bloomsbury Handbook to Katherine Mansfield* (2020), she has published two stories in the journal *Katherine Mansfield Studies* (2010, 2022). Additional short fiction has been widely published and collected as *The Real Louise and Other Stories* (2009). From its inception in 2011, she has been the editor of the peer-reviewed journal *Short Fiction in Theory & Practice*. She has also edited the collections *The Short Story* (2008) and *Teaching the Short Story* (2011).

Corinne Bigot has been publishing on Alice Munro's short stories for some fifteen years. She is currently Maîtresse de Conférences of postcolonial literatures at Université Toulouse Jean Jaurès in Toulouse, France, where she has been teaching full-time since 2016, having previously taught at Université Paris Nanterre for twelve years. She is the author of *Alice Munro, les silences de la nouvelle* (2014), and, with Catherine Lanone, *Sunlight and Shadow, Past and Present: Alice Munro's* Dance of the Happy Shades (2014). In addition, she has edited or co-edited two other volumes on Munro: *Alice Munro: Writing for Dear Life*, a special issue of *Commonwealth Essays and Studies* (2015), and, with Catherine Lanone, *"With a Roar from Underground": Alice Munro's* Dance of the Happy Shades (2015). Corinne has published work on Alice Munro's stories in a variety of books devoted to Munro and frequently in periodicals such as *Commonwealth Essays and Studies* and *The Journal of the Short Story in English* and *Short Fiction in Theory & Practice*. She has also been working on memory work in diasporic short fiction and life writing by women – including co-editing the two critical collections *Women's Life Writing and the Practice of Reading* (2019) and *Text and Image in Women's Life Writing: Picturing the Female Self* (2021).

Catherine Sheldrick Ross was Emerita Professor in the Faculty of Information and Media Studies at Western University in London, Ontario, Canada. Her previously published work on Alice Munro includes four critical articles, one interview, a television script for TVOntario and a brief biography, *Alice Munro: A Double Life* (1992). Her research expanded from a critical evaluation of literary works to studying the contexts of textual production and reception. Catherine and her graduate students conducted over 300 open-ended, qualitative interviews with pleasure readers on the reading experience. She drew on this corpus in numerous keynote speeches, presentations and workshops given worldwide and in four books: the co-authored *Reading Matters* (2006); the co-authored *Reading Still Matters* (2018); the chapter on 'The Readers' Advisory Interview' in *Conducting the Reference Interview* (3rd ed., 2019); and her equally instructive and delightful *The Pleasures of Reading: A Booklover's Alphabet* (2014). She also wrote a trilogy of educational books for children, later collected as the single-volume *Shapes in Math, Science and Nature: Squares, Triangles and Circles* (2014).

Recognition of Ross's contributions includes: the Science Writers of Canada Award (1996) for best science book written for children in Canada for *Squares*; the Margaret E. Monroe Award (2013) presented annually by the American Library Association for 'significant contributions to library adult services'; and Fellow of the Royal Society of Canada, Arts and Humanities (2018).

Acknowledgements

It's near-impossible in a short space to convey the range and the depth of our gratitude to so many good souls who have so strongly supported our work – and us personally – over the years we have taken preparing this book, not to mention before and beyond. To dear family members and dear friends, to much-appreciated critical and creative joint-labourers at home and at a distance, to enthusiastic admirers of Alice Munro and the short story everywhere, to generous library personnel in different parts of the world and notably at the University of Guelph, to the appreciative assessors of this book and the skilful folk at Edinburgh University Press. And especially to J.R. (Tim) Struthers' long-time very good-humoured but fierce personal editor, Kelsey McCallum, and his new adept and supportive additional personal editor, Zariha Fatima.

The following permissions have been kindly granted for the use of the epigraph by Alice Munro chosen to begin this book and the epigraphs by Catherine Sheldrick Ross and Eudora Welty used at the opening of the chapter by J.R. (Tim) Struthers.

By Jenny Munro on behalf of Alice Munro for the use of the quotation from the version of Munro's story 'Home' published in *74: New Canadian Stories*.

By Simon R.R. Davies on behalf of Catherine Sheldrick Ross for the use of the quotation from Ross's essay '"At the End of a Long Road": Alice Munro's "Dear Life"' published in *Alice Munro Everlasting: Essays on Her Works II*.

By Penguin Random House LLC for the use of the quotation from the version of Welty's 'How I Write' originally published in *The Virginia Quarterly Review*, 1955 (revised and reprinted as 'Writing and Analyzing a Story' in THE EYE OF THE STORY by Eudora Welty, copyright © 1978 by Eudora Welty). Used by permission of Random House, an imprint and division of Penguin Random House LLC. All rights reserved.

For Our Family Members and Dear Friends
Here and Beyond

'I want to do this with honour if I possibly can.'
Alice Munro, 'Home', *74: New Canadian Stories*

Introduction:
Catch and Release – Alice Munro and 'the human palimpsest'

Robert Thacker

In August 2001 I spent two days in Clinton, Ontario for my first formal interviews with Alice Munro towards the writing of a biography, *Alice Munro: Writing Her Lives* (2005; updated 2011). I had first met Munro in early 1983 in New York when Alfred A. Knopf had just published its edition of her fifth book, the story collection *The Moons of Jupiter* (1982), and had talked to or seen her a couple of times since, but the meeting in 2001 was the first one expressly for the biography. That book was not authorised but rather showed Munro's recognition that someone would come along and write a literary life soon – given that eventuality, she thought she would be better off to co-operate with a scholar known to her, so she agreed to talk to me as questions amassed. We met for this purpose in 2001, 2003 and 2004 – two days at a time – and she concurrently opened doors for me among her editors, agents, family and friends. We also talked on the phone.

I begin here with this first meeting for several reasons. Looking back now, it is clear that just then Munro was at what has been called a *caesura* moment by scholars of late style – a fulcrum point in her career. I have recently detailed these issues in my critical study *Alice Munro's Late Style: 'Writing is the Final Thing'* (2023). That August Munro was seventy years old. She had recently finished two of the new stories that were to appear first in 2002 in *The New Yorker* and then in what she called her 'family book', *The View from Castle Rock* (2006), 'Lying Under the Apple Tree' and 'Fathers'. Meeting me then Munro told me that she was not working on new stories but rather revising older pieces which had already appeared in serials (she mentioned memorial pieces like 'Home' [1974] and 'Working for a Living' [1981]), stories that she wanted to have better versions of since, just then too, she was thinking about her own mortality (see Thacker, *Late Style* viii, 3–5). Reasonably so, since that October she was due for heart surgery. And the day before our first meeting her author copies of her latest book, *Hateship, Friendship, Courtship, Loveship, Marriage* (2001), had arrived in Clinton. When we spoke, Munro had not yet opened them, a characteristic hesitation.

I had only learned of the title of that book a few days before when I had stopped in Toronto on my way to Clinton to meet with Douglas Gibson, Munro's editor at McClelland & Stewart. Laughing upon hearing it – the title story had not yet appeared in print, so this was my first knowledge of it – I commented to Gibson at once that, if you are Alice Munro, you can call a book anything you want.

When I got to Clinton I said the same thing to Munro, who schooled me in the children's game it referred to and asserted its aptness. Even so, once the book was published there came much comment – and a bit of confusion, really – about that title. So far as I know she herself never wavered as to its aptness, though her next book, *Runaway* (2004), featured nothing but single-word titles. The sort of wry joke she has shown herself inclined to.

During our August 2001 conversations, sessions during which Munro and I truly began to get to know one another, I offered her another title, one that I had recently noticed on a sign along a trout stream in Wyoming: Catch and Release. Remembering it, I told her it had then occurred to me that it sounded like a good Munro title. What her stories were about and did: capturing moments of being which, though held briefly, ultimately passed or were let go as life went on. Hearing it, joking, she replied: 'Catch and Release, wonderful. Just let me see about the *Hateship* business – can I get it cancelled?'

In numerous ways *The Moons of Jupiter* (1982) was harbinger to Munro's emerging and deepening style, a style accreting and expanding in the collections she published in the 1980s and 1990s. Acclaimed American short story writer Lorrie Moore sharply captures its qualities in her 2002 and 2004 reviews of Munro's *Hateship* (2001) and *Runaway* (2004), but in looking back to *Moons* subsequently, drilling into its more various offerings, she captures just where Munro was then, what she was doing and where she was going. A passage from Moore's introduction to the 2006 Penguin edition of *The Moons of Jupiter* gets right at these processes. With *Moons*, 'Munro began a transition to a kind of story that was less linear, more layered with the pentimento of memory, a narrative able to head through and into time, forward or backward, pulling in somewhere as a car might do simply to turn around. These are the haphazard migrations of life and love, she seems to say, and the theme of accident – happy or unhappy or both or neither – is something she visits in story after story' (Moore 214). Aptly too, given this, Moore alights on Munro's 'Accident' (1977) by way of her summation, noting how Munro shapes the whole of her character's life there to create her own conclusion. Catching the character Frances in her story, releasing her to the balance of her life at its end – 'But inside she's ticking away, all by herself, the same Frances who was there before any of it' (*Moons* 109) – Munro peels back the layering Moore sees, deepening her story of accident and its life-changing consequences as she offers it, creating, in Moore's phrase about the story 'Family Furnishings' in *Hateship*, a 'willing trade of the human for art' (Moore 138).

That 'Accident' is the story mentioned here is fitting, for that story was part of what was arguably Munro's first truly fecund period, a time characterised by great personal discovery and enormous productivity. By 1975 she had left her marriage (1951–76) in British Columbia and returned to her native Huron County, Ontario and there found her material, the place and the culture she had long contemplated and had written about from the West Coast (1952–73), lying all about. Judging by the outpouring of writing this move occasioned, this was, imaginatively, a critical change to her career (see Thacker, *Alice Munro* 224–90; Thacker, 'Alice Munro Country'). Another story from this period, 'The Ferguson Girls Must Never Marry', was published in *Grand Street* in 1982 but went uncollected despite enormous attempts at revision. Very importantly, however, discussing it with me in 2004, Munro said that when she wrote it she 'was on the verge of writing the complicated stories that came later', and she 'hadn't quite grasped how to do it' (Thacker interview 2004; see Thacker, *Late Style* 7–9, 184 n.2).

The title story of *The Moons of Jupiter* was in fact left over from the first, nearly published version of *Who Do You Think You Are?* in 1978. It is narrated in the first person in *Moons* by Janet, the same person who tells the two connected 'Chaddeleys and Flemings' stories that open the book. She is a writer who seems a very good deal like Alice Munro (though she was a painter in the *New Yorker* version), and each of the three stories ends without clear resolution, though a sung song is remembered and a clear recollection is left unconfirmed by subsequent searching. Janet's life, after the episodes told, continues. In 'The Moons of Jupiter' the reader last sees her returning to a hospital where her father will undergo heart surgery the next day. The reader never learns what happens.

These three stories and others beckon from *The Moons of Jupiter*, foretelling what Munro called 'the complicated stories' to come from the middle-phase collections highlighted in this book. Munro's phrasing, 'the complicated stories that came later', points directly to the effects produced by certain stories in *The Moons of Jupiter* and, following it and amplifying its effects, especially in the four collections studied in this book: *The Progress of Love* (1986), *Friend of My Youth* (1990), *Open Secrets* (1994) and *The Love of a Good Woman* (1998). Without venturing into the critical discussions offered here other than to express congratulations to each of the four authors for the work published in this book, I will now turn this introduction towards what I see as the salient biographical contexts surrounding the making and the reception of these four books. Together, they constitute what I would call a middle style within Alice Munro's career.

'The Moons of Jupiter' was Munro's third story to appear in *The New Yorker*, arguably the premier North American commercial magazine for serious short fiction. By the time of its publication there in May 1978 Munro had one of *The New Yorker*'s vaunted right-of-first-refusal contracts, so while the magazine saw most of the stories in *Who Do You Think You Are? / The Beggar Maid* (1978, 1979), it bought and first published only two ('Royal Beatings' [1977] and 'The Beggar Maid' [1977]). Besides the title story of *Moons*, *The New Yorker* bought four other stories of the twelve that were later collected in that volume ('Dulse' [1980], 'The Turkey Season' [1980], 'Prue' [1981] and 'Labor Day Dinner' [1981]). With the next collection, *The Progress of Love*, the first volume taken up in this critical study as a breakthrough book, Munro's placement rate at *The New Yorker* solidified. Of that book's eleven stories, five were bought and appeared in *The New Yorker*, the others going elsewhere to commercial magazines. With *Friend of My Youth*, eight of ten were first in *The New Yorker*, the other two in *The Atlantic Monthly*. *Open Secrets* saw all of its eight stories but one in *The New Yorker* – with these last two books, especially, Munro was on a tear at that magazine. Fewer stories from *The Love of a Good Woman* first appeared there (five of eight), but the title story was in *The New Yorker*'s 1996 holiday fiction issue connected to its cover illustration with almost thirty text pages given over to it. A singular fact.

This treatment for Munro's stories in such a well-regarded venue illustrates and emphasises just how her reputation had been established and was growing through and after *The Moons of Jupiter* during the 1980s and 1990s. With each volume too, individual stories drew immediate critical commentary from, it seemed, the moment of their first serial appearance. This was so especially of 'The Progress of Love' (1985) and 'Miles City, Montana' (1985) in *The Progress of Love*; 'Friend of My Youth' (1990) and 'Meneseteung' (1988) in *Friend of My Youth*; 'Carried Away' (1991) and 'The Albanian Virgin' (1994) in *Open Secrets*; and, most especially, 'The Love of a Good Woman', both in its showcased first appearance in *The New Yorker* and through its subsequent appearance as the opening story – all seventy-six pages of it – as the title story to its volume. What was also evident through these emergences was that Munro had set about remaking the short story as reading experience in ways that no one else has done. Writing in *The Guardian* in 2017, for instance, Tessa Hadley pointed to *Open Secrets* as 'The book that had the greatest influence on my writing', asserting that it 'helped me to begin. She's an extraordinarily innovative writer. The illusion of her stories is richly alive; and yet she's found a way of putting her authorial hesitations down on the page: is this really how it was? You can feel Munro's influence everywhere in contemporary fiction.'

All the stories just mentioned had such effects, probably most emphatically 'The Progress of Love', 'Meneseteung', 'The Albanian Virgin' and 'The Love of a Good Woman'. That last story, which saw a protracted editorial disagreement between Munro's agent Virginia Barber and the then fiction editor at *The New Yorker*, Bill Buford, as well as the magazine's chief editor, Tina Brown – they thought Munro's story just too long, despite its evident affecting powers – proved ultimately to be another harbinger of Munro's imaginative direction from her middle to her late style (see Thacker, *Alice Munro* 474–7). Beginning with *The Love of a Good Woman* each of her collections included a piece of novella length and texture.

Another way of gauging the provenance of the four volumes treated here is through the lens of biography. This shift should be seen in two ways, imaginatively and practically. Once Munro left her marriage in 1973 and returned to Ontario for good, she found herself newly confronting the sights, surfaces and culture of Ontario – and ultimately her native Huron County – in an entirely new and imaginative way. The effects of this were seen immediately in the three memoir stories she published in 1974: 'Home', 'The Ottawa Valley' and 'Winter Wind' – in them, Munro reasserts the details of her girlhood self in the last two and that of her contemporary remembering self in the first, but she does so in utterly new ways. In each of these stories, then in an ultimately failed photo text made up of descriptive vignettes entitled 'Places at Home', and then further in the fiction following in *Who Do You Think You Are? / The Beggar Maid* and in parts of *The Moons of Jupiter*, Munro was sharply engaged in a profound exploration of specific surfaces and depths of her native place, Huron County. She was seeing them anew, living among them as a then much more mature and experienced woman and writer than she had been when she was growing up there, the place she left in late 1951 when she was twenty. Munro did so in ways she had not done before. There, once she was back after 1975, Munro's subject was essentially a rediscovery of the mores, culture, sights and sounds, and history of her own home place, which, in an early interview, she described as 'RURAL Ontario. A closed rural society with a pretty homogeneous Scotch-Irish racial strain going slowly to decay' (Munro in Stainsby 30; see Thacker, *Alice Munro* 284–303; Thacker, *Late Style* 14–17; New; Weaver).

Speaking practically, by the time Munro turned to the making of *The Moons of Jupiter* what I have called her 'literary triumvirate' was in place. That is, her New York agent Virginia Barber who monitored her career and offered first response to completed stories; her Canadian editor Douglas Gibson at Macmillan of Canada and then at McClelland & Stewart; and her New York editor at Alfred A. Knopf, Ann Close. As stories were completed and were published in serials, they envisioned the next book and, when the time came, they worked together effectively to produce it in response to Munro's growing reputation and the evolution of her art. The three had first worked together on the making of *Who / The Beggar Maid* and then established working relationships. And with the right-of-first-refusal contract at *The New Yorker* its editors were, after Barber first saw Munro's new stories, her initial editorial response. Given the requirements of that contract and the editorial methods at the magazine, the *New Yorker* editors as a group responded to all the stories Munro completed and submitted through these years too.

What such circumstances did was to create a space that lent itself wholly to Munro's artistry. Attended to by professionals who knew that in her work they had something singular – talking about the *New Yorker* editors, for instance, Munro commented, 'Oh, that's it. Their belief in you, once they've subscribed to a belief in you, they really are going to go the limit with you' (Thacker interview Aug. 2001) – they all responded to her finished stories with verve, directness, and mostly, though not always, enthusiasm. Munro, in return, responded to them with revisions, fixes and her perpetual revised endings. By the time *The Moons of Jupiter* was completed all of them were off towards *The Progress of Love* and the ensuing three middle-style volumes highlighted here, as well as the further five beginning with *Hateship* in 2001, those I have seen as making up Munro's late style.

But whichever Munro story we choose to read, she is presenting there what Lorrie Moore calls 'the human palimpsest' (215), a story layered, one written to render the very facts of being itself. After having been caught by the story, having appreciated its details and felt its resonant correspondences to the feelings of being, we are released by Munro once more into the layers of the human palimpsest to continue our own lives within the mysteries of being we all share. So Alice Munro, so her supreme and everlasting art.

Seeing in Circles: The Fierce Originality of *The Progress of Love* (1986)

J.R. (Tim) Struthers

And it has been a long road – J.R. (Tim) Struthers notes that Munro has pulled off her magic trick of storytelling 148 times, and that's counting only the collected stories published in the fourteen volumes from *Dance of the Happy Shades* (1968) to *Dear Life* (2012). 'Dear Life' stands on its own as a dazzling story. But when considered in context, it's like throwing a stone into a still lake and watching the expanding circles extend out and out.
– Catherine Sheldrick Ross, '"At the End of a Long Road"' (39)

The eye is the first circle; the horizon which it forms is the second; and throughout nature this primary figure is repeated without end. It is the highest emblem in the cipher of the world. St. Augustine described the nature of God as a circle whose centre was everywhere, and its circumference nowhere. We are all our lifetime reading the copious sense of this first of forms.
– Ralph Waldo Emerson, 'Circles' (186)

Criticism can be an art too and may go deeper than its object, and more times around; it may pick up a story and waltz with it, so that it's never the same.
– Eudora Welty, 'How I Write' (245)

1. Welcome to My House!

Everybody knows what a house does, how it encloses space and makes connections between one enclosed space and another and presents what is outside in a new way. This is the nearest I can come to explaining what a story does for me, and what I want my stories to do for other people.
– Alice Munro, 'What Is Real?' (332)

As I see it, Munro's writing *as writing* can be divided into three phases: a first five strong but nevertheless in some respects (as laughable as this notion may sound) apprentice books beginning with *Dance of the Happy Shades* (1968), followed by a series of four breakthrough books, artistically speaking, starting with *The Progress of Love* (1986) through *Friend of My Youth* (1990) and *Open Secrets* (1994) to *The Love of a Good Woman* (1998), then by a final five mature and in places dazzling books concluding with *Dear Life* (2012). When I speak of four breakthrough books, I am in fact echoing the metaphor that Munro herself used in the first of my two interviews with her in which she described 'Royal Beatings', the opening story of her fourth book, *Who Do You Think You Are?* (1978), or as it was called outside Canada, *The Beggar Maid: Stories of Flo and Rose* (1979), as 'a *big* breakthrough story' (Munro in Struthers, 'The Real Material' 21; emphasis in orig.) for her artistically speaking – rather than in terms of it launching her international renown as a consequence of it being the first story she published in *The New Yorker*. And when I say that my concern is with Munro's writing *as writing*, what I mean, as I told my university students for a full fifty years, is that what we need to address as we read and discuss literature is not the still tiresomely cited aspects of 'representation' (which was given its own chapter – the very first, by the renowned scholar W.J.T. Mitchell – in Lentricchia and McLaughlin's influential *Critical Terms for Literary Study*) but rather those key features of what I like to call 'transfiguration' (a topic which was not included in that volume). Our attention, I propose, needs to be given wholly to the wonderful arrangements of actual and imagined details made possible by the astonishing skill with which writers handle elements of form and technique and style. For it's by those means that Alice Munro has so fully developed her art and allowed it to have the immediate and the profound impact on us that it does.

In examining a group of eleven stories written by the same author over a period of just a few years then collected in a single book, as is the case in studying *The Progress of Love* (1986), one might expect those stories to have major similarities and therefore assume that it would be easy to find a single approach relevant to discussing all of them. But to make this assumption is to forget that we are reading a writer who once good-humouredly chose to give a story with a highly metafictive opening the title 'Differently' in order to suggest the way Munro wanted to approach the short story as a genre: a writer whom we might therefore expect to approach every story at least a bit differently. Accordingly, classic approaches to reading the short story such as looking for commonalities in terms of the beginnings or the endings of the stories prove unsatisfying. Similarly, matters such as the overall narrative structure of each story or the narrative point of view from which each story is told are handled differently from one work to the next. For me as a reader, the challenge in finding a single means of approaching these stories consequently leads me to imagine myself, as I have frequently done from childhood through adulthood and as I like to consider Alice Munro having regularly done, standing on the beach at Goderich, Ontario, tossing a stone into Lake Huron, and watching the circles expand from the point where the stone entered the water. It's the widest, the most inclusive, of the circles, I tell myself, that I need to discern – as my old friend from the University of Western Ontario Catherine Sheldrick Ross, author of a book called *Circles: Fun Ideas for Getting A-Round in Math* (1993), likewise understood in pointing out the expanding nature of the closing title story of Munro's final collection *Dear Life* when it is seen in context. For me, that's reading Alice Munro's stories in these ways: as allegory, as meditation, as metafiction; as form, as technique, as style; as an act of narration, as an order in which a story is told, as a succession of weights; as wordplay, as metaphor, as allusion – acts of the imagination involving a consistent manner of writing that nevertheless has the flexibility to employ a variety of approaches in order to focus story by story on related but often different subjects.

As to my conception of *Reading Alice Munro's Breakthrough Books*, the idea goes back years and years to all those occasions repeated once or twice annually when I chose *The Progress of Love* as the story collection by Munro that I most wanted the students in my core second-year university seminar course in Critical Practices to read. Together with the steadily increasing significance for me of the *first* of this quartet of breakthrough books, *The Progress of Love* (1986), was my old friend and long-time fellow Munro critic Catherine Sheldrick Ross's alerting me to the profound importance artistically of the *fourth* of this quartet, *The Love of a Good Woman* (1998). My own and Catherine's excitement respectively about these two collections brought into focus a strong sense that, filled in by the two titles, *Friend of My Youth* (1990) and *Open Secrets* (1994), published in between, this group of four boldly innovative mid-career collections represented a set of breakthrough books not only for Munro but also for writers, readers, enthusiasts of the short story worldwide. I, along with Catherine, could write the opening and closing commentaries of the now-imagined book – and who better, I thought, to write the middle commentaries than Ailsa Cox, the founding and still-serving Editor-in-Chief of the leading-edge British critical journal *Short Fiction in Theory & Practice* (2011 ff.), long a superb critic of Munro, and herself a short story writer, and the distinguished French critic and Munro connoisseur Corinne Bigot. The subtitle for *Reading Alice Munro's Breakthrough Books* – so important, I believe, for immediately conveying the originality of the form of our book – occurred to me later: *A Suite in Four Voices*. 'Sweet' indeed, as my longtime personal editor, Kelsey McCallum, warmly and wittily replied when I told her.

And finally in these introductory comments, by way of a coda to this section devised in sonata-like form as a tip of the hat to the structure, I believe, of both the opening story, 'Walker Brothers Cowboy', and the closing story, 'Dance of the Happy Shades', of Munro's début volume *Dance of the Happy Shades* (1968), I wish to invite readers to take into account a favourite theory of mine as they consider the stories by Munro that we have chosen to emphasise through the design of each successive commentary in this book. It's a theory that extends an analogy offered by Alice Munro herself first in her brief essay 'What Is Real?', then again in the Introduction to the paperback edition of her *Selected Stories* (1996) later republished as *A Wilderness Station* (2015), where she described thinking of each story that she writes as a house. Building on Munro's analogy, I believe that we may view each story collection as a house and therefore may regard the opening piece of the book as the entrance way, a foyer, the place where your host greets you with an enthusiastic 'Welcome to my house!' and offers some sense of what you will find upon visiting the house's other parts – its mysteries, its intricacies, even its possible horrors such as 'the black room' that Munro warns us can be found 'at the centre of the house' (Munro, 'What Is Real?' 334). The place which she depicts so forcefully in the story 'Fits' from *The Progress of Love* through the older couple's dramatic murder/suicide and the intricate responses of the younger couple living next door. The room which metaphorically or allegorically speaking – as the Italian Munro critic Oriana Palusci states of the opening story, 'Dimensions', in Munro's *Too Much Happiness* (2009) – represents the powers of destruction or even 'the contaminating touch of evil' (Palusci 111).

2. Epic Inclusiveness in 'The Progress of Love'

I begin my actual analysis of *The Progress of Love* with the first story in the collection not out of simple convenience because it comes first but because of my long-held view that first stories have a special significance in story collections – as works that the author deliberately offers us first. In this way, we are invited to read the opening story as metafiction: as a consciously articulated and consciously placed statement and example by the author suggesting 'Here's a guide to how the stories that follow – as different as they are from one another in important respects – need to be read.' Beyond this very significant quality, the book's first story, 'The Progress of Love', also has a special connection to its last story, 'White Dump', though we don't realise that until we reach the final story. For both stories present the lives of three generations of women, a device that I believe gives *The Progress of Love* the expansive character of a Nordic saga or what Catherine Sheldrick Ross, speaking of these framing stories, calls its 'epic inclusiveness' (Ross, *Alice Munro* 88), a style newly developed by Munro here. Nor is it surprising that these two stories resemble a Nordic saga for the oldest woman in the final story, Denise's grandmother Sophie, is nicknamed 'Old Norse' after the name of that language because she reads *The Poetic Edda* each summer. And just as I believe that first stories (and last stories) have a special function in collections through conveying the author's sense of how the various stories work and how they need to be read (and of what the author wants us to continue contemplating), I believe that second and third stories are frequently chosen for special reasons, too. My theory of first, second and third stories derives from an analogy I favour to baseball: with the opening story or first pitch represented by a mesmerising fastball; the second story or second pitch being an off-speed curveball, that is, something different from the first and the third pitches; then the third story or third pitch, the strikeout pitch, represented by a confounding hard slider. Consequently, the third story often is the most challenging of the first three stories in a collection, as I believe 'Monsieur les Deux Chapeaux' and 'Meneseteung' and 'The Albanian Virgin' and arguably 'Cortes Island' are in the four volumes we discuss.

Definitely all stories must be read not simply in terms of plot but in terms of what Francine Prose emphasises in *Reading Like a Writer*: an act of narration designed for purposes that need to be closely considered (Prose 85–108) because, as E.D. Blodgett emphasises about Munro's methods, 'The narrative act ... is ... intimately related to the making of the self' (Blodgett 146). As Munro told Catherine Sheldrick Ross in response to a question about her approach to reading – and consequently, we may infer, her approach to writing – 'I don't think plot line ever mattered that much to me' (Munro in Ross, 'An Interview' 19). Emphasising story as an act of narration is a strategy Munro foregrounds in 'The Progress of Love' through the process of reconsideration of past events by the protagonist-narrator who since she has started working calls herself Fame, who as a youngster was known as Phemie, but who had originally been named after her maternal grandmother, Euphemia. Of the function of names, Magdalene Redekop argues that 'Names are ... places from which a close reader can trace historical corridors stretching far back in time' (Redekop, *Mothers* 28) – including back in literary history. Hence, it strikes me, the name that Munro has chosen for Fame's aunt Beryl surely represents an acknowledgement of the importance to Munro of her predecessor the lyric story writer Katherine Mansfield, whose novellas 'Prelude' and 'At the Bay', each including a character named Beryl, Munro has cited for special praise (Munro in Struthers, 'Remembrance Day 1988' 80). As Ailsa Cox observes, in Munro's stories 'Names are often charged with secret meanings' (Cox, *Alice Munro* 73). And of course, later in this collection the fascinating ramifications of different choices of words, names and even letters are highlighted by Munro through the way Jessie and her high-school friend MaryBeth adopt the fictional names with 'the special spelling' (166) identified in the title of the story that features them, 'Jesse and Meribeth'.

Beyond their general functions, names can also have more specific functions: here, for example, in Munro's choice of the name 'Euphemia' as a metaphor for what the act of narration can reveal or can suppress. Importantly, that name calls attention to the form of language known as a 'euphemism' by which individuals consciously or unconsciously substitute a pleasant, consoling term in place of a word or a phrase signifying something they find disturbing, even dreadful. Suggestively, at the very outset of 'The Progress of Love' Munro chooses to have Fame's father telephone his daughter and say, '"I think your mother's gone"' (3). As we come to realise, this brief instance of the use of a euphemism – replacing the harsher word 'dead' with the gentler word 'gone' – serves to introduce the way in which Fame herself, in narrating this story, chooses to substitute for the truth a personally much preferred though wholly imagined episode between her parents because the story that she eventually admits she has made up is so much more gratifying psychologically to her. Stories, in short, are not just what we read on the printed page but are also what we tell ourselves – often with great urgency and with significant implications – as Thomas King conveys so forcefully in *The Truth about Stories: A Native Narrative*.

As to the appropriateness of Munro's choice of the name Euphemia, on a strictly autobiographical level Munro herself, as Robert Thacker has pointed out, 'had a great-aunt named Euphemia' (Thacker, *Alice Munro* 24). Moreover, anybody travelling in Alice Munro Country and entering the lakeside town of Bayfield from the south as I have often done would notice that Euphemia is the name of the second street on the right as you come into town. The street, my friend and Huron County historian Reg Thompson informs me, was named after long-ago Bayfield resident Euphemia Cameron (McGregor), b. 1768 d. 1822 (Thompson, Message). In addition, it's interesting to note, given Munro's strong interest in her own Scottish background, that her choice of the name Euphemia may be viewed as an allusion to the late fourteenth-century Scottish queen consort, Euphemia de Ross, who, as the first Stewart (later Stuart) queen, was a direct ancestor of the famous sixteenth-century Scottish queen, Mary, Queen of Scots. And still more intriguingly in literary terms, the name Euphemia recalls that of a late third-century, early fourth-century saint and consequently suggests that here Munro may well be constructing a modern-day female version of the genre of the saint's legend. Reinforcing this notion is a detail Munro provides about how at one point as an adult Fame envisages changing her name to Joan – another link, we suspect, with a historic saint, the subsequently canonised fifteenth-century historical figure Joan of Arc. That figure is referenced later in this collection seemingly jokingly but in fact seriously by Munro in the novella 'A Queer Streak', where, in a further deft allusion by Munro, Violet explains to her nephew Dane that a new haircut she has been given is in '"a Joan of Arc style"' (247).

As significant as we appreciate the overall act of narration to be, the specific order in which different portions of a story are told or revealed can be all-important both in terms of what is gradually comprehended by the narrator and in terms of what is initially then eventually learned by the reader, which may be something more or different. This feature is especially noteworthy if the story is told in first person, as is the case not only with 'The Progress of Love', which in fact starts with the word 'I' (3), but also with, as Ailsa Cox points out in her commentary in this volume, the opening title story, 'Friend of My Youth', of Munro's next collection, which likewise begins with 'I' (3). Munro's choice of material for this story's first section, though it runs for less than a page, serves as a very effective beginning, since the details given about the narrator – that she works in a real-estate office, is divorced, and has two boys – prove to be much more telling than we at first realise. None of these details, as we eventually come to interpret them, functions merely literally or realistically; they are all metaphorical or allegorical – just as W.R. Martin argues of 'The Progress of Love' that 'The title itself points to an allegorical structure' (Martin 177). By way of suggesting Munro's interest in matters allegorical, we may note that much as her very important predecessor James Joyce considered himself to be strongly influenced by the great allegorist Dante Alighieri, so she has chosen to call one character here simply Mr Florence – a surname identical to the birthplace of Dante. In what we may regard as the story's widening circles of meaning, Fame's position working in a real-estate office stands as a metaphor for her continued psychological search for a home; her status as a divorcée accounts for her need to see her parents' marriage as wholly devoted and happy; and the fact that she has two sons allows a three-generational female family curse to be ended.

Another important quality that we need to appreciate when reading – besides the act of narration and the order in which a story is told – is what Kent Thompson in his brief essay 'Academy Stuff' has called the respective 'weights' (Thompson 74) given to different parts of a story – with those 'weights' being determined by the length and the kind of attention given to each and by the order in which they are presented. For example, the fact that early in 'The Progress of Love' Munro devotes a full five pages (one-sixth of the story) to Fame's mother Marietta's childhood and the particular incident involving Marietta's mother Euphemia's near-hanging or mock-hanging as experienced by Marietta and her younger sister, Beryl, back when the two of them were both little girls. Fame recounts first one version by her mother then a second version by her aunt of the story about her grandmother, beginning – misleadingly we might say, on the part of both Fame and Munro, the former for psychological reasons and the latter for artistic reasons – with the comment by Fame suggesting that the incident involved an actual attempt by her grandmother at 'hanging herself' (9) not a probable melodramatic theatrical gesture. As we learn, Euphemia decided to get even with her husband for his presumed philandering by apparently hanging herself in the barn – Euphemia being discovered with a rope strung over a beam by the young Marietta, who in her desperation went tearing off downtown in search, unsuccessfully, of her father. Upon returning home, she found her mother recovering in the care of their next-door-neighbour Mrs Sutcliffe, but for the rest of her life Marietta continued to experience both the unmitigated terror of this event and a resulting undiminished hatred for her father.

With the gradual unfolding of what Magdalene Redekop aptly terms 'the *now* of narration' (Redekop, *Mothers* 180), we are invited to consider the two versions – or the two stories we may say – of Euphemia's apparent suicide attempt or mock-suicide. Here, as I have suggested, the order in which the protagonist-narrator or Munro chooses to present events is of great significance. The fact that Marietta's terrified response is depicted pages before Beryl's light-hearted response is all-important; as it turns out, Marietta had been fooled by the seeming dreadfulness of the scene that Euphemia had staged with the intention of shocking her husband. But Beryl hadn't been fooled: as she asserts during the no doubt by Munro symbolically if ironically set Sunday dinner to which Beryl and Mr Florence – her 'man friend' (14), another euphemism – treat the young Fame and her mother and father at the Wildwood Inn, '"I was just a little squirt, but I was the one noticed that rope. . . . I saw it was just hanging over the beam, just flung there – it wasn't tied at all!"' (22). Beryl characterises their mother's action as a '"game"' (22), yet acknowledges that their mother '"could carry a joke too far"' (21); Marietta, however, contends that their mother '"meant it more than you give her credit for"' (22).

But deciding one way or another is for Munro and consequently for the story's readers far from a simple matter of black versus white; hence, I believe, Munro's decision to have a symbolic 'black-and-white cat' (13) present at the home of Mrs Sutcliffe when she comforts Marietta following the episode in the barn. During the Sunday dinner at the Wildwood Inn, Fame's father remarks that '"People are dead now"' and '"It isn't up to us to judge"' (22). But judgement – allegorically, the equivalent of a Last Judgment – is precisely what Fame in the acts of recollection and meditation and narration finds herself struggling to reach. An opportunity for meditation on Munro's part, on Fame's part and on the reader's part is what the story permits; hence on one level, as Robert Thacker remarks, the story presents 'a comparison of the lives of three women' that allows for 'a meditation on mothers and daughters' (Thacker, *Reading Alice Munro* 234). Yet furthermore, on arguably a still more important level, 'The Progress of Love' invites reflection on the very nature of judgement, which, as Clark Blaise emphasises in his essay 'The Justice-Dealing Machine', is precisely the force that the short story as a genre is meant to wield.

Fame reflects at length on the two accounts or interpretations of the story about her grandmother Euphemia's apparent suicide attempt or mock-suicide: Fame's mother Marietta's version as recounted presumably during the scene when the two of them wallpapered the front room of the family farmhouse and Fame's aunt Beryl's version as told by her during the meal at the Wildwood Inn. 'I didn't have a problem right away with Beryl's story' (23), Fame notes, a comment that prompts us to speculate why Fame might subsequently have had 'a problem' with Beryl's light-hearted version of the impact that her father's presumed dalliances had on Euphemia – based perhaps on the sorrowful nature of Fame's own marriage and divorce and her resulting increase in empathy for her grandmother, we may wonder? Like a significant number of subsequent stories in this volume – including the next four, 'Lichen' and 'Monsieur les Deux Chapeaux' and 'Miles City, Montana' and 'Fits', along with the book's final selection, 'White Dump' – the title story can in one respect be said to belong to the subgenre of what I'll term 'divorce stories'. Of Marietta's and Beryl's accounts, Fame observes: 'Why shouldn't Beryl's version of the same event be different from my mother's?' (23). Fame adds that 'It was my mother's version that held, for a time. It absorbed Beryl's story, closed over it. But Beryl's story didn't vanish; it stayed sealed off for years, but it wasn't gone' (23) – suggesting that with time Fame came to replace a more tragic and ironic view with a more comic and romantic view.

Alice Munro has always felt that a necessary quality of a short story for her, indeed perhaps the most important quality of a short story for her, is 'the tension' (Munro in Struthers, 'The Real Material' 15), a feature of her writing represented in this opening story in various ways. Perhaps most noticeably by the two versions – Marietta's much darker gothic-like conception (to invoke one genre) and Beryl's much lighter farce-like conception (to invoke another genre) – of Euphemia's apparent suicide attempt. But also by the two versions (the invented one that Fame maintains for so long in her mind as being true and the real one that Fame eventually admits as being true) of her mother's burning of the money. And by the distinction between Fame's imagined view of her parents' relationship and the real view of it which she eventually gains: 'where love and grudges could be growing underground' (31), with the phrase 'love and grudges' so concisely capturing Munro's fascination with and use of tension. But why, we ask, did the much darker gothic-like version carried and transmitted by Fame's mother Marietta eventually relinquish its hold on Fame? Has she, through the act of narration, attained some new knowledge, reached some new resolution, in terms of her relationship with her significantly now-deceased mother, which allows Fame to embrace something closer to the comic and romantic vision modelled and promoted by her aunt? No doubt there's something appealing personally to Fame (and aesthetically to Munro), in terms of a way of perceiving the world, about the fact that everything to do with Beryl, as Fame comments, 'was slanted, seen from a new angle' – the likely allusion there metafictively by Munro being to Emily Dickinson's advice to 'Tell all the truth but tell it slant' (Dickinson, '1263 Tell'). On the other hand, could Fame, and certainly readers of the story, retain some suspicion about Beryl's version of the near-hanging or the mock-hanging because her version may have been influenced not only by what she actually saw but also by what her obviously biased father later told her about the incident? '"Daddy told me all about it, but I can remember anyway"' (21), Beryl declares perhaps over-assuredly.

The significance to Munro of sustaining strong aesthetic tension in story-writing is also clearly evident in her representation of the two versions of Marietta's burning of her entire share of the money that she and Beryl inherited from their father. Important, too, in terms of the order in which different portions of a story are told or revealed, is Munro's decision to present first the story of the grandmother's apparent suicide attempt or mock-suicide and then to proceed with the story of the burning of the money – in that the hate felt by the grandmother was no doubt the source of the hate felt by Fame's mother. The truth of what Marietta has done with her inheritance comes to the fore when Mr Florence is driving the five of them back from their Sunday dinner at the Wildwood Inn. To increase the emphasis given to what is revealed, Munro sets this scene in the confined space of Mr Florence's car – such vehicles to my mind functioning regularly in Munro as a metonym for the confined space of the short story as a genre (Struthers, 'Traveling with Munro' 164–5). Moreover, the very use of a scene is a literary device of great importance to her. Significantly, Fame's father takes a seat in the front ostensibly to give him more legroom but possibly, since he does so at Beryl's suggestion, to ensure her desire to have the three females seated together in the back, with Fame both literally and metaphorically 'in the middle' (27).

As they drive, Beryl raises the matter of the two sisters' inheritances from their father. '"Speaking of money"', Beryl begins – a non sequitur, another playful use of language to which Munro calls our attention through having Fame comment in the narration that 'nobody actually had been' (28). Continuing, Beryl remarks that she put her share into real estate out in California where she had moved with her father, then with pretended innocence asks her sister what she did with hers. Marietta replies 'cheerfully' that '"we don't actually have the money"' (28) – a comment that catches everyone by surprise, seemingly most dramatically her sister Beryl but equally Marietta's husband. As Fame notes, her father turns halfway around and asks his wife '"What money are you talking about?"' (28). By way of explanation, Marietta declares simply but emphatically to Beryl: '"I burned it"' (28). At this point, as Fame reports, her father resumes looking ahead, presumably in silent bewilderment at, but to Fame evidently respectful acceptance of, his wife's decision. Beryl groans angrily, then demands of Fame's father, '"Why did you let her?"' – at which point Marietta interjects, asserting that '"He wasn't there ... Nobody was there"' (29). Her husband immediately supports his wife's choice – lovingly, though one might well add magnanimously – saying '"It was her money, Beryl"' (29). Yet the story of the burning of the money isn't resolved there – at least not for Fame – and hence we move on from what short story theorist Susan Lohafer would term a 'preclosure point' (Lohafer 4) to the necessary final page or so of the narration of the story.

And here in terms of the considerable significance of an author's decisions about the ordering of different sections of a work, it's well worth emphasising that the subject which Munro chooses to revisit in the concluding section of this unnumbered fifteen-part piece is the significance to Fame of the two versions of the burning of the money story. Hence we are left to consider that for a long time Fame has insisted on substituting a fictional version of the story for the true story told by her mother in the car, exactly as the linguistic form of a euphemism involves an act of substituting – meaning that each particular euphemism that Munro employs in this story is a metaphor for the overall workings of the mind of her protagonist-narrator. Fame repeats this act because psychologically she needs to hold on to what the fictional version of this story represents in terms of the supposed devotedness that she imagines existing in her parents' relationship. Fame needs to see her father not only literally standing beside but also metaphorically standing in support of her mother as Marietta feeds the money she has inherited into the wood stove in their farmhouse kitchen. For Fame, the imaginary episode reinforces her need to maintain as an ideal and as a reality in her mind an abiding sense of a devotedly loving relationship between her parents in the face of her own divorce. And she continues to need to repeat this version of the story, at least up until and including the time when, close to the narrative present, she is able to come back and visit her old family home (and whatever childhood demons it represents) because the sale is being handled by the real-estate office for which she works.

At this point Fame gives an account of returning to her childhood home, the farm that has since passed through different hands, most recently becoming a commune for hippies. Eventually, 'The commune disintegrated' (24) and the place was put up for sale, at which point – significantly on another Sunday – Fame, in the company of her then-current boyfriend Bob Marks, visits her old home. The kitchen now has one wall 'painted a deep blue' – the Virgin Mary's colour we may suggest – 'with an enormous dove on it' (25), presumably white – representing the Holy Spirit – to view these two descriptions allegorically if necessarily also ironically. While in the kitchen, Fame tells Bob Marks her preferred version of the story of her mother Marietta burning the money: '"She brought it home and put it in the stove. She put it in just a few bills at a time, so it wouldn't make too big a blaze. My father stood and watched her"' (26). Fame explains that the money was an inheritance from her mother's father, whom Marietta hated. When Bob Marks, ignoring the detail stressed by Fame that '"My father stood and watched her"', replies '"That's a lot of hate"' (26), Fame quickly asserts that for her the scene doesn't represent hate but its opposite (namely the other half of the allegorical pairing that the story explores and the subject announced in the title of both the story and the collection) – love. '"That isn't the point. Her hating him, or whether he was bad enough for her to have a right to hate him. Not likely he was. That isn't the point"' (26), Fame declares. Rather, '"My father letting her do it is the point"' (26); and indeed more than that, it seemed to Fame as if her father was 'protecting' (30) her mother. Fame then concludes emphatically for the benefit of Bob Marks and we may assume especially herself: '"I consider that love"' (26).

Moments later Fame goes into the front room and next into the front bedroom where she sees painted on the wall larger-than-life images of a naked man and woman – allegorical images evoking however ironically the paradisal figures of Adam and Eve in the Garden of Eden. There, looking closely beneath different layers of more recently applied wallpaper – surely, as Magdalene Redekop proposes, a fitting description of 'Munro's way of seeing the process of storytelling' (Redekop, *Mothers* 177) – Fame sees 'an edge' of the old wallpaper containing 'cornflowers on a white ground' (27). Like the kitchen wall 'painted a deep blue' (25), the characteristically blue cornflowers represented on the old wallpaper evoke the colour blue regularly associated in Christian iconography with the Virgin Mary, while the white ground evokes the purity associated with her. Then, too, the layers of wallpaper represent a metafictional metaphor guiding us to read this story as Dante in his work *Il Convivio* (known in its English translation as *The Banquet*) encourages us to read allegory as many-levelled and as ultimately redemptive in the manner in which Dante's own allegory *The Divine Comedy* proceeds from the *Inferno* through the *Purgatorio* to the *Paradiso*. Moreover, to the extent that we regard Fame's experiences including her activity narrating this story as being personally somewhat hellish, profoundly if perhaps only partly purgative, ultimately if perhaps not fully redemptive for her, then we may find ourselves envisioning a parallel between 'The Progress of Love' and the allegorical movement in Dante from Hell through Purgatory to Heaven.

The scrap of wallpaper noticed by Fame is from the batch with which she, at the impressionable age of twelve, and her mother had decorated the room together, the time when we imagine Fame's mother telling hateful stories about men to her daughter – specifically about Fame's grandmother and namesake's reportedly treacherous treatment by her husband. As a consequence of her mother's remarks, Fame's own attitudes are coloured – as if by 'a drop of black ink in white milk' (6), to borrow the analogy that her mother employs. When Bob Marks remarks of this room and the hippies that '"I guess this was where they carried on their sexual shenanigans"' (27) – a supposition that represents another euphemism or substitution for the actual truth – Fame loses her temper and, as Freud would have it, displaces on to Bob Marks the anger that she feels consciously towards her mother but probably unconsciously in other ways. In a discussion of this story during one of the 148 sessions – one per story collected by Munro – of the Alice Munro Reading Group in which I have had the great pleasure of participating on Wednesday evenings in recent years on Zoom, Jennifer Pangman observed astutely that Fame's reactions, as suggested by the intensity in particular places of Fame's language, seem to come from a deeper source emotionally than any that is acknowledged directly in the story (Pangman, Conversation).

Fame, however, in the interest of immediately softening her flare-up at Bob Marks – and in the interest of suppressing whatever distressing memory or memories of that room may be arising in her conscious mind now – allows him to maintain the illusion of his mistaken interpretation '"Was this your room when you were a little girl?"' (30). As Fame reflects at the start of the final paragraph of the story, 'And I thought it would be just as well to let him think that' (30). Notably, this statement fails to explain why Fame decides it would be best to permit Bob to misinterpret the significance for her of the front bedroom in her childhood home. And as a consequence Fame is able to avoid disclosing to the story's readers, and likely able to suppress for herself, the true memories she has of her childhood experience in this equivalent to 'the black room' so favoured by Munro. Fame reports that in reply to Bob's question she declared 'yes, yes' (30) – Munro here perhaps gesturing, we would assume ironically, towards Molly Bloom's affirmative closing to Joyce's *Ulysses*. For Fame's reactions derive from a dark, unstated, possibly only half-conscious source: from a malaise much deeper than her frustrating childhood and presumably adulthood exchanges with her mother or her difficult marriage to Ben Casey ending in divorce or the current vexations of her job and personal life. We sense that there's something much more troubling for which Fame as a girl felt she needed to obtain her mother's forgiveness – likely incest, Jennifer Pangman suggested (Pangman, Conversation). In this vein, I would argue that this front bedroom was the place where – as we come to suspect of the dark and troubling living room described in the opening pages of the collection's third-last piece, 'A Queer Streak' – a far more distressing event, presumably sexual violation, than Bob Marks's euphemistically described '"sexual shenanigans"' (27) occurred to Fame as a young girl. Just possibly – as we gradually discern in the case of the middle daughter, Dawn Rose, in 'A Queer Streak' – at the initiative of Fame's own father whom she seems all too willing to cast into an old age home rather than to care for him herself and whom we see symbolised more than by any other detail in terms of his life-long, attractive, but, it might be thought, demonically suggestive black hair.

Fame describes how in the past 'I would beat my head against my mother's stomach and breasts, against her tall, firm front, demanding to be forgiven' (13). Fame states that 'My mother would tell me to ask God. But it wasn't God, it was my mother I had to get straight with' (13). Why does Fame need to fix this deep, possibly dark, mysterious matter with her mother? For what, exactly, does Fame think she needs her mother's forgiveness? Fame states of her mother that 'It seemed as if she knew something about me that was worse, far worse, than ordinary lies and tricks and meanness; it was a really sickening shame' (13). What knowledge might this be? Is it because Fame participated, albeit presumably altogether unwillingly, in an act that represented a betrayal of her mother's marriage? And this same challenge for Fame of reconciling herself with her mother, and indeed with her entire maternal legacy descending from her maternal grandmother, continues to press urgently upon Fame still. As it does upon her creator, if we are to consider stories – and here I'm employing a couple of terms used by both critic Harold Bloom (Bloom, 'Criticism' 405–6) and poet Daphne Marlatt (Marlatt 206) – part 'facticity', part fictional autobiography, part 'ficticity', part dream-vision allegory. Thereafter, Fame elects to alter her tone towards Bob Marks from rage to warmth, explaining in retrospect that 'Moments of kindness and reconciliation are worth having, even if the parting has to come sooner or later' (30–1). But in the end for Fame herself, there can be no sustaining of illusion at the expense of the truth – at least not, we assume, without the significant psychological consequences of keeping the most difficult moments in one's personal history entirely or at least largely repressed, a secret even to oneself.

Returning to her childhood home of course also evokes for Fame the image that she cherishes of her mother standing at the old kitchen wood stove and slowly burning the money she had inherited from her father while her husband looked on supportively. Narrating the story at whatever point in the future, Fame admits, however, that 'My father did not stand in the kitchen watching my mother feed the money into the flames. It wouldn't appear so. He did not know about it – it seems fairly clear, if I remember everything, that he did not know about it until that Sunday afternoon in Mr Florence's Chrysler, when my mother told them all together' (29). For Fame, this illusory image that she holds of her father lovingly supporting her mother 'seems so much the truth it is the truth; it's what I believe about them' (30). Fame admits 'I made that up' but asks herself: 'Why, then, can I see the scene so clearly, just as I described it to Bob Marks (and to others – he was not the first)?' (29). The answer is because psychologically speaking Fame needs to believe and therefore to picture this fictional version rather than the factual truth, at least until she completes the act of narration that this story most deeply involves. Fame adds that while she hasn't stopped believing the story, 'I never told it to anyone again after telling it to Bob Marks' (30) – presumably an important departure. In one respect, Fame's not telling the story anymore represents an admission of its untruthfulness. Yet the reason she quit telling her preferred version of the story, she explains, was not because it wasn't precisely true. 'I stopped because I saw that I had to give up expecting people to see it the way I did' (30).

Could the act of narration comprised by this story be considered, therefore, to be Fame's effort to rid herself finally of the contaminating influence passed through successive generations from her grandmother and namesake, Euphemia, through her mother, Marietta, to Fame herself? – with Fame representing the end of the line or saga because, as she happily reports, her children were boys. That is to say, on one level we may consider this story as taking the form and serving the purpose of an autobiography – as Fame's effort to make her peace not so much with God but with her mother and, we conclude, most importantly with herself. In the opening chapter of James Joyce's epic *Ulysses* the Englishman Haines remarks humorously – but for Joyce we must assume seriously – about Shakespeare's *Hamlet* to Stephen Dedalus and Buck Mulligan, 'I read a theological interpretation of it somewhere, he said bemused. The Father and the Son idea. The Son striving to be atoned with the Father' (Joyce, *Ulysses* 18). And just as I argued long ago (and Margaret Atwood has emphasised recently) that with great originality and great power Munro had succeeded in rewriting Joyce's *A Portrait of the Artist as a Young Man* as a portrait of a young woman as a young artist in what I now like to term her 'novel-in-stories' *Lives of Girls and Women* (1971) (Struthers, 'Reality and Ordering' and Atwood, '*Lives*'), I find myself wondering if here Munro might not be rewriting Joyce again, with 'The Progress of Love' serving, allegorically, as a story of the Daughter striving to be atoned with the Mother.

Overall, Fame's psychological state and her actions appear to have been strongly influenced by her mother, as much as Fame has sought to resist her mother's strident religious beliefs and fierce personal opposition towards men. The mother/daughter scene between Marietta and Fame that presumably has by far the most damaging impact on Fame socially and psychologically – specifically in terms of her ongoing relations with men, including her ultimately failed marriage to Dan Casey and her eventual break-up with Bob Marks – occurs during 'the summer of 1947' (7) in advance of Beryl's visit when Fame is at the impressionable and sexually formative age of twelve. In this psychologically and symbolically crucial scene Fame helps her mother redo with new wallpaper 'the downstairs bedroom, the spare room' (7). It is the uniquely isolated period of time together while hanging new wallpaper in the downstairs bedroom that Marietta presumably uses to tell Fame her gothic-like version (as distinct from her sister Beryl's farce-like version) describing their mother Euphemia's apparent suicide attempt or mock-suicide. Here the gothic nature of Marietta's version is reinforced by Munro's undoubted allusion to Charlotte Perkins Gilman's late nineteenth-century American gothic tale 'The Yellow Wallpaper'.

We do learn one important part of the exchange between mother and daughter, namely a song (another example of Munro's fascination with oral traditions), 'a song she said her own mother used to sing when she and Beryl were little girls':

'I once had a sweetheart, but now I have none.
He's gone and he's left me to weep and to moan.
He's gone and he's left me, but contented I'll be,
For I'll get another one, better than he!' (8)

What sort of song, we may ask, is this one by a then presumably unhappily married woman (Fame's grandmother and namesake, Euphemia) or a now perhaps not so happily married woman (Fame's mother, Marietta) to be repeating evidently as pre-adolescent advice to her presumably optimistic daughter? What sort of potentially life-long harm secreted into Fame's then-imagined joyful future does this song represent? As well, we must consider the special significance that Munro gives to this scene by choosing to make it the very first of her memories that Fame records. Why? Because Marietta's song, and everything else that she may have said to Fame along that line while they were wallpapering the downstairs bedroom and later, illustrates the consequences of the remark by Marietta about the workings of 'One drop of hatred in your soul' (6) that Fame recalls in the act of narrating this story. Namely, the consequences that 'One drop of hatred in your soul will spread and discolor everything like a drop of black ink in white milk' (6).

At age twelve, Fame takes what her mother says (as some readers take what Alice Munro writes) simply literally, thinking, 'I was struck by that and meant to try it, but knew I shouldn't waste the milk' (6). But attentive readers will interpret the passage differently – that is, metaphorically. And indeed Fame herself will in time learn to think metaphorically, an activity that Mark Levene rightly states is 'at the core of selfhood' (Levene, 'Alice Munro's *The Progress of Love*' 151). Levene comments on the mix in Fame's rendition of a very small amount of 'factuality' together with a very large amount of 'metaphor': 'Contextual details, which are rare in Munro's work – "in the summer of 1947, when I was twelve" – confirm the factuality of the mother at the stove. But the rest is metaphor, the expression of Fame's newfound freedom. "She put it in just a few bills at a time, so it wouldn't make too big a blaze," she tells Bob. "My father stood and watched her"' (Levene 147). As Levene declares, 'Fame is a metaphorist in training' (Levene 147). We want to imagine that this newly developed trait will save her, though we may suspect that even by the end of her narration it doesn't fully.

Fame explains that 'There was a cloud, a poison, that had touched my mother's life' and that as a result of her mother's influence psychologically on Fame, 'when I grieved my mother, I became part of it' (13) – possibly forever, but hopefully not. This poison, Fame subsequently reveals, has to do with her mother Marietta's view of men: 'A bunch of men standing out on the street, outside a hotel, seemed to Marietta like a clot of poison. You tried not to hear what they were saying, but you could be sure it was vile. If they didn't say anything, they laughed and vileness spread out from them – poison – just the same' (11–12). Fame says of her mother, 'Her heart was broken. That was what I always heard my mother say. That was the end of it' (13) – with Munro here employing phrases common in standard speech, that is to say, clichés, a device that again draws attention to Munro's interest in the limits we unknowingly put on the language we use and therefore on what it is able to represent and to communicate. At the same time, the phrases Munro has chosen here arguably layer her writing with an allusion to the title story, 'My Heart Is Broken', of Mavis Gallant's 1964 collection *My Heart Is Broken* and perhaps another allusion to the final story, 'The End of It', of Hugh Hood's 1962 collection *Flying a Red Kite*. Fame reflects that 'My brothers weren't bothered by any of this' – adding, importantly, 'And when I just had the two boys myself, no daughters, I felt as if something could stop now – the stories, and griefs, the old puzzles you can't resist or solve' (14), though likely they do not cease. The family legacy has proceeded tragically, from generation to generation of different women, but happily, or in Northrop Frye's sense of the word comically (Frye, *Anatomy of Criticism* 163–86), can now end with Fame. Or, alternatively, and in keeping with the value Munro places on sustaining tension throughout a story, perhaps we should conclude that in this way Munro stresses that for her neither a strictly tragic vision nor a strictly comic vision (that of Sophocles versus that of Aristophanes, say, amongst the classic Greek playwrights) will suffice.

Indeed, what I find most interesting, boldest, newest and most complex about this opening story – especially for a writer who has shown herself to be so fascinated with the metaphor of 'the black room' as a representation of what is at the centre of her works – is the fact that here she chooses to emphasise, often together, imagery and hence a vision of *both* black *and* white, in order to make our responses much more challenging to articulate. By way of a postscript to what we observed earlier about the scene at the Wildwood Inn, where Mr Florence and Beryl take Fame's parents and herself for Sunday dinner, we may note the repetition of the symbolic colour white – as opposed to black – in connection with various details describing the inn and the luncheon there. The Wildwood Inn is said to be 'a white frame building' (19) and to have a dining room that is 'all in white, white tablecloths, white painted chairs' (19–20). Fame's father jokes with her about the size of a (presumably white) table napkin that she explains is as large as a (presumably white) baby's diaper. And in addition to everyone having (presumably white) 'roast chicken' with (presumably white) 'mashed potatoes' as their main course, Fame tells us that for dessert 'The others had plain vanilla ice cream' (23) while she treated herself to 'a butterscotch sundae' (23) prepared with the same white ice cream but topped with butterscotch sauce, a symbol of Fame's desire to attain something different from, and we may say something more celebratory than, anything her mother stood for.

Nevertheless, images of black seem to dominate much of the story from the outset onward, beginning with Fame's father telling her euphemistically that '"I think your mother's gone"' and Fame reporting that 'for a second or so I saw my mother in her black straw hat setting off down the lane' (3). The early and for Munro characteristic emphasis on deeply psychological and metaphysical blackness is strongly conveyed in the scene when Beryl and Mr Florence are visiting Fame's family and Beryl remarks to Fame before falling asleep for the night, '"I've never known a dark that was as dark as this"' (17). When Fame recalls that 'I was slow to understand that she was comparing country nights to city nights' (17), we realise that her response was not only delayed but also literal-minded, that there is a further metaphorical level to Beryl's and Munro's sense of the dark that the literal-mindedness of both the younger Fame and apparently the older Fame does not grasp. Remembering the closing section of the last story, 'Vandals', in the volume *Open Secrets* (1994) that Munro published two collections after this one, we find ourselves calling attention, as my co-author Corinne Bigot does in her commentary on that book, to the ominous words with which that volume ends: 'you could feel the darkness collecting, rising among the trees, like cold smoke coming off the snow' (294) – another revisiting and rewriting by Munro, I think, of Joyce, in this case the ending of his novella 'The Dead'.

How we evaluate the weighting of black or white or black-and-white images, complicated by their tragic or comic or tragi-comic overtones, is of considerable significance to our interpretation of Munro's overall aesthetic intentions. In describing Munro's aims, or we could say her vision, it would seem appropriate to cite a statement that Robert Thacker discovered in Southern United States writer Eudora Welty's essay 'How I Write': 'Brutal or lovely, the mystery waits for people wherever they go, whatever extreme they run to' (Welty, 'How I Write' 250; qtd in Thacker, *Reading Alice Munro* 158). Ultimately, the contrasting images or notions or principles in this title story, indeed throughout this collection, invite us to consider what we're reading as a contemporary variation on what C.S. Lewis described in his classic book *The Allegory of Love* (1936): but here as an allegory of love and forgiveness or an allegory of their opposites, hate and grudges – or indeed a depiction of all of these. During the dinner at the Wildwood Inn, we find ourselves pointed in the direction of considering the story as an allegory in part of love and forgiveness by the reference to Fame's mother looking at Mr Florence 'as if he was the one to be forgiven' (23) – though we may well question whether there could be any reason why Mr Florence might require forgiveness and indeed wonder if the other man present, Fame's father, was the person needing forgiveness. Here it would seem relevant to recall Blake's comment in *The Marriage of Heaven and Hell* that 'Without Contraries is no progression. Attraction and Repulsion, Reason and Energy, Love and Hate, are necessary to Human existence' (Blake, *The Marriage* 34, Plate 3). And to remember Blake's description of his own writing as 'Allegory address'd to the Intellectual powers' (Blake, '33. To Thomas Butts' 69).

In my view, the opening story 'The Progress of Love', indeed the collection as a whole, in addition to being an allegory reflecting on the nature of human love and hate, represents – like The Book of Job, which I have long held to be the ur-form of the short story – an allegory reflecting on the nature of divine love and punishment. Here it may be mentioned that Munro's choice of the make of Mr Florence's car, a Chrysler, is not so different from the word Christ and therefore represents a detail which, combined with other features, leads us to consider the story in the context of Christ's acts of redemption, seemingly reinforcing the sense of the presence of Christian allegory (or perhaps some mocking of it) here. A fact that Fame discovers only after her mother has died and her father has gone willingly into the Netterfield County Home is the resentment that her father felt towards the extreme severity of her mother's Anglicanism. We learn from Fame that her mother attended revival meetings for a number of years starting at age fourteen (interestingly, 'the same summer that her own mother – my grandmother – died') then went 'back to being just an Anglican', but 'a serious one, by the time she got married' (4). In contrast, although Fame's father was Anglican himself, he 'was not religious in the way my mother was' (4). Fame's mother prayed fervently throughout each day. Hence Fame's recollection of how, once when she visited her aged father at the Home, he mistook Fame for her mother and stated sarcastically that he was surprised she hadn't worn the skin off her knees entirely. Fame, having initially laughed and said '"What doing? Scrubbing floors?"', was then taken aback by her father's reply '"Praying!"', made in what she describes as 'a voice like spitting' (6).

Considered in allegorical terms, as a response to any readily assumed vacuous notions of the nature and the comfort of religion, it would be difficult to imagine a stronger dissenting voice or statement – be it that of Fame's father, or, behind it, we might assume, that of Alice Munro herself. In the title story, Fame, upon realising that the grades she received on her high school Entrance Examinations wouldn't matter, that she wouldn't be continuing her schooling since her parents didn't have the money to pay the necessary costs of boarding her in town, speaks with her mother. In reply Marietta, despite having been a schoolteacher herself, tells her daughter matter-of-factly, and we may think cruelly, that 'God didn't care' (8), that 'God isn't interested in what kind of job or what kind of education anybody has' (8–9). Fame herself, to the contrary, reflects that 'This was the first time I understood how God could become a real opponent, not just some kind of nuisance or large decoration' (9). Marietta's lifelong embrace of this fierce religious position strikes Fame more and more as being essentially black, life-denying (allegorically, the Freudian death drive or *Thanatos*), whereas Fame wishes to define herself in terms of a position that is brightly coloured, life-celebrating (allegorically, the Freudian life force or *Eros*). Of Fame's action of dying her hair with a colour called 'Copper Sunrise', we may note that this choice represents a further attempt to define herself not only symbolically but also in reality as an individual separate from and different from her mother.

During the scene when the family goes out for Sunday dinner, Fame's mother insists, before the group begins to eat, on 'quietly but audibly' saying grace: '"Lord bless this food to our use, and us to Thy service, for Christ's sake. Amen"' (20) – with the notion of grace reinforcing the idea of story as allegory and with grace being a word that James Joyce used, albeit with supreme irony, as the title of the story which he originally planned, before writing 'The Dead', to be the final piece in *Dubliners*. Margaret Atwood has noted the frequency of Munro's presentation of situations that evoke the concept of grace: 'In religion, this intersection of the transcendent with the mundane would be called "grace" – a redemptive quality that comes from elsewhere and is bestowed on you, despite the fact that you haven't caused it and don't deserve it. Grace of this kind occurs often in Munro's work, and though it isn't always connected with art, its root model is religious' (Atwood, '*Lives*' 97). In this context I find myself recalling Hugh Hood's remark in conversation with me that he considered the story 'Tell Me Yes or No' in Munro's third book, *Something I've Been Meaning To Tell You* (1974), to be a prayer expressed to God (Hood in Struthers, Personal Conversation). And in the same vein, I therefore wonder if the act of narration performed by Fame in 'The Progress of Love' can be viewed as an analogue to the search for religious redemption, as a means of personal atonement – yet not something, we ultimately suspect, that Fame is able by this point to carry far enough, unable as she seems to be still to identify, to sort out, to absolve herself fully of the hate or grudges that she herself still evidently and probably unadmittedly has 'growing underground' (31), as she says of her parents. Coral Ann Howells judiciously asks about Fame's retelling of her grandmother's and her mother's hateful stories, 'Is this a story about love, as [she] wants [it] to be? Or is it a story about hatred . . .?' (Howells 91). Could the story represent 'an expression of her own inability to forgive her mother, as well as her attempt to forgive her?' (Howells 91). And in the end does Fame's act of narration continue to involve some degree of 'the secular advance of repression' that Freud found in the later figure of Hamlet in contrast to how Freud saw psychological fantasy being 'brought into the open' in the earlier figure of Oedipus (Freud, *The Interpretation of Dreams* 366)?

Viewed as an analogue to the search for religious redemption, the opening story of *The Progress of Love* reflects – though with an undercurrent of satire – the form of what Frye terms a 'romance' or a 'secular scripture' (Frye, *Anatomy of Criticism* 186–206 and Frye, *The Secular Scripture* passim). In this way Munro strikes a balance between romance and satire, what we might term the tradition of Spenser and the tradition of Swift, with the title of this story alluding, as Magdalene Redekop and Robert Thacker have also noted, to Swift's poem 'Phyllis; or, The Progress of Love' (Redekop, *Mothers* 175 and Thacker, *Reading Alice Munro* 233). Beverly J. Rasporich makes the important claim that Munro 'belongs to a growing tradition of female authors who are beginning to fuse the realistic, the mythological and the metaphysical' (Rasporich 88). And in the considered judgement of contemporary Southern United States writer Richard Ford, speaking of Munro in his Introduction to the Penguin edition of *The Progress of Love*, 'There really *are* just those few unrivaled writers . . . for whom the story as mysterious and beautiful as it might be . . . is but gleaming evidence of a great presence, an authority, a spirit, an expanding opulent intelligence' (Ford xvi). To my mind, then, allegorically speaking, what Alice Munro mobilises so powerfully from beginning to end of this first of four breakthrough books is a fierce debate about the supposedly caring nature versus the seemingly uncaring nature of what we consider to be divine interventions in human lives. In this context we may note that Bernard Shaw's play *Saint Joan* ends with a plea by Joan – a name, we recall, Fame thought of choosing for herself (7) – that we can imagine haunting Munro: 'O God that madest this beautiful earth, when will it be ready to receive Thy saints? How long, O Lord, how long?' (Shaw 159).

3. Verbal Play in 'Lichen'

The playfulness, the doubleness, the language-centred nature of the very title of the story 'Lichen' – a word which, as it is *spelled*, 'lichen', suggests the literal (though we immediately think also metaphorical) physical plant that attaches itself to something else for nourishment, but which, as it *sounds*, 'liken', suggests an act of the imagination involving a choice of language – emphasises from the outset of this story Munro's all-important concerns with form and technique and style. Hence as we read the very first sentences of 'Lichen' we recall Munro's remark that for her a short story is 'more like a house' (Munro, 'What Is Real?' 332) and note in particular her reference in the story's opening lines to the importance of 'words': 'Stella's father built the place as a summer house, on the clay bluffs overlooking Lake Huron. Her family always called it "the summer cottage." David was surprised when he first saw it, because it had none of the knotty-pine charm, the battened-down coziness, that those words suggested' (32). And thus Munro cautions us, metafictively, that as good-humoured, indeed as comic a story as 'Lichen' will prove to be, we should not expect any sort of clichéd 'charm' or 'coziness' from her writing.

At a certain stage in one's life and education one may respond literally to 'the clay bluffs' that Munro describes – as I did as a youngster when struggling to climb back up from swimming in Lake Huron, slip-sliding on my hands and knees on steep clay paths to the cottage called Blue Top on Smith's Farm a mile south of St Joseph that my parents rented for three weeks every summer. Or at a different stage in one's life and education, one may respond allegorically to 'the clay bluffs' that she describes: interpreting them in a Biblical context as suggesting God's creation of Adam from dust in Genesis 2: 7 of which Job later says, 'I also am formed out of the clay' (The Book of Job 33: 6). And if only in passing, we might also note that 'bluffs', too, is an intriguing word, one arguably involving the same playfulness, the doubleness, the language-centred nature of the story's title, 'Lichen' – with 'bluffs' having the additional meaning of acts of verbal deception, sleight-of-hand, word-magic that different characters perform for various reasons and that we might well view Munro as practising for comic ends.

The range of literary associations prompted in this story both by remarks made by individual characters and by the names Munro has chosen for them is significant in the way it contributes to what I'll call the 'literary archaeology' of 'Lichen'. Not an inappropriate analogy, I believe, given that Munro's second husband, Gerald Fremlin, was an important physical geographer – the Editor-in-Chief of the fourth edition of *The National Atlas of Canada* (1974) and the co-author with Arthur H. Robinson of *Maps as Mediated Seeing: Fundamentals of Cartography* (2nd ed., 2006) – and given Munro's acknowledgement of how Gerry greatly increased her appreciation of geographical details or what she calls 'the landscape' (Munro in McCulloch and Simpson 249). By way of an example of such literary associations, when Catherine, David's girlfriend of eighteen months (Stella and David have been married for twenty-one years and separated for eight years), is preparing to return to the cottage from the beach and sees Stella and David watching from the cottage's living-room window, there's the line 'She waves, and Stella waves back' (43). Then on three more occasions in a single paragraph and once more just a little later we're told about Catherine's experience that afternoon down at the Lake watching 'the waves' (44–5, 45) – surely, we appreciate through Munro's repetition of this image, a reference to the 1931 novel of that name by Virginia Woolf whose lyric style clearly stands as a precursor to Munro's own stylistic practice. And although Eva Mendez does not reference this particular story in her book on Woolf and Munro, 'Lichen' definitely supports the strong connections Mendez observes between the concerns and the styles of these two authors.

Later on, after Stella and David and Catherine have supper, and David departs to make his thwarted phone call to his new girlfriend Dina, Munro again would appear to allude to Woolf's *The Waves* and its lyric style. Following supper, Catherine confides to Stella that '"I feel a change coming in my life.

I love David, but I've been submerged in this love for so long. Too long"' (44). Catherine explains: "'I was down looking at the waves and . . . I thought, The waves never, ever come to an end. So then I knew, this is a message for me"' (44–5). In sum, Catherine – like her creator, Alice Munro, and before her Virginia Woolf (here again evoked through Catherine's two further references to the waves) – possesses the capacity to think and to understand not simply literally but in or through metaphor. Echoes here of Woolf – in other instances of her 1927 novel *To the Lighthouse* – would certainly seem to be reinforced by the fact that Stella, as she tells David, is currently writing an article '"for the historical society and the local paper"' about '"the old lighthouse"' (35), which she informs Catherine can be seen from the end of Stella's living-room window. The fact that the setting of Woolf's *To the Lighthouse* is itself a summer residence (in that case on the Isle of Skye, a detail that I believe would catch Munro's attention both because the Isle of Skye is part of her ancestral homeland of Scotland and because Munro is endlessly fascinated with islands) reinforces the variety of connections that Munro creates between her own work and Woolf's. Hence Magdalene Redekop, speaking of the allusions that she hears in reading Munro, declares: 'Fragments of Woolf float in and out of "Lichen" as I read – the image of Mrs Ramsay sitting at the window in *To the Lighthouse*, that famous dinner party, and through it all the waves and time passing' (Redekop, 'On Sitting Down To Read' 296–7).

Allusions of all kinds to literature, to folklore, to myth and – as Munro's biographer Robert Thacker would be certain to emphasise – to an author's own life appear throughout Munro's stories, including specific references that can be identified in different names that she chooses. Names may have an intensely autobiographical significance – in this case Catherine being the name of Munro's second child who, Catherine Sheldrick Ross explains, lacking functioning kidneys lived only briefly and then haunted Munro's dreams (Ross, *Alice Munro* 53). In addition, Catherine's name undoubtedly evokes that of the heroine, Catherine Earnshaw, in Emily Brontë's gothic romance *Wuthering Heights* (1847), a book greatly beloved by Munro which she told Catherine Sheldrick Ross she read '"constantly for four or five years"' (Munro in Ross, *Alice Munro* 44) beginning at age fourteen. Moreover, Munro would continue to draw on details pertaining to Emily Brontë and *Wuthering Heights* in the mature years of her writing career. The name Almeda chosen by Munro for the fictional nineteenth-century Southwestern Ontario poetess Almeda Joynt Roth depicted in 'Meneseteung', a story in Munro's next breakthrough book, *Friend of My Youth* (1990), is identical to one of the names chosen by Emily Brontë to use for herself in the fictional play-world of Gondal invented by the three Brontë girls and their brother. And the surname that Munro gives to the missing girl, Heather Bell, in the title story of Munro's third breakthrough book, *Open Secrets* (1994), matches that chosen for their pen names by the three Brontë sisters when they co-authored their collection *Poems* (1846) and when each subsequently published her first and in Emily's case her only solo volume.

In terms of the range of allusions that we discern in 'Lichen', we may note that Stella reminds David of how he once described Catherine as '"inclined to be fey"' (40), a phrase whose importance is underlined by Munro's using it three times in just half a page. Especially interesting is the fact that Catherine, though she only teaches part-time at an art college and therefore has a very limited income, nevertheless makes a special trip to Ireland – a land of the faeries, many people including Lady Gregory and W.B. Yeats would say – in order to view *The Book of Kells*. That magnificent illuminated manuscript was produced about 1,200 years ago and, since it contains parts of all four New Testament gospels, directly evokes the concept of allegory and hence promotes the idea of reading Munro's stories allegorically too. We learn that at dinnertime Stella and David and Catherine 'drink mead' (44), something regarded in Norse myth as a source and a symbol of poetic inspiration, indeed, as Gertrude Jobes calls it, the 'Norse drink of the gods' (Jobes 1081) – a detail that anticipates the featuring of Old Norse in the final story of this collection, 'White Dump'. This allusion reinforces the ritualistic, indeed mythic nature of the story 'Lichen' and again carries the range of Munro's literary references back a number of centuries. Also interestingly, in speaking of the echoes contained in individual names, Redekop observes that 'Catherine was a martyr' (Redekop, *Mothers* 187), a notable detail in the context of the given name, Euphemia, of the protagonist-narrator of the collection's immediately preceding title story being that of a martyr and saint. The reference in 'Lichen', as the many readers of Leonard Cohen's novel *Beautiful Losers* (1966) would not forget, recalls Cohen's portrait there, employing her full name, Catherine Tekakwitha, of the young seventeenth-century Iroquois woman (or, to use the now regularly cited version of her first name, Kateri Tekakwitha) canonised after Munro wrote this story but long regarded as a saint.

Of course, many of the allusions in 'Lichen' only serve to stress how far characters or situations are from their often romanticised Biblical or Classical or literary or historical counterparts. Stella, as Marianne Micros aptly discusses, is a far more realistically depicted character than her namesake in Sir Philip Sidney's late sixteenth-century sonnet sequence *Astrophil and Stella* (Micros, 'Et in Ontario Ego' 45–7) that portrays the ill-fated relationship between Stella and her besotted admirer Astrophil, whose names we may note mean 'star' and 'star-lover' in Latin and Greek respectively. And given Munro's long fascination with Southern United States writing, as I have detailed in my essay 'Alice Munro and the American South', the name Stella may well involve too an allusion to the name of the much-beleaguered wife of the brutish Stanley in Tennessee Williams' 1947 play *A Streetcar Named Desire*. The name David draws largely ironically on that of the Old Testament shepherd and later King of the Jews celebrated as a poet and singer of songs. For although both men are adulterers, Munro's David is still a far cry from his Old Testament namesake – or the splendid marble *David* (1501–4) sculpted by Michelangelo. Yet Munro's David has his comic moments, though generally unintended by him, such as when he is deciding how to speak when calling his new girlfriend Dina at her former boyfriend's, imagines not using 'his own voice' or even 'a man's voice at all', and recalls that 'He used to be able to do different voices on the phone. He could even fool Stella at one time' (48), with the word 'fool' and David's past performances and even possibly present performances conceivably reminding us of one or another fool in Shakespeare – Feste from *Twelfth Night* we might think, based on allusions elsewhere in 'Lichen' to a song that Feste sings.

These references, including elements of the pastoral genre and of the poetic form called a blazon discussed by Marianne Micros, deepen what I am calling the 'literary archaeology' of this story – literary references extending back several centuries and including, I believe, an allusion to a famous metaphor from a play by a contemporary of Sidney's, the 'star-crossed lovers' of Shakespeare's *Romeo and Juliet* (Prologue, l. 6). Of the use here of the tradition of the blazon in particular, Micros explains that 'Munro subverts and demolishes the blazon form by describing women's bodies literally or by using metaphors ironically' with the intention of suggesting 'the difficulties inherent in human image making' (Micros, 'Et in Ontario Ego' 47). Munro's tone here is indeed ironic, or satiric we might suggest, given that Stella shares a first name with the subject of several poems by Jonathan Swift, the author, as I have noted in discussing the opening story for Munro's collection, of the poem 'Phyllis; or, The Progress of Love', from which she drew the title of that story and of the book itself. Munro's references can be seen to carry back even further when one considers the Classical models for Renaissance writing – including, I believe, and I am sure my co-author Corinne Bigot would agree, the important source for Munro, Ovid's *Metamorphoses* – in addition to the Biblical sources invoked so fully by Munro as James Carscallen has attested in his monumental study *The Other Country: Patterns in the Writing of Alice Munro* (1993).

If, then, we are to consider Munro's writing as allegory, work that draws profoundly on metaphor and allusion and wordplay, then we may very reasonably wish to ask: as allegory of what? For W.R. Martin, 'Lichen' represents 'a portrait of the contrasted modes of love – something like the sacred and the profane' (Martin 177) – a subject, we may add, that Munro treats later in this collection in 'The Moon in the Orange Street Skating Rink'. More broadly, I would argue that 'Lichen' represents an allegory of the twin forces of love and hate, of personal salvation and personal destruction. Catherine remarks to Stella that when love takes the form of dependence (as in the relationship between lichen and a rock, we might emphasise), '"Love can make you mean"' (44). In this way, Beverly J. Rasporich notes, Munro recognises and issues a warning about the 'danger for women in this kind of dependent love with its corollary, hate' (Rasporich 81). That is, 'Lichen' represents an allegory showing diametrical ways of being, what philosophers call ontology.

But just as importantly it's an allegory showing diametrical ways of knowing, what philosophers call epistemology. Hence Munro's parodic representation through David's misconceived portrayal to Stella the preceding summer of the mode of understanding of his then new girlfriend, Catherine: '"I don't think she's ever read a newspaper. She hasn't the remotest idea of what's going on in the world. Unless she's heard it from a fortune-teller. That's her idea of reality"' (41). For David, Catherine is '"all instinct"' (41). And just as he described Catherine as '"fey"' (40), he characterises his current new girlfriend, Dina, as '"The little witch"' (42). A further association for Dina is supplied by Marianne Micros, who links her with the mythical Diana by dropping the first 'a' in the goddess's name just as David has told Stella that Dina is spelled '"without an 'h'"' (42) (Micros, 'Et in Ontario Ego' 53).

Here Munro is making an important distinction between a more intuitive way of knowing and a more rational way of knowing – a choice, we might say, between focusing on the characteristics and the approaches pertaining to what has been termed 'ficticity' versus 'facticity', the method of the artist as opposed to the method of the sociologist one might suggest ('without prejudice', as my old friend here in Guelph Douglas Killam good-humouredly taught me to write). It's a distinction that we see repeated a couple of stories later in 'Miles City, Montana' through the contrast between the capacity on the part of the protagonist-narrator for what her husband Andrew describes as '"some kind of extra sense that mothers have"' (105), as distinct from his own rationalising. While Andrew's name clearly links him with the patron saint of Scotland, his mode of understanding arguably links him with the empiricism of the eighteenth-century Scottish philosopher David Hume discussed by Munro in *The View from Castle Rock* (Munro, 'No Advantages' 22–3), with whom the character David in 'Lichen' notably shares a first name. It's a philosophical distinction that even David seems to come to appreciate when, late in the story, he jokes about Stella's recognition of his squeamishness over a young nurse's spotting the two of them embracing as they leave the nursing home after visiting her father there: '"Madam Stella, the celebrated mind reader"' (54). Through this comment Munro not only calls attention once more to the act of reading but also reinforces subtly (because the remark is made comically rather than seriously) her explorations of different ways of knowing and ways of being.

A question that I regularly ask myself about any part of a short story which doesn't at first appear to fit the story or at least to fit an initial interpretation of it is: What would be lost if this section were taken out of the story (or ignored in analysing it)? Then I say: Having momentarily removed but then restored this part of the story, what seems to have been gained? A case in point in 'Lichen' would be the trip that Stella and David make to visit her father in order to celebrate his ninety-third birthday. Of the nursing home where Stella's father resides, 'the Balm of Gilead Home', the story states that 'It is named after the balm-of-Gilead trees, a kind of poplar, that grow plentifully near the lake' (50). But even if that is literally or factually the truth, is it the truth metaphorically or allegorically? One thinks of the question posed by the prophet Jeremiah, '"Is there no balm in Gilead . . .?"' (Jeremiah 8: 22), a question which might be viewed as a reasonable epigraph for this story or indeed others by Munro, especially when we find their vision and their tone darkening. The prophetic nature of Jeremiah's writing reminds us of the qualities that fiction can possess, as my old friend Dennis Duffy has said of Hugh Hood's work, not only as memory but also as prophecy (Duffy, 'On Fact and Fiction'). Here the notion of a balm can be seen as applying to the actions, call them rituals, performed by various characters in the story, particularly by whoever – Stella, presumably – is considered to be what Henry James regarded as a work's 'centre of interest' (James, 'Preface to "Roderick Hudson"' 16) or centre of consciousness, and also by the story's readers, whose imaginative or psychological or emotional journeys may well be the most profound of all. In this regard, it would seem appropriate to consider first what different characters are shown as experiencing and perhaps learning in different scenes, then what we ourselves have gained through engaging with, in John Metcalf's words, 'the story as *thing to be experienced* rather than as *thing to be understood*' (Metcalf 63; emphasis in orig.).

The scene when Stella and David visit her father is placed second-last in the story, immediately before the brief four-paragraph section that we may consider the story's epilogue, and it covers about one-fifth of the entire story. Here what seems to me most interesting is the way in which Munro, through her treatment of Stella's drastically speech-impaired father, probes the related subjects of language and communication. When they arrive, her father utters the one word '"David?"', evidently recognising, as Stella points out, '"his step!"' (50). This initial utterance by Stella's father is described not as a word but as a 'sound': 'The sound seemed to come from a wet cave deep inside him, to be unshaped by lips or jaws or tongue' (50). Momentarily we learn that he produces 'further sounds, a conversational offering' (the last word used by Munro here having a definite religious and therefore allegorical association) and that 'It was the core of each syllable that was presented, a damp vowel barely held in shape by surrounding consonants' (51). Speaking of metafiction, could a writer call attention more precisely or more beautifully to the letters and words needed for her art? Similarly, in David's unsuccessful attempt to reach Dina by phone at the residence of 'her last, and perhaps not quite finished with, boyfriend' (47) named Michael Read, the metafictive surname 'Read' (or perhaps 'Reade') is made much of comically by Munro through the lengthy conversation that she reports David having with the telephone operator in which he is told '"I have no listing for a Michael Read"', replies '"All right. Try Reade, R-E-A-D-E"', then when that's unsuccessful asks 'Is there an M. Read? Read?' and finds out 'there is an M. Read, living on Simcoe Street. And another M. Read, R-E-A-D, living on Harbord' (47). His first name, Michael, seems relevant allegorically since in Milton's *Paradise Lost* it was the archangel Michael who directed Adam and Eve out of the Garden of Eden after the Fall. All this in case we didn't fully appreciate Munro's attention to the practice of her art not simply word by word but letter by letter and hence Munro's investment in ourselves as readers.

As greatly as Munro's work deserves to be praised as writing, we need at the same time to recognise the great importance to her stories of the quality that Walter J. Ong identified as orality. Stories not only take the form of the short story but of the stories, the conversation, the dialogue that the short story regularly features. And in the case of Munro, a short story regularly includes other oral and aural modes. Music, for example: a topic that Megan LaPierre has discussed in stories by Munro including the final and title piece of her first collection, *Dance of the Happy Shades* (1968), the final piece 'My Mother's Dream' of the last of our four 'breakthrough books', *The Love of a Good Woman* (1998) and the 'Finale' to Munro's fourteenth and last volume, *Dear Life* (2012). Here in 'Lichen' we find what Marianne Micros points out is the twice-referenced song beginning 'O mistress mine, where are you roaming?' from Shakespeare's *Twelfth Night* (II, iii, 38) – a song alluded to first when David sings a version of the opening of it (39) and subsequently when another line from it, 'What's to come is still unsure!' (II, iii, 48), is recalled emphatically by Stella (46) (Micros, 'Et in Ontario Ego' 44). Importantly, *Twelfth Night* is a comedy that features the verbally gifted fool named Feste, a character who sings both the aforementioned song and later a different song beginning 'Come away, come away death' (II, iv, 51). As previously stated, the use of the word 'fool' in the description of David's past verbal performances and present plan for calling Dina suggests a possible association between David and Feste. Furthermore, Feste is a character whose performance skills or tone or verbal sleight-of-hand Munro might be thought of as consciously and playfully emulating in 'Lichen'. Then, too, the allusions here to *Twelfth Night* reinforce our sense throughout Alice Munro's work of story as allegory because the play's title reminds us that the next day after the Twelve Days of Christmas is the Feast of the Epiphany on which the baby Jesus was shown to the Magi.

But to cite a different oral mode – conversation – there's the previously described very funny conversation between David and the telephone operator involving, appropriately, the surname R-E-A-D or R-E-A-D-E. Then there's the haunting story that Stella's father manages to volunteer, in obviously compressed form, involving a supposed episode in his youth: '"Gray. Dort. Gray-Dort. First car – ever drove. Yonge Street. Sixty miles. Sixty miles. Uh. Uh. Hour"' (52). In this instance, although Stella firmly refutes her father's story when speaking a little later with David, claiming '"It's his fantasy"' (52), what matters is that Stella's father is able to delight mentally in a possibly factual or possibly fictive – but even in the latter case, no less real – experience involving a time when he acted with the energy and the boldness of youth. Or to mention another oral mode: jokes or verbal play or simply wry remarks such as when – following a brief discussion of an unnamed Ingmar Bergman film (the one, we learn upon checking, with the Biblically allusive title *Through a Glass Darkly* echoing 1 Corinthians 13: 12) in which, as David states, '"God was a helicopter"' – Stella, very possibly speaking metafictively for Munro herself, comments: '"I can't say I ever really appreciated Bergman movies. I always thought they were sort of bleak and neurotic"' (37). Or when David identifies himself as '"just a civil servant"' to friends of Stella's and one of them, Mary, displaying a love of wordplay undoubtedly shared by Munro replies: '"A simple serpent! . . . I used to work in Ottawa . . . and we used to call ourselves simple serpents! Civil serpents. Servants"' (38), with the repetition of the word 'serpents', along with the choice of name for Mary, also conjuring up associations with Biblical allegory.

Language, wordplay and still more precisely simile, the figure of speech by which we *liken* one thing to another, to echo the pun, yet another figure of speech, introduced by Munro in the story's title, 'Lichen', is the subject that Munro emphasises in the story's epilogue. At that point, 'A week or so later' (55), following the visit by Catherine and David, Stella happens upon the pornographic 'Polaroid snapshot' (55) or more precisely crotch shot (to employ the title of a short story by Munro's fellow Southwestern Ontario writer George Elliott) of his new girlfriend, Dina, which David had tried to give to Stella earlier because he was afraid he would succumb to his wish to hurt Catherine by showing the picture to her. When David first displayed the photo to Stella, we are told that she says '"It looks like lichen . . . Except it's rather dark. It looks to me like moss on a rock"' (41). The relationship between lichen and a rock functions metaphorically to suggest David's continuing dependence on Stella and perhaps equally her continuing dependence on him – as lichen and rocks are mutually sustaining – for although they have been separated now for eight years, they still haven't divorced. On another level, as Héliane Ventura notes suggestively, Munro's treatment here of the pornographic snapshot of Dina may be viewed as a revisitation and reinvention of the notorious painting *L'Origine du Monde* (1866) by French painter Gustave Courbet (Ventura, 'Le tracé de l'écart' 269 ff.).

After being upbraided by David for incorrectly (or perhaps only supposedly) identifying the image as lichen, Stella looks more closely, seeing the woman's 'legs spreading into the foreground' and in between them 'the dark blot she called moss, or lichen' (42). Then Stella, altering her description through the use of a different simile – for a probably unconscious but certainly hostile reason – substitutes something more bestial and more violent for the image, thinking that 'it's really more like the dark pelt of an animal, with the head and tail and feet chopped off' (42). Reinforcing this image of Dina is what we're told of her failure to get a part in a pornographic film 'because of some squeamishness about holding a tame rat between her legs' (49). Munro's choice of a rat prompts us to think of Freud's early history of the Rat Man concerning which, Patrick J. Mahony explains, 'Freud was bent on making a psychoanalytic showpiece' (Mahony, *Freud and the Rat Man* 212). In that case study, Freud described matters central to his thinking such as *Eros* and *Thanatos*, dream symbolism and the unconscious, all of which figure prominently in various stories in this collection.

As noted, Munro likes to work with oppositions because she believes that for her the short story form requires what she calls 'the tension' (Munro in Struthers, 'The Real Material' 15). Here in 'Lichen', by contrast to the actual Polaroid of Dina, there's the imaginary 'picture' (52) of Stella 'as she had been twelve or fifteen years before' (52–3) that David holds in his mind to this day. 'He saw her coming across the lawn at a suburban party, carrying a casserole' (53), a picture reminiscent of a particular Diane Arbus photograph of suburbanites relaxing in a back yard that Munro told me was a favourite of hers (Munro in Struthers, 'The Real Material' 6 and see Arbus, *A Family On Their Lawn One Sunday in Westchester, New York*). The question 'Why did this picture please him so much?' is answered this way: that in addition to 'wonderful' food, Stella 'brought . . . the whole longed-for spirit of the neighborhood party' (53). This scene, as Ailsa Cox would appreciate, calls to mind Katherine Mansfield's classic story 'The Garden Party' and therefore evokes the lyrical style of that important predecessor of Munro's as a short story writer. The everyday picture of Stella as a rich spiritual presence – 'With her overwhelming sociability, she gathered everybody in' (53) – stands in strong contrast to the pornographic picture of Dina as a mere physical presence.

Further to our perception of Munro's absorption with the subject of language, her juxtaposition of 'like' and 'lichen' in Stella's statement '"It looks like lichen"' (41) reminds us of the verbal play on the noun 'lichen' and the verb 'liken', along with a larger point about the often multiple dimensions of language, that Munro introduced by means of the story's evidently punning title. By choosing here to use similes beginning with 'like' twice in rapid succession – '"like lichen"' and '"like moss on a rock"' (41) – Munro invites us to hear, then to consider, the homonym, or to use the term employed by Isla Duncan, the 'homophone' (Duncan, *Alice Munro's Narrative Art* 42), namely the verb 'liken', a comparison that Redekop also notes (Redekop, *Mothers* 184). A further example of Munro's enjoyment of puns is provided when David refers disparagingly to the pills that Catherine takes and Stella replies, '"Mood elevator, going up!"' (43). Moreover, when David upbraids Stella for responding jokingly to the fact that Catherine takes pills, Stella replies '"That's your affair"' – a presumably conscious though she claims unconscious pun that prompts David to reply, ironically, '"Very funny"' (43). '"I didn't even mean it to be"', Stella declares, adding, '"Whenever something slips out like that"' – with Munro here undoubtedly using the word '"slips"' to create a joking allusion to Freudian slips – '"I always pretend I meant it, though. I'll take all the credit I can get!"' (43). In having Stella state that she pretends to mean what she says, Munro is operating realistically and metafictively: revealing not only Stella's sly method but also hinting at Munro's own technique, at times to mean the reverse of what she says.

But what about the nature of, and any development in, the relationship between Stella and David as 'Lichen' proceeds? David's memory of Stella some twelve or fifteen years earlier at the neighbourhood garden party continues to define his perception of her, of their ongoing relationship, of her present attitude towards him. 'Well, he forgave her – he loved her – as she walked across the lawn' (53), a remark that strikes us as peculiar in that it's only David's insecure ego, not some action by Stella, that requires any need on his part to forgive her for ostensibly eclipsing him at the gathering. We learn of David's 'unexpected delight in Stella just as she was, the unusual feeling of being at peace with her' (53) that David experienced at the party even while he was flirting with Rosemary, the first woman with whom he would have an affair while married to Stella. To David it 'seemed profound, this revelation about himself and Stella – how they were bound together after all' (53). Furthermore, it struck David that 'as long as he could feel such benevolence toward her, what he did secretly and separately was somehow done with her blessing' (53). Here the words 'revelation' and 'blessing', as ironically as they are used by Munro, again alert us to the overall allegorical nature of the actions described. Yet of Stella's position vis-à-vis David's, we're told: 'That did not turn out to be a notion Stella shared at all' (53). We learn that for David, 'All his ordinary and extraordinary life . . . seemed stored up in her' and, as a consequence, 'He could never feel any lightness' with Stella, since she 'knew so much' (54) about him. And yet, as David and Stella leave the Balm of Gilead Home – visiting which evidently, if mysteriously, provides some metaphorical balm for them – we're told that 'Nevertheless he put his arms around Stella. They embraced, both willingly' (54).

In the conclusion to the story, Stella sees that after the Polaroid's exposure to the sun where David had left it – 'but not hiding it very well, behind the curtains at one end of the long living-room window, at the spot where you stand to get a view of the lighthouse' (another allusion to Woolf's *To the Lighthouse*) – the photograph 'had faded' (55). We learn that 'the black pelt in the picture has changed to gray. It's a bluish or greenish gray now' (55), presumably a colour meant to convey symbolically that Stella's life – by means of her interactions with Catherine and David and her father and her reflections during the week or so afterwards – has finally reached a point emotionally that appears to be if not radiantly white like the pile of left-over candy that provides the title image for the book's final story, 'White Dump', then certainly not gloomily black, and perhaps even hopeful: 'She felt the old cavity opening up in her. But she held on' (55). As for the lichen, we're told: 'She remembers what she said when she first saw it. She said it was lichen. No, she said it looked like lichen. But she knew what it was at once' (55), though she said something else – a fact which leads Isla Duncan to observe of Stella's reconsideration of her original statement about the photograph that 'a closer inspection of her truth-telling utterance reveals her own acknowledged self-deception' (Duncan, *Alice Munro's Narrative Art* 50).

The epilogue continues: 'She said, "Lichen." And now, look, her words have come true. The outline of the breast has disappeared. You would never know that the legs were legs. The black has turned to gray, to the soft, dry color of a plant mysteriously nourished on the rocks', that is to say, 'like lichen' (55). Then Munro adds the two-sentence paragraph 'This is David's doing. He left it there, in the sun' (55), where the original image has now faded, disappeared, signifying its eventual inconsequence. The story concludes: 'Stella's words have come true' (55), as if she and her creator have cast a word-spell as we remember from Munro's earlier story 'Spelling' where the aged and infirm character Aunty courageously spells out different words including 'C-E-L-E-B-R-A-T-E' (Munro, 'Spelling' 183). Then we read how for Stella 'This thought will keep coming back to her – a pause, a lost heartbeat, a harsh little break in the flow of the days and nights as she keeps them going' (55). And how exactly does that series of three closing metaphors – including the cautionary and even despondent images of 'a pause, a lost heartbeat, a harsh little break' but finishing with the counterbalancing and encouraging and even optimistic clause 'as she keeps them going' (55) – add up, in terms of our impression of Stella's emotional state now? Favourably, we must conclude: a response that no doubt contributes to the pleasure that many readers take in this text.

Ultimately, we may consider 'Lichen' not so much as an allegory of love and hate, but as an allegory of what at the end of the preceding story, 'The Progress of Love', was described as 'love and grudges' (31). Or very possibly in the end we may consider 'Lichen' to be an allegory of love and forgiveness. Conceivably, we could leave the final words here to the fey-like Catherine, spoken by her to Stella: '"Love is strange, it does strange things"' (44). For as Ailsa Cox has remarked concerning the influence of certain of Munro's most important predecessors, 'Stories by Joyce, Woolf or Mansfield resist closure, ending on an image, a question or a gesture', techniques that Munro 'both renews and subverts' (Cox, *Alice Munro* 35). Indeed, the tone of Catherine's statement perfectly evokes the mysteriousness and hence the elusiveness that a different Catherine, my old friend Catherine Sheldrick Ross, concludes from her analysis of 'Cortes Island' to be representative of Munro's richest writing. In this way, as Ross explains in this volume, 'a residue of uneasiness or unresolved tension or mystery draws readers back into rereading the stories', discovering details that 'often reveal significances not noticed on first reading' and that prompt an even more intense experience of 'these works' gathering sense of mystery'.

4. Ways of Knowing and Ways of Being in 'Monsieur les Deux Chapeaux'

Short story theorist and critic Charles E. May in his career-capping book *"I Am Your Brother": Short Story Studies* (2013) rightly emphasises the genre's (and Alice Munro's) twin epistemological and ontological purposes. Namely, her effort at what, in the title of this commentary, I characterise as 'Seeing in Circles' – recalling Emerson's observations in his essay 'Circles' about the sort of imaginative thinking and use of language symbolised by the figure in that title and mine. The fact that language works in many ways and on multiple levels, as we find in jokes, in metafiction, and significantly in allegory, is stressed from the outset of 'Monsieur les Deux Chapeaux', the third story, and as such for me one that I expect to be a special story, in *The Progress of Love*. Very importantly, too, 'Monsieur les Deux Chapeaux' is remarkable, indeed arguably unique, in how it invites us to contemplate various ways of knowing and ways of being. The name given to the older of the two brothers in Munro's story, Colin, would appear to involve an allusion to a key character in Edmund Spenser's pastoral poems 'The Shepheardes Calender' (1579) and 'Colin Clouts Come Home Againe' (1595). Taken together with the fact that the title of Munro's collection would appear to be an allusion to Jonathan Swift's characteristically satiric poem 'Phyllis; or, The Progress of Love', this juxtaposition of pastoral and satire leads us to anticipate different, possibly opposing, tones and modes being at play in 'Monsieur les Deux Chapeaux'.

The story's title not only refers to a character, Ross, who wears two hats while working on the yard at the school where his older brother Colin teaches – the French nickname having been given to Ross by the school's French teacher Nancy – but also involves two languages: the one, French, in which the story's title is announced, and the other into which English-speaking readers must translate it. That feature or device not only immediately calls attention to the importance of language as a medium and a subject of crucial importance for the writer (and for readers) but also involves us in performing an act of translation which reproduces the way a writer of fiction transforms so-called 'reality' into a more refined reality, art. Indeed the significance here of translation anticipates the critical use of this same motif and device at the very end of the collection's final story, 'White Dump'. Nancy's being portrayed as fluent in two languages – or as Ross tells her, '"You got double vision"' (69) – can be viewed as a metaphor for readers' need to appreciate details in Munro's stories both literally and metaphorically or, we may say, both realistically and allegorically. The fact that the title 'Monsieur les Deux Chapeaux' appears in what for solely or even primarily English-speaking readers represents a foreign language suggests the challenges that readers face in understanding anything different – including this particular story that I believe to be extraordinary even by Alice Munro's standards. Reinforcing the motifs of French and translation, Munro's choice of the story's title may be an allusion to the colourful drawing *Deux Chapeaux* (1880) by French artist Édouard Manet.

The character designated by the story's title, Colin's brother Ross, is described at the beginning as comically, even farcically, wearing two hats: 'the green-and-white peaked cap he had got last summer at the feed store' ('green-and-white' colours evoking the pastoral and the virginal) and, on top of that, 'the old floppy hat of pinkish straw that their mother wore in the garden' (56). The 'pinkish' colour evokes femininity and perhaps even homosexuality, as does the meaning in slang of the name of the French teacher, Nancy – all suggestions that prove to be seriously misleading in terms of Ross. Initially he strikes us as a wholly fool-like character; later, we realise that he is the type of individual who plays the fool in order to conceal, to distract attention from, his real intentions. Munro even uses the word 'distraction' herself, metafictively, in having the school principal Davidson describe how school kids will '"make any little thing an excuse for distraction"' (57). The question '"What's he up to?"' (56) is asked twice at the outset by Davidson upon seeing that Ross is wearing two hats while working on the grass (again suggesting the colour green and evoking the pastoral). The question at first invites us to think about it casually, to interpret it in terms of the most superficial level of Ross's actions, rather than considering the possible greater significance of the question's placement and its repetition: as a way of urging us to study him more carefully. Munro's choosing to have Ross wear two hats serves as a metaphor for his constant duplicity – his motives involving not just comic purposes but serious designs. The fact that Colin thinks, in response to the principal's initially asking what Ross is doing, 'Not much' (56), sets up a pattern by which we are regularly if temporarily tricked by Munro into being distracted from considering the serious, even insidious, behaviour of which Ross is capable. The act of interpretation or, as my co-author Corinne Bigot would emphasise, misinterpretation is further underlined when Colin replies to the school principal's twice-posed question '"What's he up to?"' by saying '"You mean why has he got the two hats on?"' (56) instead of asking a different question then or later about his brother Ross's true intentions.

Upon considering whether in tone or in form Munro's stories are either comic or tragic, either pastoral or satiric in the sense of what Northrop Frye calls 'Menippean satire' or an 'anatomy', meaning a work that 'deals less with people as such than with mental attitudes' (Frye, *Anatomy of Criticism* 309), we recognise that in the end, and even at particular moments, Munro invites us to experience simultaneously the aesthetic and emotional experience prompted by each mode. In being confronted by such a multiplicity of modes, we may find ourselves thinking of Shakespeare's hilarious but serious description of the range of styles that the acting troupe Polonius proposes engaging to put on the play-within-the-play in *Hamlet* is capable of performing: 'tragedy, comedy, history, pastoral, pastorical-comical, historical-pastoral, tragical-historical, tragical-comical-historical-pastoral, scene individable or poem unlimited' (*The Tragedy of Hamlet* II, ii, 395–8). The list of modes is all-encompassing and wonderfully applicable to the range of Munro's writing not only across entire collections but also within individual stories – the final phrase, 'poem unlimited', striking me as a particularly apt description of her astonishing handling of the short story genre, much as Harold Bloom's critical study *Hamlet: Poem Unlimited* (2003) clearly finds that term to be a perfect characterisation of Shakespeare's achievement in the play from which the phrase is taken. Of course, Munro's attention to the modes of comedy and tragedy, of pastoral and satire in the sense of an 'anatomy' resists any simple categorisation. Still, it's important not to underestimate the significance of Davidson's comment to Colin about Ross's wearing two hats, '"Maybe it's supposed to be funny"' (57) as a metafictional clue by Munro to the frequent playfulness of her own writing.

Once again of particular importance in this third story, as in the collection's opening title story, is Munro's use – I would again say allegorically – of the colour symbolism of black and white. The contrast figures in the supposed joke but in fact racist slur which Colin and Ross's mother, Sylvia, heard at work and repeats twice at a family dinner party at Colin and Glenna's. Sylvia speaks of a 'black man' and a 'white man' using a urinal, and the implied stereotypical sizes of the men's respective sex organs, a comment that Colin notes as properly giving the French teacher Nancy 'some difficulty' (71), but also a comment suggesting the importance of the erotic as a driving force in this story. Yet despite the wholly justifiable nature of Nancy's and our objections to Sylvia's supposed joke, it nevertheless represents a sly effort on Munro's part to distract us from the serious groundwork she is laying for her use of symbolism of black and white again throughout 'Monsieur les Deux Chapeaux'. Further examples referring to both black and white include '"the black and white tiles"' that Glenna and Colin have chosen to replace the '"old boards"' (81) on the floor of the kitchen in their recently purchased house. And there is the juxtaposition of black and white in the description of the dinner party held outside in Colin and Glenna's backyard 'under the blossoming black-cherry tree' for which occasion 'Glenna had spread a white cloth and used her wedding china' (71).

As for references just to blackness, there is the fact that the composer and performer of the tell-tale recording 'Show Some Emotion' (68) which Nancy chooses to play when she visits Colin and Glenna is the Black singer-songwriter from Britain, Joan Armatrading. There is another racial implication of Blackness (and, as in the racist joke that Sylvia relates, definite prejudice) in the nickname given as a first name to the school's janitor, 'Coonie Box' (57), whose full name may suggest symbolism of death if we interpret it as meaning 'black box' or coffin. Still more threateningly, there is 'the black lane' (76) that figures in the party scene recalled towards the end of the story where the boys found a loaded hunting rifle which was then accidentally discharged towards Ross, prompting him to fall down as if he had been shot dead and causing Colin to think that he had killed his own brother. And as for references just to whiteness, there is the depiction of Glenna while she is working with Ross on his Camaro: 'Glenna's jeans were cutoffs, baring her long, powdery-white legs' (65). There is the whiteness of the product from which the convenience store where Nancy drives Colin takes its name, 'Mac's Milk' (71). And there is the whiteness not only, appealingly, of Glenna's wedding dress but also, terrifyingly, of her ghost-like appearance on the eve of her wedding to Colin, 'looking very white' (80), presumably out of terror at the prospect of her marriage to him. An image that suggests yet another element being put into play by Munro here: the ghost story, as in the case of Joyce's novella 'The Dead' or the intensely haunted and haunting final story 'My Mother's Dream' of the last of Munro's four breakthrough books, *The Love of a Good Woman* (1998).

Crucial to our understanding of the dynamics of 'Monsieur les Deux Chapeaux' and many other Munro stories is the need to appreciate her sometimes light depiction and sometimes dark depiction of human sexuality. One example involves the relationship between Colin and Ross's mother, Sylvia, and her husband. Sylvia's name seems connected to the word 'sylvan' and as a result contributes to our early mistaken sense of this story as a pastoral – the word 'sylvan' or 'silvan' having appeared memorably in Milton's description of the Garden of Eden as 'A Silvan Scene' (*Paradise Lost* IV.140). The reality of Sylvia's life is, however, far different. The fact that she gave birth to her two sons after ten years then just under eleven years of marriage conveys the strong possibility that her husband was infertile or uninterested in sex or possibly gay and that she became pregnant with her two sons by some other man – conceivably, though we are given at most a hint, the police constable who figures in different scenes in the story and who is said (perhaps euphemistically) to be 'a sort of boyfriend' (79) of Sylvia's. This interpretation of Sylvia's husband is reinforced by the memory that Colin has of his father, a long-time railway man, while they were walking down the street together and his father offered a stick of gum to him. We are told that 'There was a kindly, official air about this gesture – his father was wearing his uniform at the time – rather than a paternal intimacy' (72–3), a description by which Munro implies that Colin's father may have been his father and Ross's only in terms of an 'official' (72) role, rather than by blood.

To cite a different example, we may consider Glenna's marriage to a socially acceptable but presumably a sexually less ardent man like Colin rather than to a socially unacceptable but presumably a sexually more ardent man like Ross, a decision that leaves Glenna on the eve of her wedding crying uncontrollably. I believe Munro's depiction of Glenna's choice between Colin and Ross to be a rewriting of Catherine Earnshaw's choice between the placid man she doesn't love but marries, Edgar Linton, and the ardent man she loves but doesn't marry, Heathcliff, in Emily Brontë's *Wuthering Heights* (1847). Or we might view Munro's portrayal of Glenna's relationships with Colin and Ross as a rewriting of Anna's marriage to Karenin and her affair with Vronsky in Leo Tolstoy's *Anna Karenina* (1878). Or as echoing the contrast between Gretta's now unimpassioned feelings for her husband Gabriel Conroy and her still impassioned feelings for her deceased young suitor Michael Furey in Joyce's 'The Dead'. The anxiety that Glenna feels about marrying Colin is powerfully conveyed in the section that Munro chooses, emphatically, to place second-last in the story: the description as recalled by Colin of Glenna's presumed jitters, though her feelings ran far deeper than that, when 'at nine-thirty the night before the wedding' she finally completed her work on the dresses for all five bridesmaids as well as herself and headed upstairs where Colin 'found her weeping' and 'couldn't get her to stop' (80). So serious was the situation that 'Glenna sobbed and said, among other things, that she saw no use in being alive' (80). This statement – reinforced by other situations in the story, including Ross's apparently self-destructive impulse in remodelling his Camaro with an oversized engine that is likely to explode – invites us to think of 'Monsieur les Deux Chapeaux' as an allegory depicting 'the tension' (Munro in Struthers, 'The Real Material' 15) that Munro considers necessary for her own stories between the Freudian life force or *Eros* and the Freudian death drive or *Thanatos*.

We get an initial seemingly joking picture of a possible Ross and Glenna romance the first time that Glenna comes for dinner at the home of Colin and Ross's mother, Sylvia. We read, 'The first words Ross ever spoke directly to Glenna were "Do you know the only thing that's the matter with you?"' (60) – a question that invites misinterpretation as presumably implying that it will lead to a criticism by him of Glenna. To the contrary, however, Ross's seemingly serious question, once he explains it, is regarded by all as a joke – 'A relief. They all laughed' – once Ross declares that '"The only thing the matter with you . . . is that I didn't find you first!"' (61). We learn that in time 'It became a family joke. What would have happened if Glenna had met Ross first?' (61). The answer given, again presumably jokingly, is that 'Colin wouldn't have had a chance' (61). But what's so very interesting is the conversation between Colin and Glenna that follows, including responses both visually and verbally by Glenna that are more ambiguous or many-levelled than they first appear. Colin experiences an urgent need to know what his wife's answers would be to his questions about herself and Ross, '"What if you *had* met him first? Would you have gone out with him?"' (61; emphasis in orig.). In fact Colin is so perplexed that he promptly repeats the second question. Intriguingly, though upon first reading the statement we may not pay serious attention to it, we are told that Glenna 'looked embarrassed', after which she makes a remark whose ambiguity we at first likely miss: that '"Ross isn't the type you go out with"' (61). Perhaps, however, we later imagine, Ross is the type you stay in with, the type you have an affair with, even though he is your husband's brother. We learn that Glenna 'always said, "I like Ross, though. You can't help *liking* him"' (59–60; emphasis in orig.) then quickly – or we might suggest all too quickly – would add, as if to distract Colin from an impression she doesn't want to reveal, '"I like him *and* your mother. I like her, too"' (60; emphasis in orig.).

Glenna's attraction to Ross and her sense of a choice for her between the two brothers is made evident early on through the description of how during the dinner at Sylvia's house 'Glenna suggested that Ross might like to come to the drive-in' (61) with Colin and herself that evening. The potential love triangle is then suggested by the fact that 'The three of them sat on top of Colin's car, with Glenna in the middle' (61), much as in the collection's first story Fame was caught in the middle, literally and symbolically, between her mother and her aunt in the back seat of Mr Florence's Chrysler. The clue provided by Munro to suggest that Ross and Glenna actually start an affair and are carrying on together sexually at Colin and Glenna's house while Colin is at work lies in the hint of dissatisfaction shown by Glenna and Colin's very young daughter, Lynnette, at a seeming lack of concern for her during the day that she expresses through demanding her father's attention when he returns home. Meanwhile, Glenna continues 'polishing the trim rings and center caps' (64) that had been taken off the wheels on Ross's car – the double meaning of 'rings' calling attention to her marital status and the double meaning of 'caps' calling attention to his two hats. The fact that Glenna is 'polishing like mad' (64) seems meant to display her total absorption in that task rather than anything else – a deliberate misdirection on her part that we interpret as exactly that.

Glenna explains to Colin about her polishing parts of the wheels on Ross's car that she hadn't taken the time to get her hay-fever shots that day because '"I got fooling around with these and I got sort of hypnotized"' (64). Here Munro's delightful use of the euphemism 'fooling around' in its sexually charged sense and the underlining of the joke a page later when Munro has Colin remark that '"Ross always fooled around with cars"' (65) definitely causes the reader's eyebrow to rise. Colin is aware that by the time he got home 'Ross would be there ahead of him, working on the car' (63) or, more specifically, working with Colin's wife, Glenna, on the car. And given the pleasure Munro takes in using euphemisms – to which we were first alerted by the naming of the focal character of the collection's opening title story after her grandmother Euphemia – we find ourselves wondering if the phrase 'working on the car' (63) could be a euphemism for the collaboration between Ross and Glenna on a much more intimate indoor activity. Ross's preoccupation with installing an oversized presumably symbolic engine in his car invites consideration in the context of Marshall McLuhan's commentary in the title piece of *The Mechanical Bride: Folklore of Industrial Man* (1951). There, upon observing of current advertising that 'A car plus a well-filled pair of nylons is a recognized formula for both feminine and male success and happiness' (McLuhan, 'The Mechanical Bride' 98–9), McLuhan points forebodingly to 'the widely occurring cluster image of sex, technology, and death' (McLuhan 101). More specifically, in terms of Ross's obsession with rebuilding cars, we may note Beverly J. Rasporich's comment about how in the collection's second-last story, 'Circle of Prayer', Trudy's ex-husband Dan's 'association with cars and machinery is an extension of masculine sexual control, of the sex act itself' (Rasporich 155).

Other language that Munro uses can regularly be considered to have both a literal commonplace meaning and a second sexual meaning – to involve double entendres, we may say – including the oft-repeated word 'stripper' and even the word 'sheets' in descriptions of Ross's work on the car such as 'The top coat of paint had fallen off in sheets when he used the stripper' (64). On the same page Munro repeats the word 'stripper' three times including twice in one paragraph when Colin is worried that Ross has been using stripper on the car and might have exposed Glenna and Lynnette to it, though that wasn't the case, and once more when Ross mentions '"stripper"' (64). Colin reassures himself that he can 'trust Glenna not to expose herself and Lynnette to that' (64), though again attentive readers may well catch the doubleness of this phrase: that Colin can't 'trust Glenna not to expose herself' in some other way that he would not appreciate. Even the seemingly innocent observation that there was 'No sign of either hat on Ross now' (65) raises the question of whether he might have removed his two hats somewhere else, very possibly inside the house while he '"fooled around"' (65) – to cite Colin's (but not Munro's) unknowingly euphemistic phrase about his brother – not with his car this time but with Glenna. And of course in reflecting on Munro's attention to Ross's hats, we do need to remember that in Freudian dream analysis hats are thought to be a symbol of the male sexual organ (Freud, *The Interpretation of Dreams* 478–80). Still more generally in terms of Munro's language, we may cite her description of how Ross used to follow girls down the street slowly in his car, 'sounding the horn as if in Morse code' (61), and see this description as suggesting metafictively that Munro herself is writing in a secret language, a code comprised of figures of speech such as euphemisms, metaphors and allusions.

The likelihood that Ross and Glenna are having an affair is rightly raised then wrongly dismissed when Colin, after returning home, relaxes and has two thoughts about Ross and Glenna. First, Colin thinks of how pleased he was when Glenna smiled at Ross's ostensible joke about the only problem with her being that he hadn't met her before his brother had, Colin feeling pleased because he believed that 'from now on Ross could stop being a secret weight on him; he would now have someone to share Ross with' (66). Of course, the related notion of Colin sharing his wife with his brother has a doubleness in meaning – suggesting not only emotionally but also sexually – to which Colin becomes suddenly alert but which he immediately dismisses though Munro wants us to consider it: 'The other thought that had crossed Colin's mind' (66), we are told, 'was dirty in every sense of the word' (66–7). But 'Ross never would', Colin thinks, recalling how Ross 'glowered and stuck his big lip out and looked as if he half felt like crying' – for what reason we might wonder, perhaps envy rather than the prudishness Colin supposes? – 'when there was a sexy scene at the movies' (67). In this way Munro slyly has Colin mislead not only himself but also possibly the story's readers about Ross unless we accept the interpretation by Colin which he himself has dismissed.

Glenna isn't the only woman in the story who is attracted to Ross. The French teacher Nancy says adoringly of his wearing two hats while doing yard work one day at the school: '"Ross, you were beautiful. What an inspiration on a dull dragged-out old Friday afternoon"' (69). And later Nancy declares to Colin that '"I love Ross"' (71). In addition, and disturbingly, there are even suggestions of a possible Oedipal relationship, as outlined by Freud (Freud, *The Interpretation of Dreams* 362–6), between Sylvia and each of her two sons, notably Ross – be it psychological or something else. In the case of Ross, it's certainly more than overprotectiveness on Sylvia's part, for when Nancy tells Colin that she loves Ross, Colin replies '"You better not let Sylvia hear you say that"' (71). Similarly, a description of Colin's view of his mother possesses an undercurrent of Oedipal implications: 'Colin thought there was something clumsy and appealing about her figure and her wide-open face with its pink, soft skin, clear blue eyes under almost nonexistent eyebrows, her eager all-purpose smile. Something maddening as well' (59). And the same undercurrent may be conveyed by Colin's attitude towards his mother's boyfriends, about whom 'he usually took a lightly critical tone' (59) – as if envious, we may ask? The rivalry between Colin and Ross may be intensified by competitive Oedipal feelings for their mother. Still more troubling, however, is the implication of an actual incestuous relationship between Sylvia and Ross, who continues to live with his mother. This possible very disturbing element of their relationship is suggested by Colin's question to Sylvia, '"If you're working the early shift, . . . how do you know what time Ross gets up?"' (59) – with the presumed echo here by Munro of the euphemism for male sexual arousal, 'getting it up', reinforcing the implication. As 'Monsieur les Deux Chapeaux' proceeds, its depictions of sexuality grow steadily more distressing.

The intertwining of comic or pastoral material equally with tragic or satiric material is most evident in Munro's ever-deepening portrayal of Ross. He proves to be the opposite of the sort of 'fool-saint' we encounter in the character of Mary Dempster in Munro's fellow Southwestern Ontario-born writer Robertson Davies' novel *Fifth Business* (1970) and in other characters devised by Munro, including Milton Homer in the closing title story of *Who Do You Think You Are?*

(1978), or as it was called outside Canada, *The Beggar Maid: Stories of Flo and Rose* (1979), and Kelvin in the second-last story, 'Circle of Prayer', in this volume. Rather than a fool-saint, Ross represents what, thinking of the title of Edna O'Brien's story collection *Saints and Sinners* (2011), I shall call a 'fool-sinner' – a fool whose behaviour and impact are essentially or at least primarily sinful in contrast to saintly in nature, that is, someone who, allegorically speaking, promotes reflection on the workings in our world of the forces of evil, of the demonic, as opposed to the forces of good, of the angelic. That contrast is reinforced by the description of Glenna on her wedding day as 'angelically pretty' (80) – though that may well represent the light side rather than the dark side of her. As for Ross, our sense of his psyche and actions alters drastically over the course of the story: from his initial preposterously comic appearance wearing two hats to the accounts of his past and present erotic exploits to the apparently death-driven impulse represented by his installing a presumably dangerously oversized engine in the Camaro that he has started rebuilding. On the subject of Ross's changes to his car, alterations which Nancy prophetically thinks will eventually kill him (as Ross undoubtedly foresees), Glenna astutely points out to Colin that '"I think he started thinking about the car when he realized he wasn't going to live with us in the house"' (65) – meaning that Ross's thoughts darkened drastically as soon as he grasped that he would be denied proximity to the woman who had become the love of his life, his brother's wife, Glenna.

In contrast to, but perhaps not entirely separate from, Ross's death drive is the strong but illicit and in various respects perverse and harmful nature of Ross's sex drive. The extreme nature of his erotic impulses is emphasised by means of the story about his obsession in Grade Nine with Wilma Barry – described for us, from Colin's point of view, as Ross's 'persecution of Wilma Barry' (62) – and through the hints, whether disguised as jokes or concealed by distracting descriptions of everyday actions, of Ross's intense feelings for and probable sexual activity with Colin's wife Glenna now. After reference is made to Ross's Grade Nine infatuation with and persecution of Wilma Barry, we wonder why Ross says, '"Colin, tell Glenna about me and the piece of pie!"' (62). Is it because on Ross's part for other characters, and on Munro's part for readers, this story would offer a comic '"distraction"' (57) from material with far more serious implications? Concerning Ross's behaviour overall, the subsequent statement about work on the car that 'Ross had all this planned out' (67) leads us to speculate whether that comment might well be true of everything that he plans or does – even those comic or seemingly comic statements or actions that he claims are without intent, certainly without serious intent. We think, 'Ross had all this planned out' and then wonder, what else?

Certainly there are allegorical implications to the seemingly purely comical incident when Ross was caught during lesson time at school sneaking from his lunch a piece of apple pie (suggesting Adam's eating of the forbidden fruit), allegorical implications underlined by the use of the word 'devil' in the teacher's response to Ross, '"What in the devil do you think you're doing?"' (62). We also need to consider how, at the end of this episode, Ross slips the piece of pie underneath his bum and then brings 'his sticky hands together in a clap of innocence' (62) or, rather, in a show of innocence. Again characteristically, Ross claims that '"I didn't do it to be funny!"' (62) – misleadingly suggesting that, by extension, none of his actions or statements are deliberate, self-interested, let alone calculated mischievously or maliciously when in fact they are. The end of the story about Wilma Barry has an important implication in the present, for the answer that Ross gives to the question about his first fixation, Wilma, a question posed significantly by Glenna, '"Where is she now, Ross?"' is the same answer '"Gone. Married"' (62) as Ross would give if he were asked about his new fixation, Glenna. Ross's answer – like much else about how he behaves and how Munro writes – works on two levels, be that moral duplicity on his part or aesthetic doubleness on her part.

The final story contained in 'Monsieur les Deux Chapeaux' is focused on Sylvia's twenty-fifth wedding anniversary party and is related by her during the outdoor dinner party hosted by Colin and Glenna. Sylvia's story is told at the prompting of Ross over the objections of Glenna, who says '"It's horrible"' (74), and told to the dismay of Colin, who is humiliated by what it reports. Presumably the reason that Glenna so strongly objects to hearing again the part of the story which Sylvia is going to tell next is because it makes Glenna imagine the possibility of Ross dying, the possibility of losing her strong emotional and presumably sexual connection with him. As for Colin's response, he simply refuses to listen once again to an account of events that continue to have a deeply negative emotional affect on him, electing instead, part-way into his mother's story, to head out into the yard with his mother's newest boyfriend, Eddy, 'a retired garage owner and car dealer' (58) and therefore an expert about cars, to assess the safeness of the work Ross is doing on his Camaro.

Sylvia states that in other cases the result of what she is about to describe '"has been worse. Tragic"' (74). Then we read, '"It sure could've been tragic," Ross said, laughing' (74) – a line that reinforces the perplexing mix of modes that Munro draws on in this story. The foreboding nature of Ross's laughter at the incident's potentially turning tragic is emphasised not only by his laughter being mentioned twice more on the next page when Colin hears it while standing outside with Eddy but also by the fact that it was 'In the dark he heard Ross laughing again' (75). Colin asks Eddy to judge the possible danger of the much larger Chevy engine that Ross is installing in his Camaro, a judgement for whatever reason that Eddy hesitates to make. Eddy's name represents an allusion to the long-established Canadian-based Eddy Match Co. and thus connects with other images here of fire, a standard symbol of sexual excitement, images including Glenna's tape of the soundtrack for the 1981 film *Chariots of Fire* that we are told Ross chooses to play. And surely Eddy's name represents another pun on Munro's part, chosen at least in part because he represents Sylvia's latest 'flame'. But the point of Colin's involving Eddy here is that he is meant to pass judgement on Ross's work on his car and by implication on Ross's psychological state – judgement being a matter, allegorically speaking, of significant Biblical import.

One way of reading 'Monsieur les Deux Chapeaux', specifically Colin's responsibilities for his younger brother Ross, is to see Munro's story as an allegory about the line from Genesis spoken to God by Cain about his brother Abel that asked 'Am I my brother's keeper?' (Genesis 4: 9). This topic seized the imaginations of the authors of the two most important books on the short story, Frank O'Connor's *The Lonely Voice: A Study of the Short Story* (1963) and Charles

E. May's *"I Am Your Brother": Short Story Studies* (2013). In Munro's story it is announced in the very first sentence when the school principal, Davidson, asks Colin: '"Is that your brother out there?"' (56) and, as E.D. Blodgett argues, the story's opening question indeed represents 'the kernel' (Blodgett 137) of all that follows. More specifically, Ildikó de Papp Carrington finds an archetypal connection between the seeming shooting of Ross by his brother Colin recalled in the final pages and the Biblical story of the actual murder of Abel by his brother Cain (Carrington, *Controlling* 66) – as well as an allusion in Davidson's question for Colin to 'the one God asked the guilty Cain: "Where is Abel, thy brother?"' (Carrington 67). Yet as Carrington emphasises, what we discern upon comparing the two stories is a direct contrast both in the sense that Colin, unlike Cain, does not kill his brother and in the sense that Colin, unlike Cain, takes responsibility for being his brother's keeper, something which, Carrington notes, 'Cain ... protests to God he cannot be' (Carrington 66). The line spoken to God by Cain about his brother Abel – 'Am I my brother's keeper?' – does not involve a fond statement of fraternal commitment but rather a vexed and resentful question.

The moral issue raised in the Biblical question 'Am I my brother's keeper?' takes on increased moral weight over historical time for Colin and, because of the order in which Munro chooses to have different scenes in the story narrated, takes on increased aesthetic weight over narrative time for the work's readers. Ross's motive in wanting to have the story about when Colin supposedly shot him dead told over and over seems vindictive, a deliberately guilt-inducing though seemingly at most mischievous reminder to Colin of the cruel joke that Ross played on his brother. We learn that the rifle had been loaded but 'The bullet hadn't come near him. It had hit the shed a little way down the lane' (77). And 'everybody, knowing Ross, believed or suspected that he had put on an act on purpose, on the spur of the moment' (77), pretending that Colin had shot him dead.

Allegorically, this incident reinforces the story's depiction of 'the tension' that Munro says is so important to her, in this case between a celebration of life in terms of the Freudian life force or *Eros* and a rejection of life in terms of the Freudian death drive or *Thanatos*. But far more gravely this situation emphasises the story's own apparent movement by this point from a celebration of life to a rejection of life. Colin's motive in not wanting to hear the story told over and over would appear to be guilt, for at the very end of 'Monsieur les Deux Chapeaux' we are told of Colin's recognition that his responsibility in life going forward will be to prevent anything dreadful from happening to Ross and therefore to himself. Or perhaps we should say that what Colin feels is not exactly guilt but a need, for his brother's sake and for his own sake, to conduct himself honourably, generously, lovingly – in the eyes of God, we might suggest, when Colin would in allegorical terms face a presumably favourable Last Judgment. By contrast, Colin's brother Ross would appear to require being judged unfavourably. As readers, then, however much we may find our attention directed towards Colin, we need to be sure to give equal attention to the two brothers, most especially to the story's title character. We consistently need to heed the advice given in the story's final scene by Sylvia (and through her metafictively by Munro), when all eyes including the readers' are on Colin: '"Get those stupid lights off him ... Turn the lights on Ross if you want to turn them on something"' (79).

The story's final pages continue the earlier segment depicting the pursuit of Colin by various people from Sylvia's twenty-fifth wedding anniversary party, including the group of boys who had witnessed the apparent shooting of Ross by Colin, including the resurrected Ross himself – I say 'resurrected' because near story's end we read, presumably parodically, of 'Ross risen up' (83) – who are heading along with Sylvia and the constable to where Ross suggests they can likely find his brother, at Tiplady Bridge. We learn of the innermost reflections by Colin, who still thinks he has murdered his brother, that the idea 'that they had come to blame him . . . didn't interest him. He knew what he had done' (81) – though in fact he didn't. Moreover, 'He hadn't run away and cut down here and climbed the bridge in the dark so they couldn't punish him' (81). Then why did he proceed there, we wonder – to think about what philosophers would call matters of ontology, ways of being, that are as much a concern of the short story genre as what philosophers would call matters of epistemology, ways of knowing? We learn that 'he wasn't shivering with the shock' (81) – but presumably from something else: from a new understanding of existence we suspect.

There is the hugely important question, for Munro here and in possibly all her stories, '"How do you know?"' – a question posed by one of the boys to another who declared (as it happens, incorrectly, like certain of our own initial misinterpretations of situations and details) of the rifle they discovered, '"It isn't loaded"' (76). And beyond that we ask: What do you know? Hence Colin found himself contemplating 'all the jumble of his life, and other people's lives in this town, rolled back' (81), as Munro describes it through a favourite analogy for her own writing (as I and Lorraine M. York and others have noted) but here newly reconfigured as 'just like a photograph split and rolled back, so it shows what was underneath all along' (81–2). But the answer to 'what was underneath all along' – as we may recall from Shakespeare's *King Lear* or T.S. Eliot's *The Waste Land* – lies in the seemingly nihilistic single-word sentence that Munro has Colin offer next, 'Nothing', in the two-word sentence that she has him offer soon afterwards, 'Still nothing', and in Munro's emphatic use of the word 'nothing' (82) for a third time half a page later. That third instance echoes the earlier simile 'just like a photograph split and rolled back' (81): we learn of Colin that 'His life had split open and nothing had to be figured out anymore' (82). And if that was the case, what way of being, of understanding might follow for him?

In a metafictional critique first of the limitations of language itself, Munro – seemingly pushing to the side any thoughts that readers may have had about the significance of her having chosen Colin's name by way of alluding to pastoral poems by Edmund Spenser – has Colin reflect 'How silly it was that he should have a name and it should be Colin, and that people should be shouting it' (82). And further, in a metafictional critique of the very logic that all of us regularly employ, she has Colin observe 'What was silly was to think in these chunks of words. Colin. Shot. Ross. To see it as an action. Something sharp and separate, an event, a *difference*' (82; emphasis in orig.). As opposed to seeing it preferably as what, we ask. Not, as I first found myself considering, as destiny, inevitability or, more emphatically, 'doom', to borrow a word that Southern United States writer William Faulkner used as the name of the character Ikkemotubbe or *du homme* or Doom in several of his short stories including 'Red Leaves' and that Munro employs in the opening story of her third breakthrough book, *Open Secrets* (Munro, 'Carried Away' 26). But rather, I now find myself contemplating, to see the thing we seek to represent as something indescribable, something that is part of a grand unknowable continuum. A mystery. Or 'The Great Mystery', as ethnologist and mythographer Basil H. Johnston translated the Ojibwe name for God, *Kitchi-manitou* (Johnston 350).

While Colin remains for the time being up on the bridge, we learn that he 'felt dizzy, and sick with the force of things coming back to life, the chaos and emotion' (83) – with the phrase about 'things coming back to life' reinforcing the sense of this story as an allegory of life and death, death and rebirth. James Carscallen asks what this experience of Colin's is like and replies 'it is like nothing and everything' (Carscallen, *The Other Country* 112), words which underline this scene's deep philosophical implications for Munro, for Colin, and for ourselves. As Colin does what he has been told and starts to climb down from the bridge, we learn that 'he had to keep himself from thinking, too suddenly, about what had just missed happening' (83). What, we ask: not only the possible death of his brother Ross but also the possible death of all of Colin's feelings, hope, faith. And just as Colin feels drained and uneasy, so do we. For our opening sense of the story as comedy or as pastoral has narrowly avoided, if perhaps only temporarily avoided, turning into a closing sense of the story as tragedy or as satire should Ross succeed in the act of self-destruction that he seems to have envisaged for himself, an act that would undoubtedly have deep emotional consequences for all of the story's other principal characters. In the story's emphatic and portentous single-sentence final paragraph we learn of Colin's sobering awareness 'that to watch out for something like that happening – to Ross, and to himself – was going to be his job in life from then on' (83). Will Colin succeed in protecting Ross and himself, we wonder? Does the story operate both as memory and as prophecy, to echo once more Dennis Duffy's terminology (Duffy, 'On Fact and Fiction')? Can we infer how the story will end 'beyond the ending' as Rachel Blau Duplessis would phrase it? As comedy or as tragedy? The act of interpretation involves our recognising that, as James Carscallen states, 'a whole story is a single epiphanic happening' through which 'centre has become circumference' (Carscallen, *The Other Country* 114). Or, in my and Catherine Sheldrick Ross's terms, a stone tossed into a lake creating ever-widening circles.

In the end we must ask if the Nothingness that Colin contemplates towards the conclusion of 'Monsieur les Deux Chapeaux' represents the philosophical view that Munro herself finally adopts here. Or at least by implication does she counterbalance that, as we have recognised her as being fond of doing, with some sort of celebration of Being – the first concept given in the title in English translation, *Being and Nothingness* (1956), for Jean-Paul Sartre's classic philosophical study *L'être et le néant* (1943)? For surely a celebration of language and stories and Being – or to borrow a phrase of James Carscallen's, 'the mystery of transformation' (Carscallen, *The Other Country* 398) – is what Munro finally through the act of writing 'Monsieur les Deux Chapeaux' and giving us this 'poem unlimited' to read accomplishes so resolutely and so admirably.

5. Did You Enjoy Your Visit?

Reflecting on several critical studies of Munro in an essay collected in *Reading Alice Munro 1973–2013*, Robert Thacker argues that fundamentally Alice Munro's stories present us with what Louis K. MacKendrick stressed through the subtitle he chose for the first book-length study of her work, published under his editorship in 1983, called *Probable Fictions: Alice Munro's Narrative Acts*. Thacker then states good-humouredly of Munro's stories that 'What we do with them . . . is largely whatever we want' (Thacker, *Reading Alice Munro* 188). As a result, he says, in the choice of the topics or the elements different critics feature, we all end up 'privileging this, downplaying that, exaggerating here, ignoring there' (Thacker 188) – to what I would call our conscious, half-conscious or even unconscious purposes. Each individual critic therefore constructs what Thacker calls one or another 'version of the Munro critique' (Thacker 188). To circle back to my own list of preferences stated in the opening section of this commentary for ways of reading Munro most effectively, that would involve viewing her stories in the following terms: as allegory, as meditation, as metafiction; as form, as technique, as style; as an act of narration, as an order in which a story is told, as a succession of weights; as wordplay, as metaphor, as allusion. Early in this discussion of *The Progress of Love*, I also drew attention to the theory I have long held, derived from an analogy to baseball, about the opening three stories of a collection as frequently being arranged in a special way with particular purposes. More recently I have found myself wondering if the closing three stories of a collection might be arranged in much the same way but in reverse. Namely, with the third-last story (here the novella 'A Queer Streak') being the most challenging of the final three; with the second-last story (here 'Circle of Prayer') being different from both the third-last story and the final story; and with the last story (here the saga-like 'White Dump') circling back to, and in this case actually being a companion three-generation piece to, the opening work 'The Progress of Love'.

To attempt in the necessarily briefest of ways to convey some sense of what I have called 'The Fierce Originality of *The Progress of Love*' in terms of Munro's achievements in each of these final three stories involves difficult personal choices. Here I find it helpful to recall Munro's own comment that her story 'Images' started with a 'picture in my mind' (Munro, 'The Colonel's Hash Revisited' 189) – that is, with a detail that for me opens up possibilities – though admittedly these notions might be the last that Munro herself would consciously consider – of reading that story and others by her first and foremost as allegory, as meditation, as metafiction. Sometimes Munro explains in author's commentaries or in interviews what the seed that prompted the writing of a particular story happened to be. But in the cases of many stories, Munro may not provide such an explanation – and, in any event, very possibly what needs to be stressed is not the seed that inspired Munro but the particular sentence or passage or scene that stimulates the individual readings that each of us performs. For me, the meeting-places for Munro's mind and mine tend to involve especially rich and forceful scenes – and within them, of course, images. In fact, I frequently think that the best description of the central technique found in her work would be the title which Allan Wade used in 1946 for the collection of theatre criticism by Henry James that he edited and which Hugh Hood subsequently echoed in 1984 in the title of one of the novels in his twelve-part epic cycle *The New Age / Le nouveau siècle* (1975–2000): *The Scenic Art*. There, in such scenes, we discover the most powerfully immanent and the most powerfully transcendent.

As allegory, 'A Queer Streak' by definition works on several different levels: the personal, representing the lives and the fates of individual characters; the erotic, involving courtship, diverse sexual orientations, but also presumably abusive interfamilial behaviour; the historical, representing the evolution of social life in Ontario over most of the twentieth century; and the literary, involving Munro's own choices of form and technique and style in her writing. We can readily imagine different sorts of readers, from those absorbed with realism to those delighting in metafiction, being intrigued by one or another – indeed perhaps by more than one – of these subjects. Yet transcending, though still informing, this group are what I believe to be Munro's most pressing concerns – with questions of epistemology, involving the nature of knowing and particular ways of knowing, and with questions of ontology, involving the nature of being and particular ways of being – or to express that allegorically, her concerns with what Hamlet calls 'a divinity that shapes our ends' (Shakespeare, *The Tragedy of Hamlet* V, ii, 10). For me, the most mysterious scene in the novella 'A Queer Streak' is the very deliberately placed opening two-page passage about the typically darkened front parlour at the family's home and in particular the description of the surely symbolic and disturbing painting of three princesses around a king – the dark-haired Violet's presumed stepfather and her two red-headed sisters' actual father goes by the nickname of 'King Billy' – who may be dead or possibly asleep, conceivably following coitus we hesitantly speculate. The painting represents the key to the puzzle that Munro wants us to spend the entire novella pondering and that I believe she answers, at least initially for us in a way that is completely perplexing when, in the final conversation between Violet and her nephew Dane, Munro has Violet declare bizarrely but employing the symbolic language that interpreters of dreams and of literature can appreciate, '"There is a wild pig running through the corn"' (253) – or however else one might describe a father who presumably molests his own daughter. What does Violet know or suspect to have occurred years earlier in this 'black room' with which Munro, presumably forebodingly, begins this story? Something that has happened to Violet, we may wonder, especially if we think we hear the word 'violate' in her name? Or something that has since happened or that could soon happen to one or both of her younger sisters – very possibly to thirteen-year-old Dawn Rose, who 'was a big stout girl now, with loose breasts jiggling inside her dress', though probably not yet to twelve-year-old Bonnie Hope, who 'was still childish in body' (214)?

A second story and a second-last story in a collection each seeks to portray, to reach for, something different, ideally something more. In 'Circle of Prayer' Munro gives extended attention to the interchange of questions and answers, particularly between Trudy and her teenage daughter Robin, a dynamic which can be seen as working both on a personal and on a metaphysical level, as realism and as allegory. Yet for me the most haunting part of the story comes not long before the ending, when we're offered a two-page recollection by Trudy of the time she and her once-husband Dan spent on their honeymoon at the island residence of Trudy's mother-in-law. Specifically, one afternoon while Dan was out fishing and Trudy stayed back, heard the sound of a piano, and followed the music until she reached the front veranda of the closed-down hotel where Dan's mother lived, 'stopped at a window' (272) – windows always possessing a metafictive value for Munro – and looked inside. There Trudy discovered Dan's mother playing the piano, notably 'without any lights on, in the half-dark, half-bare room' (272) – just as, I find myself thinking metafictively, Munro herself memorably told her fellow Canadian writer Adele Wiseman, as Catherine Sheldrick Ross relates, that '"I work in the dark"' (Munro in Ross, *Alice Munro* 84). Dan's mother 'wasn't playing a classical piece' (272) as might have been expected based on her having studied piano in her youth, but rather 'Three O'Clock in the Morning', a waltz referenced in F. Scott Fitzgerald's *The Great Gatsby* (1925) that finishes with the romantic line 'I could just keep on dancing forever dear with you' and played here – both hauntedly and hauntingly – by a woman whose beloved husband has been claimed by death. Also remarkably, we learn that Dan's mother didn't stop playing when she reached the end of the piece, but began again. We're told: 'Maybe it was a special favorite of hers, something she had danced to in the old days. Or maybe she wasn't satisfied yet that she had got it right' (272–3) – an explanation that speaks metafictively of Alice Munro's own intense creative practice. But we can't help but wonder if maybe Dan's mother resumed playing not out of personal enjoyment or artistic perfectionism but because the piece operated on an even deeper emotional level for her, as the act of remembering this scene does later for the now separated and like her mother-in-law now bereft Trudy. And we can't help but wonder if maybe the significance for Trudy of this memory resides in the depth of emotion with which the music so strongly resonates both for the performer and for the listener – as is the case for this scene and its creator and each reader.

The story 'White Dump' – and the collection that it concludes – ends with a series of three separate sequences, involving, as short story theorist Susan Lohafer would note, a first 'pre-closure point' (Lohafer 4) then another 'pre-closure point', and finally the story's actual ending. The first sequence depicts Isabel's return the day after her husband Laurence's fortieth birthday to see and to begin an affair with the pilot of the four-seater plane in which Laurence had enjoyed a flight with his daughter Denise and his mother Sophie as a birthday present. But the first sequence also flashes forward several years to include a later conversation in which Isabel describes that affair to Denise as both '"the most passionate"' and '"the most sordid"' (308) of the love affairs that she would have during the years ahead. The second much briefer sequence refers to how the family played a game of charades that represents not only a suitable metaphor, realistically, for all the acting people choose to do in their often not-so-ordinary lives but also, like the game of Scrabble earlier in this story, a suitable metaphor, metafictively, for the care, not just word by word but syllable by syllable, with which Munro chooses her language. Hence, we learn of Peter, in acting out the word for the constellation Orion (a word which he has presumably chosen for himself), that 'He did the second syllable by drinking from an imaginary glass, then staggering around and falling down' (309). Denise makes a joke of Peter's choice, '"Space is Peter's world, after all"' (309), causing their parents to laugh. Significantly, however, the line that Munro gives Denise only takes the form of a joke; in actuality, it's a serious point disguised as a joke, the way that Munro often conveys important suggestions or allusions. Munro adds that 'This remark was one that would be quoted from time to time in the household' (309) – the emphasis given by her to the joke being repeated 'from time to time' suggesting, I believe, that just as we are asked to think allegorically of Space as Peter's world, so too we are asked to think allegorically of Time as Denise's world. And in that way, Munro expands the range of 'White Dump' and all the stories in the collection that precede it to force our engagement in not just a philosophical, not just an aesthetic, but a deeply personal meditation on the workings in our individual lives of Space and Time.

Then in the third and very last sequence of the saga-like story 'White Dump' we learn that 'Sophie, who never understood the rules of charades – or, at least, could never keep to them – soon gave up the game, and began to read' (309): specifically, *The Poetic Edda*, the Old Norse saga 'which she read every summer' (309). We may wish to consider as well that Sophie's first name evokes that of Sophia, the goddess of wisdom who in Gnosticism represents the female counterpart to Jesus, thereby affirming that in all three final stories in this collection Munro is inviting us to consider how a matriarchal society, as opposed to a patriarchal society, would work. Sophie, having finished her evening's reading, headed for bed, leaving her book where, at story's end, we learn that 'Isabel, picking it up before she turned out the light, read' the following:

*Seinat er at segia;
svá er nu rádit.* (309)

At this point we get a translation from an unknown presumably omniscient source of the preceding two-line passage into a single line of English – the act of translation in this instance, I believe, serving as a metaphor for art's re-creation of life. '(It is too late to talk of this now: it has been decided.)' (309), we are told, in parentheses – the additional punctuation not only replacing the expected traditional quotation marks but presumably indicating a change in narrative point of view or at least in narrative tone. Of this allusion, Héliane Ventura points out that 'these lines belong to the "Lay of Atli," a lay which is part of the heroic poems of the *Codex Regius* dating back to the thirteenth century' – adding, 'The lay describes the disastrous fate of Gudrun: she marries Atli (Attila), has two sons by him, whom she roasts and feeds to her husband in revenge for his murder of her brothers, and she later attempts to commit suicide' (Ventura, 'The Female Bard' 168).

That voice from 'Beyond' (to echo the title of another short story by William Faulkner), that point of view, that other-worldly vision strikes me as equal to what we would find in the most forceful plays of ancient Greek theatre, in the most riveting scenes of Icelandic saga, in the most compelling novels by Thomas Hardy. And while it is generally considered to be poor form to finish a piece you are writing with a quotation, let alone to repeat one you presented at the beginning, I'm going to take that risk here and – having stressed the value of seeing in circles – return to the extraordinarily apt sentence I quoted earlier by Eudora Welty, a writer greatly admired by Munro. For there Welty beautifully and convincingly advises us that 'Criticism can be an art too and may go deeper than its object, and more times around; it may pick up a story and waltz with it, so that it's never the same' (Welty, 'How I Write' 245). And so the four of us, myself and Ailsa and Corinne and Catherine, in our individual but complementary ways, strive to read, to dance with Alice Munro's stories.

'The Old Order Changeth': Change, Renovation and Modernity in *Friend of My Youth* (1990)

Ailsa Cox

1. Looking Through Binoculars: The Short Story Genre and Moments of Change

Readers new to Alice Munro often ask me where is the best place to start? Each one of her fourteen books is rewarding, but I usually suggest beginning with *Friend of My Youth* (1990). Two of the stories in Munro's seventh volume – the title piece and 'Meneseteung' – are amongst her most studied texts, having attained canonical status with relative ease. But that is not the only reason for my recommendation. *Friend of My Youth* encapsulates many of the key techniques and motifs that constitute Munro's literary signature, alongside subject matter that has defined her career – the relationship with the maternal; the workings of memory; the urge to dramatise personal experience like a fictional story.

Indeed, the book's title story is, arguably, the paradigmatic Munro text. As Deborah Heller has pointed out, 'The opening story, "Friend of My Youth," immediately points in several directions at once, introducing strategies and motifs . . . that will be picked up throughout . . . while also returning to material familiar from earlier "autobiographical" stories' (Heller, *Literary Sisterhoods* 70). Later in this commentary I shall identify some of the ways in which the individual stories speak to each other, picking up on just a few of the recurring motifs employed by their author. But I shall begin with an in-depth reading of the story 'Differently' as an example of Munro's unique creative practice, focusing on concepts of radical change both in the lives of Munro's characters and as a structuring principle for the short story genre, which she has made so much her own.

Munro is fascinated with the process of change, as she herself revealed in a radio interview with Eleanor Wachtel recorded soon after the publication of *Friend of My Youth* (Munro in Wachtel, 'Alice Munro' 109). Not only are her characters' lives subject to sudden crises and changes in direction; radical change is also embedded within narrative structure, the stories unfolding as a series of disruptions, discontinuities and temporal dislocations. The second half of the twentieth century was a period of rapid social and cultural transformation, challenging assumptions about sexuality, class and gender. Technological changes and counterfultural forces accentuated a drive towards what was new and modern, and a cult of youth; yet there was also a feeling of nostalgia and a desire to preserve the traces of the past. Throughout my discussion, I shall examine how Munro's stories reflect those contemporary moods from the vantage point of a twenty-first-century reader and how she uses the short story's ability to engage with the ever-changing present moment.

In its responses to change and mutability, Munro's fiction provides something more profound than social documentary. As historian John Weaver explains, 'Munro offers not only a verifiable reality, but also ... mythic insights' (Weaver 155) – an emotional history of her time, emerging from her fictional enquiries into direct experience, reminiscence and other traces of the past. W.R. Martin and Warren U. Ober share this view of Munro as 'artist-historian of small-town Ontario' (Martin and Ober, 'Alice Munro' 250), concluding that 'she transfigures daily life and gives her readers universal experience' (Martin and Ober 251). Additionally, they point out that 'Munro's interest in change extends far back beyond individuals and society into the eons of prehistory' (Martin and Ober 238), as shown by the many geological and archaeological references running through her oeuvre. In the *Friend of My Youth* collection, 'Pictures of the Ice' ends with the image of gigantic frozen waves on the shoreline. The uncanny frozen shapes elude efforts to capture their true effect on camera, while deep snow remodels the human-centric landscape, obscuring the playground and the boardwalk. Seasonal extremes are also evoked in 'Meneseteung', as the poet-protagonist struggles to represent a protean and timeless reality through the image of the eponymous river. On a macrocosmic level, human mutability is one small element within a universe prone to natural upheavals: 'The changes of climate are often violent', she reflects, 'and if you think about it there is no peace even in the stars' (70).

The clearest articulation of the human place in the cosmic cycle is the passage in 'Oranges and Apples' where Murray contemplates the shaping of a lakeside boulder by geological processes dating back to before the first Ice Age. These thoughts lead to a consideration of how the lake itself erodes the shoreline, which, in turn, is likened to the ageing of the human body. Thus the physical changes undergone within a single lifetime are juxtaposed with the equivalent, but differently paced, alterations wrought in the natural environment. The repetitive rhythms of the tide evoke a permanent state of instability informing every law of nature. Passing fashions in human attitudes, whether they concern matters of architectural taste or codes of moral behaviour, are equally subject to the relentless turning of the wheel. In the sixties, when Murray's peace of mind was overturned by his wife's infidelity, 'Everybody alive seemed to be yearning toward parking lots and shopping centers and suburban lawns as smooth as paint' (133). Now everyone aspires to the homespun and the rural.

Munro's generation – the generation to which most of her protagonists belong – was a transitional one, caught between the traditional values of their elders and the permissive attitudes first introduced by youth culture. A memoir by Munro's daughter Sheila Munro gives a vivid account of the eruption of countercultural values, sexual liberation and second-stage feminism in the late sixties and early seventies, when Sheila was a teenager and her mother approaching middle age. Describing the break-up of her parents' twenty-year marriage in the early 1970s, Sheila notes how many of their friends were going through the same process: 'It was as if there was some centrifugal force at work in the culture, splitting families asunder, scattering children like leaves. The generation who had married in the fifties now had children who were almost grown up; they still had a chance to make up for what they had missed out on in their twenties' (Sheila Munro 225–6). Alice Munro's ability to take a longer-term perspective on drastic shifts in attitude that seem purely personal is announced in the opening story, 'Friend of My Youth', where the narrator's wilful acceptance of sexual desire clashes with her mother's more repressive values. Looking back on these differences, the narrator realises that despite both women's pride in their freethinking, each had unknowingly followed the progressive orthodoxies of her own era: 'It's as if tendencies that seem most deeply rooted in our minds, most private and singular, have come in as spores on the prevailing wind, looking for any likely place to land, any welcome' (23).

Despite the private suffering Murray endures in 'Oranges and Apples', infidelity does not end his marriage; by the late sixties, adultery has become commonplace, even banal. When he discovers his wife flaunting herself – most likely masturbating – for their lodger's benefit, the scene becomes absurd: 'Murray could see himself – a man with binoculars watching a man with binoculars watching a woman. A scene from a movie. A comedy' (127). The image is a fitting one. Munro herself is looking through binoculars in this collection, viewing the human species with comic detachment, as well as empathy, reading its behaviour from a longer-term perspective.

The act of reading is central to Munro's art, whether it is applied to books or to people. Munro's slow-burning reputation meant that for a long time, outside her native Canada at least, she was celebrated as 'a writer's writer'; but as Joyce Carol Oates has observed, she is also a reader's writer ('Writers on Munro'). She is a reader's writer whose own love of reading is embedded in her subtle intertextual references – ranging from the Brontës to Tennyson to Tolstoy, James Joyce and Eudora Welty, as well as folk ballads, fairy tales and passages from the Bible. Most importantly, she is a reader's writer because of the intimate bond she builds with the reader.

In various books and essays Robert Thacker stresses the autobiographical element in Munro's work (Thacker, *Alice Munro* and Thacker, '"This Is Not a Story, Only Life"'), something she has, for much of her career, been keen to underplay – if the autobiographical is understood as a literal correspondence between real life events and those on the page. As she wrote in her Introduction to the Penguin edition of *The Moons of Jupiter*, fiction is generated from numerous overlapping sources: 'The stories that are personal are carried inexorably away from the real. And the observed stories lose their anecdotal edges, being invaded by familiar shapes and voices' (Munro, Introduction, *Moons* xiv). What is striking in Munro's oeuvre is that her fiction absorbs, responds to and considers the implications of first-hand experience, whether in her own life or the lives of others – tacitly inviting the reader to join her in these wonderings.

Just as the autobiographical is a mode of writing, perhaps it is also – as Thacker implies – a mode of reading. Elizabeth Hay has said that Munro's stories about her mother 'spoke directly to me, offering a deeper and more personal truth than I was used to finding in fiction' (Hay 178). She goes on to say, 'I was picking up the scent of the real mother inside the fiction, a mother who came from the

Ottawa Valley in eastern Ontario, as did mine' (Hay 178). In this connection lies the peculiar power of Munro's fiction – the personal investment of the reader, who is induced to follow the scent of reality by actively interpreting the heightened ambiguities of a Munro text.

Additionally, she is a rereader's writer, in that her stories seem not only to read memory as a variety of fiction, but to invite rereadings of her previous texts. As my co-author Corinne Bigot has noted in 'Ghost Texts in Alice Munro's Stories': 'Munro has been composing a sequence of never-ending variations on recurring themes, so that her stories seem to be haunted by recurring figures such as the mother who is left behind, women who run away, the child who disappears, and by dead children' (Bigot, 'Ghost Texts' 143). Such variations on a theme imply that, for both the writer and the protagonist, there is always the possibility of a different kind of ending, and another viewpoint, in life, as in art.

Munro has never thought of herself as an experimental writer – especially as someone whose deceptively simple narrative style might have seemed an anomaly in the late twentieth century, when an exuberant postmodernism was all the rage. Even today she is celebrated more often as a chronicler of provincial life than as a literary innovator. Yet she stretches the inherent properties of the short story genre to the very limit. She exploits its ability to compress time and space, using a complex elliptical structure to shift back and forth between past and present and the atemporal zone constituted by letters, dreams and fantasy. Hers are polyphonic texts, in which conflicting voices overlap and different readings of experience compete with one another; Coral Ann Howells has written extensively about 'Munro's projects of textual mapping', in which external reality is 'overlaid or undermined by maps of characters' inner lives and by memory maps of nearly forgotten family or local history' (Howells 5). Crucially, Howells observes, there will always remain 'something else which is out there unmapped' (Howells 5), something indefinable that can never be fully contained by language.

These stories are metafictional in that they reflect on their own construction, but this constant self-questioning has a significance beyond literary aesthetics because it examines a human propensity to frame real life within the simplified patterns of storytelling. Peter Brooks's wide-ranging study *Seduced by Story: The Use and Abuse of Narrative* critiques a 'current hyperinflation of story' (Brooks 10), giving examples of the narrative turn in numerous forms of public discourse from TV advertisements to political speeches. He suggests that 'narrative becomes a necessary form of knowing with the emergence, in the Enlightenment, from a culture dominated by a sacred explanation of the human condition into a new secular world where humans are on their own and must explain themselves to themselves' (Brooks 17). The idea that a psychological urge to construct the self through narration is related to the rise of secular values has some relevance to Munro's protagonists, who place their faith in literature, art or romance more often than the Bible. Conceding that 'Telling the story of oneself to oneself does seem absolutely inevitable if one is not to live life unthinkingly' (Brooks 21), he nonetheless warns against the dangers of conflating narrativised versions of reality with the truth itself. Though Brooks does not include Munro in his readings of literary texts, her work performs the task that to him is so essential, reminding the reader of the constructed nature of storytelling.

Adrian Hunter regards 'Friend of My Youth' along with other examples of what he calls Munro's 'mature stories' as 'anti-narratives' (Hunter, *The Cambridge Introduction* 176), works marked by an endless process of textual unravelling. In *The Blind Short Story*, a special issue of *The Oxford Literary Review*, Timothy Clark and Nicholas Royle provide another useful approach to Munro by challenging the visual metaphors that have dominated short story theory. The concept of the short story as a fragment made whole by imagery and by the transformative insight of the epiphanic overlooks (as it were) the blindness of the reading experience. By way of explanation, Clark turns to Munro's description of her own approach to reading short fiction, from her essay 'What Is Real?':

> obviously I don't take up a story and follow it as if it were a road, taking me somewhere, with views and neat diversions along the way. I go into it, and move back and forth and settle here and there, and stay in it for a while. It's more like a house. Everybody knows what a house does, how it encloses space and makes connections between one enclosed space and another and presents what is outside in a new way. (Munro, 'What Is Real?' 224)

As Clark observes, 'Munro's image reminds us of how far the visual analogy of viewing the text as a whole really expresses a cognitive fantasy. Instead, the text consists of various kinds of "enclosed space", not commanded from outside but inhabited from within by the reading memory' (Clark 16). In his own essay, Royle returns to Munro's image, arguing that 'The model is always cryptic, haunted. . . . the space of the short story is closed and, in crucial ways, blind' (Royle 156). Knowledge, in Munro's fiction, is always incomplete; the greater the number of facts or opinions attached to an event, the less is understood.

2. Textual Instability in 'Differently'

The rivalry between sisters, triggered by the arrival of Robert in the collection's opening story, 'Friend of My Youth', is re-enacted in other sister-like relationships in the book as a whole, most notably in 'Differently', where the close friendship between Georgia and Maya is shattered, once again, by a man. And yet, despite the destructive power of these male figures, it is the complex intimacy between female characters that seems the more psychologically profound, and that resonates through memory.

As a short story title, 'Differently' prefigures the cryptic titles of Munro's later work, notably *Runaway* (2004), in which every title consists of one word. Several other titles in *Friend of My Youth* are partial quotations – 'Goodness and Mercy', 'Oh, What Avails', and even 'Friend of My Youth' – inviting the reader to complete the sentence ironically. No such context is implied for 'Differently', an adverb stranded without a verb or a subject. Douglas Glover has discussed difference as a fundamental epistemological concept, crucial to Munro's understanding of the world and to her style: 'My sense is that she doesn't compose so much by reference (to a notional reality) as by dramatic antithesis. A statement provokes a counter-statement or a counter-construct, subversion, or complication, and the sentences, paragraphs, and stories advance by the accumulation of such contraventions' (Glover 45). He goes on to explain how characterisation is affected by this antithetical stance. Characters often serve as a contrast to the protagonist, even though they may have other things in common: 'In a sense, Alice Munro stories are like assemblages of Venn diagrams: each circle defines a separate, autonomous, and different field ... But there are areas of coincidence, where the circles overlap, and where people find a solidarity (always tentative and temporary), usually in opposition to someone or something else' (Glover 56).

In his discussion, based on *Lives of Girls and Women* (1971), Glover remarks on how often Munro uses the word 'difference', inscribing these complex points of opposition and comparison within the language itself. As he points out, signification is by its nature grounded in difference; and while he does not take the argument in this direction, it is worth noting that psychoanalytical theory traces the origins of the signifying process to the subject's separation from the maternal body, and the construction of an autonomous self. The daughter's need to break free from the figure of the mother is a key element in *Lives of Girls and Women* and in the title story, 'The Progress of Love', of the collection before this one. 'Friend of My Youth' revisits those earlier conflicts, achieving a tentative reconciliation with the past.

Munro's antithetical approach to characterisation, so well described by Glover, is especially striking when it comes to pairs of sisters or to close friendships between women. In these relationships, the tension between intimacy and rivalry may sometimes resemble that between mother and daughter. Munro pairs contrasting characters, breaking up the pattern with points at which the expected roles cross over or contradict conventional assumptions. In 'Friend of My Youth', Ellie is the younger sister, but, unlike in fairy tales, she is not the most attractive. Flora is the sensible, practical one; yet even after she has had to make way for Ellie, she has the looks and bearing of 'A gypsy queen' (8).

In 'Differently' these contradictory patterns are especially complicated in the characterisation of best friends, Georgia and Maya. The writer Tessa Hadley has commented on the particular demands this convoluted story makes on the reader – the need to check back and forth across its pages, orienting yourself to constant time shifts, digressions and elaborations: 'The texture of her writing is so mobile, flickering, intricately woven. It's like the texture of thought itself, of memory' (Hadley, 'Tessa Hadley on Alice Munro').

'Differently' opens with what seems, on a first reading, to be an irrelevance – a description of how Georgia met her current partner, a character who is never named and scarcely features in the plot. The narrative then shifts to Georgia's previous marriage, to Ben – a time when she lived in British Columbia and was friends with Maya, who is now deceased. The story is framed by Georgia's visit to Maya's widower, Raymond, still living in Victoria with his new wife, Anne.

Put simply, the elements of the story set in the present day are narrated in the present tense, while the analeptic passages that make up the bulk of the story are told in the past tense. But within that basic structure, linear progression is constantly destabilised by further temporal and geographical dislocations. Inside the present-day narrative, Raymond is assigned an unusually lengthy passage of direct speech, giving his account of the garden Maya built when she was dying – or more specifically, her friendship with the young artist who put her ideas into practice. The story of how Georgia found out about Maya's death then follows, preceding the account of their first meeting at a dinner party.

Navigating multiple relationships across temporal and geographical dislocations makes hard work for the reader. While Maya was married to Raymond, she had several lovers, including Harvey, who was then married to Hilda, both of whom were present at the initial dinner party. The story is also saturated with descriptive detail – from the older Raymond's touchy-feely goodbyes to Georgia's use of a knife to scrape the grease from kitchen tiles. On a second reading, the relevance of the opening passage is apparent. This is a story that deliberately flouts the orthodoxy of the creative writing classroom. The instructor who later became Georgia's partner warned her against 'Too many things going on at the same time; also too many people' (216), but how can the story be told otherwise? None of the characters is surplus; Hilda serves an important plot function by writing the letter with the news of Maya's death.

Whether it is the quietly satirical jibe against minimalism or the farcical aspects of the sexual shenanigans, in this story, as in 'Wigtime' and 'Oranges and Apples', comedy comes to the fore in this collection. The names Hilda and Harvey echo one another like something from a comic strip. (There is a more subtle homophony in Raymond/Maya.) Hilda's choice of 'another, presumably more trustworthy doctor' (223) as her second husband confirms the impression that, as in farce or Shakespearean comedy, love and sex is a game, in which the couples are swapped around and rearranged. Across the whole collection, close relationships are frequently bonded by theatricality, in-jokes and role-playing. In 'Oh, What Avails', the two children, Joan and Morris, share an exclusive culture based on jokes and nicknames. The friendship between Georgia and Maya is consolidated by their mutual love of masquerade, which they use to subvert conventional notions of femininity.

Georgia 'thought of herself as a girl – and then a woman – who didn't much like other girls and women' (223–4). Her husband's naval career having taken them from their native Ontario to British Columbia, she calls the other wives '"the Navy *ladies*"' (224; emphasis in orig.). In Maya, she seems to find a likeminded companion; their solidarity, based on a sense of intellectual superiority, is reminiscent of the friendship in 'Jakarta', from *The Love of a Good Woman* (1998), between Kath and Sonje, whose name for the slightly older, more fully domesticated mothers on the beach is 'the Monicas' (Munro, 'Jakarta' 79). In that story, the mutual bond is signified by reading; in 'Differently', the impetus behind the friendship between Georgia and Maya is, in its first stages, a more generalised resistance to convention that marks them out from their peers. This difference is first represented by Maya's somewhat startling appearance at the dinner party – barefoot in a shapeless robe, her eyebrows plucked out in favour of blue-painted lines (224). Unlike Georgia, she does not wear any other make-up. The detail about the blue lines, 'Not an arched line – just a little daub of blue over each eye, like a swollen vein' (224), is unusual, though it may have been a fashion of the time. Overall the impression, as Maya's name implies, is of a goddess or a priestess, a suggestion reinforced by the idea that Georgia's husband has introduced her new friend 'as an offering' (224) and the fact that her own husband, Raymond, '"worships"' (225) her.

Georgia and Maya are described as 'friends on two levels. On the first level, they were friends as wives; on the second as themselves' (226). On the first level, they form a quartet with their husbands in conversations that often focus on boyhood memories. Their activities on the second level could, perhaps, be inspired by this talk of schoolboy pranks; they conduct elaborate role-playing in restaurants, pretending to be aristocratic widows from the days of the Raj, or groupies attached to a fictitious folk singer. Georgia and Maya are not like other women. Nor do they have very much in common with their husbands, who in adult life are polite and well-behaved – innocents, secretly mocked by their spouses.

The job Georgia takes in a bookstore also involves an element of role-playing. She changes her image: 'Sitting on her stool at the front of the store, showing her bare brown shoulders and sturdy brown legs, she looked like a college girl – clever but full of energy and bold opinions' (229). Her affair with a customer, Miles, seems at first to be another game, an escapist fantasy with no repercussions in real life:

> And Georgia herself, watching her children on the roundabout, or feeling the excellent shape of a lemon in her hand at the supermarket, contained another woman, who only a few hours before had been whimpering and tussling on the ferns, on the sand, on the bare ground, or, during a rainstorm, in her own car – who had been driven hard and gloriously out of her mind and drifted loose and gathered her wits and made her way home again. (233)

I have already mentioned the proliferation of descriptive detail throughout the story; this labyrinthine sentence replicates its analeptic narrative structure at a microcosmic level, compressing the multiple occasions on which Georgia has committed adultery within the singular, yet habitual, moment when she handles the lemon or watches the children. (Georgia's children scarcely figure in this story, remaining nameless, numberless and silent throughout.) Tessa Hadley's comparison of Munro's prose style to 'the texture . . . of memory' (Hadley, 'Tessa Hadley on Alice Munro') holds true, in that the younger Georgia is savouring her double life through reliving sensual experience. But the lemon is not a Proustian madeleine; sense-impressions do not transport either the younger or the older Georgia back in time. The image is spatial rather than temporal; Georgia 'contained another woman' (233).

Whether at the level of an individual sentence or the narrative as a whole, Munro thwarts causality by means of complexity. There is no simple logic behind characters' actions, no linear chain of cause and effect. Georgia must navigate these complications in life, just as the reader steers through textual complexity. During her affair with Miles, the boundary between reality and make-believe begins to blur:

> Trouble began, perhaps, as soon as they said that they loved each other. Why did they do that – defining, inflating, obscuring whatever it was they did feel? It seemed to be demanded, that was all – just the way changes, variations, elaborations in the lovemaking itself might be demanded. (233)

At their next assignation, Miles acts brutishly, fantasising about a foursome with their spouses, and accusing Georgia of being '"a squeamish little slut"' (235).

Baffled and distressed, she orders him out of the car. The following night, Maya calls with some exciting news: Miles, whom she has heard all about but not met, is coming round to see her.

Assuming Miles wants to confide in Maya about their own romance, Georgia waits for hours by the phone, just as she has waited for Miles himself to ring. Leaving the children by themselves, she even drives over to Maya's on a spying mission. (Raymond is conveniently at work.) She stays awake all night, describing her condition to herself as *'a paralysis of grief'* (237; emphasis in orig.). She is self-aware enough to know that the phrase is hyperbolic, her feelings out of proportion. Yet she also knows that a phone call from Maya with the news that Miles loves her 'would have given her a happiness that no look or word from her children could give her. Than anything could give her, ever again' (237). She rings Maya first thing in the morning; Maya's voice is 'sleepy (pretending to be sleepy?) and silky with deceit' (237). A shame-faced apology soon follows; Georgia slams down the phone, their friendship at an end.

To Maya, a fling is an inconsequential diversion: '"I've been rotten, but I didn't mean to be. I offered him a beer"' (238). It is hardly out of character; telling Miles all about her friend's erotic escapades, Georgia has naively 'offered wild Maya up for his entertainment' (236), just as Ben introduced Maya to Georgia 'as an offering' (224). The connotations of 'offered' and 'offering' knit together opposing concepts of a casual transaction, whether it involves taking a beer from the fridge or having sex in the garden, and of appeasement, as in sacrificial ritual.

On the fatal evening, it is a phone call from Maya – the imagined melodrama of hearing how madly Miles is in love with Georgia – rather than a call from Miles himself that Georgia longs for. When Miles does eventually call her, she puts the phone down. Maya is rather more persistent in her efforts at reconciliation, but Georgia refuses even to look at her when she's sitting in her own kitchen. (Georgia has been obliged to let her in, since their children are playing together.) Although Georgia believes that she is using Maya as a scapegoat for Miles's bad behaviour, the emotional energy is focused on Maya herself; Georgia feels 'a vengeful pleasure' (241) out of studiously ignoring all her friend's pleadings. The phrase used, 'breaking with Maya' (241), foreshadows the words used to describe the end of Georgia's marriage a few months later: 'She broke with Ben' (241). The break with Maya is a kind of divorce.

The names Miles and Maya are even more comically homophonous than Harvey and Hilda, but they are not yoked together syntactically until after the sudden break in the friendship, when Georgia conceives of them as 'two pale prodigies. Miles and Maya. Both of them slippery, shimmery – liars, seducers, finaglers' (241). 'Miles' has previously evoked travel and distance, the romance of the highway, embodied by the motorbike he rides. But the term 'prodigies', usually applied to children, introduces further connotations, recalling for me the unsettling little boy in Henry James's 'The Turn of the Screw' (1898); in that novella, Miles has a sister called 'Flora', a name whose pagan connotations are not so very far away from 'Maya'. (Flora is, of course, the name of the older sister in 'Friend of My Youth', where the name is firmly linked to the character's Scottish identity, rather than Jamesian spectrality.) The 'pale prodigies' in James's novella inhabit an exclusive supernatural reality beyond the control of a governess who becomes obsessed by the ghosts they claim to see. Georgia, however, congratulates herself on her ability to keep control, inflicting a strict punishment for the transgression.

These intertextual suggestions link Munro's story to a work that is one of the best-known examples of narrative instability and irresolution, mostly achieved through the device of the unreliable narrator. But in Munro's hands textual instability is extended to lived experience. Reality itself, especially the motivations of individuals, the choices they make and their true desires, is impossible to fathom, as becomes clear in Georgia's subsequent behaviour. Far from retreating into the safety of her marriage, she renounces both Maya's promiscuity and her previous conventional lifestyle, rewriting her own history in the process:

> Never, never. I was never happy, she said.
> People always say that.
> People make momentous shifts, but not the changes they imagine. (242)

Carol L. Beran has noted how frequently notions of happiness are invoked by Munro, as a challenge to the storybook notion of marriage as living happily ever after and to the unrealistic expectations women have grown up with (Beran, 'The Pursuit of Happiness' 331). Munro herself has expressed scepticism about concepts of personal growth and self-development:

> There are just flashes of things we know and find out. I don't see life very much in terms of progress. I don't feel at all pessimistic. I rather like the idea that we go on and we don't know what's happening and we don't know what we'll find. We think we've got things figured out and then they turn around on us. No state of mind is permanent. It just all has to be there. (Munro in Hancock 214)

The word 'flashes' appears several times in this interview, conducted in 1982, a few years before the stories in *Friend of My Youth* were first published. The term, my co-author J.R. (Tim) Struthers has suggested to me, no doubt echoes L.M. Montgomery's use of 'the flash' in her novel *Emily of New Moon* (1923), which Munro long admired and about which she later wrote an Afterword (Struthers, Message 31 January 2023). Here, Munro relates the concept of 'flashes' to her preference for the short story as a genre more suited than the traditional novel to depicting fragmented lives. Munro's characters do not become older and wiser, remaining more or less the same throughout the contradictions and discontinuities they experience. They compulsively reinterpret the past rather than overcoming obstacles on the road to enlightenment.

The final section returns to the present moment, Raymond seemingly making a clumsy pass at Georgia as they bid their farewells. It is here that the story's title emerges after Georgia observes that '"we never behave – we never behave as if we believed we were going to die"' (242). The broken syntax implies inarticulacy, possibly as a ploy to make the remark seem offhand; Raymond is nonplussed and Georgia embarrassed by the gravity of her own words. Asked how '"we"' should behave, she simply answers '"Differently"' (242). Much is left unsaid; it is not clear whether Georgia is thinking of Maya, of her own actions towards her or of the wider perspective middle age might have on youthful experience. In the closing passage, none of this is relevant: 'She doesn't think about Raymond, or

Miles, or Maya, or even Ben' (243). The final image, recalling Georgia's job in the bookstore, is detached from personal relationships, casting the protagonist as observer rather than participant: 'She thinks about sitting in the store in the evenings. The light in the street, the complicated reflections in the windows. The accidental clarity' (243). The understated visual image evokes the diffuseness and complexity of external reality, along with a readiness to respond to the random, perhaps even inexpressible, insights it generates.

During a television interview with Paula Todd, Munro described working in the bookstore she ran with her then husband in Victoria as a way out of the writer's block that afflicted her for a time when her children were young (Munro in Todd). Although an explicit link is not made at the end of the story with Georgia's creative writing, her recollection of an intuitive response to these inchoate sensory stimuli implies an artistic sensibility at work. The suggestion means that 'Differently' is not just about the unpredictability of lived experience, but about the reading of it, and its transmission on the page. The narrative voice in 'People always say that' (242) does not belong wholly to the character or to the implied author, but somewhere in between. Reading, writing and remembering are all intertwined, the ambiguities of viewpoint inviting the reader's complicity.

3. Approaching the First Three Stories

3.1 'To the memory of my mother': 'Friend of My Youth' and the Munro Paradigm

The collection *Friend of My Youth* is dedicated 'To the memory of my mother', and the fictional reimagining of the mother-daughter dyad is another reason why this particular volume is so representative of Munro's work as a whole. Interviewed by Jeanne McCulloch and Mona Simpson in 1994, Munro called the relationship with her own mother 'my central material in life' (Munro in McCulloch and Simpson 237). Magdalene Redekop has devoted a full-length critical study to this subject, *Mothers and Other Clowns: The Stories of Alice Munro* (1992), to which I am indebted. 'Dear Life', the title story closing Munro's final volume, affirms the centrality of that material.

A former schoolteacher, an active and, by all accounts, strong-minded woman, Anne Laidlaw was afflicted by Parkinson's disease – an illness far less easily diagnosed and more difficult to treat at that time than it is today – when her daughter was not yet in her teens. She died some fifteen years later, when Munro was living in Vancouver, two thousand miles away. Difficulties between mother and daughter are not so unusual, as Munro herself remarked in the 1990 radio interview with Eleanor Wachtel recorded soon after the book's publication (Munro in Wachtel, 'Alice Munro' 106). But the desire to break free, establishing an autonomous identity with different needs and values, was complicated by the nature of Anne Laidlaw's illness, the attendant guilt and shame, and the challenges it posed to Munro as a writer.

Munro regards 'The Peace of Utrecht', written following her mother's death and collected in *Dance of the Happy Shades* (1968), as a moment of creative liberation, because, for the first time, she felt able to respond to the emotional devastation wrought by Anne Laidlaw's disease and its effect on her caregivers. The specific effects of the illness also forced a crisis of representation, undermining notions of fixed identity, a stable reality and a logical sequence of cause and effect. These were the disfigurement, paralysis and slurred speech that seemed to obliterate her mother's personality, but also the random periods of remission that seemed to restore her old self temporarily. During the 1990 Wachtel interview, Munro points out that in the early stages, before Parkinson's was diagnosed, the illness appeared to some members of the family to be 'a neurotic, self-chosen affliction' (Munro in Wachtel, 'Alice Munro' 106) – a cause for embarrassment rather than the compassion one might expect.

In 'The Peace of Utrecht', present-day impressions of the narrator's home town are intercut with fragments of the past as, haunted by guilt, the protagonist, Helen, tries to deal with disturbing memories of her dead mother. She recalls 'Our Gothic Mother, with the cold appalling mask of the Shaking Palsy laid across her features, shuffling, weeping, devouring attention wherever she can get it, eyes dead and burning, fixed inward on herself; this is not all' (200). It 'is not all' because on better days the sick woman revives, as if 'wakened out of a bad dream' (200), even baking and sewing as she did before. Helen goes on to refer to her own dreams, in which her dead mother's symptoms are ameliorated, just as they are in 'Friend of My Youth'.

The later story foregrounds these dreams by introducing them in the opening line: 'I used to dream about my mother, and though the details in the dream varied, the surprise in it was always the same' (3). Because the reader is entering the story blind, this sentence is free of the guilt that pervades the earlier dream. This narrator is 'astonished' (3) to find so much of her mother's health restored, particularly her 'liveliness of face and voice before her throat muscles stiffened and a woeful, impersonal mask fastened itself over her features' (4). However tone remains relatively light-hearted, mining the comic incongruity of the situation: 'I would say that I was sorry I hadn't been to see her in such a long time – meaning not that I felt guilty but that I was sorry I had kept a bugbear in my mind, instead of this reality' (4). The image of the mask is familiar from 'The Peace of Utrecht', and a carnivalesque humour is not altogether absent from the earlier story; but the notion of 'a bugbear' suggests unfounded childish terror rather than the full-blown horror of 'Our Gothic Mother' (200). The mood established in this first paragraph of the later story is one of bemused wonderment.

In his biography of Munro, Robert Thacker compares the opening story of this collection to the closing story of *Something I've Been Meaning To Tell You* (1974). 'The Ottawa Valley' ends that collection with 'Munro's inability to fictionalize and so "*get rid*" of her very real historical mother' (Thacker, *Alice Munro* 433). The transformation that opens both the title story and the collection *Friend of My Youth* is of a kind only possible in dreams – a phantasm that leads the way through the artistic and emotional impasse announced by 'The Ottawa Valley'.

The dream opening also introduces a temporal and spatial indeterminacy that continues throughout the story. Dreams are atemporal; time is suspended during sleep, and chronology abandoned so that the first-person narrator can be 'the age I really was' (3) and her mother still alive. Dreams also dissolve spatial boundaries, transporting the dreamer instantly from one space to another. In this case, the narrator says she sometimes finds herself in her old kitchen, sometimes on the street or even at the airport. Sudden, seemingly random transitions of this kind also characterise Munro's fiction; the text itself is structured like a dream, an aspect I shall return to in my discussion of 'Meneseteung'. Chronology is, to some extent, embedded in that first sentence through the modal verb 'used to', implying a frequent experience in a past that is now discontinued: 'I used to dream' (3). When that past was, at what remove from the undetermined present moment, is left unexplained, with few clues available about the narrator's current circumstances, except for the implication, later on, that she is a fiction writer.

After the dream introduction, another version of the mother is introduced with an abrupt shift in time and space to the Ottawa Valley where she was a young teacher with 'a soft, mischievous face' (4) – a version that existed before her daughter was born, and that is reconstructed in the dialogue between the mother's anecdotes and the narrator's imaginings. The mother's recollections of a strictly religious farming family she boarded with in those days, and her speculations about what happened to them subsequently, form the narrative spine of the story, the closest it comes to a conventional external plot.

During the mother's time there, the house is already divided between Flora and the younger sister Ellie, who is married to Robert. According to local gossip Robert had been engaged to Flora, but was obliged to marry Ellie upon making her pregnant. After losing that child and many other disastrous pregnancies Ellie becomes incurably ill, and is eventually attended by Nurse Atkinson, one of the various conniving nurses that feature in stories by Alice Munro. Once the narrator's mother leaves the area and is herself married, news reaches her that Robert has taken the nurse as his bride following Ellie's demise.

Flora is not quite the 'Friend of My Youth' the reader might assume from the story's title. The phrase appears near the end of the story, as the narrator describes her mother's struggles to keep up her correspondence in the later stages of her illness, when she has difficulty handling a pen. Unfinished letters are scattered round the house, addressed to '*My dearest Mary,*' '*My darling Ruth,*' and so forth (24; emphasis in orig.). The one beginning '*Friend of my Youth*' does not seem to have been addressed to Flora, and 'I don't recall one that began with *My dear and most admired Flora*' (24; emphasis in orig.).

The Russian thinker Mikhail Bakhtin has described the dialogic properties of language; whether at the level of an individual word, a sentence or an entire text, meaning is derived from the clash and interplay of different voices, from multiple connotations and by the context of what is said before and after the individual utterance. The polyphonic qualities of Munro's fiction are evident in this story, as she mingles autobiographical discourse, letters, oral history, direct speech and romantic fiction. Silence, which is an aspect of that fundamental blindness discussed by Clark and Royle, is also part of the signifying process. What is not said, or is withheld – the 'don't recall' (25) that does not necessarily rule out the possibility – is as important as words said out loud.

According to psychoanalytical theory, speech arises in the infant as a compensation for separation from the maternal body; it fills the void left by the absent mother. This story is very clearly an attempt by the adult narrator to fill that void, and to revive the mother doubly removed from her, first by illness and then by death. Stories fill the empty spaces left by the silences, omissions and absence. Flora's final letter provides the information that she has left the farm, and is working at a store, without giving any reasons for her decision and 'Nothing in it about God's will or His role in our afflictions' (24). The reader might wonder why the narrator thinks that Flora should add anything of this kind; the reason, in fact, is that the narrator, her expectations shaped by fictional convention, is searching in vain for narrative closure and for a consistent character with clear motivations.

Flora's story – this lurid tale of love, deception and betrayal – has been transmitted not just through the letters the mother receives from Flora herself, but through the gossip passed on by her other friends in the Ottawa Valley and the oral testimony handed down from mother to daughter. These multiple voices blur into one another, as the tale is dramatised in the telling. Is it the mother, or is it the collective voice of local gossip, that stages the melodrama, furnishing it with vivid details from a scene that only the participants could have witnessed first-hand?

> Some people, seeing the names in the paper, thought the editor must have got the sisters mixed up. They thought it must be Flora. A hurry-up wedding for Flora! But no – it was Flora who pressed Robert's suit – it must have been – and got Ellie out of bed and washed her and made her presentable. It would have been Flora who picked one geranium from the window plant and pinned it to her sister's dress. And Ellie hadn't torn it out. Ellie was meek now, no longer flailing or crying. She let Flora fix her up, she let herself be married, she was never wild from that day on. (10)

Towards the end of the story, the narrator tells us, she was too preoccupied with fiction-writing to be especially interested in her mother's tales about Flora; yet numerous details are recalled, complete with passages of direct speech and character description. The use of such fictive techniques is especially pronounced in the passages concerning Nurse Atkinson: 'Audrey Atkinson raised her pinkish-orange eyebrows at my mother behind Flora's back, and my mother was furious' (13). Ultimately it is impossible to disentangle fully the multiple voices and viewpoints in the reconstruction of past recollections, even though the mother's version is sometimes challenged, for instance its omission of Robert: she 'never reports anything that Robert said, never has him contributing to the scene' (12).

If she'd been a writer, the mother says, she would have written a story about Flora called '"The Maiden Lady"' (19). However, it is not the mother's fictionalisation that is incorporated into the text, but the narrator's summary of this supposed account, in which Flora is cast as a character redeemed by sacrifice: 'That was what I believed my mother would make of things' (20). The narrator imagines what she would put into a novel, reversing Flora's portrayal as a martyr into that of gothic villainess: 'Rejoicing in the bad turns done to her and in her own forgiveness, spying on the shambles of her sister's life' (20). Surprisingly the climax of this narrative is the triumph of the modernising Audrey Atkinson who not only takes over the entire house but also consigns Flora's books – the gloomy Calvinist literature she reads to the ailing Ellie – literally and symbolically to the fire.

For the narrator, these contradictory readings are rooted in contrasting attitudes to sex. The sex drive is repressed in her mother's version, just as the figure of Robert is obscured; but in the narrator's imagination the figure of Robert is eroticised, 'black-haired, heavy-shouldered, with the strength of a plow horse, and the same kind of sombre, shackled beauty' (12). The generational clash of values recalls a similar conflict running through *Lives of Girls and Women*, between the mother's type of feminism that aims to free women from the dangers of illicit sex and the daughter's fascination with sexual desire as a kind of liberation in itself.

As 'Friend of My Youth' reaches its ending it becomes apparent that for the narrator, in Isla Duncan's words, 'the subject of her mother's tale has become the mother herself' (Duncan, *Alice Munro's Narrative Art* 55). Returning to Flora's story some time after her mother's death, the narrator imagines what might have become of her, even picturing a chance meeting between them in a department store. 'Of course', she says, 'it's my mother I'm thinking of, my mother as she was in those dreams' (26). Flora has become an avatar for the mother herself, just as the skittish younger sister stands to some extent for the narrator, the syllables of her name, 'Ellie', echoing the first name of the author.

The imaginary meeting involves reconciliation, acceptance, forgiveness; it is also a manifesto for an alternative approach to storytelling – a kind that does not build towards closure or definite conclusions, but is a narrative constructed from endless possibilities. Before settling on the department store fantasy, the narrator speculates about exactly what kind of shop Flora might have worked in:

> A hardware store or a five-and-ten, where she has to wear a coverall, or a drugstore, where she is uniformed like a nurse, or a Ladies' Wear, where she is expected to be genteelly fashionable? She might have had to learn about food blenders or chain saws, negligees, cosmetics, even condoms. She would have to work all day under electric lights, and operate a cash register. Would she get a permanent, paint her nails, put on lipstick? She must have found a place to live – a little apartment with a kitchenette, overlooking the main street, or a room in a boarding house. How could she go on being a Cameronian? (24–5)

The important words here are 'might', 'would' and 'must', each verb recalibrating degrees of liberty and compulsion. To say 'might' implies possibility, the naming of different types of stores and products offering examples from a list that is far from exhaustive. Yet 'might have had to' (24) also denotes unwelcome outcomes, in the light of Flora's supposed ignorance of modern technology and objections to birth control. 'She would have to work all day' (24), like earlier uses of 'would' in the text, such as 'They would only heat the main room of the house' (12) and even 'That was what I believed my mother would make of things' (20), conveys a certain amount of determinism. Social conditions are for the most part a matter of fact, and non-negotiable, but within those conditions small, yet significant, personal choices are on offer – for instance those concerning hairstyle and make-up.

There is always a small element of doubt in the construction 'must have'. The implication is that all the evidence points to a strong probability, but 'She must have found' (25) is more provisional than 'She would' (24). In this passage, a clear connection has been drawn between the idle speculation of everyday gossip and the transformation of life into art. In most fiction, character is clearly delineated from the start; the openness of the short story genre, which, as Frank O'Connor says in *The Lonely Voice*, is 'by its very nature remote from the community' (O'Connor 29), less tied to the external, social world than the conventional novel, liberates the author from definition. In 'Friend of My Youth', the decision-making behind characterisation is exposed at the surface of the text, like the unfinished workings of a mathematical puzzle. For Munro, character is always a work in progress – less a set of fixed attributes than an experiment in human behaviour.

Taking a flight of fancy, the narrator travels back in time to a 1950s department store where she is served by 'a tall, handsome woman, nicely turned out' (25), that she instinctively knows must be Flora: 'I would have wanted to tell her that I knew, I knew her story, though we had never met. I imagine myself trying to tell her' (25). The imaginary figure listens politely, yet ultimately resists whatever version the narrator imposes on her life with a knowing shake of the head. The dead, like Banquo's Ghost in *Macbeth*, rarely speak, communicating most eloquently through gesture. In the passage that follows, speech is restored to the dead mother, but her voice is restrained, even diffident:

> Of course it's my mother I'm thinking of, my mother as she was in those dreams, saying, It's nothing, just this little tremor; saying with such astonishing lighthearted forgiveness, Oh, I knew you'd come someday. My mother surprising me, and doing it almost indifferently. Her mask, her fate, and most of her affliction taken away. (26)

The narrator is pleased to see her mother restored to health, yet also admits to feeling 'slightly cheated' (26) because the assumptions of the narrative she has constructed have been fatally undermined. This moment is revelatory in terms of the psychology of the story's narrator; it also transforms her approach to storytelling:

> My mother moving rather carelessly out of her old prison, showing options and powers I never dreamed she had, changes more than herself. She changes the bitter lump of love I have carried all this time into a phantom . . . (26)

I shall end this analysis of 'Friend of My Youth' by returning to the 1990 Wachtel radio interview, during which Munro read from the story's ending. Here Munro made clear that the story was originally inspired by the tale of Flora's misfortune. Only during the process of writing, 'trying to figure out what the story is all about' (Munro in Wachtel, 'Alice Munro' 108), did the material about the mother unexpectedly displace these original intentions. The imaginary novel the narrator weaves around Flora is reminiscent of the melodramatic novel Del wants to write about her neighbours in 'Epilogue: The Photographer' in *Lives of Girls and Women*. There, too, a gesture from a real-life character implies that language cannot contain lived experience – and especially subjective experience – in all its complexity. The moment of realisation comes as Bobby Sherriff, relieving the would-be novelist of her dessert plate, 'rose on his toes like a dancer, like a plump ballerina. This action, accompanied by his delicate smile, appeared to be a joke not shared with me so much as displayed for me, and it seemed also to have a concise meaning, a stylized meaning – to be a letter, or a whole word, in an alphabet I did not know' (Munro, 'Epilogue: The Photographer' 253–4).

Here, again, silence and gestures play a crucial part in the dialogic process, which produces meaning through an ever-changing context.

In the 1990 Wachtel interview, Munro spoke about her fascination with ongoing change:

> Cherished beliefs change. Ways of dealing with life change. The importance of certain things in life changes. All this seems to me endlessly interesting – that is the thing that doesn't change or that I certainly hope doesn't change. (Munro in Wachtel, 'Alice Munro' 109)

Bakhtin identifies an affinity between prose fiction and the boundless process of change, praising 'an indeterminacy, a certain semantic openendedness, a living contact with unfinished, still-evolving contemporary reality (the openended present)' (Bakhtin, 'Epic and Novel' 7). That 'semantic openendedness' is especially pronounced in Munro's stories. It is linked not just to the diversity of voices at play in the text, but also to a narrative viewpoint that is grounded in empathy. During the 1990 Wachtel interview, Munro spoke about changes in her own attitude to her mother, as she matured; and how most of us come to appreciate, often only after our parents' deaths, that they are human beings, not so very different from ourselves: 'Often, when I'm enjoying something, I think of how meagre her rewards were and how much courage, in a way, she needed to go on living' (Munro in Wachtel, 'Alice Munro' 107). For both reader and writer, that empathy with, and curiosity about, other lives is at the heart of Munro's fiction, as it embraces the workings of change, predictable only in its inevitability.

3.2 Settlers and Cultural Identity: 'Five Points'

As we have seen, Munro's fiction draws on her Scots Presbyterian heritage. Her maternal forebears, also Protestant, emigrated from Ireland in the nineteenth century, around the same time that her paternal ancestors were leaving the Scottish Borders (Thacker, *Alice Munro* 15). In 'Friend of My Youth', the length of time the members of the Grieves family have spent in the Ottawa Valley is not disclosed, but, clinging to their 'freak religion from Scotland' (5), and rejecting modern conveniences, they are still living the pioneer lifestyle.

Most of Munro's characters are conscious, to some degree, of their European ancestry. An exception, curiously enough, would appear to be Almeda Joynt Roth in 'Meneseteung', the story in the collection that comes closest to historical fiction. Almeda's account of her family begins with their move from what was then the Province of Canada's capital, Kingston, in 1854. She has a brother, William, and a sister, Catherine, both of whom die young; the parents' first names, however, are not given on their gravestones. While the siblings' names could not be more Anglo-Saxon, the surname, 'Roth', is German or Jewish in origin, 'Joynt' possibly Irish. The full name is rich with connotations, explored at length by my co-author J.R. (Tim) Struthers in one of the two essays he has written on this story (Struthers, 'In Search' 182–5). I will simply add how odd it seems that the narrator speculates about 'Meda' as a family nickname for the protagonist, yet remains incurious about the rest of her name.

Other stories in the collection, however, depart significantly from representing Munro's Scots and Irish background and her Southwestern Ontario upbringing. In 'Five Points', the book's second selection, Neil, the lover of the protagonist Brenda, is indifferent to the country's colonial heritage, and lacking in curiosity about the recent immigrants who are adding to its cultural diversity – as is revealed in a story he tells about a part of Victoria close to where he grew up. Brenda's impressions of the city, some two thousand miles away, on the west side of Canada, are based entirely on picture postcards. Victoria, the capital city of British Columbia, is, in fact, on Vancouver Island, a ferry-ride away from the mainland. It still retains what, to the visitor's eye, is an old-fashioned charm – dismissed by Neil as '"all just tourist shit"' (27). Five Points is a fictional area of the city, which is hazily described, but contains a school and, importantly, a candy store which was once Chinese but was taken over by 'Europeans, not Poles or Czechs but from some smaller country – Croatia; is that a country?' (28). The family's nationality is never confirmed, though their Catholicism is consistent with Croatia (which would have been part of Yugoslavia at that time). Because the older daughter, Maria, speaks English, she is effectively the person in charge of the store. At thirteen, with sagging breasts, glasses and old-fashioned braids wound round her head, she looks 'about fifty years old' (29). Neil goes on to tell Brenda how Maria used money from the till to pay for sex with her teenage customers.

These analeptic passages, summarising Neil's version of events, but potentially embellished from Brenda's perspective, are deeply disturbing. No wonder 'The story ... stays with her like a coating on the tongue, a taste in the mouth' (42). Within the store, Maria takes on adult authority, and business is flourishing as it turns into a café serving the kind of Eastern European pastries that were a novelty at that time. But even before the sexual misbehaviour comes to light, local children make fun of her behind her back. The boys she pays for sex taunt her to her face, extorting extra cash. Maria is said to be 'forking over' (39); an immediate association is 'fucking over', though in fact it is Maria who is being fucked over by her exploiters.

The phrase 'forking over' (39) also suggests Neil's speech, interwoven with the authorial voice. His language yields to something closer to Brenda's language and viewpoint, as the narrative shades into a more empathic reconstruction of the girl's ordeal: 'Maria's matronly, watchful calm was gone – she looked wild and sullen and mean. She gave them looks full of hate, but she continued giving them money. She kept handing over the bills. Not even trying to bargain, or to argue or refuse, anymore. In a rage she did it – a silent rage' (39). Inevitably her parents find out all their money is gone and, as a result, they are forced to close the store. They prosecute their own daughter, who is sent to juvenile detention. The boys deny everything, and remain unpunished.

Maria's eventual fate is left undetermined, Brenda's hopes for a positive outcome contrasting with Neil's callous indifference:

> 'Well, maybe she got married,' she says. 'After she got out. Lots of people get married who are no beauties. That's for sure. She might've lost weight and be looking good even.'
>
> 'Sure,' says Neil. 'Maybe have guys paying her, instead of the other way round.' (42)

As with Miles in 'Differently', Neil is unwittingly revealing a deep-seated misogyny, triggering a vicious row with his lover. Maria can be dehumanised even more than other women because she is also an immigrant. The authority she ought to gain as an entrepreneur is taken away thoughtlessly by a group of young males who are able to act with impunity. Neil, who is only sixteen when he leaves British Columbia, portrays her simply as a grotesque. Like Teresa Gault in the collection's final story, 'Wigtime', Maria suffers from male contempt towards women, especially the female body.

Similarly, Neil attacks Brenda for wearing dressy shoes 'so every step you took would show off your fat arse' (44), a remark for which he later apologises. Unlike Miles and Georgia, he and Brenda are reconciled after their argument. Far from ending, their affair is transformed into something analogous to Brenda's relationship with her disabled husband. Munro's technique of doubling and substitution applies to these characters too. Just as Maria and Brenda seem entirely different, yet are linked by male degradation, so the young lover Neil and the older husband Cornelius are paired with one another through the dynamics of heterosexual relationships. Brenda realises that she derives the same perverse pleasure from arguing with Neil that she experiences in rows with Cornelius. She even points out, much to Neil's resentment, that his name ultimately derives from the same Dutch root as her husband's: '"Yeah, but I'm not Dutch, and I wasn't named Cornelius, just Neil"' (43).

In this story, as in so many others, Munro handles the balance of power between the sexes with great subtlety. Male entitlement is exposed in all its toxicity – the double standard that has potentially ruined Maria's life; the sexual harassment Brenda endures from passing motorists – yet women are, to some degree, complicit with patriarchal attitudes. The motives for the characters' behaviour are obscure, both to themselves and to the reader; their desires are contradictory, driven by primal urges that cannot be rationalised.

Brenda castigates both her husband and her lover for their eagerness to pick a fight:

> Men wanted you to make a fuss, about disposing of vegetable babies or taking drugs or driving a car like a bat out of hell, and why was that? So they could have your marshmallow sissy goodness to preen against, with their hard showoff badness? So that they finally could give in to you, growling, and not have to be so bad and reckless anymore? Whatever it was, you got sick of it. (46–7)

Yet Brenda is equally reckless and as much of a show-off, taking numerous risks during the affair with Neil, even having sex on the roadside. In an early row with Cornelius, he reprimands her for smoking marijuana; yet during the argument with Neil, sparked by his story about Maria, one of her concerns involves his drug-taking. She is emotionally invested in masculinity, fascinated by the conventionally masculine world of mines and building sites and hard physical labour: 'She loves to get a man fresh from all that' (31).

Finally, Neil admits to taking money from Maria, but – like the pretext for those arguments with Cornelius – this seems not to be the issue any more, and Brenda ignores his confession. This closing section is preceded by a passage in which Brenda thinks about the salt mine beneath the lake, where Cornelius worked underground until the accident that, it is implied, has impaired his sexual performance. Since leaving that underground world he has described it vividly to Brenda – a masculine space, both an eerie natural landscape and a workplace full of heavy machinery, a space she can only experience vicariously.

The juxtaposition between this forceful passage and the final section gives an ending to the story that relegates Neil's confession to secondary importance. The closing section of the story plays out with Neil at the wheel of his 'old blue Mercury' (35): his physical presence representing 'an energy, a quality of his self . . . That's what she has set herself to follow – the sap, the current, under the skin, as if that were the one true thing' (48). Even though Brenda is far from blind to Neil's flaws, and to the mutual damage inflicted irrevocably by the argument, she is bound to him. The bond is forged partly through an inevitable intimacy, duplicating the marital relationship, and partly through her fascination with what she perceives as an essential masculinity. Her revulsion at Neil's participation in the mistreatment of Maria is not enough to make her break with him.

For many of us, perhaps especially for those, like myself and Alice Munro, who are non-drivers, cars are emblematic of masculinity – and for women who learn to drive, and purchase their own cars, no doubt emblematic of sexual equality and personal independence. Brenda can drive; she drives the dangerously conspicuous van used in the family's second-hand furniture business on her assignations with Neil. But the affair, usually consummated in Neil's trailer near Lake Huron, is primarily located in the car that takes her there, Neil's 'old blue Mercury – dark blue that can turn into a pool, a spot of swampy darkness under the trees' (35). One of the associations with the god Mercury, my co-author J.R. (Tim) Struthers has reminded me, is his role guiding souls down into the underworld (Struthers, Message 20 April 2023). Here, man and machine almost merge, acquiring an erotic mystique: 'At a distance – in the car, waiting for her – he's always been a bright blur, his presence a relief and a promise' (48). This 'presence', sensed from the passenger seat, becomes an almost metaphysical 'energy' (48). When Neil begs her not to get out of the car, power is suspended briefly between them, as he awaits her crucial decision.

The closing sentences provide one of Munro's most ambiguous endings, as the two of them sit there with the engine still running: 'She feels his heaviness and anger and surprise. She feels that also in herself. She thinks that up till now was easy' (49). For me, that closing sentence implies that the relationship will continue, that it will probably end her marriage and become a serious commitment, in a reversal of the reader's expectations. Whatever happened to Maria is now irrelevant; there is no further speculation about her fate. Although her story is central to the plot, she remains a marginal character, whose voice is never heard.

Following immediately after 'Friend of My Youth', 'Five Points' suggests changes in a landscape shaped by colonial settlements. In *The View from Castle Rock* (2006), Munro has described how, in her father's time, the land worked by the pioneers remained very much the same (Munro, 'Epilogue: Messenger' 343). The farmsteads, fences, orchards and barns created by them endured until much later in the twentieth century. Despite the improvements insisted on by Nurse Atkinson, this situation must have been the case for the Grieveses' farm in 'Friend of My Youth'. In 'Five Points', the road has displaced local landmarks, and the old way of life is giving way to the new. Brenda and Cornelius have repurposed a farm as a place to sell second-hand furniture: 'It's called Zendt's Furniture Barn. Locally, a lot of people refer to it as the Used Furniture on the Highway' (29).

Yet the compulsion to work hard persists through these changes. In 'Friend of My Youth', the Grieveses are assumed to be prosperous, their self-denying lifestyle a deeply felt cultural preference. Flora has to be persuaded to keep back some cream for her sickly sister rather than selling it all. The business of money-making, subsistence, profit and loss is much more to the fore in 'Five Points'. The entire family pulls together to make their shop succeed, but it is the thirteen-year-old Maria who 'understood English and money' (29). What she has not understood is that the standard economic rules of supply and demand do not apply to sexual transactions. When the business is closed, no trace is left behind, the shop replaced by a laundromat. The only member of the family whose fate is known is Maria's younger, conventionally attractive sister. Like the imaginary version of Flora in 'Friend of My Youth', Lisa finds herself a job in a department store – in her case working in the cosmetics section. In both instances, the store stands for empowerment through assimilation into mainstream Canadian culture, though whether that empowerment is true or false remains to be seen.

Other recent immigrants feature occasionally in Munro's stories, for instance Greta's Czech-born husband and mother-in-law in 'To Reach Japan' from *Dear Life* (2012), but their details remain incidental, an exception being Charlotte/Lottar's foreign-born husband Gjurdhi in 'The Albanian Virgin' from *Open Secrets* (1994). In 'Five Points', Maria has no voice; she is speechless in 'a silent rage' (39). Yet, symbolically, she stands at a threshold between tradition and modernity; she is old-fashioned in appearance, yet the family's renovation of the café introducing ordinary Canadians to exotic pastries heralds a more globalised and inclusive culture. The Eaton's store in Victoria, where Lisa found a job, we learn from independent research, is now long gone, making way for a new shopping mall. Evidently, you can eat sushi there. You can even visit a cannabis boutique.

3.3 Dreams and Altered States of Consciousness: 'Meneseteung'

Munro's female protagonists frequently experience liminal states of consciousness, such as intoxication, hallucination or the frenzy of sexual desire. Dreams, like these other altered states, offer the reader access to a diffuse and complex interiority. They may also leak into reality, suspending time and undermining the stability of the material world; in 'Friend of My Youth', the narrator's recurring dream, bringing her dead mother back to life, merges with daydreams and the fiction-making process, just as the imaginary figure of Flora merges with that of the mother herself. Ultimately, the entire text resembles a dream, in its sudden shifts through time and space, and in the skewed logic of events that resist interpretation.

The collection's third story, 'Meneseteung', is divided into six numbered sections, each introduced with a few whimsical lines quoted from *Offerings*, a volume of verses by Munro's fictional nineteenth-century poet-protagonist, Almeda Joynt Roth. As I have observed elsewhere, these sub-divisions resemble a series of tableaux, or staged exhibits from 'a virtual museum' (Cox, 'Thoughts from England' 284) – the opening section beginning with a forensic examination of Almeda's book, the second continuing the discourse of the local historian, before moving into the more impressionistic language of the fiction-writer, which is sustained for most of the story. In these passages, describing a succession of profoundly altered states, the narrative is focalised largely through Almeda, as reconstructed through the narrator's imagination.

We learn that the entire town is enduring the debilitating heat of a Southwestern Ontario summer, its denizens succumbing to various illnesses, including mental instability. Almeda herself lives alone in a comfortable middle-class home whose backyard nonetheless overlooks the slum quarter, on the edge of the insalubrious 'Pearl Street Swamp' (55). Almeda has not apparently taken the 'nerve medicine' (62), most likely laudanum, that she has been prescribed as a cure for insomnia, because she finds that it induces unwelcome and 'disturbing' (62) dreams. Awakened, therefore, by the pandemonium of Pearl Street on a hot Saturday night, she at first watches the brawling with detachment: 'it is always partly a charade with these people; there is a clumsy sort of parody, an exaggeration, a missed connection' (63–4). Later she is shocked by the sound she hears from a man and a woman, fighting one another she thinks, who finally collapse against Almeda's fence: 'The sound they make becomes very confused – gagging, vomiting, grunting, pounding. Then a long, vibrating, choking sound of pain and self-abasement, self-abandonment, which could come from either or both of them' (64). Most readers would hear these sounds as rough sex, or possibly rape; Almeda construes them as murder. She is considering what to do next when she falls asleep abruptly.

Munro then describes what might appear to be simply an example of the false awakening, in which the dreamer thinks she is no longer sleeping:

> She wakes, startled, in the early light. She thinks there is a big crow sitting on her windowsill, talking in a disapproving but unsurprised way about the events of the night before. 'Wake up and move the wheelbarrow!' it says to her, scolding, and she understands that it means something else by 'wheelbarrow' – something foul and sorrowful. Then she is awake and sees that there is no such bird. (64)

Louis K. MacKendrick (MacKendrick, 'Giving Tongue' 320), Marianne Micros (Micros, '"Pearl Street ... is another story"' 326), and Kim Jernigan (Jernigan 59) hear several echoes of Lewis Carroll in 'Meneseteung'. Almeda's photograph as a young woman was taken in the year *Alice's Adventures in Wonderland* (1865) was first published and we may note that coincidentally Carroll photographed Alice Liddell, the model for his Alice, as 'The Beggar Maid', a phrase used by Munro for the title of an earlier story and book. Almeda resembles Carroll's Alice as a mostly sensible character encountering a bizarre and distorted reality, possibly under the influence of potions she consumes along the way. Almeda's comic vision of 'Tombstones ... marching down the street on their little booted feet, their long bodies inclined forward, their expressions preoccupied and severe' (69) comes after she has finally added a few drops of laudanum to her tea. The earlier figure, the talking crow, is equally reminiscent of Carroll; his Alice is constantly bossed about by opinionated creatures. However, the crow in *Through the Looking-Glass* stands for something rather more mysterious and threatening than his more loquacious animals. Tweedledum and Tweedledee are terrified by 'the monstrous crow' (Ch. IV), which suddenly swoops down from the air. Alice herself never sees the bird, perceiving it as a black cloud, though she can sense its wings beating like a premonition of nightfall.

On one level, Almeda's false awakening is ridiculous, the incongruity of the talking bird and the wheelbarrow as silly as the Mad Hatter's riddle in *Alice's Adventures in Wonderland*, '"Why is a raven like a writing-desk?"' (Ch. VII). But the crow is, in most mythologies, a prophetic creature. Meanwhile the wheelbarrow contains multiple associations, most particularly the wheelbarrow employed by youths in town to parade the town drunk, Queen Aggie, before dumping her in a ditch. In time to come Almeda's obituary will refer to hooligans tormenting Almeda, driving her into the Pearl Street Swamp where she catches pneumonia. The crow's urging is thus a kind of prophecy, as becomes apparent on a second reading.

Venturing outside, Almeda discovers a woman's body by the fence. Straight away, she fetches Jarvis Poulter, her neighbour and putative admirer, who soon establishes that the woman is, contrary to Almeda's belief, not murdered, just '*dead drunk*' (67–8; emphasis in orig.), as the coy report in the local paper has it. He 'nudges the [woman's] leg with the toe of his boot, just as you'd nudge a dog or a sow' (66). The woman is continually described in bestial terms. When Almeda first spots the supposed corpse, she notes 'a bare breast let loose, brown nipple pulled long like a cow's teat, and a bare haunch and leg', the grey tint of bare skin reminding her of 'a plucked, raw drumstick' (65). Once the woman is roused, she bangs her head deliberately against the fence, releasing 'an openmouthed yowl, full of strength and what sounds like an anguished pleasure' (66). She is a monstrous id, a slave to primitive drives, in opposition here to the cultured poet. According to the values of nineteenth-century society, there is a binary opposition between them: '"A lady oughtn't to be living alone so close to a bad neighborhood"' (67), Poulter declares.

Not surprisingly, Almeda is repelled by the drunken woman, feeling nauseous and faint. Much preoccupied with cleanliness, having taken up housework both at home and at the church as a remedy for her nerves, she has come face to face with abjection. In her analysis of the abject, Julia Kristeva has described how, in the distinction between the self and the other entailed in the infant's separation from the maternal body, and the need to regulate one's own cleanliness, certain substances become taboo. These include human waste and bodily fluids – the blood and the vomit matted in the woman's hair – but the corpse, Kristeva claims, is 'the utmost of abjection' (Kristeva 4). Consequently, she argues, 'In that compelling, raw, insolent thing in the morgue's full sunlight, in that thing that no longer matches and therefore no longer signifies anything, I behold the breaking down of a world that has erased its borders: fainting away' (Kristeva 4).

The abject is that which is neither self nor other, and can never be fully expunged – repulsive yet also fascinating. This ambivalence is evoked by Almeda's reaction to the sounds she hears in the night:

Two voices gradually distinguish themselves – a rising and falling howling cry and a steady throbbing, low-pitched stream of abuse that contains all those words which Almeda associates with danger and depravity and foul smells and disgusting sights. (63)

The word 'foul' of course recurs in the 'foul and sorrowful' (64) something connoted by the crow and the wheelbarrow in Almeda's dream. In this lengthy, hyperbolic sentence, the rhythmic repetitions and sound patterns – 'danger and depravity', 'disgusting' – evoke a breathless excitement, a loss of control.

The topographical location of Almeda's house, on the margin between respectability and dissolution, mirrors the various kinds of liminal states she experiences internally, including, as is later revealed, the effects of menstruation. In this condition, she is paradoxically more sexually attractive to Jarvis Poulter than she has been within the constraints of their embryonic courtship. Almeda is, however, feeling too unwell to keep the arrangement he makes to walk her to church – an arrangement that readers accustomed to nineteenth-century novels may well interpret as the prelude to a marriage proposal.

Much has been made of the home-made grape juice that Almeda has left to strain overnight, the image of the purple juice overflowing its basin juxtaposed with her menstrual flow. The title, 'Meneseteung', taken from the name given to the Maitland River by the First Nations, itself becomes a mangled version of the word 'menstruation', used in this context. Coral Ann Howells suggests that 'We may even see such imagery as Munro's version of *écriture féminine*, a way of writing the biological rhythms of the female body and so moving through metaphor beyond the body into the spaces of imagination' (Howells 112). Howells links Almeda's hypersensitive drugged state to the Dionysian connotations of grapes (Howells 110, 112), an association pursued in much greater detail by Klaus P. Stich who has even considered the likelihood of wild grapes growing in the Pearl Street Swamp (Stich 109).

Deborah Heller finds a further connection with the bloodied woman Almeda discovered earlier: 'In a series of interlocking images, the blood that has congealed in the woman by the fence begins to flow in Almeda, as her menstrual flow merges with the grape juice overflowing its container, and both with the flow of words in her mind' (Heller, *Literary Sisterhoods* 82). The laudanum that she has by this time added to her tea contributes to a hallucinatory state in which the physical senses are heightened and the imagination highly charged, the boundary between mind and body, fantasy and reality, seeming to collapse: 'Almeda looks deep, deep into the river of her mind and into the tablecloth, and she sees the crocheted roses floating' (70).

This collapse of boundaries recalls Kristeva's belief that creative literature is 'rooted ... on the fragile border (borderline cases) where identities (subject/object, etc.) do not exist or only barely so – double, fuzzy, heterogeneous, animal, metamorphosed, altered, abject' (Kristeva 207). Almeda's creative delirium releases 'a flow of words somewhere, just about ready to make themselves known to her' (69). These words will form themselves into 'one very great poem' called '"The Meneseteung"', a 'poem that will contain everything and, oh, that will make all the other poems, the poems she has written, inconsequential, mere trial and error, mere rags' (70).

I have always taken the statement 'She doesn't leave the room until dusk' (70) to imply Almeda's absorption in the drafting of her masterpiece; and her consequent avoidance of her suitor, Jarvis Poulter, as the pursuit of a life dedicated to her art. Now I wonder if she ever completed it or if the goal of the great, all-encompassing poem is a chimera, like its counterpart, the great novel. The verses from earlier poems by Almeda that are quoted in the story are clumsy little ditties, their dreams and fancies constrained by convention. Howells believes that Almeda's ecstasy enables her to transcend such limitations, though she points out as well that Almeda's transfiguration also heralds her erasure from history until the newspaper account of her death many years later (Howells 110–13). Regardless of what may or may not have become of Almeda's destiny as a poet, through these passages in 'Meneseteung' Munro has acknowledged the inevitable gap between that first inchoate vision and the words on the page. But more than that, she has explored creativity itself as a state of delirium. Whether the poem is committed to paper or not, Almeda's altered state makes her particularly receptive to a fluid, multiplicitous reality, and responsive to creative stimuli. The pearl itself evokes transformation, in its journey from the oyster shell: and even the rubbish-strewn Pearl Street Swamp can become 'a fine sight' (56) in the morning mist. Munro's description of the night-time noises on the street, focalised through the fictionalised Almeda, is synaesthetic: 'It's as if there were a ball of fire rolling up Pearl Street, shooting off sparks – only the fire is noise' (63).

The French philosopher Henri Bergson argued that real time was immeasurable, our consciousness constrained by the clocks and timetables needed for social relations. Real time exists as boundless duration, something which now and then, perhaps through art, can be grasped at a deeper level of existence: 'Could reality come into direct contact with sense and consciousness, could we enter into immediate communion with things and with ourselves, probably art would be useless, or rather we should all be artists, for then our soul would continually vibrate in perfect accord with nature' (Bergson 150). Under the influence of her 'nerve medicine' (62), Almeda is mesmerised by the fabrics, objects and ornaments in her nineteenth-century dining room: 'For every one of these patterns, decorations seems charged with life, ready to move and flow and alter' (69). Is this the perfect communion Bergson imagined? 'Of course', the story goes on to say, 'Almeda in her observations cannot escape words' (69). But words will always fail to contain the deeper reality that is touched only fleetingly, in dreams.

Kim Jernigan describes this story as one that is 'doubly haunted, first by an underlying cultural narrative which circumscribes, defines and informs the choices of the central character and then by the figure of an unnamed narrator gathering material towards a telling which will redefine and reinscribe what the story *is*, what importance it has, what it might mean to those who live it, tell it, or receive it' (Jernigan 46; emphasis in orig.). She reminds us so little is revealed about the narrator that nothing can be taken completely for granted, not even her gender, logical though it may be to regard this authorial figure as a proxy for the biographical author.

The guise of the amateur historian is adopted by the narrators of both the title story and 'Hold Me Fast, Don't Let Me Pass', the story that immediately follows 'Meneseteung'. 'Friend of My Youth' concludes with a coda, giving the factual background to the Cameronians, the Calvinist sect that the narrator has heard about through her mother's anecdotes. Like 'Hold Me Fast, Don't Let Me Pass', 'Meneseteung' begins with a reading of the sources – Almeda's poetry collection, including her preface and a photograph, and the newspaper archives that will conclude Almeda's story with her 1903 obituary. The first word in 'Friend of My Youth' is 'I' (3); in 'Hold Me Fast, Don't Let Me Pass', the name of the protagonist, Hazel, is revealed on the first page. By contrast, in 'Meneseteung' the first person is almost entirely withheld until it is reinstated in the closing passages. Despite that assumed objectivity, the truths behind the historical record are open to speculations from the very start:

> *Offerings* the book is called. Gold lettering on a dull-blue cover. The author's full name underneath: Almeda Joynt Roth. The local paper, the *Vidette*, referred to her as 'our poetess.' There seems to be a mixture of respect and contempt, both for her calling and for her sex – or for their predictable conjuncture. (50)

Speculations of this kind are inevitable in the biographical research mimicked by Munro, but with the movement from generalised notions to the re-enactment of the past, the balance tips from historical discourse towards fictional invention. In character descriptions, details based on hard evidence or the well-informed guesswork of someone familiar with the period mingle with the purely imaginary, such as the wart on Jarvis Poulter's eyebrow: 'This is a decent citizen, prosperous: a tall – slightly paunchy? – man in a dark suit with polished boots. A beard? Black hair streaked with grey. A severe and self-possessed air, and a large pale wart among the bushy hairs of one eyebrow?' (57). The question marks suggest the fiction-writer's notes; as in 'Friend of My Youth' the inner workings of the fiction-maker's engine are replicated in full view, on the surface of the text. The transmutation of history into fiction seems to be completed by the passages of intense subjective experience in the section labelled V, but there is a return to the historian's language towards the end of the story, with the *Vidette*'s accounts of the deaths of both Almeda Roth and Jarvis Poulter. The narrator uncovers Almeda's gravestone, with the single-mindedness of a detective, grubbing with her bare hands and finding an inscription, 'Meda', that seems to confirm possibilities the narrator has already considered about the poet's use of a shortened version of her name.

The first published version of 'Meneseteung', as it appeared in *The New Yorker*, ends with a statement of optimism about others who, like herself, might save the dead from obscurity: 'You see them going around with notebooks, scraping the dirt off gravestones, reading microfilm, just in the hope of seeing this trickle in time, making a connection, rescuing one thing from the rubbish' (38). The version in *Friend of My Youth* qualifies that optimism with an additional paragraph, closer to what Munro originally submitted to *The New Yorker*:

> And they may get it wrong, after all. I may have got it wrong. I don't know if she ever took laudanum. Many ladies did. I don't know if she ever made grape jelly. (73)

This coda in 'Meneseteung' is a firm reminder that the past is always open to reinterpretation, and that every story is just one version of a tale that is always subject to revision. In the next section, I shall look at Munro's use of a coda in more detail through a reading of the collection's last story, 'Wigtime'.

4. The Coda: 'Wigtime'

Munro often ends a story with a few extra lines or some additional information, after the tale might seem to have reached its natural conclusion. Sometimes the coda to a short story undermines the reliability of what has been established, as in 'Meneseteung', where the reader is reminded that the past is always open to reinterpretation. The coda at the end of the collection's first story, 'Friend of My Youth', places slightly more faith in the historical record – relaying a number of facts about the Cameronians in Scotland, not least their armed resistance against state authority – and strikes a bleakly comic note. And at the close of the collection's last story, 'Wigtime', we find ourselves asking about the main characters, Anita and Margot: Are these two friends better off without their illusions? Each of these examples, in its own way, invites the reader to reconsider the meaning of the story from a different angle.

The very brief coda to 'Wigtime' reaffirms Munro's challenge to the conventional happy ending:

> Margot and Anita have got this far. They are not ready yet to stop talking. They are fairly happy. (273)

Carol L. Beran argues that this pragmatic ending 'explodes the myth that only a happy marriage can bring happiness to a woman' (Beran, 'The Pursuit of Happiness' 331) and consequently that 'Wigtime' is another of the stories in this collection that subverts the tropes of romantic fiction. Margot is very definitely married, though whether happily or not is for the reader to decide. Her husband is mentioned within the first page, describing the return of her old friend Anita after thirty years away. The husband is conspicuously successful as a businessman; Margot shows off the grand house he has built overlooking the harbour. In material terms she has everything she wants. The attentive reader can make the appropriate connection between her husband's business, running a fleet of buses, and Reuel, the driver of the school bus, described in the analeptic passages that return to Reuel and Margot's earlier relationship. His involvement with her while she was still a schoolgirl is disclosed two-thirds through the story; the pattern is repeated when Margot discovers his fling with a teenage babysitter.

Whereas Margot, in mid-life, has become a matriarch, with four children and at least one grandchild, Anita is divorced and childless. Like Hilda in 'Differently', Anita has been married to a doctor, a conventional love object in romantic fiction: 'This should have been the end of her story, and a good end, too, as things were reckoned in Walley' (255). Now she has no clear plans, having just completed a PhD. For Anita, social disapproval is to be expected – yet there are exceptions amongst the older women in the town, admiring the freedom of a younger generation. Her schoolgirl ambitions were divided between the conformist dream of becoming a fashion model and the rather more eclectic vocation of archaeologist. The PhD is in anthropology, close enough to serve as a partial fulfilment of that secret desire.

The binary opposition between these dual protagonists is quite systematic, though blurred by doubling and substitutions; it was originally Margot's plan to train as a nurse in order to travel, an ambition thwarted because of her relationship with Reuel which keeps her stuck in Walley. The pattern is made more complex by a third female figure – Reuel's first wife, the immigrant Teresa, who keeps the store running while he drives the school bus. Their wartime romance has been tarnished by the reality of life in Teresa's adopted homeland, and by her subsequent ill health. The teenage Anita and Margot linger by shopfronts, imagining their own stylish weddings. But Teresa's wedding dress, fashioned out of a lace tablecloth, has been turned into rags for the garage: 'How could Reuel know?' (254).

Margot has a difficult home life; both girls endure the hardships of winter and a regimented life at school. Yet, as adolescents, their lives are charmed, perhaps to a degree that can only be appreciated retrospectively: 'They could never be deeply unhappy, because they believed that something remarkable was bound to happen to them. They could become heroines; love and power of some sort were surely waiting' (253). Neither of them realises that she is living under a spell that will be broken with the advent of sexual maturity, or understands that Teresa – an object of pity, if not of downright scorn – might stand as a warning of what lies (almost literally) in store. The miscarriages that have distorted Teresa's body have also damaged her sex life, a topic she discusses frequently in public. Her garrulousness is only making her situation worse, breaking the taboo against women talking openly about sex. That taboo is broken again with further consequences when the girls imitate a saucy song they have learned from Reuel. He issues a reprimand when he picks them up the next morning: '"A girl saying certain things is not like a man saying them. Same thing as a woman getting drunk. A girl gets drunk or talks dirty, first thing you know she's in trouble"' (258). His words are an unwitting prediction of what happens to Margot, who initiated the singing, and who does indeed get '"in trouble"' with Reuel.

Yet Margot is far more knowing than Reuel supposes:

Margot's mother dreaded Margot's father's lovemaking as much as the children dreaded his cuffs and kicks, and had once slept all night in the granary, with the door bolted, to avoid it. Margot called lovemaking 'carrying on.' She spoke disparagingly of Teresa's 'carrying on' with Reuel. But it had occurred to Anita that this very scorn of Margot's, her sullenness and disdain, might be a thing that men could find attractive. (251)

Margot voices disdain at Reuel's risqué song: '"Big fat nerve he's got, singing that song in front of us. Big fat *nerve*"' (258; emphasis in orig.). But the superficial meaning of words said out loud is undercut by looks and demeanour. Context is crucial in the construction of meaning, and ambiguity inherent in the changing connotations of language. The phallic connotations of '"Big fat *nerve*"' may escape Anita, who is mortified by Reuel's sanctimonious lecture, fearing that 'They had displeased Reuel and perhaps disgusted him, made him sick of the sight of them, just as he was sick of Teresa' (259). She makes 'a face at Margot', who pays no attention, 'looking demurely and cynically at the back of Reuel's head' (259). The oxymoronic coupling of 'demurely and cynically' conveys Margot's skill at manipulation, self-consciously assuming a mask of femininity.

Nonetheless Anita has the insight to intuit that Margot hides 'how it must really be at home, with her father' (255), making light of the way he chases her around the house like 'a hapless comedian, racing around in vain pursuit (of fleet, mocking Margot) and rattling locked doors (the granary) and shouting monstrous threats' (255). The reference to the granary, where the mother also locked herself away, may suggest some element of sexual abuse. Reuel's house is a refuge for her; the police refuse to intervene, acting only to penalise her father for vandalism at the garage.

Perhaps because of her experiences with her father, Margot has learned to play along with male games, to read sexual codes and to turn them to her own advantage. Even as a teenager she has acquired 'a bold lassitude that Margot showed sometimes in movement, with the serious breadth of her hips and the already womanly curve of her stomach, and a look that would come over her large brown eyes – a look both defiant and helpless, not matching up with anything Anita had ever heard her say' (251). Again, Margot is described through the incongruous yoking together of contradictory terms – 'bold lassitude', 'defiant and helpless'. Speech is not a fixed code, but a shifting network of meanings, changing according to both verbal and non-verbal contexts – a look or a gesture.

When the older Margot says to Anita, '"Do you want to know really how I got this house?"' (263), Margot's mastery of gendered power play becomes fully apparent. The tale she tells, narrated first through reported speech, then through free indirect discourse, is full of narrative tension and vivid descriptive detail. After an anonymous tip-off, Anita discovers that Reuel is spending the weekend at a beachfront campsite, and not where he's supposed to be, on a fishing trip. Donning an ingenious disguise, she tracks him down to the cabin he is sharing with, as it turns out, their teenage babysitter, Lana.

Like Margot, Lana comes from a disadvantaged family, but in this case it is her mother's reputation for promiscuity that is the source of her social exclusion. Lana has been brought up by her grandparents and, again like Margot, is not, at first glance, strikingly attractive: 'But she did have a chunky, appealing little figure, well developed front and back, and chipmunk cheeks when she smiled, and silky, flat, naturally blond hair' (267). The 'chunky, appealing little figure' recalls a similar broadness in Margot's body; evidently Reuel's earlier predilections are being re-enacted. Spying on the pair of them, Margot sees a parody of the father-daughter relationship: 'He touched his cheek to her flat blond head, then rubbed his nose in her hair, no doubt to inhale its baby fragrance' (268). The malicious notes Margot leaves on his car are very public accusations of child sexual exploitation. It is not clear from the story whether Lana actually is under the age of consent, which would have been fourteen in Canada at that time; whatever their sexual relationship, Reuel has contrived a ruse almost as clever as Margot's in order to disguise Lana as his daughter. Rage surges through Margot's body after she discovers the two of them together. Like Georgia's anger at Maya in 'Differently', the feeling is dangerously euphoric, even bacchanalian: 'She felt that she had been cut loose, nothing mattered to her, she was as light as a blade of grass' (269).

Margot's intoxicating rage gives way to a cool rationalism. Rather than turning her life upside down by ending her marriage, she decides that her interests are best served by exploiting the power she holds over Reuel – starting with the new house he builds as atonement. Her pragmatism contrasts with the impulsive decisions made by so many Munro protagonists, including Anita. Yet when Anita considers the succession of fleeting relationships that constitute her own love life, it is in language that similarly invokes the financial balance sheet: 'She felt regret about some of them but no repentance. Warmth, in fact, spread from the tidy buildup. An accumulating satisfaction' (272). As a teenager, Anita had an overwhelming crush on Reuel. When, married to the doctor, she encounters a man with, by implication, a faint resemblance to Reuel, she realises 'she could feel more for a phantom than she could ever feel in her marriage' (272). The word 'phantom' recalls the 'phantom pregnancy' in the title story – 'something useless and uncalled for' (26). Anita's happiest moments in the story are the solitary ones she spends in hospital after her emergency operation, drugged and cosseted, daydreaming and reading magazines. Her erotic fantasies about Reuel are part of that daydream, cut short by the news of the scandal over Margot. The girls' friendship is disrupted but not destroyed by rivalry over a man; it is easily resumed when Anita comes back home. The title story opens the collection with an affirmation of the enduring power of the maternal bond; 'Wigtime' closes *Friend of My Youth* by asserting the endurance of female friendship, which may not entirely displace the maternal bond, but survives its destructive potential.

As the story nears its end, it returns to the figure of Teresa, whom Margot has been visiting at the County Home. In her confused state, Teresa believes she is the war bride she once was:

> 'We're all on the boat,' says Margot. 'She thinks we're all on the boat. But she's the one Reuel's going to meet in Halifax, lucky her.' (273)

These lines immediately precede the final three-sentence coda, providing the story's closing image. The sarcasm in '"lucky her"' is palpable. Yet Teresa is happy in her delusion, just as Anita was happy in her daydreams when she was in another hospital all those years ago. Are Anita and Margot better off without their illusions? Is being 'fairly happy' (273) good enough?

Thirty years after 'Wigtime' was first published, Reuel seems a more sinister character than the hapless figure I once took him for, his interest in young girls a warning flag for the twenty-first-century reader. The story is a comedy, and can still be read in that way, as Tracy Ware argues in his discussion of 'its humour and its form' (Ware, 'A Comic Streak' 229); far from being a bogeyman, Reuel is kept in order every time Margot calls out '*Wigtime!*' (270; emphasis in orig.) to remind him of how he was caught. Yet, like Maria's story in 'Five Points', the collection's coda leaves a nasty 'taste in the mouth' (42). As in the case of Heather Bell in the title story of Munro's next book, *Open Secrets* (1994), you can't help wondering what happened to Lana.

5. Reading Across a Short Story Collection

The book-length collection is not the natural habitat of the short story, which is usually composed and, in the first instance, published, as a stand-alone text. The single-author volume has developed as a means of consolidating the author's reputation and keeping the work in circulation long after its first appearance in more ephemeral media such as magazines and radio. In Munro's case, the magazines themselves conferred literary status; all but two of the stories collected in *Friend of My Youth* had made their debut in *The New Yorker* in the period between November 1987 and January 1990 – the exceptions being 'Hold Me Fast, Don't Let Me Pass' and 'Pictures of the Ice' which appeared in *The Atlantic Monthly* (Thacker, *Alice Munro* 567). Once the stories are assembled between the covers of a book, they also become the definitive version of texts that may exist in different forms. 'Meneseteung' is perhaps the best-known example of Munro's habit of making adjustments to closing lines, this time with the restoration, rather than excision, of her final paragraph (see my earlier discussion here and Thacker, *Alice Munro* 434–5). In that new context, the stories also speak to one another, as determined by the choice of title story and their arrangement.

Two of Munro's earlier books, *Lives of Girls and Women* (1971) and *Who Do You Think You Are? / The Beggar Maid: Stories of Flo and Rose* (1978, 1979), can be considered story cycles, linked by the recurring figure of the protagonist and by topics pertaining to the life experiences of her generation. Allan Weiss has written about the 'Juliet Triptych' in *Runaway* (2004) – 'Chance', 'Soon', and 'Silence' – as a prime example of the mini-cycle (Weiss 65–84). But, for the most part, the connections in *Friend of My Youth* are looser and more subtle. As in earlier volumes, the stories are set mostly in semi-rural and small-town Ontario, around the fictional towns of Logan and Walley, both inspired by Munro's birthplace, Wingham (Thacker, *Alice Munro* 43–4). Attentive readers may also notice recurring details. For example, the local property developer, Morris Fordyce, a major character in 'Oh, What Avails', has already been briefly mentioned as Karin and Brent's landlord in 'Pictures of the Ice' (143). Neil's employer in 'Five Points' is 'the Fordyce Construction Company' (30). The 'man from Logan' (110) who receives government handouts for taking on old buildings in 'Oranges and Apples' could be Morris Fordyce yet again.

As in every collection, the individual stories are placed in dialogue with one another, sharing the artistic, cultural and personal preoccupations that shaped their composition. The title story, the last to be published individually (Thacker, *Alice Munro* 567) but the first in the book, serves, to use Rolf Lundén's term, as an 'anchor story' (Lundén 124–5) introducing themes, motifs and techniques that are essential to the volume as a whole. These elements include, as we have seen, the addition of a coda, the evocation of dreams and the relationship between mother and daughter. An interest in local history, the Scottish cultural heritage, orality and storytelling may be added to that list, along with the numerous intertextual echoes, especially those relating to old-fashioned verse.

In various stories, characters whose choices are restricted by sickness or disability struggle to maintain control over their own lives and those of others, sometimes through manipulation, sometimes through outright resistance. The endless miscarriages suffered by Ellie in 'Friend of My Youth' turn the careless young girl into a demanding patient, endlessly complaining, and regaling visitors with embarrassing medical details. The '"crosspatch"' (11), as Flora describes her, is a childlike counterpart to the 'bugbear' (4) that is the narrator's sick mother. Amongst the local community, Ellie's illness is regarded as divine retribution for sexual transgression. Nor is there much sympathy from her caregivers. Flora carries out the task efficiently, but her choice of material for reading out loud – including hellfire sermons and Scottish tales recited in an impenetrable dialect – seems questionable. Both Flora and Nurse Atkinson infantilise Ellie, scolding her when she complains, and Nurse Atkinson extends that strictness to Flora as well: '"Now, when I'm here alone with her, she behaves herself quite nice. I don't have any trouble at all. But after you been in here I have trouble all over again because she sees you and she gets upset. You don't want to make my job harder for me, do you?"' (15). In terminal cases such as Ellie's, the conflict between physical debility and strength of will is accentuated even further in the patient's desperate fight against the inevitable. If the figure of the nurse stands for any kind of angel, then it must be the angel of death.

Despite the parallels between the bugbear and the crosspatch, the narrator's mother is aligned with Flora, rather than Ellie, in the compelling passage that liberates one figure from her sickness, the other from a repressive upbringing:

> Of course it's my mother I'm thinking of ... My mother moving rather carelessly out of her old prison, showing options and powers I never dreamed she had, changes more than herself. She changes the bitter lump of love I have carried all this time into a phantom – something useless and uncalled for, like a phantom pregnancy. (26)

'[T]he bitter lump of love' endured by the narrator recalls Ellie's failed or phantom pregnancies – and the new growths that were intimations of death. 'Nobody then spoke of cancer' but instead used a euphemism – which is why Flora speaks of '"a growth"' (8) when Ellie's illness is finally revealed as something more serious than routine gynaecological problems. Even within the contemporary framework of 'Oranges and Apples', Barbara uses the word '"cancer"' (112) in a preliminary consultation with her physician, but not, apparently, in conversation with her husband. Barbara also has a lump; and that unspeakable sickness may be associated with 'the bitter lump of love' in 'Friend of My Youth' and with Ellie's doomed pregnancies as well as her cancer.

I have returned to this penultimate paragraph in 'Friend of My Youth' because its ambivalence towards sickness, maternity and storytelling makes it a key passage in the collection as a whole; and yet it is also a passage that defies explication. On one level, it reconciles the narrator, both personally and creatively, with the figure of her dead mother. But the final sentence of that paragraph, like much that has come before, is built on negations and contradictions. '[U]seless and uncalled for' (26) is a surprising choice of words to describe any kind of phantom, let alone a phantom pregnancy – dismissive, even a little bathetic. Is something being suppressed? Or left deliberately unfinished, like the phantom pregnancy itself that is never brought to term?

Storytelling is often used by Munro's characters to regain control over the narrative of their own lives, if only in their private fantasies. In 'Goodness and Mercy', a story set on board a transatlantic passenger-carrying freighter in the late 1970s, storytelling, song, voice and breath are interconnected. Part way through the story, Averill hears her mother Bugs singing Zerlina's aria 'Vedrai carino' from Mozart and Da Ponte's opera *Don Giovanni* (1787). This song, one of the favourites in Bugs's repertoire, celebrates love as a cure for all ills; yet for Averill the siren song heralds danger, the sick mother calling her back down below, to her cabin. Averill has concealed herself on deck in a position where she is able to watch the captain take his solitary walks late at night. Psalm 23, 'The Lord Is My Shepherd', the hymn later recalled by the captain, goes through Averill's head. (The coincidence may not be as startling as the narrative implies; the psalm is a very popular choice at funerals.) A counterpoint is set up between Averill's voiceless solo and the aria that is transmitted so clearly that it can be heard on deck. When the hymn is reprised in the captain's story, it is as if he has somehow tuned into unspoken desires that accompany the silent song: 'Averill believed that it was her story he had told' (178). Perhaps the two songs, the voiced and the silent, are not so much two solos as a single duet.

Averill's 'silent singing' of the psalm is 'wrapped around the story she was telling herself' (169) out on the deck each night. That story is her own erotic fantasy about the captain, as she watches him from her concealed position, its details withheld from the reader until the captain's yarn has been coaxed out of him at the party. The singing is also 'a barrier set between the world in her head and the world outside, between her body and the onslaught of the stars, the black mirror of the North Atlantic' (169). Beyond the surface of 'the black mirror', the sea is boundless and unfathomable, the space where corpses are consigned. The boundary Averill's internal song constructs against the shapeless eternity of dark sea and sky is the border she needs to establish between her own self and the all-encompassing maternal body. Yet this primeval ambience is also the site of the imagination, the darkness that brings forth the light.

Illness or disability can be used to frame the narrative or to trigger significant plot developments. 'Oh, What Avails' opens with a section titled 'Deadeye Dick' – a nickname Morris is cruelly given after he is half-blinded and disfigured by a childhood accident. His mother's, and later his own, fatalism is encapsulated in the response to this incident. His mother claims she cannot afford treatment, and is unwilling to ask for help. In adult life, so his sister Joan believes, Morris has no such worries, and would in any case be entitled to free medical care. But his reluctance to change is grounded in a belief that it is 'shameful, to try to turn in the badge misfortune has hung on you' (182). The story closes with Morris's gesture of removing his glasses, with the blacked-out lens that usually conceals the injury; this act is a sign of intimacy with Joan, of relinquishing the self-regard and the insularity that have shaped both their lives. That new feeling is reinforced by their shared recollection of a poem from their childhood, Walter Savage Landor's 'Rose Aylmer'.

Illness also serves as a catalyst in 'Wigtime', where Anita is summoned back to her home town by her mother's rapidly deteriorating health. Anita's teenage friendship with Margot was initially disrupted by her own stay in hospital, recovering from appendicitis, which also, incidentally, prompted her decision to go into nursing. Meanwhile, Anita's absence has left Margot alone with Reuel on the journey to school, giving them the opportunity to start an affair.

As I suggested in my discussion of Ellie's illness in 'Friend of My Youth', the various physical afflictions endured by the characters raise questions of power, control and helplessness. In 'Pictures of the Ice', the collapse of Karin's marriage to Brent is hastened by their baby's death from meningitis. Simultaneously, Brent's guilt about the death drives him towards Christianity, as a result of which Karin meets the minister, Austin, who employs her to look after a wife with terminal cancer. Brent wallows in his own remorse, but Karin finds consolation in the fatalism that some Munro characters find reassuring: 'Even if he'd been a fussed-over precious little baby in a home where the father didn't get drunk and the mother and father didn't have fights, he might have died; he probably would have died, anyway' (151).

Illness is not exceptional in Munro's fiction; it is normal, even mundane, and it does not necessarily alter the dynamics of a relationship, though it may sometimes bring tensions to the surface. The dying mother in 'Wigtime' remains largely the same spiteful person she has always been, though at one point she remarks to Anita, '"So glad to have – a *daughter*"' (256; emphasis in orig.). Is she being manipulative or are her words an expression of genuine affection? Her antagonism towards her daughter's best friend, Margot, may even have substituted for disappointment in her own daughter. Visiting the younger Anita in hospital, she exulted in the teenage Margot's shameless behaviour, speaking so forcefully it was experienced as an attack on the helpless patient: 'her mother's face, her mother's voice came pushing at her like a fist through gauze' (261). Towards the end of her life, the resentment against Anita unleashed by dementia, she accuses her, with equal venom, of throwing her '"*Life* ... Down the *drain*"' (256; emphasis in orig.). The violence of the mother's speech contrasts with the restrained authorial voice in the lines quoted previously that end both the story and the collection: 'Margot and Anita have got this far. They are not ready yet to stop talking. They are fairly happy' (273).

Whatever Anita's mother may believe, a human life is not a single, well-defined object that can be quantified or even wasted, and the human body is not enclosed either, but is always in process. Munro's presentation of the embodied subject can be understood through the concept of the carnivalised, grotesque body discussed by Bakhtin in his analysis of Rabelaisian humour, 'a body in the act of becoming. It is never finished, never completed; it is continually built, created, and builds and creates another body' (Bakhtin, 'The Banquet' 233). The human body is an individual site of change, but as the grotesque body is also integrated into the cosmos. Bakhtin's claim that such a 'body can merge with various natural phenomena, with mountains, rivers, seas, islands, and continents' (Bakhtin 234) could not be better illustrated than by this passage from 'Pictures of the Ice', in which Austin's disintegrating body becomes a kind of landscape: 'That downward slide is what's noticeable on him everywhere – face slipping down into neck wattles, chest emptied out and mounded into that abrupt, queer little belly. The flow has left dry channels, deep lines' (146).

The bodies of Munro's characters are frequently remodelled or curated, through costume or self-adornment, either as disguise or in line with their personal self-image. Austin is one of several characters who present themselves as younger or, as with Maria in 'Five Points', older than their actual age. At the beginning of 'Pictures of the Ice', Austin is trying on incongruously youthful attire in preparation for his supposed wedding, an image he poignantly tries to sustain until his disappearance from the town. Antoinette in 'Hold Me Fast, Don't Let Me Pass' claims to have been '"born in 1940"' (85), even though she has been clearly identified as the wartime sweetheart of the protagonist's husband. Antoinette also claims to be a natural blonde, contradicting the artificial impression given by the earlier description of her on duty at the hotel, 'alert, upright, hair stiff in its net of spray' (81). In 'Oh, What Avails' Morris Fordyce's sister Joan 'looks younger than she did ten years ago' (194), thanks to the youthful fashions of the early 1970s.

'Oh, What Avails' is unusual in that it focuses largely on a male character, Joan's brother Morris. Yet it is Joan's adolescent crush on their neighbour's child, Matilda, that ties the narrative together, providing the story's title and its closing imagery, through allusions to Landor's poem 'Rose Aylmer'. As a young girl, Matilda is blessed with 'the beauty of storybook illustrations' (186). Her blonde tresses cropped, her looks conforming to the fashions of the time, the adult Matilda has become far less conspicuous. Yet throughout the travails of Joan's love life, the fascination she once felt for the pale figure of the storybook princess lies dormant in her imagination. Later in the story, she is shocked to discover the ageing Matilda has become a lone eccentric, wandering the streets, acting 'weird' and 'dressing sloppy' (209).

The nature of female friendships – even in one-sided relationships such as this one – is often more psychologically profound and long-lasting than short-term obsessions with male objects of desire. Here in 'Oh, What Avails' both the allusions to nineteenth-century poetry and the figure of the elderly outcast recall the fate of Almeda Joynt Roth in 'Meneseteung', who, neglecting her appearance, also becomes *a familiar eccentric, or even, sadly, a figure of fun* (71; emphasis in orig.). Similarly in 'Wigtime', Teresa, believed to be older than she claims to be, has 'funny spells' (272) later in life, eventually ending up in the Psychiatric Wing at the County Home.

Additionally, 'Oh, What Avails' offers some of the most powerful juxtapositions of the human body with the built environment, breaking down the borders between the internal self and the outside world; just as the self is always being remodelled, so the town itself is permanently under construction. The fashion-conscious Joan has nonetheless taken a dislike to the 'spruced-up properties' (196) dominating her home town, preferring the transitory spaces of the past to modern-day improvements. She reflects on how, unfortunately, 'The town of her childhood – that haphazard, dreamy Logan – was just Logan going through a phase. Its leaning board fences and sun-blistered walls and flowering weeds were no permanent expression of what the town could be' (196). The town she remembers from her younger days was living through its own adolescence – a period so often associated with freedom in Munro's fiction. The changes Joan encounters in contemporary Logan also generate a deeper awareness of transience, connecting personal experience with the natural world, the built environment, and mutability:

suddenly, without warning, Joan is apt to think: *Rubble*. Rubble. You can look down a street, and you can see the shadows, the light, the brick walls, the truck parked under a tree, the dog lying on the sidewalk, the dark summer awning, or the grayed snowdrift – you can see all these things in their temporary separateness, all connected underneath in such a troubling, satisfying, necessary, indescribable way. Or you can see rubble. Passing states, a useless variety of passing states. Rubble. (208; emphasis in orig.)

There will be literal rubble in the streets, thanks to developers such as Joan's brother Morris, whose persistent reappearances upon rereading this collection act as a reminder of social and material changes in the landscape; but 'rubble' also stands for the inevitable collapse of the present day into the oncoming future that itself will soon be absorbed into the past. The word 'rubble', foregrounded typographically and by repetition, is only one syllable away from 'rubbish'. Joan's need to protect her composure, perhaps even her sanity, by keeping 'this idea of rubble at bay' (208) recalls the important phrase in 'Meneseteung' about 'the hope of seeing this trickle in time, making a connection, rescuing one thing from the rubbish' (73). '[M]aking a connection' suggests the modernist search for those elusive moments of insight that generate meaning, if only for an instant, and recapture impressions of the past. Such endeavours are psychologically necessary but at best create only a facsimile of the past and an approximation of experience as the passing moment is absorbed into time gone by.

'"The old order changeth, yielding place to new"' (149) proclaims the elderly Austin in 'Pictures of the Ice', quoting from Tennyson's poem 'Morte d'Arthur', as he disposes of his redundant property. His admiration for the computer at the Auction Barn, where much of his furniture is bound, only highlights his own obsolescence. The Auction Barn in this story recalls Zendt's Furniture Barn in 'Five Points', run by Brenda and her husband on the site of 'a worn-out farm with good buildings' (29). Flora's final letter in 'Friend of My Youth' does not reveal whether Nurse Atkinson has renovated her half of the Grieveses' farmhouse in the same way as she refurbished her own side following her marriage to Robert; but she does mention that '[T]he old stable is all fixed up with milking machines and the latest modern equipment, it is quite a marvel' (23). Flora herself has abandoned the harsh, Scots Presbyterian way of life she grew up with for the modern conveniences of her job in a city department store. Both the department store and the latest farming equipment are themselves doomed to become anachronistic in due course. Perhaps the Grieveses' farmhouse in the Ottawa Valley has become another worn-out building glimpsed from the highway.

In 'Oranges and Apples', Murray chooses the wrong moment to modernise Zeigler's Department Store just as a mall is being built out of town. He loses his business, and is forced to sell the family home, becoming embittered when he learns that 'a man from Logan, a dealer and developer, was getting government money for restoring old buildings when the fact of the matter was that he was tearing the old buildings down and preserving only a remnant of the foundation to incorporate into his new, ugly, badly built, profitable apartment blocks' (110). Whether or not the 'man from Logan' (110) really is Morris Fordyce, he is a man who reads the landscape purely in terms of material value, as we learn of Morris in 'Oh, What Avails': 'Not just houses and buildings but fields and trees, woodlots and hills appear in his mind with a cash value attached to them' (198).

The seemingly unstoppable march of progress is disrupted by nostalgia for tradition and the increased curiosity about the past that motivates the amateur historians in 'Meneseteung' and 'Hold Me Fast, Don't Let Me Pass'. But tradition itself may be misremembered, reconstituted or newly invented. The older Joan notices 'something here that is strained, meticulous' (208) in the restoration or recreation of original features in the Logan houses, as tastes change from modern to traditional – a phenomenon also remarked upon in 'Oranges and Apples'. In that story, the supposedly ancient tradition of seeing the sun set in two different places by the lakeside has been invented for the benefit of tourists, along with '[t]he old-fashioned bandstand in the park' (133) nearby. The lake itself, like the river in 'Meneseteung' or the sea in 'Goodness and Mercy', stands for endless change, yet the eternal in Munro is also the particular. Seen from Margot's house in the final story, 'Wigtime', the lake is miniaturised (like the genre that Munro has made her own): 'From up here on the deck the two long arms of the breakwater look like floating matchsticks. The towers and pyramids and conveyor belts of the salt mine look like large solid toys. The lake is glinting like foil' (273). Munro's art is the art of changing perspectives, the world close up and far away, both sublime and ridiculous. And there is always something new to see, something you missed on a previous reading.

The Art of Misreading; or, The Driving Force of Misunderstanding: *Open Secrets* (1994)

Corinne Bigot

> Voici un principe d'esthétique ... une règle, dis-je, pour les artistes[:] Soyez réglé dans votre vie et ordinaire comme un bourgeois, afin d'être violent et original dans vos oeuvres.
>
> – Gustave Flaubert, 'A Mme Tennant', jour de Noël 1876

1. Introducing a Dark Collection

Open Secrets is at once a strikingly appealing, coherent, yet rather chilling collection. All eight stories were first published within the same time frame – 1991 to 1994.[1] In 'Darkness Collecting: Reading "Vandals" as a Coda to *Open Secrets*' Nathalie Foy observes of these stories that 'The similarities ... are striking enough to encourage juxtaposed readings. There is a way in which, when the stories intersect in their similarities, they shed light as well as shadow on each other' (Foy 148). Foy's comment shows that coherence does not arise from social realism, even when it comes to the six stories here that are set in the fictional towns of Carstairs or Walley that Munro locates in Southwestern Ontario. Incidentally, with 'Vandals', the last story in the collection, Munro also shows her hand, as she has her characters 'follow the river track as far as Highway 86' (277) to reach the (fictional) 'nature preserve' (266) that is situated outside of but not far from the (fictional) town of Carstairs – Highway 86 passes through Wingham, the author's birthplace.

'The Albanian Virgin', the third story, is evidence that the cohesiveness does not only hinge on geographical coherence. Although the source of 'The Albanian Virgin' was a story Munro had heard about a Clinton, Ontario librarian who claimed that she had been captured by bandits in Albania in the early 1900s (Munro in Gzowksi, Interview 9 Oct. 1996), what strikes me is that Munro, thinking that the story may not have been true – back then the word 'Albania' fuelled people's imaginations – remarked, 'Albania is a country of the mind' (Munro in Gzowski). The name of the country itself, as Georgiana M.M. Colville points out, evokes a 'white (alba) fabric' (Colville 83), and I have no doubt that Munro must have loved this suggestion. The collection forcefully demonstrates that Alice Munro is a *'geomancer'*, as Robert McGill has it: 'one who arranges spaces artfully, drawing them into resonant relationships with one another'

(McGill 32). The various spaces in the collection, including Victoria and Albania, are all placed in 'resonant relationships', as my introductory section intends to show. For instance, while the Albanian story starts with an Albanian guide who is killed in Montenegro and whose decapitated head is probably carried away by his killers, the collection debunks the idea that such violence only happens in faraway countries.

The second and third parts here will focus on five individual stories – the title story; the first, second and third stories; and the final story, the coda to the collection. The other stories – 'The Jack Randa Hotel', 'A Wilderness Station' and 'Spaceships Have Landed' – will be discussed in the introductory and concluding sections, which weave together the major motifs in the collection.

1.1 Mapping Doud County

Six of the eight stories are set in the fictional towns of Carstairs, a factory town in a river valley, or Walley, a lake town, which is not very distant from Carstairs. The name Carstairs is probably derived from the Gaelic word *Caer* referring to a fortified place, so it is a fitting name for a town that is dominated by a factory which in the first story, 'Carried Away', is compared to a medieval stronghold: 'The piano factory . . . stretched along the west side of town, like a medieval town wall' (25). 'Spaceships Have Landed' provides us with information that Carstairs originated on the flats by the Peregrine River in the nineteenth century. In that story, too, the social geography of the town is mapped: the main character Rhea, her childhood friend, and the town's bootleggers live 'on the edge of Carstairs' (229), not too far from the river, where the poorer social classes reside.

As argued by Coral Ann Howells, in 'Open Secrets' Munro starts with referencing points on what could be a map of Carstairs, only 'to focus on what is left out of this map' (Howells 121), leaving readers with blank spaces, absent clues and isolated pieces of evidence. This characteristic holds true of most of the stories. I find Gilles Deleuze and Félix Guattari's definition of the process of mapping particularly relevant to Munro's evocations of Carstairs and Walley, and more generally, the area she conjures up in the collection. They posit that contrary to tracing, 'the map . . . is entirely oriented toward an experimentation in contact with the real', and go on to point out that the map 'fosters connections between fields' (Deleuze and Guattari 12), which aptly describes Munro's process. I propose to call the area that Munro maps in the collection 'Doud County', after the leading family of Carstairs. Martin and Ober argue that in this collection Munro plays the role of a 'small-town historian' (Martin and Ober, 'Alice Munro' 237). With the mentions of the factory – Douds – and the family, Munro offers social commentary about life in a small town. In 'A Real Life', Millicent is eager to be known to the leading ladies of Carstairs such as Mrs Doud, and the Douds are shown to have a strong influence in 'Carried Away' and 'Spaceships Have Landed'. The Douds are the owners of a factory that maimed or even killed different workers (26) and in 'Carried Away' Munro soon involves the factory and the family in a web of violence that permeates the collection.

The name Doud is of Gaelic origin, and the first part of the word, *dubh*, meant black or dark-complexioned, which suggests that Doud is a fitting name for the family, the factory and the area – Doud County is a dark country. The heir, Billy Doud, we learn in 'Spaceships Have Landed', marries a girl who has probably been the victim of a mysterious assault. In 'Open Secrets' a girl mysteriously vanishes during a hike organised by a woman who used to have a job in the office at Douds Factory (133) and the main suspect 'used to be the piano tuner at Douds' (146). Even women such as Louisa Doud, who married the factory owner, and Bea Doud, his daughter, are caught in the web of violence: in 'Vandals' Bea is shown to be the silent accomplice of a paedophile. Bea is therefore one of the vandals the title alludes to, so I see a promising but puzzling connection with Louisa, her stepmother, who in 'Spaceships Have Landed' is 'known as the Tatar' (240), since Vandals were originally members of a Germanic tribe that in the fourth and fifth centuries invaded Western Europe (*OED*) and Tatars were inhabitants of Central Asia before the Western world used the word 'Tatar' to refer to peoples who devastated much of Asia and Eastern Europe (*OED*). Interestingly, in 'Vandals' Bea Doud will bring the paedophile to Carstairs – after his death she has Ladner buried 'in the Doud plot' (262).

Robert Lecker explains that 'Carried Away' is 'about a postwar, postindustrial fall' (Lecker 103) and its effect on utopian ideals; however, other stories in the collection intimate that violence started much earlier. The collection creates a sense of connection to the Canadian wilderness and to Ontario's history through allusions to European settlements, with the names of Carstairs and Walley. In 'Spaceships Have Landed', a mysterious mark on Eunie's face suggests that she was raped and left lying on the ground, on the very spot where the nineteenth-century town started – the former fairgrounds – which the narrator refers to as 'that first mistaken settlement' (259). The adjective 'mistaken' may recall the error of judgement made by the founders of the town, but we should bear in mind that the verb 'mistake' also means to take improperly or wrongfully, to transgress, to do wrong (*OED*). 'A Wilderness Station' directly emphasises the violence and danger inherent to settlers' lives in the 1850s, whether Simon Herron's death was caused by an accident when he was logging trees, or whether he was murdered. In 'Vandals', as Héliane Ventura observes, the paedophile's work on his pristine land, a 'nature preserve' (266), is evocative of the domestication of the bush by early settlers (Ventura, 'Aesthetic Traces' 310). The books on Ladner's bookshelves reveal his interest in wars and violence – Michael Trussler notes Thucydides' *History of Peloponnesian War* (Trussler 87) and Lucile Bentley draws attention to *The French and Indian Wars*, the only book on Canadian history, which serves as a reminder that Canada's settler history is a history of violent invasions (Bentley, '"A body"' 54–5).

Many of Munro's stories have featured and reflected on Ontario's glacial landscape and its lakes, as a way to emphasise connections between human history and Ontario's history.[2] Curiously, the glacial landscape is not prominent in *Open Secrets* and there are only three allusions to Lake Huron – in 'The Jack Randa Hotel' (189), in 'A Wilderness Station' (225), where it is not named, and in 'Spaceships Have Landed' (241). Rivers are given more prominence. The Peregrine River that evokes both Sir Peregrine Maitland (Thacker, *Alice Munro* 451)[3] and a bird of prey[4] is at the very centre of the town of Carstairs and the county – and like the factory, a place where violence can happen, both in 'Open Secrets' and 'Spaceships Have Landed'. At the end of 'Spaceships Have Landed' when the older characters drive to where the old fairgrounds used to be, Rhea's noticing that the wild landscape of the riverbanks has been tamed, civilised and beautified, and that a parkland and 'a shorn and civilized riverbank' (259) have replaced the fairgrounds and racetracks, implies more than loss, even if Rhea regrets that the places of her childhood have disappeared. The place where Eunie's misadventure occurred has also disappeared, erasing all trace of it, all the more so because Eunie's 'low grumble' (260), which only her husband hears and interprets, is not to be deciphered.

In 'Open Secrets', the girl disappears in the woods, near the river. In 'A Wilderness Station', a man dies in the woods, either by accident or at the hands of his brother or perhaps his wife. Yet the most frightening place in the collection is perhaps the 'nature preserve' in 'Vandals': the work of the paedophile, the preserve that is anything but natural is located outside the town boundaries 'in the northern part of the county' (266), and it casts its dark shadow onto Doud County, with the word 'preserve' suggesting that the violence that was perpetrated there remains trapped, never to be forgotten.

1.2 The Fact of a Body

Mark Levene argues that starting with *Open Secrets* (1994) and continuing in *The Love of a Good Woman* (1998), Munro introduces 'terrible acts of willed or accidental violence' (Levene, '"It was about vanishing"' 854). The very structure of the collection highlights this increased representation of violence, opening with the discovery of Jack Agnew's decapitated body in 'Carried Away' and ending with the revelation of a man raping children in 'Vandals'. There are many acts of destructive violence: a man is killed and probably beheaded in 'The Albanian Virgin'; in 'A Wilderness Station' it is suggested that Simon Herron was murdered, either by his brother, George, or by his wife, Annie, partly because Simon physically and sexually abused her, and in the Walley jail one hears the incessant screams of a woman who was raped. 'Open Secrets' hinges on the possibility if not the probability that Heather Bell was raped and murdered.

Although Munro has often evoked and described maimed bodies in her previous collections, I am tempted to think of *Open Secrets* as a variation on 'the fact of a body'.[5] First, attention is drawn to bodies that bear the marks of violence, bodies that are maimed (or even decapitated) and to corpses. Many stories imply that some truth could be discovered, provided these bodies were examined. For instance, in 'A Wilderness Station', Annie Herron's secret letter to her friend mentions the 'black and blue marks' (213) on her arms and upper legs, which could be evidence of domestic violence. Munro purposely makes Annie's body silent and undecipherable by having the Clerk of the Peace examine Annie when she arrives in Walley (201) and refrain from commenting on any mark. In 'Spaceships Have Landed', the narrator mentions the marks on Eunie's body and face when she returns home – 'she had scratches and smears of blood on her arms and forehead ... One side of her face was dirty, too, from being pressed against the ground' (254). The use of the passive voice implies that someone might have pressed her face on the ground and the marks on her body all indicate a sexual assault. However, when Eunie arrives home, none of the many people in the house comments on these marks; Eunie's story of having been taken to a spaceship by alien children is not disputed; and the Chief of Police is relieved that 'There was nothing to be followed up, nobody to be charged' (255), which indicates a blatant desire to see and to do nothing. By contrast, pictures will be taken of the racetrack, which is now said to be the trace or 'the mark left by the spaceship' (257), conjuring up inexistent visions of the spaceship.

Dead bodies disappear from view, either because they morph into something else or because they are hidden away. In 'A Wilderness Station' Annie Herron first mistakes her husband's body for 'a log' (196) because it is covered in snow, a mistake that announces the central issue of the story – the (in)visibility of Simon's body. In the conflicting accounts that the man's brother and wife write, the body disappears since it was buried during the snowstorm that cut them off from the town. George explains that he could not get help because of the snowstorm and had to bury Simon next to the shanty. He claims that subsequently he 'put up a wooden marker' for Simon's grave, but erected 'his stone' (196) in the local cemetery, although he did not move Simon's body. Annie claims that she and George purposely erased all traces of the grave after they buried Simon: 'George beat [the dirt] down flat with the shovel as much as he could. Then we moved all the wood back searching where it was in the snow and we piled it up in the right way so it did not look as if anybody had been at it' (210). Consequently, Simon's body was never examined, which is of crucial importance to the story, since examining it would have determined whether Simon was killed by a branch or an axe.

'Open Secrets' is centrally concerned with a girl's inexplicable disappearance and the disappearance of her body, although extensive searches are conducted (159–60). Yet although Heather Bell's photograph eventually fades in public places, her vanishing act haunts the memory of the main character and informs the story. In 'Carried Away' Munro stages a complex vanishing act that turns the dead worker into an elusive, haunting presence. As both Ildikó de Papp Carrington (Carrington, 'What's in a Title?' 557–8) and Robert Lecker (Lecker 111) have shown, the story hinges on Jack's invisibility; he is 'enigmatic, invisible, and therefore powerful by virtue of his physical absence' (Lecker 111). Although there is tangible evidence of Jack's visits to the Library both before and after the war, namely a note Jack left under the blotter and the books he borrowed, the librarian never saw him (37). It is only when he dies that he is seen, albeit briefly: Arthur Doud covers Jack's body with his own jacket, and then presses Jack's head 'out of sight' (34) against his chest.

The fact of the body is also inherently linked to a central concern in the collection – (not) looking at violence. Arthur Doud does not fully comprehend what he sees when he reaches the scene of the accident. As he is shown the scarlet, brilliant blood on the floor, he fails to see the body, mistaking it for 'A pile of work clothes soaked in blood' (33). Yet Arthur is also the one character in the collection who takes responsibility for a death when he picks up and cradles Jack's head. By contrast, in 'The Albanian Virgin' the Canadian woman who has been kidnapped seems reluctant to see that the rusty bundle the size of a cabbage which she is looking at could be her guide's decapitated head. In *Open Secrets*,

Munro draws attention to the role played by silent witnesses and to those who fail to understand what they are meant to see.

1.3 The Driving Force of Misunderstanding

The collection is peppered with verbs such as 'does not notice', 'doesn't see', 'confused with', 'mistook for'. Munro often tells stories through the eyes of characters who fail to understand other people, or misread the world around them, or are reluctant to see what they are supposed to notice. Evoking Millicent in 'A Real Life', Munro explained that she was interested in seeing everything through her eyes: 'so it's mostly what she'd understand' (Munro in Thacker, *Alice Munro* 448), or, as I would rephrase it, misunderstand. Coral Ann Howells' remark that in 'Open Secrets' 'things are seen, but they are not understood' (Howells 124) works for the whole collection – from stories in the comic mode such as 'A Real Life' whose humour depends on Millicent's reluctance to understand the facts of life, to 'Vandals' that raises the question of whether people misunderstand situations or decide not to acknowledge what is going on. Andrea F. Szabó's comment about 'The Jack Randa Hotel' that Gail 'constantly misreads the world' (Szabó 116) actually sheds light on the collection as a whole.

The motif of misunderstanding provides unity to the collection regarding structure, style, plot and characterisation. Many characters are readers (of letters, of books) but the more texts and letters they read, the less they understand the world around them. 'Carried Away' is a case in point: Louisa, the librarian, reads Jack's letters and all news of the war most attentively, yet she fails to notice the blanks in Jack's letters or to understand the significance of his absence after the war. Louisa herself is often judged and misunderstood by men. For instance, Jim Frarey is quite surprised to discover that she is a virgin – '"I got a wrong impression"' (20) – and Arthur Doud never understands what Jack's death, and therefore Jack, meant to Louisa. When Arthur brings back the books Jack took away, he believes that Louisa is 'unhinged' (28) by the thought that the dead man might have left something in the books. He then assumes that her interest in the victim is due to his 'making off with her books without her knowing about it' (37). He misunderstands the point of her questions about Jack, believing that she is blaming him (36), and then mistakes her interest for a morbid fascination with death (38). Finally, he fails to understand what her 'peculiarly quivering, shamed, and determined voice' (40) means. Their relationship, then, is based on misunderstandings. Interestingly, it is only when Arthur accepts that he does not understand Louisa that he proposes to her: 'He realized that he knew hardly anything about her – what kind of person she really was or what kind of secrets she could have' (40).

The most intriguing aspect of the collection is that there is no pattern, no clear journey towards understanding. *Open Secrets* explores the consequences of various acts of misunderstanding and misreading, be they comic or tragic. In 'The Jack Randa Hotel' Gail's mistakes are highlighted – for instance she failed to see that Will was falling in love with another woman, although there had been signs that indicated it, and in Brisbane she fails to understand that her neighbours, an old man and his young companion, are lovers, taking them to be father and son.

At the end of the story Gail looks back at her 'journey' (189), which is also a metaphorical one. In her analysis of the story, Szabó contends that Gail's decision to leave behind the books she had borrowed from the Library when she flees shows that she abandons her preconceived notions of love and relationships: 'Gail opts out of the romance' (Szabó 118). Similarly, Coral Ann Howells argues that Gail is probably ready to let go of Will, since in the ambulance, when she is holding the old man's hand, she 'suddenly realises that she is hanging on to someone – and something – which is already dead' (Howells 132). I personally tend to see Gail's journey as the journey of a woman who finds herself marooned in Walley after Will left her, pursues Will to another island, only to opt for freedom when he comes to her door to claim her back.

When Gail hears (or thinks she hears) Will behind her door, she finds that the words she previously longed for have now turned into a kind of chain which could bind her forever: '*Love – need – forgive. Love – need – forever.* The sound of such words can become a din, a battering, a sound of hammers in the street' (188; italics in orig.). The dashes that look like chains and the 'battering' sound of hammers make the words sound oppressive, synonymous with prison, so that she is 'driven to escape' (188). I am interested in the way Munro uses the words 'loose' and 'maroon' together in the story. In Brisbane, Gail wears 'loose flowered cotton dresses' (174) and I remember that Munro drew attention to the word 'loose' in 'Oranges and Apples' in *Friend of My Youth* when a husband recalls that his mother sees his wife as 'A loose woman' (Munro, 'Oranges and Apples' 132). Although he understands what she means, he wonders whether the word could not describe 'A woman who could get loose, who wasn't fastened down, who was not reliable, who could roll away' (Munro 132). As pointed out by Deborah Heller, many female characters from *Friend of My Youth* 'get loose from the roles expected of them by other characters in their fictional lives and from the roles that readers may expect them to play in predictable plots' (Heller, 'Getting Loose' 60), and this pattern holds true of Gail. According to the *OED*, 'loose' also means 'free from bonds, fetters, or physical restraint' and 'allowed to run free in travelling or marching'. Noticing that when Gail dyes her hair the result is said to be 'a deep maroon' (169), I cannot help thinking of the Maroons – the communities of black slaves who had escaped from captivity to settle in the mountains and forests of the West Indies; and I picture Gail as a Maroon.

'Spaceships Have Landed' is less ambiguous since it describes a seventeen-year-old girl's sexual awakening as she learns to listen to what her body is telling her. Rhea has been courted by the Doud heir and she is aware that the town thinks that 'She was lucky: Billy Doud had chosen her' (244). Yet Rhea experiences a discrepancy between what she is supposed to feel and what she feels – a 'fogged-in feeling' (247) that leaves her feeling 'cut off and bewildered' (244) – and she gradually realises that body language is more trustworthy than words. Although Billy says he wants to have sex with her, his body shows that he does not: 'He pressed his lips tightly against hers as if it was his job to keep both their mouths shut' (242). Rhea eventually understands that Billy dislikes women's bodies and sex. She also understands that *she* is a sexual being, with sexual urges, when she realises that she is attracted to Billy's friend Wayne. When they kiss, their embrace bears little resemblance to the sessions with Billy, and Rhea experiences the kiss through her entire body, which opens up – in direct contrast to what happened with Billy: 'She had the idea of herself, at this juncture, being opened and squeezed, opened and squeezed shut, like an accordion' (248). With this short scene, Munro reminds us that teenagers experience sexual desire too – and she does so without adding any gloss onto the fact. The kissing scene in the corridor is a crude exploration and admission of Rhea's experience (she is drunk and vomits in the corridor) but it shows how Rhea's body clears up the confusion that social pressure introduced: 'Some crowding and snorting, inside or outside of her, *trying to make itself understood*' (248; emphasis added). In this respect, 'Spaceships Have Landed' does depict a journey towards better understanding.

By contrast, 'Vandals', the last story, explores the devastating consequences of misunderstanding a situation and misreading signs – whether we consider children who did not read the signs that Ladner placed around his property, or Bea Doud's failure to (literally) read the signs that the children showed them, or, perhaps, her capacity to look the other way. Bea Doud is seen to make mistakes from the moment she enters Ladner's nature preserve – she confuses rotten apples for mushrooms, and fake animal bodies for real ones – and her mistakes announce the major motif in the story, her failure or reluctance to understand what is happening with the children that spend their afternoons with Ladner. Whether Bea turns a blind eye or fails to see what is happening, the abuse goes on in the nature preserve and is never exposed.

2. 'Open Secrets': Death by Landscape

'Open Secrets' is set in 1965 in Carstairs; it starts with the account of how a teenage girl disappeared during a hike in the woods, and focuses on the town's reaction to this disturbing event that shatters the town, as well as the main character's reaction. The narrative is characterised by a cacophony of sounds, voices – rumours and gossip – and silence.[6] The story is told from the point of view of Maureen, a character whose powers of observation go hand in hand with her reticence to say or to do anything. Maureen listens to her cousin telling her about the disappearance of the teenage girl, to gossip in the village and to testimony given to her husband, Lawyer Stephens. As the story unfolds, it becomes clear that Maureen feels some empathy or even connection with the girl who disappeared but does not voice her interest or concern. She will also remain silent even though she has a suspicion as to what happened to the girl, which encourages readers to shift their attention from Heather, the girl who vanished, to Maureen. The story suggests that the main character can perceive the truth and simultaneously opens up the possibility that she is driven by her capacity to imagine stories.

The story begins with a floating segment in italics, a foreign voice so to speak, that disturbs the main story. Four other italicised segments inexplicably and randomly intrude upon the narrative until the confusion is cleared up when Frances tells Maureen, '"There is a poem already made up and written down . . . I've got it here typed out"' (156). Munro creates a complex multilayered polyphonic narrative: the paragraph that follows the first italicised segment is the oral, second-hand account of an incident that happened during the Canadian Girls in

Training's annual hike: 'Frances *said* that Mary Kaye *said* Heather Bell had been the worst one, the boldest' (130; emphasis added). The main character, Maureen, hears 'two new reports' (140) at the Post Office, and the words of the people who claimed they heard a cry are quoted so that other words, other voices are added: 'Who was that? they remembered saying to each other. . . . *Who was that?*' (140; italics in orig.). The repeated phrase is set in italics, conveying the people's tone, evoking all that is implied behind these words.

Another report is then added, by a woman living on a nearby farm. Marian Slater reports the strange behaviour of her neighbour, Mr Siddicup, mimicking his 'wheezing and growling noises' (146): '*Ah, ahh* was all he said . . . still making these noises – *ah, ahh* – that would never turn into words' (148; italics in orig.). Since Marian Slater's testimony clearly casts suspicion on this man, Maureen then imagines the words that the people in town would spread: 'people would say in horrid, hushed voices that no, they weren't surprised. *I wasn't surprised, were you?*' (152; italics in orig.). As the italics show, Maureen has the ability to hear what people could say, and although these words have not been uttered yet, they somehow add to the polyphony of the text. The narrator also mentions the gossip that circulates about Heather's mother. After the case gets cold, since Heather is never found, rumours persist – some people think that she left of her own free will and others remain suspicious of Mr Siddicup: 'Many people will continue to believe that he did something or saw something. *He had something to do with it*' (160; italics in orig.). Through these devices, we are able to hear the gossipy voice of a small town, but the result amounts to nothing since the truth will never be heard and the devices eventually mark off Maureen's silence.

Maureen is depicted as someone who listens to others, and can choose silence. In this gossipy town where people remind Maureen that she is only a 'country' girl who married up, Maureen did keep one of her intimate secrets: her 'only misfortune was a hidden one – her tubes had been tied up to make her infertile' (134). A brutal scene with her husband shows that she is used to silencing her own voice during abusive sex: 'And she had to keep her mouth closed not on any howls of protest but on a long sickening whimper of complaint' (156). In general, Maureen's silence may amount to a complicit one: although the story of Heather Bell's disappearance is never solved, one passage offers a clue as to the identity of the man who, it would appear, raped and murdered her. After they gave their testimony to Lawyer Stephens, Marian and Theo Slater leave his and Maureen's house and sit down a short distance away. Maureen, who observes their silent communication, sees the husband caressing his wife's hat in a compulsive gesture:

> He stroked that hat made of horrible brown feathers as if he were pacifying a little scared hen.
> But Marian stopped him. She said something to him, she clamped a hand down on his. The way a mother might interrupt the carrying-on of a simple-minded child – with a burst of abhorrence . . .
>
> Maureen felt a shock. She felt a shrinking in her bones. (153–4)

Munro added this passage for the book version after she was told by Douglas Gibson, her publisher at McClelland & Stewart, that some of the readers there found the story '"a little too opaque"' (Gibson in Thacker, *Alice Munro* 453). The 'shock' (154) Maureen experiences which attacks her own body suggests that she understands something is wrong; and Marian's abhorrence implies a reaction to something immoral on Slater's part. What I personally like about the clue[7] is the impressive way it reaches the surface even though the reverberations of silence are so strong. Marian silently stops her husband, as if she intended to silence him, clamping her hand on his. Maureen's 'shock' echoes Marian's reaction, suggesting that Maureen too feels abhorrence when witnessing this compulsive gesture. The shock is also a shock of recognition since, as previously noted, another passage shows that when Maureen's husband forces himself on her, she is used to silencing her own sounds in order to hide his lewd behaviour much as Marian Slater conceals her husband's presumed crime. A passage at the end of the story confirms the hypothesis that Maureen knows that Theo Slater is guilty and his wife his silent accomplice. As she is stirring custard on her stove that same day, Maureen 'sees' Theo Slater's hand 'pressed down, unresistingly, but by somebody else's will – it is pressed down on the open burner of the stove . . . and held there . . . just long enough to scorch the flesh' (158). Since she sees that this branding, recalling ancient practices to punish guilty people, is done 'In silence' and 'by agreement' (158), her vision implies guilt and complicity – evoking both her own and Marian Slater's complicit silence.

The end of the story also implies that Maureen is aware of her own choices. The narrator transports readers into another part of the country, in the future, after Maureen has left Carstairs. She will be making custard and 'she'll watch the soft skin form on the back of a wooden spoon and her memory will twitch, but it will not quite reveal to her this moment when she seems to be looking into an open secret' (160). The image of soft skin on the back of a spoon aptly evokes a closed eyelid, and serves as a reminder that Maureen is not keen to look at any open secret. Maureen's paying attention to the skin on the spoon suggests that a sticky liquid remains when one lifts the spoon. The image of the skin can evoke Maureen's turning a blind eye. Yet I find the image to be versatile as it can also symbolise the impossibility of getting free of the memory – whether that be the story of Heather's disappearance, Maureen's own silence or simply her own reaction to Heather's fate – since the skin sticks to the spoon. Similarly, the story sticks to her memory, long after Heather Bell 'is old news' (160) and the thing that the town wants to forget. Maureen also feels a connection with Heather Bell, after she disappears, for her fate fascinates Maureen if not haunts her. It is only when Heather disappears that Maureen gets interested in her.

With 'Open Secrets' Munro creates her own Southwestern Ontario version of a 'Death by Landscape' – to cite Margaret Atwood's short story of that name first published in the Canadian magazine *Saturday Night* in 1989 and then in Atwood's story collection *Wilderness Tips* in 1991. Atwood's Lucy and Munro's Heather both vanish in the woods, never to be found. In both stories the peace of the scene – a lake in Atwood's story and rocks by a river in Munro's – is disturbed by a scream or shout no one can identify. Atwood's Lucy disappears during a canoe trip at summer camp and Munro's Heather disappears during a CGIT hike – outings that are in both cases organised by an older woman to keep the tradition alive until the incomprehensible horror of the disappearance disturbs these traditions. By setting her story in a place that everyone is familiar with – Miss Johnstone had been taking girls along the same paths for at least two decades – Munro shows that ordinary familiar places can be as dangerous as the trackless wilderness of Northern Ontario that Atwood evokes. Furthermore, in both stories attention is drawn to the absence of the body:

> What can be said that makes any sense? 'Girl vanishes in broad daylight, without a trace.' It can't be believed. ... But a dead person is a body; a body occupies space, it exists somewhere. You can see it; you put it in a box and bury it in the ground, and then it's in a box in the ground. But Lucy is not in a box, or in the ground. (Atwood, 'Death by Landscape' 125, 128)

> Heather Bell will not be found. No body, no trace. (Munro 159)

Spectrality informs the stories and the emphasis shifts to the one who stays behind. Lucy's friend, Lois, collects paintings by the Group of Seven that represent the Northern Ontario wilderness. The survivor responds to the horror of having literally lost her friend by imagining that Lucy lives in a painting, which she haunts. As for Munro's Maureen, she pictures herself in Heather's place, wondering what it means to vanish in the woods:

> From the chintz-covered hassock at her husband's side [Maureen] looked out at the old copper-beech trees, seeing behind them not the sunny lawn but the unruly trees along the river – the dense cedars and shiny-leaved oaks and glittery poplars. A ragged sort of wall with hidden doorways, and hidden paths behind it where animals went, and lone humans sometimes ... She could imagine vanishing. But of course you didn't vanish, and there was always the other person on a path to intersect yours and his head was full of plans for you even before you met. (139–40)

Carrington reads the final lines of the paragraph as an allusion to Heather's fate – her encounter with Theo (Carrington, 'Talking Dirty' 604). Yet what strikes me is that the passage allows for both literal and figurative meanings, not only an allusion to Heather's fate but an allusion to Maureen's life too. Overall, the scene conveys a sense of unease, hinting at Maureen's silenced dissatisfaction with her present life. Maureen conjures up the wild trees at the moment when she is about to take dictation, which in her mind means playing the part of the dutiful wife or the efficient secretary (138), and is sitting at her husband's side.

As noted by William Butt, architecture and interior design play a discreet but central role in the story (Butt 255). The narrator draws attention to the fact that Maureen is in 'the sunroom' (136), sitting on 'the chintz-covered hassock' (139). The sunroom is one of the few rooms Maureen has managed to modernise – she has 'put new chintz' (132) there – so the room and the piece of furniture may symbolise domesticity and a role that Maureen is not used to. Yet it can also provide her with a liminal space, opening up towards the outside. The mental image of the woods Maureen pictures is similarly ambivalent: it is a site of entrapment, with someone stopping 'you', but it is also synonymous with freedom, providing one can 'vanish' (140) – implying Maureen's desire to leave her life behind, to the point of envying Heather's fate. Thus 'a path to intersect yours' (140) could also refer to Stephens deciding that he was going to marry Maureen and turn her into a respectable homemaker and a lawyer's wife. As she recalls the hikes she took part in and her own rebellious acts, it seems that Maureen feels empathy for Heather, if not a connection to her. Frances criticised Heather's bold behaviour but Maureen's memories suggest, as William Butt argues, a similar 'need to transgress. To rebel' (Butt 256), which one day vanished when she became older.

This passage also illustrates Maureen's ability mentally to wander off and escape from the roles she plays: 'Maureen could still enjoy being the Jewel. ... Part of her thoughts could slip off on their own' (138). Although her thought process could be construed as escapism, a way for her to deal with her boring life, the rest of the passage insists on Maureen's ability to conjure up mental pictures from the stories that spread across town: 'Maureen remembered now some story about Marian's getting [her husband] from an advertisement. *Woman with farm, clear title. Businesswoman with farm*, it could have been' (142; italics in orig.). As Maureen remembers that Marian sold corsets, she 'imagine[s] her taking measurements' (142). Finally, she recalls that Theo Slater used to drive the old people to their swimming lessons: 'And now another story surfaced, a less malicious one ... Maureen had another picture of him, too – carrying the old father in his arms, into Dr Sands' office' (142). There is a strong emphasis on Maureen's ability to imagine these pictures, and the combination of the words 'story' and 'picture', together with the italics quoted previously and the single dash quoted here, all allow for the intrusion, or surfacing, of these pictures and stories in readers' minds. As I will demonstrate later, they open up pathways into other stories that remain to be told. They highlight the workings of Maureen's imagination and of storytelling, which can suggest that her belief that Theo is a murderer could be the result of her own imagination.

3. Approaching the First Three Stories

3.1 Wonky Hearts in 'Carried Away'

The collection opens with 'Carried Away', a story of about fifty pages, whose time frame spans from 1917 to the mid-1950s. The opening story also introduces the town, Carstairs; Douds, the piano factory; and the owners, the Douds. Although there is no indication as to when Douds was founded, the narrator briefly traces its history – it 'started out making pump organs' (25) then switched to player pianos. At first sight, this description introduces a realistic dimension, a sign of changing times, which is later confirmed when Douds switched to 'radar cases for the Navy' (47) during the Second World War. Yet, to me, the 'pump organs' irresistibly evoke a pumping organ, as if Douds were the town's main organ – a heart pumping blood and oxygen.

I also believe that the 'pump organs' and the depictions of the factory and the Library nod to the Victorian social novel. The portrait of Arthur Doud's father dominates the Library (28) from his central and unmovable position between the two front windows. When we consider that *'the Working Man'* (italics in orig.) in the story is killed by the factory, the plaque provides a clear example of irony:

> A. V. Doud, Founder of the Doud Organ Factory and
> Patron of this Library. A Believer in Progress,
> Culture, and Education. A True Friend of the Town
> of Carstairs and of the Working Man. (28)

All of these details and Arthur's vision of his role as Douds's owner – he feels he is expected to provide work, to give money to the town's churches, to fund the Memorial Park and to continue helping the town's boys go to university – are reminiscent of Victorian social novels depicting the relationships between factory owners and a town.

Although Louisa mentions Thomas Hardy as a favourite author (6), I personally hear Dickensian echoes in Munro's evocation of Douds. First, Douds produces pianos, perhaps a nod to Dickens' famous musical metaphor in *Hard Times*: 'Let us strike the key-note, Coketown, before pursuing our tune' (Dickens 65).[8] Dickens' description of 'the piston of the steam-engine [that] worked monotonously up and down' (Dickens 65), informing the rhythm of people's lives in Coketown, is recalled in Munro's story by the evocation of the factory whistle that defined life in Carstairs:

> The factory whistle dictated the time for many to get up, blowing at six o'clock in the morning. It blew again for work to start at seven and at twelve for dinnertime and at one in the afternoon for work to recommence, and then at five-thirty for the men to lay down their tools and go home. (25)

While Dickens' repetitive pattern when he describes the people 'who all went in and out at the same hours, with the same sound upon the same pavements, to do the same work, and to whom every day was the same as yesterday and tomorrow' (Dickens 65) is, arguably, stronger, Munro's phrasing also suggests repetition, regularity and monotony, using polysyndeton – a device Dickens was famous for.

Dickens' narrator alludes to the fact that Coketown's factories chopped up their workers' limbs and Munro's narrator alludes to different accidents, including a worker who lost an arm, before proceeding to describe the major calamity at Douds. The evocation of Douds, then, strikes the key-note, anticipating the death of Jack Agnew, the event that haunts the lives of the librarian, Louisa, and Arthur Doud, the factory owner and patron of the Library – as demonstrated by Carrington (Carrington, 'What's in a Title?') and Lecker. To me, another relevant aspect of the story is that other forms of indirect violence surface as Louisa is constantly under male scrutiny. When she starts speaking about Jack, Jim Frarey, the travelling salesman she befriends at the hotel, silently dismisses her as a type: 'This was it, he thought – the usual. Women after they have told one story on themselves cannot stop from telling another' (19). The men who look at her – Jack before he left, Jim Frarey, and finally Arthur Doud – all comment on her looks, wondering whether she has a lover and whether she is still suitable marriage material. Jim Frarey, who notices that Louisa wears more dashing clothes than she used to, assumes that she is on the look-out for a husband (14). When Arthur Doud starts coming to the Library, he silently comments on her clothes, hair, lipstick and 'eye-catching style' (35). When they start talking, he hears 'a humility in her voice', which he assumes is 'sexual' (38) – another mistake that announces the many misunderstandings in their relationship.

Arthur starts spending time in the Library, a visible, unwanted presence that annoys Louisa to the extent that she envisions hitting 'the back of his neck' (48). As she later concludes, she first failed to see that a relationship, a marriage, could result. What Louisa senses, however, is that the man who disappeared and the one who keeps coming to the Library are connected, and Arthur does adopt Jack Agnew's role as Louisa's watcher when he starts visiting, after Jack's death. The connection was initiated when Arthur picked up Jack's head and 'felt like a wounded man' (34) as Jack Agnew's blood seeped through his clothes. Quite striking are the echoes between the scene when Arthur proposes, on a rainy Saturday, a few moments after Louisa locked the door (39–41) and the scene evoked by Jack's first letter involving a rainy Saturday afternoon after Louisa had unlocked the door (7). Arthur looks at Louisa and the image that describes what he feels – 'like the scorch of electricity' (40) – recalls Jack's evocation of Louisa shaking her hair next to the radiator: *the water sizzled like grease in the frying pan* (7; italics in orig.). Louisa herself, who laughs when Arthur proposes, connects the two men: '"I thought – that's the last I'll see of him"' (41). Yet it is unclear whether Louisa assumes that Arthur would disappear, just as Jack did, or whether she is thinking that by marrying Arthur, she will stop thinking about Jack.

The uncertainty is never cleared up. The final section of the story, 'Tolpuddle Martyrs', starts with Louisa's visit to her doctor in London, Ontario in the 1950s. A sense of confusion permeates the final part from the moment Louisa leaves the doctor's office and goes to a nearby park. She hurriedly leaves the park and then gets lost as she fails to remember where the temporary bus depot is (43–4). She is then forced 'to detour' (44) and finds herself in residential streets with buildings that are pulled down. While the scene evokes a realistic depiction of the type of changes urban centres underwent, what interests me is the confusing cityscape (43–5) that prepares for Louisa's vision, whether it be a dream or a hallucination. There, on that street, nothing is what it should be and everything is something else – the bus depot is an old house; old houses have been turned into a parking lot; two men from the bus company are sitting on old car seats on what used to be the veranda of a house. In the waiting area for the buses, one finds old kitchen chairs, and strips of old carpets and bathroom mats, then a sheep that turns out to be 'a dirty-white dog' (45).

The nightmarish, unreliable cityscape is the perfect setting for Louisa's vision or hallucination. She sees and hears Jack, who then morphs into Jim Frarey, the man who was her lover after she learned that Jack lied to her. The general impression of confusion that pervades the whole passage allows Munro to challenge realistic conventions and conjure up an alternative life for Jack. I am personally interested in the way the passage makes perfect, marvellous sense, linguistically speaking, revealing Louisa to be in a muddle, still. When Louisa reads about a local union leader named John (Jack Agnew) in the local newspaper, she also reads about the Tolpuddle Martyrs, so that when 'Mud' (she tells Jack this is her nickname) sees a group of oddly dressed people, she assumes they are the Tolpuddle Martyrs, whom she then sees melting 'into a puddle' (49). Mud (her nickname), the Tolpuddle Martyrs and the puddle all prepare us for her sense of confusion, her feeling that she is up against 'a devouring muddle' (50).

The whole passage reveals Louisa's oscillation between passion and reason, and her indecision about the three men to whom she was attracted. Although she acknowledges Jack's good looks, she dismisses them, preferring 'the kind of looks Arthur had' (45). Towards the end, Jack morphs into Jim, the man who briefly became her lover in 1919. In this respect, I wonder whether Munro is not suggesting that Louisa had a fickle heart in that 'The doctor, the heart specialist, said that her heart was a little wonky' (41). Louisa's comment on his choice of words, her interpretation of them – 'She thought that made her heart sound like a comedian' (41) – reminds us that Munro keeps exploiting the ambiguities of language, its plasticity; or, in Laurent Jenny's words, 'le jeu du "figural"' (Jenny 13). As Louisa considers this word, she also unlocks the word 'wonky', and her comment liberates possible meanings and interpretations. In turn, I am encouraged to engage with it too, and I reflect that 'wonky' also means indecisive, irresolute or wavering – a fickle heart. For although Louisa may dismiss Jack's cliché that '"Love never dies"' (48) with a down-to-earth statement, she nevertheless feels 'a widespread forgiveness of folly . . . An amorous flare-up of the cells, of old intentions' (48–9), which indicates that her feelings for Jack might resurface. Thus, Louisa hesitates between horror and forgiveness. After Jack morphs into Jim, and 'He' (49) is nowhere to be seen, an isolated sentence summarises her conclusion, with the adverb 'helplessly' introducing the possibility that Louisa sees Jack's betrayal as something that could not be avoided: 'A traitor, helplessly. A traveller' (50). Since it is unclear who 'He' is, the binary structure also reveals similarities between Jack and Jim that Louisa's conscious mind may not have been aware of.

When Louisa pulls herself together and the vision disappears, the narrator explains that 'She . . . was left with a cold sheen on her skin, a beating in her ears, a cavity in her chest, and revolt in her stomach' (50), a curious image that allows for multiple interpretations. It could convey Louisa's horror at remembering Jack's deception and her understanding that she spent three decades mourning a traitor and a liar. The 'cavity in her chest' could also be a physical representation of her pain, recalling Arthur's idea that Louisa could be 'one of those people full of mended cracks that you could only see close up' (37) – this fact would show how mistaken Arthur's belief that these cracks were mended was since the cracks turned into a huge cavity. Yet the image of the 'cavity in her chest' changes: 'It was anarchy she was up against – a devouring muddle. Sudden holes and impromptu tricks and radiant vanishing consolations' (50). Carrington sees 'consolations' (50) as 'the key word', and sees Louisa's hallucination as 'healing' (Carrington, 'What's in a Title?' 562). I personally see the words 'up against' (50) as evidence of Louisa's strength. From the beginning her agitation and the reaction of her body – her 'giddiness' (48), a 'flare-up' (49) of her cells and then 'a cold sheen on her skin, a beating in her ears, a cavity in her chest, and revolt in her stomach' (50) – are counterbalanced by her ability to fight: 'She would not have it. She pulled herself up tightly . . . She would not have it' (49). Most importantly, Louisa's pride at having managed the factory first with Arthur and then on her own after his death is emphasised: '"I am always thinking about the factory, that is what fills my mind. What should we do to stay afloat?"' (47).

Since 'wonky' also means unreliable and shaky, I believe that Louisa's wonky heart is also the beating heart of the piano factory she managed to keep afloat, a wonky heart that stopped beating when she died, as suggested by the narrator's remark in 'Spaceships Have Landed' that 'After Billy's mother died, problems multiplied and Billy sold out' (260). In my reading, Louisa's wonky heart reveals strength and resilience.

I am also tempted to think that Munro invites her readers to look into her character's wonky heart to show that she resists interpretation. The picture is always wonky, or always incomplete. With Louisa, Munro creates a complex, multifaceted character whose journey she traces. The opening sections conjure up a rather naïve Louisa, who may have been influenced by her reading since she felt like 'a heroine of love's tragedy' (9) for falling in love with a married doctor. When she is writing to Jack and then waiting for him to return, Louisa behaves like a girl in love, directing her walks to Jack's house (7); she reads about the war in the newspapers, perusing the maps the newspapers publish; and after the war, she keeps the Library open, waiting for him to appear there – at times making 'a pact with herself not to look up till she had counted to ten' (17). Yet, as argued by Maria Löschnigg, Louisa is not a victim (Löschnigg 103). The ending, a flashback to the moment when Louisa applied for the library position as soon as she heard of the librarian's death, shows how resourceful she had always been. She applied because 'she believed in the swift decision, the unforeseen intervention, the uniqueness of her fate' (51). Her belief in 'the uniqueness of her fate' strikes me as a sign of her resilience, especially as all the men she meets see her as a type.

Löschnigg contends that Louisa's experience of writing to Jack 'may even have endowed her with an additional, if imaginary, life parallel to her actual one' (Löschnigg 103), which the dream or hallucination episode could confirm. Yet I find that the ending shows that Louisa always had the ability to see the world around her differently, to picture what is not here. The narrator adopts young Louisa's perspective as she looks from her hotel at 'the snow-covered hills over the rooftops', the town streets and 'big blinkered horses with feathered hooves' (51) pulling sleighs. The nostalgic image of pre-war, pre-industrial Carstairs with horses pulling sleighs seems to spring from fiction – I personally hear an echo of the opening pages of George Eliot's *Middlemarch* depicting Maggie Tulliver looking at a horse pulling a wagon across a bridge. Most revealing is the fact that Louisa pictures what she cannot see or hear: the horses 'pulled the sleighs across the bridge, past the hotel, beyond the streetlights, down the dark side roads. Somewhere out in the country they would lose the sound of each other's bells' (51). The ending conjures up a vanishing act, thereby prefiguring the remark the narrator makes in the third story, 'The Albanian Virgin' – 'It was about vanishing' (126). At the very moment the narrator provides new information about Louisa, the story ends with an impromptu trick, and a radiant vanishing vision.

3.2 Extra-Ordinary Bodies and the Facts of Life in 'A Real Life'

Martin and Ober argue that 'A Real Life', along with 'The Jack Randa Hotel', illustrates Munro's 'brilliance as a comic writer' (Martin and Ober, 'The Comic Spirit' 41). The story parallels three women's fates, highlighting small-town pretensions and showing these women's reactions to marriage and sexuality. 'A Real Life' mocks one of the women's belief that her friends should marry because '"Marriage takes you out of yourself and gives you a real life"' (75). In this respect, the first pages of the story amount to an ironic revision of Jane Austen's *Pride and Prejudice*, which focuses on marriage and examines social pretensions and class issues. Munro's Millicent believes that marriage is based on material possessions, which explains why her fiancé did not promise her love or happiness but a bathroom and a dining-room suite and living-room furniture (53). However, this marriage, to a farmer, ruined Millicent's social dreams. Her carefully arranged suppers allow her to display her damask, china and silverware, but also signal her disappointed dreams of socialising with the leading people in Carstairs, as cruelly indicated by the parentheses: 'Sometimes Millicent asked people to supper (though not the Finnegans or the Nesbitts or the Douds)' (60).

The story begins with a dinner party which Millicent has meticulously planned, only to be disrupted by the late arrival of one of the guests. Dorrie's arrival at Millicent's house, which is witnessed by the hostess, another female friend and two guests, the local pastor and an English visitor called Mr Speirs, is reminiscent of Elizabeth Bennet's arrival at Netherfield in *Pride and Prejudice*, which is witnessed by Bingley, his two sisters and Darcy. Austen's Elizabeth Bennet finds herself to be 'at last within view of the house, with weary ankles, dirty stockings, and a face glowing with the *warmth* of exercise' (Austen, *Pride and Prejudice* 25; emphasis added), and in the next chapter, the Bingley women comment on Lizzie's dirty petticoat, which everyone could see, and her wild appearance, Mrs Hurst remarking pointedly that '"I shall never forget her appearance this morning. She really looked almost *wild*"' (Austen 27; emphasis added). In Munro's story, Dorrie's unkempt appearance when she arrives in view of the house similarly horrifies Millicent: 'Dorrie came around the side of the house, looking *warm* from her walk across the field, or from excitement.... Threads showed where she had pulled the torn lace off the collar [of her dress] instead of mending it, and in spite of the hot day a rim of undershirt was hanging out of one sleeve' (63; emphasis added).

In the same way as the Bingley sisters fail to understand the appeal a woman's glowing face and healthy body has for their male companions (Darcy in particular), Millicent fails to understand why Speirs is fascinated by Dorrie: 'perhaps he saw Dorrie as a novelty, a Canadian *wild* woman' (64; emphasis added). In the same way as Lizzie Bennet's wit is part of her charm, Dorrie's conversation fascinates the male guests, which 'mystified' (67) Millicent. Dorrie's first words, however, challenge conventions in a much more radical way than Austen's heroine did: '"I would have been on time ... but I had to shoot a feral cat"' (63).

Munro's heroine is not a nineteen-year-old gentleman's daughter but 'a big, firm woman with heavy legs' and 'a broad bashful face' (54). As Munro draws attention to Dorrie's body, the story departs from the romance plot to introduce a reflection on women's bodies, specifically bodies that do not fit the norm. Millicent focuses her attention on Dorrie's unsuitable clothing: 'She was wearing her good summer dress, a navy-blue organdie with white dots and white collar, suitable for a little girl or an old lady' (63). However, the description of Dorrie's arrival through Millicent's eyes reveals that Millicent is more horrified by Dorrie's body than her clothing: 'With [her wet hair], and her pink shiny face, she looked like a doll with a china head and limbs attached to a cloth body, firmly stuffed with straw' (63). Millicent's vision of 'a cloth body, firmly stuffed with straw' is a perfect simile to convey her attempts to metaphorically contain Dorrie's large body, which is later evoked when Millicent and her friend Muriel cut Dorrie's wedding dress, struggling against 'the eccentricities of Dorrie's figure' (68).

Throughout the story, Dorrie's body takes centre stage, forcing Millicent to be aware of its flesh and blood reality. Attention is drawn to Dorrie's silent resistance to Millicent's attempts to contain her body, and to Millicent's reaction: 'There stood Dorrie in the dim window light – mulish, obedient, childish, female – a most mysterious and maddening person' (77). The asyndeton 'mulish, obedient, childish, female', which is contained inside a pair of dashes, reveals a connection among femininity, childhood and animality that profoundly disturbs Millicent. Through internal focalisation Dorrie's body is aligned with animals, as previously suggested when Millicent notices that Dorrie 'stood like a docile beast in her woolen underwear, which smelled quite frankly of her flesh' (69). I am interested in the way Dorrie's smell that even Millicent cannot ignore is paired with an animal simile. Munro blurs boundaries between the human and the animal worlds, especially when it comes to sexual drives. Both Dorrie and Speirs are compared to animals: during dinner, Millicent notices that he 'listen[s] like an old dog' (66) to Dorrie's trapping stories, and on their wedding day, she sees that Speirs is as 'wolfish as [she] remembered' (77). 'A Real Life', in a comic mode, debunks the idea that human beings and animals have little in common.

The comic (and at times bawdy) tone of the story comes from the opposition between Millicent's obsession – getting Dorrie married so that she can have '"a real life"' (75) – and her dislike of the facts of life. Munro mocks her character's naivety, as Millicent seems unaware of the sexual undertones her own words may have. For instance, during the wedding preparation she wonders why Mr Speirs would have a sword (71). Another comic effect is achieved by Millicent's assumptions (and misunderstanding) regarding the reason why Speirs fell in love with Dorrie as she assumes 'it was the way that Dorrie used her knife and fork that had captivated the man' (52). Millicent actually mistakes one knife for another – Speirs was fascinated by a knife, a skinning knife, and by Dorrie's pleasure at skinning animals: 'He asked about the skins, saying they must have to be removed very carefully, and Dorrie said that was true and you needed a knife you could trust. She described with pleasure the first clean slit down the belly' (66). Clearly, there is a sexual energy in the scene that Millicent either ignores or fails to see.

The story also shows that Dorrie is an extraordinary woman, something Millicent does not appreciate. During dinner Dorrie reveals that she is a hunter (65), which creates a connection with Speirs, whose name probably originated with spear-carrying hunters. As he listens to Dorrie's tales of her life – she traps muskrats – he gradually morphs into a hunting dog: 'And Mr Speirs listened like an old dog, perhaps a hunting dog . . . Now he has got a whiff of something nobody else can understand – . . . his nose quivers and his muscles answer, ripples pass over his hide' (66). Millicent, who assumes that Dorrie's life is neither real nor suitable, fails to understand the magical, mythical quality of this life, which is precisely what captivates Speirs. He does not see Dorrie 'as a novelty' or 'a

Canadian wild woman' (64), as Millicent wrongly assumes; he sees her as the epitome of a mythical way of life in the Canadian wilderness, one of the last trappers. Dorrie may recall other Munro characters such as Ben Jordan in 'Images' from *Dance of the Happy Shades* (1968) and the father in 'Working for a Living' from *The View from Castle Rock* (2006), but Dorrie is Munro's only female trapper. Speirs's morphing into a hunting dog also implies that Dorrie can be seen as a (hunting) goddess, which eludes Millicent who can only think of Dorrie as unhinged or eccentric.

Millicent eventually talks Dorrie into marrying Speirs and into abandoning her house and her life. It seems that Dorrie gives in to Millicent's persuasion, to allude to another Austen novel. Yet resistance is implied at the very moment when Millicent believes she has triumphed over Dorrie: 'a most mysterious and maddening person whom Millicent seemed now to have conquered, to be sending away' (77). Secondly, Millicent's failure to understand Dorrie surfaces when she peruses the letter and the picture that Dorrie sends from Australia, trying to figure out whether Dorrie (and her life) changed after she married Speirs. In her letter Dorrie compares herself to a Polynesian queen: '"I have grown as fat as the Queen of Tonga"' (78). She is making fun of her own weight, but her words recall the words Millicent said when she talked her into marrying Speirs: '"He'll make you a Queen!"' (78). There is a twist, however, as Queen Sālote Tupou III, a powerful woman,[9] was a queen by birthright, not marriage. Ironically, Dorrie's married life in Australia was similar to the life she had had in Carstairs with her sick brother Albert, as Speirs became ill after the Second World War. Dorrie did have an adventurous life, travelling abroad, riding horses and even flying an airplane – after her husband's death. Thus, the woman that Millicent pictured as 'the Pillar of Salt in the Bible' (77), a petrified statue on her wedding day, becomes loose and free of bonds after her husband's death. Dorrie's own death also eludes the confines of the conventional life Millicent sent her to as she dies 'climbing up to look at a volcano' (78) in New Zealand, a curious woman to the end.

By contrast, the story's closing draws attention to the narrow confines of Millicent's mind and comprehension. She is said to forget 'the way she had wept, not knowing why' (78), when Dorrie got married, implying that although she felt her actions were wrong, she survives by forgetting unpleasant things. Many years after Dorrie left, Millicent still believes that she 'created happiness' (78) and 'was right' (80) to force Dorrie to leave and give up her life. Yet Millicent seems to be on the verge of understanding that she was mistaken as the narrator underlines her curious behaviour and her bafflement. Although she does not look at Dorrie and Albert's house, she knows it is there, and while she does not gather the fallen chestnuts as they used to, Millicent thinks about it, which reveals her awareness that such rituals mattered, as part of the siblings' real life. Her bafflement at her own behaviour suggests there are cracks in her reasoning: 'I ought to knock [the house] down and sell the bricks, she says, and seems *puzzled* that she has not already done so' (80; emphasis added). A previous incongruity had actually been noticed: although she once 'saw a pile of dog dirt at the head of the stairs' inside Dorrie's house, '*strangely*, Millicent herself found less and less need to see it as anything but something that had a right to be there' (54; emphasis added). Her strange reaction, which is very much at odds with her sense of propriety, introduces the possibility that Millicent half perceived that Dorrie's house, and by extension, Dorrie herself, 'had a right to be there' and as they were.

In turn, I find myself wondering whether the very odd image she has of Dorrie on her wedding day, 'like the Pillar of Salt in the Bible' (77), that is to say a petrified statue, is a revealing mistake, suggesting that Millicent somehow perceives that marriage could indeed turn Dorrie into a lifeless, inanimate object. The ending of the story, though, keeps Millicent on the verge of understanding and acknowledging this possibility.

3.3 Metamorphoses and Vanishing Acts in 'The Albanian Virgin'

'The Albanian Virgin' takes place in Victoria and Albania, two 'real' places, and the many references to Albania are clearly the result of research. The (alternative) names of the Albanian lake and town – Scutari, Sckhoder, Skodra – are given, as is the name of the language spoken in this region, Ger, and the ancient name of Maltsia e madhe, a northern region bordering Montenegro, is correctly given as Cran Gora. Regarding Victoria, the narrator mentions specific streets such as Pandora Street and Johnson Street. However, her impression of Victoria undermines its realistic description by drawing attention to the world of storytelling: 'Like a town in a story, I thought – like the transplanted seaside town of the story set in New Zealand, in Tasmania' (107). And although there is an actual Johnson Street in Victoria that is quite close to Yates Street where the Munros opened their first bookstore (Thacker, *Alice Munro* 176–8), the bookstore in 'The Albanian Virgin' plunges characters and readers into the world of books and fiction, turning into 'a temporarily suspended place where stories are shared, identities exchanged, provisional transformations completed', to borrow from Andrea F. Szabó's analysis of Australia in 'The Jack Randa Hotel' (Szabó 111).

The narrator of 'The Albanian Virgin', Claire, fled Ontario after her marriage fell apart and probably because her lover, Nelson, saw them as a couple, and opens a bookstore in Victoria, intending to start a new life in this 'strange place' (106). The door of the bookstore is symbolically left open, and Claire encounters several '"characters"' (94), including an odd woman named Charlotte. 'The Albanian Virgin' weaves two stories – Charlotte's and Claire's – and two lives together, although initially distance is suggested. Claire does refer to Charlotte as 'the sort of friend I had in my early days there' (85), but young Claire's prejudices do surface. For instance, recalling Charlotte and her husband when they came to her bookstore, Claire describes their clothes as 'discards from a costume box' (117), metonymically equating the old couple with discards. When Claire goes to Charlotte and Gjurdhi's place for dinner, she compares the building's vestibule to a public toilet, calls their apartment 'horrendously untidy' (118) and fixes her attention on the stains on Gjurdhi's dressing gown (119).

Claire is in fact extremely prejudiced and judgemental when it comes to Gjurdhi, who seems to repulse her. When she first sees him in her bookstore, she thinks he is out of place; she sees him looking around 'as if trying to figure out what sort of place this is or what the books are for' (117). Her first description dismisses him as a parasitic bird: 'I thought he was . . . just one of a number of shabby, utterly uncommunicative old men who belong to the city somewhat as the pigeons do' (117). She next compares him to 'a dog or a donkey' (117), highlighting her belief that he is dependent on Charlotte. Each interaction between Claire and Gjurdhi emphasises miscommunication and misunderstanding, in part because she largely deprives him of a voice. Generally speaking, Claire interprets his nods, tone, facial expression and sounds: about another bookstore 'He made a sound of disgust, maybe indicating that he knew well enough where it was' (95), and when questioned by her about Charlotte's illness 'He smiled disdainfully, tapping himself on the chest – perhaps to show me the source of Charlotte's trouble' (97).

Claire is also disappointed by the evening she spent at their place – not only did Gjurdhi try to sell her old books, but she felt that there had been no exchange of confidences, no sharing of life stories with Charlotte. As argued by Georgiana M.M. Colville, the name of the street where Charlotte lives, Pandora Street, is significant and ironical (Colville 87), since Charlotte does not open a Pandora's Box. However, Charlotte gave Claire something more valuable: the story she claims to have made up for her – the story of a Canadian woman who in the 1920s was abducted by Albanian villagers and then rescued by a Franciscan priest. The hospital nurse tells Claire that Charlotte and Gjurdhi are '"really quite the characters"' (94), which is a polite way to say that they do not fit in, but with the Albanian story Charlotte becomes a storyteller and, if we believe that she is the woman in the story and Gjurdhi the priest who rescued her, the odd and old couple become characters in their own rights.

The story Charlotte tells Claire is also reminiscent of captivity narratives, since the Canadian woman was abducted, remained and lived with a local tribe, and was ultimately rescued by a man. Yet when Claire asks Charlotte where she got the idea for the story, Charlotte's answer – '"From life"' (125) – allows for different readings, including the possibility that she is telling her own story. Clues indicate that Charlotte is Lottar, and Gjurdhi the Franciscan who rescued her. Apart from the fact that 'Lottar' (as the villagers called the Canadian woman) sounds close to 'Charlotte', the most obvious clue is the 'large, wooden crucifix' (97) that Gjurdhi wears and Claire notices, recalling the 'wooden crucifix' (82) the Franciscan wore. The story, then, restores the odd couple their dignity.

In the story, the Canadian woman seems to have been quite adventurous; she had set off to explore Southern Europe on her own, evoking female travellers or explorers of the early twentieth century. Her story is given an ironic twist: her being kidnapped was brought about by her hesitation to break with social codes and conventions. She did not go to Cetinge as planned, because the couple she had met and befriended thought 'it was not wise' (84), and, ironically, it was her short walk behind the hotel, '*a little* way up the road behind the town, *just* to see the ruins' (84; emphasis added), in the company of a man, a local guide the man at the hotel had recommended, that endangered her. From this moment on, she will need a man to rescue her.

The Albanian story reverses the dynamics in the couple since the priest is depicted as a powerful man, to whom Lottar is attracted, and whom she depended on: the name that Lottar uses for him, *Xoti*, is translated as '"leader" or "master"' (128). The story grants him the role of a saviour, which contradicts the image Claire conjures up of Gjurdhi through her animal similes. Most importantly, the Franciscan's linguistic skills allow him to communicate with Lottar and to rescue her, first by saving her from being married off to a Muslim villager, and then by guiding her to the town. Thus, Charlotte gives him back his voice and reverses the negative portrait Claire paints of the old man. Lottar's memory of 'the flourish of his black mustache' (109) contrasts with and repairs Gjurdhi's 'unsavory, struggling mustache' (117). As the beginning and the ending of the short story make clear, the narrator is an older woman who looks back at younger Claire, and her including Charlotte's story within her own is probably a way for Claire to atone for mistakes and misconceptions of hers when she first met the old couple.

To me one of the most interesting aspects of the story is that the narrator acknowledges the old couple's humanity by drawing attention to their corporeality and animality, stripping them naked, so to speak – in spite of the emphasis on clothing and costumes. Animal similes and references to smell and skin throughout the Albanian story also suggest a resemblance between the old and the young. The Franciscan is first and foremost a physical presence, as his height, black eyebrows, mustache and 'rank smell' (82) are the first elements Lottar recalls and Charlotte mentions. The cigarette the Franciscan gives Lottar is said to smell 'of his skin' (94) and, later, Lottar recalls his body and smell, revealing her desire: 'She had not understood how much she depended on the smell of his skin, ... the flourish of his black mustache' (109). A parallel with Claire's lover, Nelson, is introduced when Claire muses, 'Nelson would still be Nelson to me. I had not changed, with regard to his skin and his smell and his forbidding eyes' (114). When Claire thinks of Nelson, he is remembered as a strong, bodily presence, by his skin and his smell – clearly, the fact that her husband is a dermatologist, whose job is to treat skin problems, to scrub another person's skin clean, so to speak, is no coincidence; it further separates the husband from the lover, and aligns Nelson with the Franciscan, whose strong smell and bodily presence are repeatedly emphasised.

Claire's remarks also amount to an admission that one's smell and skin are traits that human beings share, whatever their social position and age are. This suggestion prepares for the moment when Claire acknowledges that the old and the young experience similar sexual drives. When Claire is leaving, she notices on Charlotte's face 'A savoring and contented look that I knew had to do with Gjurdhi although I hardly wanted to believe that' (123). The look reveals sexual desire on Charlotte's part for an individual whom Claire sees as a shabby old man with an 'unsavory, straggling mustache' (117) – and, in turn, prompts Claire to respond with a feeling of desire for her lover, Nelson. To describe Charlotte's look, Claire uses an animal analogy that highlights what Héliane Ventura calls 'the inextricable tissue of animality and humanity' (Ventura, Introduction 7) common to both the young and the elderly. Claire reflects: 'It made me think that ... some hot and skinny, slithery, yellowish, indecent old beast, some mangy but urgent old tiger, was going to pounce among the books and the dirty dishes and conduct a familiar rampage' (123–4). Claire acknowledges that *she* is familiar with such desires and urges and that Charlotte and Gjurdhi are sexual beings who experience the same desires she does. As Colville notes, smell and bodily sensations do link the two stories and the two women (and the two couples) together (Colville 89). In this respect it is no coincidence that after

Nelson confessed to his wife about the affair, 'she told him that she would rather be escorted by a skunk' (113).

Comparing the Albanian story to Claire's life shows that Claire becomes a mirror image of Lottar. Claire's tiny apartment, whose bed is never folded up into the wall and whose window is left open, oddly resembles the *kula* that Lottar stayed in. Claire's favourite clothes, a *black* sweater and a *red* dressing gown (106), evoke the black-and-red clothes Lottar was made to wear. And the image of young Claire as 'underfed and shivering' (106) in her tiny cave-like apartment is reminiscent of Lottar's situation in the village. The embedded story thus pervades the framing narrative.

Another way to read the story is to focus on storytelling and Charlotte's ability to move boldly between fictional worlds as well as between fiction and life. Charlotte and Gjurdhi seem to occupy a different space than other people do, what Ulrica Skagert calls 'an ambiance of make-believe' (Skagert 58). The text is peppered with cinematic references: Charlotte tells Claire that she has '"been making up a story, for a movie"' (86) and points out that she and Gjurdhi could have '"Got work in the movies"' (122). When she learns about the PhD thesis that Claire is supposedly writing on Mary Shelley's later novels, she tells her that *The Fortunes of Perkin Warbeck* '"would make a movie"' (120) but also remarks, '"Mary Shelley's own life is the movie"' (120). Incidentally, the book that Charlotte picks up in the bookstore, *The Dud Avocado* (117), follows the adventures of a young woman who left America to go to Paris, finds herself entangled in complicated love affairs, and triangles, all the while trying to break into the film industry. By contrast, when Claire recalls the final confrontation amongst her husband Donald, Nelson, his wife and herself, she finds the similarities with the cinema disturbing: Donald's reacting 'so much the way someone would do in a movie' makes her feel 'embarrassed for him' (112), and she heads west soon after this 'scene' (113). Having a bookstore, with books on shelves and tables, then, is perhaps a way for her to keep the fictional and the real worlds separate, until she encounters Charlotte.

Although Charlotte comes across as odd – Claire's customers dislike and distrust her due to her strange appearance and visible lack of money – her talent at storytelling transfers to and transcends her real life. As pointed out by Skagert, 'Charlotte transfigures time and space' (Skagert 54), turning the depressing space of the hospital ward into the world of fiction as she embarks on her story. The short story, which Colville describes as following 'a cinematic structure of alternate and at times parallel montage of two stories' (Colville 83), also pays tribute to Charlotte's talent as a storyteller. Interrupting Charlotte's story and switching to her own, the narrator creates dramatic pauses in her narrative that mirror Charlotte's own pauses. When Charlotte stops, adding '"That part is not of interest"' (109), the narrator also pauses, returning to her own love story. But she later picks up on and repeats Charlotte's words, using italics to highlight the effect Charlotte's words had on her: '*That part is not of interest*' (124; italics in orig.). A few paragraphs later the words 'she recovered, and she told me more' (125) are followed by a blank space, then by the account of Claire's last visit to the hospital. The very end of the short story – the last four paragraphs – picks up on Lottar's story, filling in two gaps in Charlotte's narrative, but at this stage it is unclear who chose the ending – Charlotte or Claire, or even the world of fiction.

Lottar's story ends with a brief paragraph that calls to mind a fairy-tale ending: 'She called him and called him, and when the boat came into the harbor at Trieste he was waiting on the dock' (128). As Ulrica Skagert reports that Munro commented in an interview by Peter Gzowski at the time of the collection's publication in 1994, Lottar's story '"is in a way the ultimate love story"' (Munro in Skagert 59). The ending also draws a clear but improbable connection with the moment when Claire sees Nelson waiting for her. On her way back she pictures a life with Nelson, creating a scenario in her mind, and then becomes aware of a man standing near the door who looked like 'someone disguised. Jokingly disguised' (127). Her statement, 'For this really was Nelson, come to claim me' (127), makes the apparition providential. These endings remind us, as Mark Levene has it, 'that we inhabit fantasy as much as fact, that our familiar lives are accompanied by phantom existences that must be allowed' (Levene, '"It was about vanishing"' 854). Claire could have also provided the happy ending to Lottar's story herself, since before she concludes the narrative with Lottar and the Franciscan, she provides an ending to her own love story.

The final parts of Lottar's story are preceded by five italicised statements that disturb our reading process:

We have been very happy.
I have often felt completely alone.
There is always in this life something to discover.
The days and the years have gone by in some sort of blur.
On the whole, I am satisfied. (128)

The first two lines could refer to Claire's life with Nelson, but the third one reads like a fortune-cookie piece of wisdom. The first line could also be what Claire wished for but did not happen. Mark Levene refers to the passage 'as a sort of experiential haiku, notes towards parallel lives' (Levene, '"It was about vanishing"' 856), yet the sentences mockingly sketch points in Claire's life, all the while revealing nothing about it. They also remind me that I know nothing of Lottar's life after she was rescued, and almost nothing of Charlotte's life – even if I assume that she is Lottar, there is a forty-year gap in between Lottar's story and Charlotte's presence in Victoria in 1964.

After she heard Charlotte's story, Claire seems to wish for other encounters, and she tries to locate Charlotte and Gjurdhi who have left the hospital but fails to find them, as they have 'vanished' (126). Thus, at the moment when Claire seems to get a better understanding of the old couple, they elude her. The couple's vanishing act can be understood as the last act of a series of metamorphoses – a central motif that is introduced as a joke when Charlotte, who is angling for a job in the bookstore, tells Claire, '"Ask me who wrote Ovid's *Metamorphoses*"' (117). From the beginning, understanding who Charlotte and Gjurdhi are proves difficult to everyone, including Claire. People in the bookstore pin several names and identities on them – '"the Duchess and the Algerian"' (118), '"peddlers"' (96), '"scavengers"' (118).

Charlotte and Gjurdhi protect their true selves under their garish costumes. Claire compares the couple's clothes to theatrical disguises: 'they were both wearing things that might have been discards from a costume box' (117); 'a garment that looked as if it belonged, or had once belonged, on the stage' (115). And when Claire evokes the noise Charlotte's bracelets make – 'She clanked as if she wore hidden armor' (116) – I picture Charlotte as a woman wearing medieval 'armor'. I also believe that when Charlotte tells the narrator, '"I'll just silently steal away with my tent now"' (96), she morphs into an adventurous female explorer – the word 'tent' reminds me of these female explorers posing in front of a tent (Gertrude Bell) or inside a tent (Elizabeth Sarah Mazuchelli), wearing an exotic or 'native' costume (Isabella Bird Bishop), or dressed up in men's clothing (Isabelle Eberhart).[10] This suggestion implies that Charlotte is essentially a woman of no fixed abode – a traveller.

Metamorphosis is a central component of the Albanian tale: the Canadian woman who was abducted and became Lottar in the Albanian village changed identities and gender. She lost her English words and Canadian identity, sharing the women's lives. Like many of these women she was dressed up as a bride, destined to be married to a Muslim; she then became a 'Virgin', which implied being dressed up as a man. She became the heroine of a captivity narrative too when the Franciscan rescued her and she returned to Western civilisation. Charlotte's description of how the women in the *kula* dressed up Lottar foreshadows Charlotte's final vanishing act: 'she found herself *disappearing* into a white blouse with gold embroidery, a red bodice with fringed epaulets, a sash of striped silk ... a black-and-red wool skirt, with chain after chain of false gold ... over her hair and around her neck' (91–2; emphasis added). Charlotte and Gjurdhi's ultimate vanishing act defeats Claire and prevents anyone from knowing who Charlotte is. So it is only fitting that Charlotte and Gjurdhi's building has changed beyond recognition (126), erasing the only material trace that anchored them to a place.

Charlotte's relationship to or ownership of the story also proves elusive. When Charlotte turns her umbrella into a '"tent"' (96), she conjures up the image of a female explorer. We should remember that nineteenth-century and early twentieth-century female explorers were also writers; they published travel narratives in which they depicted encounters with so-called 'native' people and wrote accounts of local customs. When Claire asks Charlotte where she got the idea for the story, Charlotte's answer is beautifully ambiguous: '"From life"' (125), which prevents us from knowing whether she based the story on her own life, or on another person's. That is until we realise Munro provides us with a clue hidden in plain sight, a purloined letter of sorts. Gjurdhi comes to the store in order to sell Claire some old books, and Claire dismisses them as 'Not so very old, and not so beautiful, either, with their dim, grainy photographs' (95). The three travelling books Claire notices in his wagon are '*A Trek Through the Black Peaks. High Albania. Secret Lands of Southern Europe*' (95).

High Albania,[11] which was published in 1909, is the account by British explorer and writer M. Edith Durham (1863–1944) of her second journey from Montenegro to Skodra. Durham's first journey took her along the Dalmatian Coast from Trieste to Cetinge in Montenegro, which is the journey that Lottar undertook until she was captured. *High Albania* describes Durham's next journey through the Skodra region in Albania – the very area where Lottar was taken – and it details customs such as blood vengeance, the role and struggles of the Catholic Church, and the activities of Franciscan priests. Durham also describes stone *kulas*, and women's clothing such as the red-and-black (or black-and-white) stockings and the black wool skirts with crimson or purple stripes and red bodices adorned with epaulettes that married women wear (Ch. III). These are precisely the items Charlotte mentions: the stockings the old women knit (87) and the clothes that Lottar is made to wear on her wedding day (91–2). Durham also mentions that she 'met several Albanian Virgins' (Ch. II) and, among the photographs included, one finds a photograph of the Albanian Virgin Rapsha (Ch. IV).[12]

The presence of the book in the wagon indicates that Charlotte found inspiration from Durham's life and book. I see Claire's silence (she does not comment on *High Albania*) as a choice to grant Charlotte the right to transform her own life, to turn it into a story. The mention of the book could also be seen as Munro's showing her hand, reminding her readers that she too found inspiration in Durham's book, which did not prevent her from turning these elements into a Munro story.

4. 'Vandals' as Coda: On (Not) Reading Signs

'Vandals', the eighth and last story in the collection, is connected to the first story since Bea, one of the main characters in 'Vandals', was mentioned in 'Carried Away' – first as Arthur Doud's teenage daughter (26–7) and later as Louisa's divorced stepdaughter (47). In 'Spaceships Have Landed', the story that precedes 'Vandals', Billy is said to have taken care of his sister Bea and to have converted the family home after her death into a residence for the elderly and the disabled (260). In that story, we learn about Bea's drinking (260), which is also mentioned in 'Vandals'. And in 'Carried Away' the narrator explains that Bea would tell friends a story about Jack Agnew's library books, but omit the fact that he had died in an accident at the Doud factory. The narrator's comment, 'Perhaps she had really forgotten' (27), foreshadows Liza's view in 'Vandals' where she wonders if Bea had 'made a bargain not to remember' (293) her lover's unpleasant behaviour towards her. These elements show that what matters most for Munro is not chronology, but a different kind of logic. Hence, as Nathalie Foy explains, 'Vandals' is a coda to the whole collection, casting not only light but also shadow on the other stories.

'Vandals' alternates between two different time periods that are connected by a place, Ladner's nature preserve, and Liza's memories of the abuse that occurred there when she was seven and that resurface at age twenty when she goes to check on the house at Bea's request. 'Vandals' explores the workings of traumatic memory and the complex relationships between children and adults – a scenario that Munro would also explore in 'Rich as Stink' in her next collection, *The Love of a Good Woman* (1998). Liza is shown to love both her abuser, Ladner, and Bea, Ladner's lover and possibly silent accomplice. 'Vandals' is also centrally concerned with silence – the children's, Bea's and Ladner's. When they were children Liza and Kenny kept silent about the abuse, and Liza does not say anything about it when she starts trashing Ladner's house, even though her husband Warren starts asking questions – she makes 'croaking noises to stop him being thoughtful' (284). Although Warren asks her why she wanted to vandalise the house, Liza gives him a cryptic and misleading answer – Bea gave Liza money to go to college – which he cannot understand.

It is possible to assume that Bea gave her the money to atone for Bea's having kept silent and having done nothing to stop the abuse, which now raises the question of a possible complicit and guilty silence on her part rather than ignorance. However, Bea's propensity to make mistakes is underlined: during her first tour of the property she confuses mushrooms with rotten apples (272) and, looking at Ladner's diorama, mistakes a wire armature for the skinned body of a deer (273). Bea's silence, her inability to see what is happening and to do anything to stop it, is perceived through Liza's eyes:

> Bea could spread safety, if she wanted to. Surely she could. All that is needed is for her to turn herself into a different sort of woman, a hard-and-fast, draw-the-line sort . . . *None of that. Not allowed. Be good.* The woman who could rescue them – who could make them all, keep them all, good.
> What Bea has been sent to do, she doesn't see.
> Only Liza sees. (293; italics in orig.)

Liza's words 'could' and 'Surely' suggest hope and trust. However, the italicised words that read as a kind of prayer, the words that Liza wishes Bea would say, are also the words that Bea will never say, as Liza also simultaneously realises.

The repetition of 'see' is a reminder of the story's main motif which is conveyed through countless allusions to eyes that do not see anything – the dead animals' eyes that Ladner destroys and replaces with glass when he stuffs the animals, the empty eyeholes – and also conveyed through the empty mouth holes in the animal heads that Bea notices (273) and that in fact announce the story's central interconnected motifs: being blind / being silent. The scene in which Liza's vandalising of Ladner's house is described (she has destroyed the stuffed animals) pursues the motif: as Warren and Liza are about to leave the house, Warren notices 'a bird in the mess on the floor', and its dislocated head, 'showing one bitter red eye' (284), draws attention to a silent witness to Liza's actions. Finally, when Liza trashes the house and throws a bottle against the stove, she yells '"Bull's-eye!"' (280), as if she were metaphorically targeting Bea's unseeing eyes. Furthermore, there are repeated suggestions that although the children do not talk, they wish that some adults would see something.

Bea is not the only character whose ignorance is questioned. The children's father, who worries because Ladner is a taxidermist, does not realise that his children are being sexually abused. Ironically, one of the few things Liza and Kenny mention to their father is that 'They had squished eyeballs to jelly. They told their father about that' (286). Most striking are the parallels between Bea and Liza's husband, Warren, that surface when Liza starts trashing the house. Significantly, Warren turns his back to Liza so that he does not have to watch what is going on: 'He was trying to be like a grownup who won't watch' (280). The comparison reminds us of Bea's inability to see. Another parallel is created when Liza shows Warren the same tree she had shown Bea so many years before, the tree that, as I will explain, literally signalled the abuse, but just like Bea, 'Warren wasn't interested' (294).

'Vandals' features an impressive number of signs and letters that the characters are meant to read and decipher, but quite clearly these characters fail to understand what the signs mean. On first meeting Liza and her younger brother Kenny, Bea was shown six letters carved on the beech tree that stood in the middle of the path: Ladner's and the kids' initials, and 'the letters P.D.P.' (289). Liza's showing Bea the initials is a telling and ambiguous action – the initials hint at the abusive relationship between Ladner and the kids, a relationship which also excludes Bea. This gesture means that Liza could either be trying to tell Bea about the abusive relationship or be warning Bea that she is not part of the special relationship and 'secret life' (289) that bind Ladner, Kenny and Liza together. Throughout the story, Liza (both as a child and as an adult) is shown simultaneously to encourage and to stop interpretations. While Liza did show Bea the initials, she did not comment on them, and neither does she when she asks Warren to look at them: '"See, it had letters carved on it"' (294).

The abuse only surfaces indirectly. First, when Liza shows Bea the initials, her brother shows the other letters, sending a loud message: 'Kenny had banged his fist against P.D.P. "Pull down pants!" he shouted, hopping up and down' (289). When Ladner corrects Kenny, the oxymoronic tension between 'serious' and 'pretend' draws attention to a disproportionate gesture that no one comments on: 'Ladner gave him a serious pretend-rap on the head. "Proceed down path," he said', then admonished Bea to '"Pay no attention to the dirty-minded juveniles"' (289). It is for readers to question their versions, and to think about what these letters could mean. For Héliane Ventura, they actually reveal the truth about the relationships: she sees the word 'PeDoPhile' (Ventura, 'Aesthetic Traces' 312). As Carrie Dawson has shown, the truth appears via the references to Ladner's work as a taxidermist and originator of the preserve. '"The kids"' (272), as Ladner calls them, are aligned with animals and consequently, Dawson argues, his 'taxidermic display can be read as a story about the violation and manipulation of bodies' (Dawson 74), which is precisely what happens to the children.

In the third section, the abuse is not described directly, but surfaces through a traumatic memory and visual images. By placing the traumatic memory after the trashing of the house, Munro indicates that the sexual assaults are the repressed motive behind the vandalising – and Warren's comment, '"Like going back in time"' (280), indicates that going back to the house actually means for Liza going back in time. Liza's traumatic memory and reliving of the assault are conveyed by a complex textual verbal-visual interface.[13] The third section returns to the period when Bea lived with Ladner and spent a lot of time with the children too. After an unpleasant scene between Ladner and Bea which distresses Liza, Liza goes to her house to pick up a present for Bea (perhaps foreshadowing Bea's gesture of giving money to atone for her silence). When Liza returns to the preserve, readers are taken on a tour of the place with her: 'But when you cross the road – as Liza is doing now, trotting on the gravel – when you cross into Ladner's territory, it's like coming into a world of different and distinct countries' (291). Affects permeate the description of Ladner's 'territory' – a telling word that recalls how he dominates the whole place. Liza sees, rather than recalls, the places where 'serious instruction' took place – Ladner teaching them about trees for instance – and where she and Kenny have run wild and free, then finally, at the very end, places that are filled with sensory memories – 'a bruise' – and affects such as 'shame' (291).

The next passage reveals that these are the places where the children have been raped. This portion deserves to be quoted in full, as the visual dimension of the text plays a crucial role. The layout indicates that Liza suddenly comes upon the tree with the carved letters, which was said to be in the middle of the path:

> And places where Liza thinks there is a bruise on the ground, a tickling and shame in the grass.
> *P.D.P.*
> *Squeegey-boy.*
> *Rub-a-dub-dub.*
>
> When Ladner grabbed Liza and squashed himself against her, she had a sense of danger deep inside him, a mechanical sputtering, as if he would exhaust himself in one jab of light, and nothing would be left of him but black smoke and burnt smells and frazzled wires. Instead, he collapsed heavily, like the pelt of an animal flung loose from its flesh and bones. He lay so heavy and useless that Liza and even Kenny felt for a moment that it was a transgression to look at him. He had to pull his voice out of his groaning innards, to tell them they were bad.
> He clucked his tongue faintly and his eyes shone out of ambush, hard and round as the animals' glass eyes.
>
> *Bad-bad-bad.* (291–2; italics in orig.)

The first italicised segments, which initially resist understanding, create surprise and disturb the narrative. Munro fully explores the visual potential of a font that disrupts the layout, associating it with haunting memories and sounds. The sole connection between the three letters (which Munro expects her readers to remember) and the next italicised segments can only be the kind of irrepressible, unconscious and affective association which, Laurie Vickroy explains, is characteristic of trauma narratives (Vickroy 3).

Coming across the tree seems to trigger the type of traumatic memories that Judith Lewis Herman notes are usually 'encoded in the form of vivid sensations and images' (Herman 38). These are first and foremost oral memories, and the ensuing verbal-visual association shows that Liza is assailed by a disjointed sensory and affective memory which then forms a sound that reverberates in her mind, with the last line indicating that Liza heard the words many times. The middle part, with a noticeable shift to the past tense, clearly evokes the abuse through images, a strategy often employed when dealing with abuse. The italicised segments all use the language of childhood, recalling and perverting a line from a nursery rhyme, '*Rub-a-dub-dub*' (292; italics in orig.), thereby providing a reminder to readers that the victims were children. The words also crudely recall actual bodily contact between abuser and victims. The last italicised segment is equally horrifying, with a repetitive pattern that testifies to a double violence. It mimics the assault and suggests that the children have internalised the blame, and therefore Ladner's logic – 'they were bad' (292). The impact of Ladner's control over them and his shifting the blame onto them is also shown in the middle part as both the children feel it is a transgression to look at Ladner. Both Liza's and Bea's memories make it clear that Ladner used to control everyone: 'He could switch from one person to another and make it your fault if you remembered' (289). Although he speaks very little throughout the story – his silences are highlighted – he controls the narrative and seems to have forced the children to remain silent and to have erased their memories. However, one of the most striking aspects of this passage is that it reveals that such memories cannot be erased but can only return – they will be remembered, recalled and relived, again and again.

Liza's vandalising of the house reminds us that, as Marlene Goldman points out, in Munro's writings, paradoxically, the antidote to violence and shame can only be found by returning to the original 'scenes of shame and transgression' (Goldman 82). There are several parallels between the memory of being raped and Liza's trashing of the house. Liza's shouting '"Bull's-eye"' (280) and targeting the animals could also be her way to protest against Ladner's way of watching them after he raped them: 'his eyes shone out of ambush, hard and round as the animals' glass eyes' (292). Quite striking are the sounds Liza makes as she wrecks the house: for instance, 'a funny noise – an admiring cluck of her tongue' (279) and 'croaking noises' (284). Liza therefore seems to morph into the birds that she is trashing, but surprisingly her reaction creates a direct echo of the sound made by Ladner after he raped the children: 'He clucked his tongue faintly' (292). The similitudes introduce a degree of complexity that corresponds to Munro's way of exploring the emotional relationship between the children and the adults, without simplifying it – Liza was emotionally attached to both Bea and Ladner, and Ladner did teach the children many lessons about trees and animals.

As a taxidermist, Ladner created dioramas, hence, stories, and in the house, when twenty-year-old Liza destroys Ladner's books and stuffed animals, throwing 'the mounted birds and animals' (279) on the floor, she clearly destroys Ladner's narrative and replaces it with her own. By using snow, dirt, furs and feathers, and eventually liquids, Liza creates an explosively graphic visual message, as Héliane Ventura convincingly argues (Ventura, 'Aesthetic Traces' 315–16), which is how she gets to tell her story. Liza makes black tracks on the floor and writes a cryptic message on the wall, '"*The Wages of Sin is Death*"' (283; italics in orig.), which turns out to be prophetic since Ladner soon dies. Yet it is unclear whether Liza's actions permit her to start the healing process that normally characterises trauma narrative. As pointed out by Mark Levene, the first sentence of the story's fourth and final section prevents us from knowing whether having vandalised the house allows Liza to leave her past behind or, on the contrary, to shut it up inside her memory (Levene, '"It was about vanishing"' 857) since 'Liza locked the door as you had to, from the outside' (293). The moment when Liza shows Warren the trees and tries to teach him about them is also extremely ambiguous. Liza's words reveal that she has retained Ladner's lessons since she can tell what the trees are by their bark (294). Most importantly, *she* still feels Ladner's presence: '"And that one with the bark like gray skin? That's a beech. See, it had letters carved on it but they've spread out, they just look like any old blotches now"' (294). The comparison '"the bark like gray skin"' creates a connection with Ladner which becomes explicit with the word '"blotches"' that recalls 'the splotch' (268) on

Ladner's face. Since 'blotch' can refer to a dog's disease (*OED*), it also recalls Bea's impression that Ladner 'was his own fierce dog' (267).

Finally, a blotch is an inflamed eruption (*OED*), suggesting a wound that never heals. What remains is 'the darkness collecting' which the characters feel, but the pronoun 'you' in the last sentence allows Munro to introduce ambiguity as to who feels the darkness and wishes to avoid it: 'you could feel the darkness collecting' (294). Quite strikingly, 'Vandals' also prefigures the dark tone of the opening title story in Munro's next collection, *The Love of a Good Woman* (1998), which takes place in Walley, the fictional town featured in 'Carried Away', 'The Jack Randa Hotel' and 'A Wilderness Station'.

5. The Art of Misreading

5.1 Munro's Intertextual Polyphony

Munro's way of engaging with literature has long interested her readers, who have long tried to find the best word to describe it. Miriam Marty Clark observes that the word '"allusion" does not adequately describe [Munro's] stories' lodgings at the intersection of many texts' (Clark 50); Héliane Ventura has used the concepts of 'sources' or 'hypotexts' (Ventura, 'The Question of Sources' 117); and Vanessa Guignery and Magdalene Redekop have used musical metaphors, allowing them to point out that each reader will hear (or pick up) something personal. Using the concept of 'intertextual polyphony' Guignery explains that 'This intertextual and intervocal space is also where the text's score can freely develop since different readers will hear different voices, depending on their culture and background' (Guignery 30). Redekop, who explains that rereading 'Lichen', from *The Progress of Love* (1986), she heard intertextual echoes she had not been aware of before (Redekop, 'On Sitting Down To Read' 298), argues that 'you can pick up the vibrations of multiple allusions . . . Other readers may be on different wavelengths' (Redekop 296). I believe that these echoes and faint voices enrich our reading experience rather than direct it.

I personally hear subtle but persistent echoes in *Open Secrets* of Ovid's *Metamorphoses* which demonstrate Munro's love of world literature, including Greek tales and myths. In my reading of 'The Albanian Virgin', Charlotte's joke, '"Ask me who wrote Ovid's *Metamorphoses*"' (117), which reveals the central motif in the story and sheds light on the animal similes, is anything but irrelevant. The reference plays a crucial role in *Open Secrets* since the whole collection is informed by the motif of metamorphosis and is peppered with animal similes. *The Metamorphoses* is a narrative poem, written by the Roman poet Ovid in the first century. The work itself is a collection of mythological and legendary stories, many taken from Greek sources, and these stories refer to various well-known myths. Transformation (metamorphosis) always plays a role, however minor. Ovid's is a vision of the world in which the only laws are impermanence and transformation.

The motif of metamorphosis is central to 'The Jack Randa Hotel', the fifth story in the collection. Gail's metamorphoses are, at first, literal since she puts on disguises when she leaves Walley for Brisbane. I believe, however, that the key metamorphosis happens at the very end when she decides not to wait for Will – the moment when Gail turns into a loose woman or even a Maroon, in my own reading. In this respect, Gail's remembering the thousands of migratory butterflies she saw in the woods in Walley is important. Butterflies themselves go through a cycle of painful metamorphoses – the caterpillar has to digest all of its tissues and to create new cells in the thousands. These butterflies were migratory butterflies 'resting before their long flight down the shore of Lake Huron and across Lake Erie, then on south to Mexico' (189) and Gail herself, who is at the airport, seems poised for flight. So it is no coincidence that Gail's memory is linked to another allusion to Ovid's *Metamorphoses*. Upon seeing the butterflies Gail had said they were like '"the shower of gold in the Bible"' (189). Will's pointing out her mistake – 'Will told her that she was confusing Jove and Jehovah' (189) – serves to draw attention to Gail's words, which actually allude to the metamorphosis of Zeus into a shower of gold, in order to seduce Danae, featured in Ovid's *Metamorphoses* (IV.604–62).

Many tales in Ovid's *Metamorphoses* are about gods and human beings morphing into another species, often animals; for instance, gods frequently change into animals when they want to seduce a woman. This process of transformation explains why, in 'The Albanian Virgin', Claire's final animal simile – she pictures Gjurdhi as a 'hot and skinny, slithery, yellowish, indecent old beast, some mangy but urgent old tiger' (123) – conveys more than her dislike for Charlotte's husband, and her disbelief that Charlotte could still be feeling desire for him. Mange is a disease – mangy animals start losing their fur – but I hear an echo of Claire's remark that coming to Victoria means that she has 'come out into the world in a new, true skin' (106). Although a cliché, the phrase evokes an animal shedding its skin or fur, which indirectly aligns Claire with an animal too. The simile reveals a close kinship with animals when it comes to sexual drives – a central motif in Ovid's *Metamorphoses* and in Munro's collection.

Open Secrets as a whole is rife with animal similes. While some comparisons are explicit, as when Dorrie is compared to a mule or a beast in 'A Real Life', other comparisons are implicit. For instance, in the title story we have to assume that Theo Slater raped and murdered Heather Bell to see that the girl is aligned with a hen when he strokes his wife's hat 'as if he were pacifying a little scared hen' (153). The most important feature to point out is that there is no table of correspondence as the same character can be compared to or aligned with two different animals: in 'Open Secrets' the girl who vanishes in the woods is metaphorically equated with 'a fox' (140) – since the witnesses are unsure whether they heard Heather or a fox – and, if we believe that Theo Slater is guilty, with 'a little scared hen'. Secondly, the same animal simile can be used with very different types of characters. Mr Speirs, the English gentleman, is seen as 'wolfish' (77) by Millicent in 'A Real Life', while Jack Agnew describes his father (and himself) as a 'lone wolf' (5) in 'Carried Away'. Several characters in the collection are compared to a dog: in 'A Real Life', when Speirs listens to and falls in love with Dorrie, he morphs into 'a hunting dog' (66); in 'Open Secrets', Maureen is compared to 'a beaten dog' (156); in 'Spaceships Have Landed', the teenager Wayne who fawns over Rhea is compared to 'some kind of dog' (247); in 'Vandals', the paedophile Ladner is said to be 'his own fierce dog' (267). These examples show that the dog simile is clearly versatile: as pointed out by Sabrina Francesconi, who looked at Munro's representations of dogs in 'Save the Reaper' and 'Floating Bridge' from Munro's next two collections, 'Munro's zoopoetics is *dynamic* and *fluid*' (Francesconi, 'Barking (with) Dogs' 82; emphasis in orig.).

'Vandals' rests on a complex network of animal similes, allusions and alignments. The fact that Ladner is a taxidermist and Liza and Kenny help him prepare the animals is a device that allows Munro to connect '"the kids"' (272), as Ladner calls them, a term also used for young goats, with the animals that Ladner skins. The fact that Bea, the silent accomplice, describes herself as '*slit top to bottom with jokes*' (269; italics in orig.) implies, as Carrie Dawson observes, that Bea aligns herself with the animals that are slit before they are skinned and stuffed (Dawson 73). In the rape scene previously quoted Ladner is also compared to the dead animals he rips open – 'he collapsed heavily, like the pelt of an animal flung loose from its flesh and bones' (292), which introduces yet another level of complexity.

My contention is that with the animal similes and, more generally, the alliances with the animal world, Munro tends to blur boundaries between human and animal species. In 'A Real Life' the animal similes are designed to convey not only Millicent's dislike of sex but also Speirs's interest in Dorrie, which is revealed when she describes how she skins animals. In 'Spaceships Have Landed', Wayne is compared to a dog when he sits by Rhea, who 'look[s] down at his wagging black head' and laughs 'because he remind[s] her of some kind of dog' (247). It is unclear whether Rhea is picturing Wayne as a friendly, dependent companion or as a randy dog, but the moment is fraught with sexual energy, which both the boy and the girl feel.

Other stories, however, are pervaded by sexual violence. This recurring feature reminds us that the main topics in Ovid's *Metamorphoses* are lust, violence, rape and the silencing of victims. These motifs also permeate Munro's collection. For instance, in 'Open Secrets', rape and murder are suggested by the scene in which Theo Slater strokes his wife's hat 'as if he were pacifying a little hen' (153), and a few pages later the sexual violence Maureen endures is crudely evoked when she is said 'to keep her mouth closed not on any howls of protest but on a long sickening whimper of complaint that would have made her sound like a beaten dog' (156). 'Vandals' is the story that best emblematises this motif since it is centrally concerned with sexual abuse and the silence that surrounds it.

In 'Vandals', when Liza passes by a display that includes an eagle and owls staring at her (289), she is, as Carrie Dawson points out, 'implicitly compared to the birds, whose silent and violated bodies are on display', and therefore evokes the myth of Philomela (Dawson 74). The story of Philomela, who is raped in the woods by her brother-in-law, the King of Thrace, is silenced by her abuser, and eventually turns into a nightingale, is featured in Ovid's *Metamorphoses* (VI.438–674). The indirect allusion may help us understand why both Ladner and Liza are compared to birds, since in Ovid's tale Philomela and her abuser both turn into birds. Ovid's tale also shows how Philomela takes part in a revenge scheme against her abuser that entails slaughtering his son. I believe that in 'Vandals' Liza is shown, symbolically, to shed blood: when she vandalises the house, the tomato sauce is described as 'fake blood' (283) and when she throws the bottle of peppermint liqueur on the floor, the liquid is likened to 'Dark-green blood' (281). Yet I would argue that 'Vandals' also departs from the myth since in Ovid's tale Procne, Philomela's sister, sees and understands the message and is the one who decides to punish Tereus, while Bea's lack of reaction is a central point in 'Vandals'. The way that Munro alters the myth in 'Vandals' and makes Bea the paedophile's accomplice, rather than the victim's avenger, shows that Munro draws inspiration from such sources yet engages with them in her own way.

A crucial element in the tale is that Philomela, after she was silenced, managed to tell her story via a tapestry. In this respect, it is tempting to see the depiction of Liza's trashing the house with the insistence on its graphic components as a visual message that is addressed to Bea. Whether or not Bea understands Liza's message, it is clear that Liza destroys Ladner's narrative and writes her own. Consequently, the focus in 'Vandals' can be said to shift towards the storyteller. Having the opportunity to tell one's story, one's version of events, is a central motif in Ovid's *Metamorphoses* and in Munro's collection. The story of Philomela is featured in Book VI, which starts with the story of a famous weaver, Arachne. This connection is why I believe that the end of 'A Wilderness Station' can also be read in relation to Ovid's tales.

'A Wilderness Station' contains many letters, including the letter written by Christena Mullen that recalls the stories that 'Old Annie', the seamstress who lived with the Mullens, told her. Christena mentions that her sister dreamt of Old Annie, 'up at the top of the third-floor stairs brandishing her measuring stick and wearing a black dress with long fuzzy black arms like a spider' (216–17). While the picture conjures up the image of a widow in black, and brings to mind the spider called the black widow which is supposed to kill the male when it mates, I cannot help seeing Annie as Arachne, the rebellious weaver who was turned into a spider by Minerva because she dared tell an unsavoury version of the gods' deeds. While Minerva wove a fable that depicted the gods' glorious exploits, Arachne wove a different version showing countless sexual assaults on women committed by Jupiter and several other gods. Although Annie's voice is difficult to hear, she challenges official versions: in the letter she hid in the curtains she had sewn, Annie contradicted the account that George wrote which was published in a local paper. The letter exposed the sexual abuse she had endured and revealed George's attempts to abuse her.

5.2 Erratic Reading

Some of Munro's storytellers are also avid readers and Munro's characters often look at a scene with their mind's eye, remembering the books they had read. *Open Secrets* features many characters who work in a library or borrow books from a library or manage a bookstore. In 'The Albanian Virgin' Charlotte, who is revealed to have read many works, engages in discussions with Claire, who manages the bookstore and who is supposedly writing a PhD thesis on Mary Shelley's later novels. Claire, however, feels 'more interested in Mary's life' (111) and in the other women in the Shelleys' lives than in the novels themselves. Claire's interest in personal details, her wandering off from the texts she is supposed to analyse, may also exemplify the way Munro turns to and brings in literary voices

122 Corinne Bigot

from the past, and dismisses literary pretentiousness, including scholarly analyses of texts. Munro's unique engagement with world literature and previous texts often encourages me to practise the type of reading that Virginia Woolf called 'The Wrong Way of Reading' – advocating that a reader can stray from the paths set by the author.

Most stories in *Open Secrets* are complex, multilayered narratives which nevertheless remain elliptical. The most complex story is probably 'A Wilderness Station' since the many diagnoses about the 'case', the many observations and accounts that several men and one woman produce about Annie, all fail to reveal the truth about her, and Annie's own letter becomes elliptical when she starts mentioning the night she and George spent together in the marital bed (213). In this story, gaps appear within a surplus of text while silences persist in the midst of clamorous voices. As Wolfgang Iser stresses, reader-response theory posits that readers '[fill] in the gaps left by the text itself' (Iser 285), or what Vincent Jouve regards as the silences in the text (*'les silences'* or *'les blancs'* in the original French, Jouve 288). Readers are enticed to attempt to fill in the gaps as they gather the different clues. Does it mean that the reading experience is akin to assembling the different pieces of a puzzle? This possibility is what Anne Wheeler's film adaptation of 'A Wilderness Station', *Edge of Madness* (2002), suggests. A very effective close-up of Mullen's hands holding Simon's skull creates the image of a man's hands assembling a puzzle (Wheeler 01.30.18). A puzzle, however, implies the possibility of completion, of a final answer, which Munro does not provide. The film often does away with the ambiguity that is crucial to Munro's story. The scriptwriters did not invent any details, but used elements from Annie's letter and filled in the blanks in the letter and the story, which we have to recognise as an interpretative process the text allows for.[14]

Another striking aspect of *Open Secrets* is that in several stories Munro plays with the surface of the text – including visual elements such as isolated italicised segments – to create the multilayered structures that characterise the most complex stories. Munro's use of italics for repetitions is always worthy of attention. The italic typeface was invented in the sixteenth century by a Venetian printer, Aldo Manucci, also known as Aldo Manuzio, and later, Aldus Manutius (1449–1515), who wanted to show that he was printing a different type of text – poetry, not prose – and the font was first used in their 1501 edition of Virgil. Visually speaking, italics disturb the layout of the page, simply because they look different from the 'normal' font, as they slope to the right. Accordingly, in his history of typography, Gérard Blanchard argues that due to this trait italics were, from the start, endowed with 'a psychological dimension' (Blanchard 38).

Munro, I believe, has often made striking use of italics to introduce and to convey a haunting effect. The italicised segments in 'Open Secrets' are a case in point. They seem to surface randomly in the course of the story – they do not fit in, they disturb our reading, capture our attention. We eventually understand what they represent when Frances tells Maureen: '"There is a poem already made up and written down"' (156). Here, another (anonymous) voice is woven into the polyphony of rumours that tell Heather's story, adding another layer to the text. Most importantly, having the five stanzas randomly intrude into the main narrative creates the effect of a refrain that suddenly surfaces in Maureen's mind or memory, disturbing her, haunting her. For me, both the emphasis given to the lines of the poem and the way they disrupt the layout of the text create the possibility that Maureen, who often keeps silent and tries not to remember what she (thinks she) knows, remains haunted by Heather's fate. Similarly, I find the italicised sentences cited previously from 'Vandals' to be a powerful device that reveals how Liza's memory remains haunted by the rape and by her relationship with Ladner. Due to the 'psychological dimension' italicised phrases always seem to possess, they imply that the words have a persistent, personal and disturbing meaning for the characters; but they also encourage readers' participation as they imply that there is more meaning.

I have also often found Munro's use of dashes to be worthy of attention, since they can add an important dimension to the layers of text. My reading is influenced by Michel Charles's theory of 'ghost texts' ('*énoncés fantômes*' in the original French, Charles 168–210), that is to say scenarios that a writer thought of, but gave up on. He argues that these ghost texts lie behind the surface of the text, as a form of lining, and that a text preserves traces of these scenarios. Following up on Charles's idea that a text shows traces of these other texts, Francine Cicurel argues that dashes in a text are the 'scars' left by these ghost texts: 'autant de "cicatrices" laissées par ces textes fantômes qui n'ont pas été retenus' (Cicurel 61). 'Open Secrets' is characterised by a very high number of dashes that interrupt the main sentences or phrases; they cut the text open, towards untold or alternative stories. Maureen remains strikingly silent during most of the story, but her thoughts occupy most of the text, and they do tend to ramble, to detour or take off in unexpected directions. In this respect they recall Maureen's vision of the wood with its secret doorways and hidden paths (139).

Dashes are used when Maureen remembers the various stories that circulate in town about the Slaters, and she starts imagining scenarios and pictures:

> And now another story surfaced, a less malicious one, about her husband. He had driven the bus that took old folks to their therapeutic swimming session, at Walley, in the indoor pool – that was how they had met. Maureen had another picture of him, too – carrying the old father in his arms, into Dr Sands' office. (142)

The dashes open up towards another storyline, one that may or may not have been true, but that Maureen can picture, adding another layer to a complex narrative structure.

These dashes cut into the surface of the text, hinting at stories that remain to be told, or the stories that Maureen can make up. Interestingly, as suggested to me by my co-author J.R. (Tim) Struthers, the description following the dashes contains an echo of Virgil's depiction of Aeneas carrying his father Anchises in Book II of *The Aeneid* (Struthers, Message to Corinne Bigot), an episode that Ovid also briefly alludes to (Ovid, *Metamorphoses* XIII.623–39). In Struthers' reading, a subtle intertextual allusion is also hidden and introduced as an aside or another layer to the text. Michel Charles argues that the presence of traces such as dashes encourages a type of reading he calls 'erratic reading' ('*lecture erratique*' in the original French, Charles 208), that is to say the possibility for a reader to wander off, a response which includes the possibility that the reading might be erroneous too.

In my reading of 'Open Secrets' the dashes that introduce the stories and pictures that Maureen imagines are also part of a web of devices that prevents me from being certain of what Maureen knows, remembers or dismisses. The device also alerts us to the process of selection, and, ultimately, reveals something of Munro's art of storytelling. For instance, when Maureen reflects on how her former friends changed, the half-submerged presence of Maureen's past is suggested by the pair of dashes: 'Having children changed you ... so that certain parts of you – old parts – could be altogether eliminated and abandoned. Jobs, marriage didn't quite do it – just made you *act* as if you'd forgotten things' (132; italics in orig.). The subsequent single dash and the italics make it clear that Maureen's youthful parts have not been eliminated and her life remains largely untold, lurking under the surface of the text. These cuts in the text, hinting at other possible stories, draw attention to the process of selection, and they shed light on Munro's art of writing stories, embracing silence and reticence.

5.3 (Mis)interpretation as Pragmatics

In *Interpretation as Pragmatics* Jean-Jacques Lecercle exposes and debunks what he calls the '*tin-opener theory of interpretation*' (Lecercle 3; emphasis in orig.), the idea that there is one 'true' meaning which is concealed in the text and which readers must discover and reveal. According to this theory, readers, 'once the layer of metal has been peeled off' (Lecercle 3) by their interpretation, can enjoy their discovery of the 'true' meaning of the text. Instead, Lecercle points out that the reading process or interpretative process does not and cannot reveal 'the' meaning of a work of art since there is no such thing. In his view, reading does not close the process of interpretation because it is in essence '*interminable*' (Lecercle 33).

The characters' many acts of misunderstanding play a central role in our reading process. First, some mistakes are shown to be pregnant with meaning. In 'A Wilderness Station', Christena Mullen points out that 'Sometimes Old Annie called the Gaol the Home' (217), which encourages me to see a possible connection or resemblance between the orphanage – 'the Home' (271) – and a jail. Indeed, Annie may be hinting at a life of uninterrupted entrapment, from the orphanage to the Herron shanty – her home when she was married to Simon – to the Walley jail, which became her home because *she* decided to remain there by making everyone believe that she was insane. Finally, I wonder whether the impression of imprisonment does not expand to the Mullen home. In Christena's memories, Annie had turned the third floor into her domain – a marginal space that could have been a safe haven or a prison. So I feel that it is only fitting that the Mullens' house subsequently became 'a Home for Young Offenders' (216). Christena's puzzling over Annie's stories or mistakes functions to encourage our own interpretative process.

In *Open Secrets*, attention is often drawn to the process of interpretation, including its pitfalls. 'Carried Away', 'The Jack Randa Hotel' and 'A Wilderness Station' include correspondence that is read by characters whose actions mirror readers' interpretative acts. The fact that the characters misread the world, misunderstand signs and fail to understand other characters is a central device that invites readers to do more detective work. This necessity is perhaps best epitomised by the three letters carved on the tree in 'Vandals' that Bea and Warren fail to understand, a response which, as we have seen, encourages readers to decode them.

The ending of 'The Jack Randa Hotel' is another case in point. At the airport, Gail picks up a box 'made by Australian aborigines' (188) that is adorned with 'a pattern of yellow dots, irregularly spaced on a dark-red ground' (188–9) and with what is described as 'a swollen black figure – a turtle, maybe, with short splayed legs. Helpless on its back' (189). Gail sees helplessness, which indicates that she fails to see that such patterns are not merely decorative. I am reminded that Aboriginal patterns usually refer to the Dreamtime stories and creation myths, and that the turtle also establishes a connection between the two continents, or 'islands' – since the turtle also has strong significance in Eastern Canada's Indigenous cultures.

The turtle is featured in creation myths in Algonquian- and Iroquoian-speaking cultures that refer to the North American continent as 'Turtle Island'. A connection between Aboriginal creation myths, Gail's world and European creation stories is created when Gail muses that the pattern reminds her of the thousands of butterflies she saw in the woods, which led her to recall the story with '"the shower of gold"' (189). Butterflies go through a cycle of metamorphoses, which creates yet another connection with the Dreamtime stories, while Ovid's *Metamorphoses* contains repeated allusions to the story of Zeus morphing into a shower of gold (Ovid, *Metamorphoses* IV, V, VI, XI). Gail's misunderstanding of the significance of the pattern on the box reminds us that a message – including an Aboriginal pattern – and a short story are always open to interpretation and misinterpretation.

Whether we hear faint echoes and pursue an intertextual allusion we perceive, fill in the blanks in the text, reflect on the psychological dimension of an italicised segment or consider that a story can open up towards different scenarios, our reactions are evidence that Munro's stories always induce us to read creatively. The dots on the box in 'The Jack Randa Hotel', the paths that feature in 'A Wilderness Station' and 'Open Secrets', and the mysterious markings and letters on the landscape and the tracks Liza makes on the floor in 'Vandals' all encourage 'erratic' or creative readings.

Notes

1 'Carried Away' first appeared in *The New Yorker* on 21 October 1991; 'A Real Life' in *The New Yorker* on 10 February 1992; 'A Wilderness Station' in *The New Yorker* on 27 April 1992; 'Open Secrets' in *The New Yorker* on 8 February 1993; 'The Jack Randa Hotel' in *The New Yorker* on 19 July 1993; 'Vandals' in *The New Yorker* on 4 October 1993; 'The Albanian Virgin' in a double issue of *The New Yorker* dated 27 June and 4 July 1994; and 'Spaceships Have Landed' in *The Paris Review* 131 (1994) (Thacker, *Alice Munro* 609–10).
2 See for instance 'Walker Brothers Cowboy' in *Dance of the Happy Shades* (1968) and 'What Do You Want To Know For?' in *The View from Castle Rock* (2006).

3 The Maitland is the name of the river in Wingham. Robert Thacker says that renaming the river the Peregrine is an Ontario joke, given that Sir Peregrine Maitland was appointed Lieutenant Governor of Upper Canada in the 1830s (Thacker, *Alice Munro* 451).
4 In 'The Love of a Good Woman', the opening (and title) story of the next collection, children stumble upon the dead body of a man in the Peregrine River.
5 I was inspired by the title of a 2017 novel by Alexandria Marzano-Lesnevich, *The Fact of a Body: A Murder and a Memoir*, in which a boy's murdered body is hidden in a cupboard. It is eventually discovered, and his murderer caught, but unanswered questions puzzle the narrator – for instance, the fact that the body remained undiscovered in the boy's bedroom for several days without anyone noticing the smell. This situation eventually leads the narrator to examine how she too came to suppress from her memory the violence her own body endured (incest).
6 Munro uses a similar device in 'A Wilderness Station', the sixth story, which is composed of texts – letters, mostly.
7 See Carrington's analysis of Slater's gesture (stroking the feathers) and the comparison to the little hen, which she reads as an intertextual allusion to John Steinbeck's novel *Of Mice and Men* since Lenny, a simple-minded man who likes to stroke animals and women's hair, eventually kills a woman (Carrington, 'Talking Dirty' 598–601).
8 Chapter 5 of 'Book the First: Sowing' introduces Coketown through its factories.
9 Sālote declared war on Germany and Japan in 1940 and 1941. She gained international attention in 1953 when she attended Queen Elizabeth II's coronation and refused a hood to be protected from the rain and rode in an open carriage. By then, she had been on the throne since 1918.
10 Isabelle Eberhart (1877–1904) travelled in Northern Africa dressed up as a man.
11 <https://digital.library.upenn.edu/women/durham/albania/albania.html>.
12 <https://digital.library.upenn.edu/women/durham/albania/virgin.gif>.
13 I have developed this interpretation in '"Locking the Door": Self-Deception, Silence and Survival in Alice Munro's "Vandals"'.
14 I have developed this point in 'Alice Munro's "A Wilderness Station" and Anne Wheeler's *Edge of Madness*: Filling in the Blanks'.

Rereading *The Love of a Good Woman* (1998)

Catherine Sheldrick Ross

1. Introduction: 'An Extra Dimension to Life'

When Tim Struthers invited me to write about *The Love of a Good Woman* (1998), the fourth and last of what he calls 'Alice Munro's breakthrough books', he suggested that I might have a head start on this project because of my earlier engagement with the title story (Ross, '"Too Many Things"' 786–810). And certainly my experience of re-engaging with these stories has been a joy, not least because I find that somehow the stories have changed – I am reading the title story differently and that change has primed me to find new elements in the volume as a whole. What strikes me this time round is the prominence of children, especially abused children. Starting in the title story with the bullied Cece Ferns and the neglected and wild Lois and Sylvie, and ending with the furious baby in 'My Mother's Dream', every story but 'Jakarta' features children who are endangered in one way or another. Unprotected by the adults who should be caring for them, these children are variously neglected, orphaned, abandoned, bullied, fought over, exposed to danger and in three stories nearly killed. In 'My Mother's Dream', a fight-to-the-finish between mother and screaming baby ends in near-death for the baby. This final story in the collection is narrated by the baby, now grown to adulthood, who is retelling the narrative of a nightmare, a struggle, a crisis and a reconciliation that must have been told to her in the first instance by her mother Jill. The narrator describes her mother post-crisis as '[s]obered and grateful, not even able to risk thinking about what she'd just escaped, she took on loving me, because the alternative to loving was disaster' (337–8). Without ever directly revisiting in this volume Munro's familiar territory of the mother with Parkinson's disease and the daughter who leaves, these stories examine, in one way or another, the relationship – always fraught and filled with landmines – between mother and child. In some stories, the relationship is seen from the mother's perspective and in others, such as 'Rich as Stink' and 'My Mother's Dream', from the perspective of the daughter. There is pain on both sides. In 'Save the Reaper', there is a doubling of mother and child in the parallel histories of two mothers, as the story teases open the delicate relationship of Eve with her daughter Sophie, Sophie's relationship with her two children Daisy and Philip, and Eve's relationship with her two grandchildren.

This commentary on *The Love of a Good Woman* is about the eight stories, but it is also about readers and about reading and rereading. There are three categories of readers in play here: Munro herself as a lifelong avid reader; the many Munro characters whose committed reading becomes an essential element in the stories in which they appear, such as 'Jakarta' and 'Cortes Island'; and we, the readers, who become engaged emotionally and cognitively with Alice Munro's stories and leave traces of that engagement in critical essays, reviews, postings on social media and book club discussions. My remarks on the stories in this volume are grounded in a view of reading as an ongoing process, involving expectations (and their undoing) and being open to revision over time, both within a single reading and between readings. In interviews conducted over almost half a century, Alice Munro has talked about the central role of reading in her own life. In a 1979 interview with Harry Boyle, Munro said:

> [B]ooks have been *very* important all through my life, and particularly when I was a teenager growing up in Wingham. And what they did then was broaden the world for me, a sense of all sorts of possibilities, of life being important because the writers took life seriously. . . . I saw that there's an extra dimension to life and people who love books feel that. (Munro in Boyle)

This statement about the special role of reading in a reader's life was made during a CBC radio interview 'Alice Munro Challenges Censorship' about a local pressure group, spearheaded by the evangelical Rev. Ken Campbell, that demanded the removal from Grade 12 and Grade 13 reading lists of Margaret Laurence's *The Diviners* (1974) and Munro's own *Lives of Girls and Women* (1971). Munro said, 'I think as soon as one step is taken you have to start resisting, because that makes the next step easier' (Munro in Boyle). The ideological fervour of the religious right to restrict the freedom to read found its way into her later story 'Comfort' in the form of a concerted attack on evolutionary theory. A whiff of the same desire to restrict reading on ideological grounds can be found in 'Jakarta', where Cottar, a Marxist journalist, rules that the only fiction his wife Sonje should read is by Howard Fast. In 'Cortes Island', the narrator is up against attitudes prevalent in Canada in the 1950s that reading was a self-indulgence and, as Munro told Louise France, 'almost considered disloyal to the idea of being a good housewife' (Munro in France). In the face of this devaluing of reading, Munro's characters who are passionate readers recognise and greet each other as part of the same tribe, as do Kath and Sonje in 'Jakarta'. And then there are the flesh-and-blood readers of Munro's stories whose puzzlements and engagements as readers are also part of this reassessment of *The Love of a Good Woman*.

The title of the volume directs our attention to the theme of love and in particular to the love of a good woman. But as we read the stories, questions arise: Who are these good women? Is the reference to the love of a good woman for someone – the love she gives to a sexual partner, for example, or the love she gives to children? Or is the good woman herself the object of love? In any case, we are primed by the title to expect the love (or absence of love) by/of the good woman to be the emotion that drives the narrative. The eight stories in this stunning collection do in fact feature women across the age spectrum giving, receiving, withholding and suffering from love. From practical nurse Enid in the title story who may become a stepmother for two little motherless girls to newly married Kath with a nursing baby in 'Jakarta' to grandmother Eve in 'Save the Reaper' to Rosemary who is the divorced mother of eleven-year-old Karin in 'Rich as Stink' to Jill who thinks she has left her forgotten baby outside overnight before it snowed in 'My Mother's Dream', these stories present mothers, stand-in caregivers and grandmothers and their complex relationships with their babies, children and grown-up daughters. But these women are also defined by their relationships with men. There are newly married wives, women having affairs, wives who leave their husbands and children, widows, a dedicated career woman who may be ready to trade in nursing for marriage and motherhood, and a daughter who makes an unwelcome discovery about her father. There are memorable depictions of women of all kinds. We are presented with good women and not-so-good women, although readers can never be quite sure which ones are which.

Something that readers and critics do agree on, however, is that Munro's stories are complex, rich, multilayered, indeterminate and always, as Georgia's creative-writing teacher objects in 'Differently' from *Friend of My Youth* (1990), about '[t]oo many things' (216) to fit into a single frame. As Munro told David Macfarlane upon the publication of *The Progress of Love* (1986), 'I want things to come in as many layers as possible, which means the stories have to come from as many people as possible, with their different baggage of memories' (Munro in Macfarlane 54). Some years later, when *Open Secrets* (1994) was first released, Munro told interviewer Stephen Smith that 'I used often to write stories that were single paths and I knew, pretty well, what I wanted to happen . . . Maybe I don't do that any more' (Munro in Smith 24). She linked the change in her later narrative style to growing older and seeing many explanations with no single reality being of greater importance: '[t]he older I get, the more I see things as having more than one explanation. I see the content of life as being many-layered. And in a way, nothing that happens really takes precedence over anything else that happens' (Munro in Smith 24). Each story in *The Love of a Good Woman* is woven together from a selection and combination of autobiographical materials, plot motifs, character types, themes, images, historic elements, literary allusions and legendary patterns.

Instabilities of interpretation arise because different elements in a particular story are noticed (or not noticed) and given differing relative emphasis by different readers and by the same reader at different times of reading. To convey the way a reader may emphasise one theme rather than another at a particular time of reading, we could use the analogy of the geographic map over which thematic overlays in different colours can be placed, one at a time, each overlay showing a different category of information – population size, immigration patterns, household income, climate zones, land use, transportation routes and so on. The story itself is the master map containing all the overlays together, but a reader may focus on one or another layer at any given reading. In each of the eight stories in this fourth and final volume of what Tim Struthers has called her 'breakthrough books', Munro has offered readers many choices about which themes to notice, which paths to follow and which patterns to privilege. Pick a story – any story – in *The Love of a Good Woman,* and you can generate a list of multiple themes and motifs, each one supported by elements within the story but with filaments that link them to other stories throughout Munro's long writing career.

Clearly a particular reader's own history of reading determines opportunities for hearing echoes of other works – reverberations either of other stories by Munro herself or of work by others. For example, someone who teaches James Joyce's *Dubliners* may read a description of lake effect snow off Lake Huron and think of snow falling all over Ireland in 'The Dead', 'falling faintly . . . and faintly falling' (Joyce, 'The Dead' 194). In her magnificent account of rereading 'Lichen', another dinner party story, Magdalene Redekop describes how she hears countless echoes – 'so many echoes that it would be overwhelming if the story were not so firmly grounded in a particular location – summer house and garden, lake and beach' (Redekop, 'On Sitting Down To Read' 297). She explains that '[t]he allusions are sometimes explicit – Hercules, Balm of Gilead, Book of Kells – and sometimes faint echoes that I can barely hear. Shakespeare's madrigal, once quoted, whispers over every line: "What's to come is still unsure"' (Redekop 294). About 'Lichen' she says, 'I always hear Virginia Woolf' (Redekop 296). Other readers with a different reading history will bring different associations, but in Redekop's case, '[f]ragments of Woolf float in and out of "Lichen" as I read – the image of Mrs Ramsay sitting at the window in *To the Lighthouse*, that famous dinner party, and through it all the waves and time passing' (Redekop 296–7).

Readers give extra attention to themes that resonate with their own lives. As author Elizabeth Poliner notes, '[o]ne of the joys for me of reading Munro is how her work often makes me stop, pause, and re-see my life, especially the place of my youth – a small, working-class Connecticut town where most of my classmates ended their educations at high school, and where our Jewish family was such an anomaly – with eyes enlarged by the sensitivity of Munro's stories' (Poliner). In addition to small-town life and outsider experience, this volume includes many other subjects that are emotionally charged: love in various forms from sexual passion to the relationship of mothers and daughters; the rewards and burdens of loving and of being loved; safe versus risky bets as husbands and lovers; sexual betrayal; the desire to escape and the vexed decision of whether to stay or leave; break-ups, bereavement and loss; guilt, shame, exposure and humiliation; and mystery, secrets and silence. Every story involves choices that alter the course of entire lives. As characters make choices that never turn out to be what they expect, the stories explore the turnarounds of chance and luck, while taking into account socially prescribed spheres for women and men, class differences and education's role in opening up possibilities.

Giving a Munro story its special signature, multiple themes are cross-cut throughout the narrative of a single story in layers and overlays. Two of these stories involve journeys and returns that are connected with mythic patterns of descent to the underworld and back, specifically the solar cycle of dawn-to-sunset and spring-to-winter and back again. Additionally, after returning from British Columbia to Ontario and moving in with physical geographer Gerry Fremlin in Clinton, Munro learned a lot about geology with its strata and layers. In this volume, Munro's fascination with surfaces and the layers beneath them takes the form of disorder that boils up into sudden gothic eruptions of craziness or violence. And finally there is the theme of the value of art, highlighted in its various forms in almost every story: pleasure reading that is both solitary and social; the writer's impossible but crucial goal of capturing every last thing; and art as represented by literary fiction, mosaic pictures in a wall, the world of theatre and plays, and music. Reviewing *The Love of a Good Woman*, novelist A.S. Byatt called Munro 'the great describer of quotidian rhythms – food, embarrassment, clothes, ageing, sex, child-bearing and child-rearing. All lives, and all great fiction, have elements of the probable combined with disruptions and disasters. Munro was always interested both in the texture of the "normal" and the shears that slit it' (Byatt).

Whichever themes a particular reader notices and gives weight to during any given reading depends on the reader's situation at the time, preoccupations, and prior commitments. And so, for example, when in the midst of Canada's second wave of the Covid epidemic I reread 'Carried Away', the first story in *Open Secrets* (1994), I found myself zeroing in on a layer in the story that had previously seemed less salient – 'in the early winter of 1919' there was 'a fresh outbreak' (14) of Spanish flu that killed Arthur Doud's wife 'when everyone had got over being frightened' (26). Despite the risk, the town librarian and central character Louisa keeps the Library open during this period, not for professional reasons, but in order to be found by returning soldier Jack Agnew, who had written to her unexpectedly from the front – '[p]*erhaps you will be surprised to hear from a person you don't know*' (4; emphasis in orig.) – and initiated what became a deepening epistolary relationship. On this later rereading, I experienced a shock of recognition over a historical detail previously unnoticed: the closed stores and schools and churches and 'the crush in the hospitals, the deaths of doctors and nurses, the unceasing drear spectacle of the funerals' (13).

I would claim that when readers read *any* work of fiction, they co-create a version of the text that differs from one reader to another and from one time of reading to another. However, this claim is true in spades for the stories of Alice Munro, an author who offers readers multiple paths to follow and multiple ways to combine the story elements. In an interview on life-changing books, novelist Amor Towles observes that in a great work 'the way in which all the various components interact creates an infinite number of harmonic combinations in the service of meaning' (Towles in Pearl and Schwager 177). Accordingly, Towles argues, 'for a book to reach many different readers, and the same reader over time, it has to be generous in its composition. Generous in the way it's designed, so that it doesn't require you to come at it from a particular angle, and insist that you leave it with a particular perspective' (Towles 177). It should come as no surprise that these qualities of generosity that Towles finds in significant books are ones that Alice Munro admires in her own reading and ones that we find in her stories.

When I interviewed Alice Munro in the late eighties about her lifelong engagement with pleasure reading, I asked her about rereading, noting that '[s]ome people say, "There are so many books out there that I don't have time for rereading"' (Ross, 'An Interview' 23). Declaring herself a committed rereader, Munro emphasised just how much a personally significant book can change, depending on your age at the time of reading, the situation you may be in and your particular life experiences:

> The books that are important to me, I figure on rereading some time. Most of the books I own I probably have reread, or reread in part. Also some books change according to your own age and your situation in life. I've read *Anna Karenina* several times and the first time I read it I really identified with the young girl, Kitty, and her illness and her dreadful humiliating love for Vronsky. And when I read it again, I identified with Anna. And then I reread it and I identified with Dolly. [laughter] This was at the height of my mother period – poor Dolly's always worried about getting the washing done and she can never rise to the occasion because of her constant preoccupations. The book had just shifted this much. And then I read it again and I didn't identify with any of the women. I read it in a much calmer, overall way. And so there are books like that that change for you. (Munro in Ross, 'An Interview' 24)

In the later story 'Passion', Munro gives her own responses to reading *Anna Karenina* to Mrs Travers, a mother figure to the central character Grace, who with her 'long, wild-looking curly dark hair' (165) and her love of pleasure reading resembles the young Alice Munro.

In the discussion that follows, I will be examining the various resources of narrative that Munro uses to fashion stories generous enough to allow readers of all kinds and nationalities – as Spanish critic Pilar Somacarrera has shown – to read themselves into the stories and then read the stories back again into their own lives.

2. 'The Love of a Good Woman': 'The Book Had Just Shifted This Much'

Of all the stories in this volume, the title story has generated the most diversity in readers' responses. As John Gerlach notes, '"The Love of a Good Woman" poses unusual problems for the reader at its conclusion – which is virtually no conclusion at all' (Gerlach 146). And it's not just the conclusion that is indeterminate. In this story, more than in most of Munro's stories, readers are presented with elements – descriptions, conversations, choices made by characters, plot turns, allusions to fairy-tale patterns, parallels to similar motifs used in other Munro stories – that can be read, as I have argued above, in various ways by different readers or in various ways by the same reader at separate times. Long-time readers of Munro have been taught by the stories themselves that every word counts and every detail is there for a reason. Attention must be paid. As her *New Yorker* editor Deborah Treisman has observed, Munro never includes anything in her stories that isn't absolutely necessary. Interviewing Alice Munro after the publication of *Dear Life* (2012), Treisman said, '[o]ften when I'm editing a story of yours I'll try to cut something that seems completely extraneous on page 3, and then when I get to page 24 I suddenly realize how essential that passage was'. Conversely, Munro is remarkable for how much she dares to leave out. Consider all the moments she knows about but *doesn't* show you. In the title story, what did the dying Mrs Quinn say to her husband that sent him from the sickroom looking 'as if he had caught hold of an electric wire' (56)? A bravura example in this volume of strategic leaving-out can be found in 'Jakarta' – some thirty-five or so years are silently passed over. Holes strategically left in the text enable differing interpretations as readers fill in the gaps in very personal ways, drawing on their own expectations of how people behave and their familiarity with how literary texts work.

In 'The Love of a Good Woman', the death of the local optometrist brings into focus the entire town of Walley, a port town on Lake Huron resembling Goderich, Ontario. Walley has the advantage of having a wider range of society than can be found in the nearby smaller town based on Wingham that appears variously in Munro's stories as Jubilee, Dalgleish and Carstairs. One Friday afternoon in April 1951, the optometrist, Mr D.M. Willens, left home, according to his wife, to drive 'out to the country . . . to take some drops to an old blind man' (30). On Saturday morning, three pre-adolescent boys see his 'arm and his pale hand' (7) floating up through the roof panel of his light-blue Austin, which has been submerged in the Peregrine River. What happened during this period of less than twenty-four hours? In section 'III. Mistake', a dying woman, Mrs Quinn, tells her home nurse Enid three different versions of what happened, but can any of her versions be believed? Has Mrs Quinn lied spitefully in order to undermine the growing intimacy between Enid and her husband Rupert? According to Mrs Quinn's shocking account, Mr Willens visited her when Rupert 'was supposed to be cutting wood down by the river' but Rupert 'sneaked back' and 'banged the life out of him' (57). Then husband and wife worked together to get rid of the car and body in the Peregrine River and hide the evidence. So what kind of man is Rupert – a murderer who may murder again or a victim himself? What will Enid decide to believe and do, after she has heard Mrs Quinn's 'wicked outpouring talk' (64) about adultery and murder? The interpretation of the story depends on the various answers readers give to these questions as they try to fill in gaps. As Gerlach points out, when stories are described as open-ended, typically 'the choices for an open ending are primarily binary, rather than continuously indeterminate' (Gerlach 149). But in this story there are multiple indeterminacies and what the reader decides about one will affect readings of the others.

The New Yorker version of the story was given a subtitle, omitted in the collected volume: 'A Murder, a Mystery, a Romance'. Readers use genre expectations as one of the basic ways of bringing disparate elements of a story into a coherent pattern. Read as romance, which is the dominant reading given by Coral Ann Howells, 'The Love of a Good Woman' is about a woman who seems to have missed out on love until she re-establishes a connection with a man from her past. Howells says that the story involves this woman's 'desire for and expectations of romantic love – though all the genres are slightly off-centre here' (Howells 149). Ailsa Cox, who sees Rupert as 'the strong, silent type – a dark, saturnine lover in the gothic tradition' (Cox, *Alice Munro* 54), says: '[t]here is no telling if Enid is playing out a masochistic fantasy or taking a bold initiative' (Cox 53). Read as a story patterned by gothic fiction, which is the approach also taken by Dennis Duffy and Judith McCombs, the story is about a woman with an attraction to self-sacrifice, who falls in love with a killer and may become his next victim. Duffy says, 'Enid [is] dicing with her own life in order to assert her power over the hatchet man ... We are in Rocky Horrorland, where we shriek out a warning to the oblivious gothic heroine lurching toward disaster' (Duffy, '"A Dark Sort of Mirror"' 182). McCombs says, 'a brutal Bluebeard murder is revealed in secret by a woman who may be crazed or lying' (McCombs 327), and wonders, '[s]hould Rupert be seen as a Bluebeard who brought a young orphan to his lonely farmhouse, then trapped her in the chambers of murder and abortion? And now, as she lies dying in the next room, quietly courts a replacement bride?' (McCombs 335). However, not everyone sees Enid as potential victim. Carol L. Beran suggests that Enid 'may have consciously contributed to the death of her patient' (Beran, 'The Luxury of Excellence' 221) in that 'Mrs Quinn's death may be a brutal form of euthanasia' (Beran 224). Isla Duncan offers a less melodramatic reading, seeing Enid 'as far from hapless or vulnerable, but rather, single minded and determined' (Duncan, *Alice Munro's Narrative Art* 102), a woman who has set her sights on Rupert and will likely marry him and take over a house 'where all order [is] as she ha[s] decreed' (77).

Genre classifications are self-reinforcing. Once a story is identified as a romance, we adopt certain expectations and reading strategies and pay closer attention to certain patterns of detail: in a love story, early hostility and misunderstandings are understood as foreplay leading to an eventual declaration of love. A story's classification as gothic horror primes readers to anticipate the darker emotions of melancholy, anxiety and fear and to pay attention to standard gothic elements such as the isolated house, atmospheric effects of light and dark, a terrible secret, framing devices in which an inset story leads the reader from the everyday daylight world into the darker world of the gothic, and disturbing dream materials that well up from the unconscious – in short, features that intensify the reader's sense of the heightened mental state of the threatened heroine (Ross, *The Pleasures of Reading* 66–74). However, expectations based on genre unravel almost immediately. A mystery story of detective fiction often begins with the familiar trope in which an anonymous dog walker (or quite possibly a group of young boys) spots an unruly body part that has got loose from its burial place. The horrified witness immediately sounds the alarm, makes a prepared statement and disappears smartly from view, giving over the story to an investigating detective. In 'The Love of a Good Woman', this narrative line is frustrated from the outset. One of the three boys *does* eventually sound the alarm and all three boys *do* disappear from the story, but only at the end of the very lengthy 'Jutland' section, which is a tour de force of deferral. Repeatedly the three boys *don't* tell what they saw. When the police finally are notified and confirm the death of Mr Willens, the entire extent of the police investigation that gets reported occurs in a brief scene in which a policeman and the Anglican minister go to break the bad news to the new widow Mrs Willens:

> Was he downhearted or anything like that? the policeman asked her.
> 'Oh, surely not,' the minister said. 'He was the bulwark of the choir.'
> 'The word was not in his vocabulary,' said Mrs Willens. (30)

Genre categories are in effect contracts with readers about the types of conflict, resolution and endings they can expect: in a romance, a happily-ever-after; in a murder story, an identification of the murderer and restoration of order; in gothic horror, a recognition of something irremediably evil at the heart of human experience. However, Munro readers are taught by the text itself to expect disruptions in genre expectations, subversions and turnarounds, as well as unpredictable insights and discoveries. As Munro remarked in an interview with Pleuke Boyce and Ron Smith concerning the stories in her preceding collection, *Open Secrets* (1994), '[t]he stories ... aren't about what they seem to be about ... the stories don't satisfy in the same way as a traditional mystery or romance would' (Munro in Boyce and Smith 225, 227). And again, fifteen years later, Munro told the Knopf Doubleday interviewer: 'I seem to turn out stories that violate the discipline of the short story form and don't obey the rules of progression for novels' (Munro in Knopf Doubleday). Continuing, she explained:

> I want to tell a story, in the old-fashioned way – what happens to somebody – but I want that 'what happens' to be delivered with quite a bit of interruption, turnarounds, and strangeness. I want the reader to feel something is astonishing – not the 'what happens' but the way everything happens. These long short story fictions do that best, for me. (Munro in Knopf Doubleday)

Consider again the puzzle to readers that is presented by the 'Jutland' section, which at twenty-seven pages is in itself as long as many Munro stories. After a five-paragraph preface that begins, '[f]or the last couple of decades, there has been a museum in Walley ...' (3), there follow four numbered sections that are divided in most cases into subsections: 'I. Jutland' in ten subsections; 'II. Heart Failure' in eight subsections; 'III. Mistake' in one long section; and 'IV. Lies' in eight subsections. Introductory paragraphs deserve special attention, as do sentences that start and end each of the subsections. The five opening paragraphs of the preface direct the reader's attention to a red box in the Walley Museum that has been preserved along with other historic artefacts such as photos, butter churns and horse harnesses. According to a museum note attached to the exhibit, this red box of optometrist's instruments once 'belonged to Mr D.M. Willens, who drowned in the Peregrine River, 1951', but '[i]t escaped the catastrophe and was found, presumably by the anonymous donor, who dispatched it to be a feature of our collection' (3).

Michael Toolan, who is interested in textual signallings, or prospections, of narrative progression, reports that his empiric studies of reader responses to the story's five-paragraph preface suggest that from there 'a reader advances ... carrying forward (and expecting to learn more about) just two or three maximally vague images, with only a very few labels attached: *Willens, drown(ed), River, red box, instruments, escape, anonymous donor, optometrist's hand, black,* and *shiny*' (Toolan, 'Narrative Progression' 112; emphasis in orig.). The appearance of other key elements, such as *car* and *children*, he says, 'is unforetold'; however, 'the reverse is true of *water* and *river* ... Repeated use of the word *water* has a place already reserved for it in advance, given the preface's main prospections; as early as the close of the preface, *water* is foreseeable (and might even be called pre-read or pre-told)' (Toolan, 'Narrative Progression' 112; emphasis in orig.).

For readers who have read many of Munro's stories, there could be an additional textual signalling in the colour red of the box itself. What seems like an apparently innocent reference to red has a habit of foreshadowing blood and violence. A drowning doesn't usually involve bloodletting, but the red box, described later as 'the dark-red box' (61), is a key element in an alternate version of what caused Mr Willens' death – not drowning but bludgeoning. In section 'III. Mistake', the third-person narrator, using a narrative style that incorporates Mrs Quinn's own idiolect and speech patterns, reports three differing versions of how Rupert came upon his wife and Mr Willens in the front room and 'banged the life out of him' (57). To hide the blood stains, Mrs Quinn burned her blouse and a stained tablecloth, then painted the floor with brown paint – the horrible smell of the burning fabric and the fumes of the paint, she claimed, 'was the whole beginning of her being sick' (61).

Readers who begin the 'Jutland' section primed to expect details of a river drowning are presented instead with elaborate details of place. 'This place was called Jutland', we are told, where there had once been a small settlement including a mill, 'but that had all gone by the end of the last century' (4). Unexpected emphasis is placed on two erroneous beliefs about the origin of the name Jutland. 'Many people believed' (4) it was named for a famous First World War sea battle that took place well after the settlement was in ruins. The three boys who came there to the river for a first swim in the icy water 'believed, as most children did, that the name came from the old wooden planks that jutted out of the earth of the riverbank and from the other straight boards that stood up in the nearby water' (4), leftover parts of the old mill dam. Right from the outset, the idea is introduced of widely shared beliefs that are plausible but in fact wrong. Next a description of the ungravelled track leading from the township road to the river sets up the related idea of important signs that are right out in the open but unremarked because attention has been drawn away by a competing interest. The narrator notes that '[t]he car tracks to the water's edge ... were easy to spot but were not taken notice of by these boys, who were thinking only about swimming', and later refers again to '[t]he tracks that they didn't notice' (5). The attention given to these two themes – commonly held beliefs that are wrong and easy-to-spot signs that are overlooked – suggests that the reader is being given advance warning about the type of attentive reading this story and others in the volume require.

Closer now to the river's edge, the boys finally 'had their attention caught by something more extraordinary than car tracks' – 'a whole car, down in the pond on a slant' (6), that they recognised by its unusual light-blue colour as belonging to Mr Willens. The third-person narrator reports the boys' gradual step-by-step piecing together of what they are seeing under the water: 'something dark and furry' looking 'like a big animal tail' (6) becomes recognisable as an arm in the sleeve of a dark heavy jacket. The narrator's account here is curiously tentative, reflecting the boys' struggle to make sense of the scene: '[i]t seemed that ...'; 'it had to be the body of Mr Willens'; '[t]he force of the water ... must have somehow lifted him ... and pushed him about'; '[h]is head must have been shoved down' (6); '[t]he window in fact must have been open'; '[t]hey could picture ...' (7). These repeated phrases and modal verbs – 'seemed', 'had to be', 'must have', 'could' – emphasise that this piece-by-piece reconstruction of events is pure conjecture. In fact, 'all they got to see was that arm and his pale hand' which was riding on the water 'tremulously and irresolutely, like a feather' (7). This first subsection of 'Jutland' – the discovery of the body – ends with the boys' exclamation: '*Son of a gun*' (7; emphasis in orig.).

As Isla Duncan points out, the second subsection, beginning '[i]t was their first time out this year' (7), undercuts readerly expectations by taking us back to the time *before* the discovery – 'a retardatory device, frequent in Munro's anachronous and fragmented narratives' (Duncan, *Alice Munro's Narrative Art* 93–4). Subsections 2 and 3 are contrastive pairs: the former describing the time *before* and the latter describing the time *after*. In the *before* time, the boys experience a joyous sense of freedom and expanded possibility as free agents 'when they got clear of town' (10) and away from adult constraints, and cross the bridge over the Peregrine River, exploring and stomping. In the *after* time, the boys put aside their '[j]umping, dallying, splashing' and 'hoots and howls' and walked 'as adults would do, . . . with the weight on them of where they had to go and what had to be done next' (11). An image 'came between them and the world': '[t]he pond, the car, the arm, the hand' (11). Subsections 4 to 9 are remarkable in their elaboration of the variety of occasions when 'what had to be done next' (11) was impossible for these boys to do, either as a group or separately. Initially they had the idea that '[t]hey would come into town yelling and waving their news around them' (11–12). Instead three boys go home to three very different families to eat their very different noontime dinners and in each case keep their mouths shut about their discovery.

When I first wrote about 'The Love of a Good Woman', what seemed most significant in the 'Jutland' section was the theme of not telling. I noted that the three accounts of the boys' Saturday noontime dinners, however different in specifics, all converged on the same silence:

> In total, there are five missed opportunities to tell their news: coming into town; at dinner with their families, repeated at three different dinner tables; receiving forsythia from Mrs Willens; at the police station; and sitting opposite Captain Tervitt, the crossing guard. The whole point of the repetition with variation of the same event – the failure to tell the news – must be that some things are untellable and some messages cannot be delivered. The central dilemma in what we might consider the story proper is a woman's decision whether or not to tell a terrible secret. How we decide to interpret her decision is shaped in our minds by the weighting we choose to give to the representation in section I of the silent boys. (Ross, '"Too Many Things"' 796)

In short, what stood out for me at that earlier time of reading was the repetition at three very different dinner tables of the '"It's hard to tell"' (32) theme that Enid articulates at the beginning of section II. Monika Lee has perceptively pointed out that this phrase '"It's hard to tell"' 'applies to the boys, Enid, Rupert, Mrs Quinn, the narrator, and the reader, all of whom find it "hard to tell"' (Lee 113). Ildikó de Papp Carrington persuasively links four instances of not telling in the story: Cece Ferns who never told anything at home; Mrs Willens who keeps quiet about her husband's failure to return home Saturday; Enid's mother who warns the four- or five-year-old Enid '"Don't tell Daddy"' (75) about the ice-cream cone incident; and Enid who realises the benefits that could bloom through collaboration in a silence (Carrington, 'Don't Tell (on) Daddy' 168). Although the theme of something untellable still seems very important, during this rereading another layer has surfaced. Now I find myself giving more weight to the boys themselves, to their very different families and to their divergent chances in life.

In the first subsection of 'I. Jutland', the three boys, who were referred to collectively as 'these boys' (5, 7) or '[t]he boys' (6, 6), were undifferentiated and indistinguishable. In subsection 2, they begin to be individualised and are given names: Cece Ferns, Bud Salter and Jimmy Box. The three boys can be considered 'tripoles', to extend a concept elaborated by Douglas Glover. Glover uses the term 'dipole' (51) to refer to Munro's frequent device of creating contrasting characters, a prime example being Del Jordan and her friend Naomi in *Lives of Girls and Women* (1971), who started off together in elementary school but then dramatically diverge in their life choices and outcomes. Glover points out that Munro often develops her stories this way by 'setting up these parallel contrasts: characters, families, ways of speaking, even homes and neighbourhoods' (48). In subsection 2, Munro is exact in placing Cece Ferns, Bud Salter and Jimmy Box and their friends along dimensions of class, expectations for future careers, and opportunities in life. This group of friends, who are between the ages of nine and twelve, will be expected soon to get jobs sweeping sidewalks or delivering groceries; none will be sent to private schools such as Appleby or Upper Canada College (11) where future leaders in politics and business make useful contacts with other such leaders; but 'none of them lived in a shack or had a relative in jail' (11). Still, 'there were notable differences as to how they lived at home and what was expected of them in life' (11). The shadow of one such notable difference appears with an apparently throwaway comment about what Jimmy Box and Bud Salter knew about Cece Ferns: 'Cece could never take anything home unless it was of a size to be easily concealed from his father' (9).

The final seven subsections of 'Jutland' go well beyond the elaboration needed to support the '"It's hard to tell"' (32) theme. In particular, subsections 5, 6, 7 are dedicated to describing, one at a time, the Saturday noontime dinners of Cece Ferns, Bud Salter and Jimmy Box respectively. Parallel contrasts are made in terms of who is present at the meal, what the families eat, who prepares the meal, the emotional climate at the dinner table and the roles performed by the adults in the household. Cece Ferns is a vulnerable only child, bullied and abused by his alcoholic father and unprotected by his clinically depressed mother. In one of the rare moments when she has not retreated to her bed, Cece's mother is introduced bending ineffectually over the stove. Her hand is 'pressed to her stomach, cradling a pain' (15), a signal that prompts Cece to take over the frying of the eggs. In contrast, Bud Salter's mother, who has made a rhubarb pie for dessert, is introduced frying apple slices and onion rings to go along with the pork chops. Meanwhile Bud's house is happily turbulent with the yelling of his five-year-old brother and the tattling of his two vain, older sisters, who have managed to take over every space of the house with their make-up, combs, curlers, nail polish, mirrors, washed sweaters being dried on towels, and ironed dresses – turbulence kept somewhat in check by Bud's mother, who, 'with a practiced, almost serene severity', says, '"Leave that pie alone . . . Stop swearing. Stop tattle-telling. Grow up"' (19). Jimmy Box lives in a crowded house with his working mother and his disabled father, his grandparents, his two young sisters, his Aunt Mary and her extraordinarily shy son Fred – a crammed living arrangement made possible only because the family culture was never to slam doors or make disagreeable comments or mention burdens or adversity: '[c]omplaints were as rare as lightning balls in that house' (20–1).

This tripole structure of parallel families throws into sharp relief 'the disabling life ... lived together' (14) by Cece Ferns and his parents. Subsection 4 of 'Jutland' closes with the one-sentence paragraph, 'Cece Ferns never told anything at home' (14), and subsection 5 dramatises why. Cece is an abused child of an alcoholic father, who dominates the household, even in his absence, with 'the threat and memory all the time of his haywire presence' (22). On this particular Saturday afternoon, Cece's father has probably gone straight from his work at the grain elevator to the Cumberland Hotel. 'That meant it would be late in the day before they had to deal with him' (14), but Cece's mother keeps an anxious eye on the street just in case. The weight of Cece's apprehensiveness is emphasised by a series of modal verbs 'might' and 'would' and constructions using 'if', 'or maybe if', 'or if' and 'or even if' – with the effect of intensifying the reader's sense of the unpredictability and peril of Cece's home life: his father 'might not be drunk yet. But the way he behaved didn't always depend on how drunk he was. If he came into the kitchen now he might tell Cece to make him some eggs, too. Then he might ask him where his apron was and say that he would make some fellow a dandy wife. That would be how he'd behave if he was in a good mood' (16). At other times, 'he would start off by staring at Cece in a certain way – that is, with an exaggerated, absurdly threatening expression – and telling him he better watch out' (16). Following that, 'if Cece looked back at him, or maybe if he didn't look back, or if ... or even if ... his father was apt to start showing his teeth and snarling like a dog' (16). Moments later, 'he might be chasing Cece around the room yelling how he was going to get him this time, flatten his face on the hot burner, how would he like that?' (16). Cece is the first of many such vulnerable children in this collection of stories. His heart-wrenching presence at the beginning of *The Love of a Good Woman* primes the reader to recognise and give weight to the appearance in this volume of other children who are afraid, alone, unnurtured and at risk.

Section 'II. Heart Failure' begins: '"GLOMERULONEPHRITIS," Enid wrote in her notebook' (31). With this shift to section II, the boys disappear, the timeline moves forward from April to the summer of 1951 and we are introduced to a new setting, new situation and whole new set of characters, including two neglected little girls. There is the visiting nurse Enid, her dying patient Mrs Quinn, Mrs Quinn's husband Rupert, Mrs Quinn's sister-in-law Olive Green and the Quinns' two daughters, Lois and Sylvie, who are 'seven and six years old, and as wild as little barn cats' (34). The introduction in the first sentence of nurse Enid with her notebook signals her centrality in the rest of the story. A practical nurse, Enid has arrived at the Quinns' farm at the beginning of summer to provide palliative care for Mrs Quinn, who is in the last stages of kidney failure. The story is told by a third-person narrator who reports Enid's interior life, memories and dreams but limits the information provided about the other characters to such behaviours and speech as can be observed by Enid. The events of the hot, humid

Souwesto summer of 1951 are told in chronological order, but with frequent analeptic scenes from Enid's past that are woven into the forward momentum of the narrative.

Subsection 2 of section II takes us back to a crucial turn-in-the-road event that occurred some sixteen years earlier, with the opening sentence stating: '[w]hen Enid was twenty years old, and had almost finished her nurse's training, her father was dying in the Walley hospital' (39). Like a character in a folk tale, Enid made a rash promise to her father not to become a registered nurse and work in a hospital. A puzzling request, but Enid's mother explained to Enid that, during his illness in hospital, her father had '"got an idea that nursing makes a woman coarse"' (39), giving them the type of 'familiarity . . . with men's bodies' that 'would change a girl' and 'spoil her good chances' (40) of marriage. Like Dorothea Brooke in George Eliot's *Middlemarch*, Enid is idealistic and attracted to the romance of self-sacrifice, hoping 'to be good, and do good' (42). Glorying in hardship and sacrificial gestures, Enid once had an ambition 'to be a missionary, at one embarrassing stage' (41) before choosing nursing. Enid's mother knew just how tempting the requested promise would be to Enid: '[t]he deathbed promise, the self-denial, the wholesale sacrifice. And the more absurd the better. . . . Sheer noble perversity' (40). What happens next could fit into Stith Thompson's *Motif-Index of Folk-Literature* under the category 'M. Ordaining the Future', where he lists story types of fatal bargains and rash promises, among them M205.0.1, '*Promise kept in deed but not in spirit*' (emphasis in orig.). So now, rather than 'a decent job in a hospital', some sixteen years after the rash promise, Enid is providing practical nursing care to dying bodies, doing what her mother described as 'miserable backbreaking work in miserable primitive houses for next to no money' while coping 'with housework and poor weaselly children as well' (43). With better hospitals and increased prosperity after the war, 'it looked as if her responsibilities might dwindle away to the care of those who had bizarre and hopeless afflictions, or were so irredeemably cranky that hospitals had thrown them out' (44). Enid, it is suggested, might be ready to choose a new course in life.

As a counterpart to the initial rash promise, the story ends with Enid at another fork in the road. Once again she is tempted by the allurement of 'wholesale sacrifice' (40) – as her mother put it about her previous sacrificial gesture, '"I can see that the worse I make it sound the more determined you get to do it"' (43). Enid concocts a plan that involves her being with Rupert alone in a rowboat in the middle of the river, making him aware that she cannot swim, asking if what she was told was true about Mr Willens' death, and promising, if Rupert confesses, that she will stick by him and visit him in jail – all this, unless of course he decides to ensure her silence by drowning her. After the funeral, she arrives at Rupert's door to put her plan into action, dressed for sacrifice in what might be 'the last clothes she would ever wear' (70). Inside the Quinn house, she enters the front room, where so many key events in the story have taken place: the alleged adultery and murder, Mrs Quinn's terrible story and Mrs Quinn's funeral. Enid hears again the words that Mrs Quinn said in that room, '[*l*]*ies. I bet it's all lies*' (emphasis in orig.), and wonders if a story of murder 'so detailed and diabolical' (74) could be the emanation of a dying person's mind. Yes, it could. The last subsection in the story begins, '[s]he hadn't asked him yet, she hadn't spoken. . . . It was still *before*' (75; emphasis in orig.). The stress on the time *before* recapitulates with variation the parallel contrast in the 'Jutland' section between the time before and the time after the boys' discovery of the body. Enid realises that through her silence she can remain in the time before. And with that silence, 'this room and this house and her life held a different possibility, an entirely different possibility from the one she had been living with (or glorying in – however you wanted to put it) for the last few days' (76). Just as her youthful notion of self-sacrifice by becoming a missionary had later seemed embarrassing, the narrator tells us that '[s]he was embarrassed now that she had dressed herself up in readiness for such a melodramatic fate' (76).

Enid's patient, the dying Mrs Quinn, is a different kettle of fish in almost every possible way. In contrast to the vibrant, full-bodied Enid, in whom 'the juices of life were so admirably balanced and flowing' (37), Mrs Quinn is 'a little bird-boned woman, queerly shaped now' (35) with 'fine, sparse, fair hair', 'large greenish eyes' and 'childish translucent teeth and small stubborn chin' (36). The dying woman with her 'ferretlike teeth' (38) resembles those other sly, scornful, knowing, sexualised and disillusioned Munro characters who are marginalised by class and by lack of education and have to fight for any advantage in life – for example, in 'The Time of Death' in *Dance of the Happy Shades* (1968), the 'pale shrewd' (92) Patricia with 'her tiny pointed teeth . . . almost transparent . . . [that] made her look like a ferret, a wretched little animal insane with rage or fear' (99). Mrs Quinn puts Enid in mind 'somewhat of girls she had known in high school – cheaply dressed, sickly looking girls with dreary futures, who still displayed a hard-faced satisfaction with themselves' and who after a few years in high school 'got pregnant' and in most cases 'got married' (38).

The relationship of the two central female characters fits the dipole structure described by Douglas Glover. With her privileged upbringing, her professional nurse's training and her leisure activities of skating, badminton, bridge games, the Book Club and the Horticultural Society, Enid has had options and choices in life. As readers, we know all we need to know about Enid's early life, but there are troubling gaps in what we know about Mrs Quinn. We are told that she was raised in a Montreal orphanage. Suggesting the orphan's cumulative losses of family, language and culture, Mrs Green remarks, '"You'd expect her to speak French, but if she does she don't let on"' (33). Even her given name has been erased: we first learn of it in Enid's notebook, recorded after her patient's death: 'July 10. Patient Mrs Rupert (Jeanette) Quinn died today approx. 5 p.m. Heart failure due to uremia. (Glomerulonephritis)' (67). Jeanette met Rupert when she was working up north as a hotel chambermaid; she married him and became pregnant, in one order or the other. In short, Munro gives readers what Judith Maclean Miller has called 'not even really clues, just bits and pieces of information that appear here and there, floating through the telling of the story' (Miller 43). Putting the bits and pieces together concerning Jeanette's past, I find myself importing into her story what is now known from reportage such as that by Sidhartha Banerjee about the widespread physical and sexual abuse of orphans and of so-called illegitimate 'children of sin' in Quebec. Between 1925 and 1972 some 75,000 children were turned over to church-run orphanages such as the house of gothic horrors operated by the Grey Nuns of Montreal. Perhaps not surprisingly, when Enid asks whether she should summon a priest at the end, 'Mrs Quinn looked as if she wanted to spit' (54). Possibly sexualised at an early age but in any case a survivor, Jeanette may have taken the initiative in cultivating Rupert. Who could blame her if she saw the shy man with the prosperous farm as a ticket to a more secure, if unexciting, future?

Motherless and unnurtured herself, Mrs Quinn seems unattached to her children and they to her. When called in by Enid from their games to 'see their mother looking pretty', Lois and Sylvie came 'obediently if unenthusiastically' but are not surprised or disappointed when their mother drives them off: '"Well, now they've seen me . . . Now they can go"' (36). She behaves as if 'these two daughters of hers were a pair of rowdy orphans, wished on her for an indefinite visit' (37). Enid, on the other hand, teaches the little girls how to brush their teeth, how to hold their spoons properly, how to say thank you and how to say grace. Finding the Quinn household lacking children's toys and books, Enid, with the help of her own mother, supplies the missing blocks, crayons, colouring books and playthings. She also gives the little girls a book of paper cut-out dolls of the two little Princesses Elizabeth and Margaret Rose and introduces them to fairy tales, notably 'Sleeping Beauty' (or 'Briar Rose' as it is sometimes called). On the steamy hot day of Mrs Quinn's death, Enid made the day special for Lois and Sylvie, with treats of Jell-O, home-made cookies and chocolate milk and with festive activities of blowing bubbles and lolling in makeshift swimming pools, 'becoming Princess Elizabeth and Princess Margaret Rose' (66). By creating 'the day's air of privilege, its holiday possibilities', Enid 'wanted them to hold something in their minds that could throw a redeeming light on whatever came later. On herself, that is, and whatever way she would affect their lives later' (64). Clearly Enid's decision whether or not to keep silent will affect the lives of many, not least of all Lois and Sylvie. Without children of her own, Mrs Green has made plans for taking the children to her place – plans that the children and Rupert will '"have to get used to"' (68) and that include eliminating such childhood exuberances as running, shouting greetings to the dog and door slamming.

These matched and opposite women Enid and Mrs Quinn repel each other like the positive and negative poles of a magnet. Enid, usually so compassionate and understanding, 'could not conquer her dislike of this doomed, miserable young woman' (38). Uncharacteristically and unprofessionally, she can't help seeing Mrs Quinn's discoloured and decaying body and her 'ferretlike teeth' as a 'sign of a willed corruption', 'sullen mischief' and 'rot' (38). Scornful, querulous and mocking, Mrs Quinn refuses to settle into the role of good wife, and loving mother, and grateful patient. Instead she makes demands, complaints and shocking accusations. Aware that Enid regards her with revulsion, she makes that knowledge into 'her triumph. // *Good riddance to bad rubbish*' (39; emphasis in orig.). But if Mrs Quinn sees Enid as a menacing invader, she may have good cause. Enid and Rupert have been attracted to each other from their schooldays – their previous encounters are described as 'teasing, or cruel flirtation, or whatever it was' (46) – and now, in the room beside the sickroom, they are deepening their relationship. Long-time Munro readers may discern, behind Enid's angel-of-mercy role, faint outlines of the practical nurses from previous stories – Mary

McQuade in 'Images' in *Dance of the Happy Shades* (1968) and Nurse Audrey Atkinson in the title story of *Friend of My Youth* (1990), who take over the household, introduce new routines and supplant the wife/mother figure.

Completing the triangle is Rupert Quinn, who remains a puzzle. Details provided about him are sparse and reveal almost nothing about his inner life or his own perspective on anything. It's another case of Judith Maclean Miller's 'bits and pieces of information that appear here and there, floating' (Miller 43). We are given Mrs Green's account of Rupert's meeting his wife when he was working in the bush up north, presumably cutting trees – '"He never had any kind of a girlfriend before that"' (33); Enid's ashamed memories of how she and her girlfriends had teased, tormented and 'picked on' (33) Rupert when they were all classmates in school ('[w]hy did they treat him this way, long to humiliate him? Simply because they could' – 33); Enid's observation that Mrs Green's inability to understand a joke reminded her of Rupert ('[t]hat was just the way Rupert would smile, in high school, warding off some possible mockery' – 33); Enid's later memory of Rupert's sitting in the seat behind her in the last year of high school ('[h]e was only at ease when he sat behind her, and knew that she could not look him in the face' – 46); Enid's apparent awareness that a request for a snippet of factual knowledge was her best bet for starting a conversation with Rupert ('Where is the Tyrrhenian Sea?' – 46; '"Bread of the Amazon' . . . Seven letters?"' – 48); and Mrs Quinn's improbable statement to Enid that Rupert '"goes out of here every night and he goes to pick up women, doesn't he"' (36).

Puzzle that he is, Rupert has nevertheless changed for me over successive readings. This time, what strikes me about Rupert is his similarity, not to Bluebeard or a demon lover, but to someone with mild characteristics of being on the autism spectrum. Rupert was bullied as a child; he avoids eye contact, has difficulty in interpreting social cues, is bewildered and out of his depth in social situations, is uncomfortable with physical contact, sticks to familiar and repetitive routines, never had a girlfriend before he married Jeanette. Like Enid, he was one of the most academically successful students in their high school and he excelled at being able to provide arcane facts and word answers for crossword puzzles. But he has trouble understanding jokes, metaphors and conversations that go beyond the factual and the literal; under stress, he engages in odd repetitive movements, 'pounding on his knees' and 'banging his big flat hands' (58); and he is flummoxed by everyday social situations such as answering the door to an uninvited caller: '[i]t seemed uncertain whether he was going to ask her in. It was bewilderment that stopped him, not hostility' (70). Rupert feels what is called in Munro's earlier story 'The Stone in the Field' 'the pain of human contact' (27) and spends as little time as possible with his wife and children. As the days get longer in June, he returns home from the fields later and later. Reported interactions with his family are limited to his brief encouragements to his daughters – '"Are you being good girls?"' (34) – and reluctant late-night visits of a few minutes with his wife in the sickroom. '"Doesn't hang around here very long, does he?" Mrs Quinn would say. . . . "Why don't we just dump her out like a dead cat? . . ."' (35).

So who is Rupert? A Bluebeard who lured a younger woman, an orphan, to his isolated farmhouse and may be about to kill a second victim? Is he, as Duffy puts it, 'the hatchet man' (Duffy, '"A Dark Sort of Mirror"' 182)? Or is he a socially awkward farmer who had no notion when marrying Mrs Quinn what marriage to her would be like and is now about to be taken in hand by a practical, managerial woman who has belatedly understood the value of expedient silence? I have been arguing that this story exemplifies to a high degree a quality that is characteristic of Munro's narrative art in general: the deliberate use of materials – images, quoted dialogue, characters' actions and literary references – that invite and can plausibly sustain a variety of interpretations. A prime example is the hatchet that associates Rupert both with death and, through the 'Sleeping Beauty' story, with rebirth and springtime renewal (Ross, '"Too Many Things"' 808–9). From the appearance of Old Joe Phippen with his axe in 'Images' in Munro's first collection to the 'crazy old woman named Mrs Netterfield' who 'had her hatchet with her and she raised it' (310) when she went after the delivery boy in 'Dear Life' in Munro's final collection, the axe-wielding or hatchet-carrying person evokes the primal fear of death. By contrast, in the solar myth, of which 'Sleeping Beauty' is the most well-known version, the bright hero with his axe chops through the briars surrounding the spring maiden's castle and awakens her – and the dormant earth – to new life with a kiss. Rupert with his hatchet can plausibly be seen in both guises. But now in this rereading, I see a third possibility that modulates, but does not erase, the other two.

The connection between the hatchet and the 'Sleeping Beauty' story is made at the end of section II when Rupert asked Enid what she wrote in her notebooks. One notebook is for the doctor, Enid told Rupert; in the other notebook, she recorded for herself 'what was happening all around' and in particular 'things to remember', an example being something that Lois had said the other day:

> 'Lois and Sylvie came in when Mrs Green was here and Mrs Green was mentioning how the berry bushes were growing along the lane and stretching across the road, and Lois said, "It's like in 'Sleeping Beauty.'" Because I'd read them the story. I made a note of that.'
> Rupert said, 'I'll have to get after those berry canes and cut them back.' (55)

Rupert's response here seems off-kilter. A person with average competence in reading social cues would know that the point to this story – and why Enid wrote it down – is not the overgrowth of berry bushes, but six-year-old Lois's cleverness in making a connection between her own life and the world of story, a story that, not incidentally, Enid herself had read to the children. A compliment was intended to Rupert's daughter, to be sure, but likely Enid mentioned this particular diary entry because she expected it to reflect well on herself and on her own suitability as a replacement mother. As the reader comes to recognise, Rupert's response about cutting back the berry canes foreshadows the reference to the 'little hatchet' that Rupert brought 'from the woodshed, to clear their path' (77) for the walk of the couple to the river and towards an unknown future. But his response also adds to the accumulating evidence that Rupert is a man who is baffled much of the time by human interaction and has therefore never been a match for Mrs Quinn with her practised verbal attacks and her mocking, derisory style. Towards the end, Enid felt that Mrs Quinn 'was building [her energy] up for a purpose' (54), in fact that she 'was building up to a display' (56). The display, whatever Mrs Quinn said, was intended to punish Rupert and it worked. After

Rupert's last visit to see his wife before she died, he fled the sickroom looking 'as if he had caught hold of an electric wire and begged pardon – who of? – that his body was given over to this stupid catastrophe' (56).

Mrs Quinn's second display the next day was mounted for Enid's benefit and occupies the whole of the third section, 'Mistake'. Isla Duncan has pointed out the strategic ambiguity of the titles of the second and fourth sections, 'Heart Failure' and 'Lies' respectively (Duncan, *Alice Munro's Narrative Art* 96), a claim that also applies to the third section, 'Mistake'. But then the reader has been warned to expect reversals – recall the narrator's unexpected emphasis in the opening paragraphs of 'I. Jutland' on widely shared, differing and erroneous beliefs about the origins and meanings of names. Mrs Quinn is the subject of focalisation in 'III. Mistake', as the narrator channels Mrs Quinn's voice and style in competing versions of what happened to Mr Willens on the day of his death. At the very end of section II, in the darkened sickroom with quilts on the windows to keep out the light, Mrs Quinn has dismissed the stories that other patients have told Enid, calling them '"Lies . . . I bet it's all lies"' (56). She then segues into her own story: '"You know Mr Willens was right here in this room?"' (56). Mrs Quinn starts out the way storytellers often begin when they want to hook their listeners with the promise of an amazing revelation: '"I could tell you something you wouldn't believe"' (56). In this case, however, the statement can be taken literally. Should Enid – or Munro's readers – believe the account of violent death and cover-up that is related in section III? Or is this display another example of the mean-spirited 'fits' and 'mulling over of old feuds' that overtook some people 'before they settled down to their dying' (37)? Could it be '"all lies"' (56)? The term 'mistake' is introduced in section III in the context of Mrs Quinn's explanation of how she and Rupert collaborated on a plan to get rid of the body: put Mr Willens in the driver's seat and push the car into the Peregrine River, making it look as if he had taken the Jutland road after dark and ended up in deep water. It would look '[l]ike he just made a mistake. // He did. Mr Willens certainly did make a mistake' (59).

What was Mr Willens' mistake? That he got unlucky after an apparently long career of making home visits that combined eye examinations with sexual dalliance? That he underestimated Rupert? And/or did Rupert make a mistake in sizing up the scene in the front room when he unexpectedly 'sneaked back' (57) to the farmhouse? What did Rupert think was happening when he saw Mr Willens and his wife playing the doctor and patient game ('[i]t was like the same game every time' – 62)? The endpoint of this practised game was for Mr Willens 'to get her down and thump her like an old billy goat. Right on the bare floor to knock her up and down and try to bash her into pieces' (62). Coming upon this scene, did Rupert kill Mr Willens deliberately in a jealousy-driven, murderous rage? Or was the death an accident as the text suggests in the very next sentence: 'Rupert just walloped him, and maybe he hit the leg of the stove, she didn't know what' (57)? Did this usually slow-moving man mistakenly think he was witnessing a violent sexual assault when he jumped on Mr Willens 'like a bolt of lightning' (57)? The close proximity of the 'bolt of lightning' (57) to the 'electric wire' (56) just one page earlier raises the possibility that what Mrs Quinn may have told Rupert behind closed doors was that Rupert, through his mistaken interpretation, was responsible for the whole 'stupid catastrophe' (56). Section III ends with Mrs Quinn's satisfied mockery of the additional mistakes made in the newspaper account: 'Mr Willens found drowned. // They said his head got bunged up knocking against the steering wheel. They said he was alive when he went in the water. What a laugh' (62).

One pole of the story is the darkened, closed-off front room, associated with the 'acrid and ominous' smell of the dying Mrs Quinn and 'the pale-lavender-brown stains appearing on her body' (31) that are linked by implication to the brown paint covering blood stains on the floor. The other pole is the outside world of nature: the cycle of seasons and the weather, the pastoral world of farm, crops and ruminating cows, and of course the river that runs through this story. In 'I. Jutland', images of the natural world anticipate renewal, rebirth and fertility: the breaking up of the river ice and the yearly flood of the river; 'patches of leeks on the ground and marsh marigolds' (5); gulls, crows, buzzards and 'the robins ... just returned, and the red-winged blackbirds ... darting in pairs, striking bright on your eyes as if they had been dipped in paint' (8). Mrs Willens, who doesn't yet know she is a widow, offers the three boys three bunches of forsythia, saying, '"It's always good to see the forsythia, it's the very first thing in the spring"' (23). And when Bud's sister Doris and a friend see the boys with their arms loaded with yellow flowers, the girls hoot, '"Where's the wedding? Look at the beautiful bridesmaids"' (24), linking references to forsythia, springtime, rebirth of the solar year and marriage.

In section II, the opening paragraph of subsection 5 establishes the outside pastoral world that is Rupert's domain in contrast with the inside world of the sickroom. Atmospheric details create the pervasive sense of 'the overflow and density' (45) of a hot, humid Souwesto summer: 'a great downpour of rain every few days' (44), 'sun ... glittering off the drenched leaves and grass' (44), '[e]arly mornings ... full of mist – they were so close, here, to the river' (44–5). With all this moisture and heat, everything is lush and overgrown: '[t]he heavy trees, the bushes all bound up with wild grapevines and Virginia creeper, the crops of corn and barley and wheat and hay' (45). As I write this during the first week of June in a city about sixty miles south of Goderich, the weather this past week has been 85°F to 90°F with high humidity and warnings of thunderstorms and possible flooding. You could say I have been primed to respond to Munro's details of a Souwesto summer. But I also have Isla Duncan to thank for drawing my attention to the importance of these details within the story. Duncan told me that when she was rereading 'The Love of a Good Woman' again recently, her response had changed somewhat from earlier readings. She felt a little 'more sympathy for the character of Enid this time around. ... I was also paying more attention to Munro's depiction of the pastoral scenes; the placid cattle cropping at the lush grass; the dense, misty mornings. I always think any kind of excess is important in Munro' (Duncan, Message).

There are two additional scenes of 'excess' whose locations – one appearing at the beginning of 'IV. Lies' and one at that section's and the story's end – signal their importance. In subsection 1, Enid has been up and awake all night, deeply troubled by Mrs Quinn's revelations. At dawn, she sat outside on the porch, trying to sort through 'what she had been told had happened' and '[w]hat to do about it' (63). With nothing decided and knowing that she should go back to check on Mrs Quinn, instead 'she found herself pulling open the gate bolt' (63). Here follow four paragraphs of what narratologist Michael Toolan calls passages of 'high emotional intensity' or HEI (Toolan, 'Engagement' 213). As Toolan defines them, HEI passages are points in the story of heightened emotional engagement in which particular stylistic elements 'cause a reader to empathize, feel moved, immersed, or involved' (Toolan, 'Engagement' 211). In the sequence at dawn, Enid took the path towards the river through the little meadow, where the cows are grazing and where the '[s]opping wet' (63) weeds brushed against her stockings. Enid's sleeplessness combined with heat and high humidity creates a hallucinatory atmosphere. 'Mist was rising so that you could hardly see the river. You had to fix your eyes, concentrate, and then a spot of water would show through, quiet as water in a pot. There must be a moving current, but she could not find it' (63). The reader becomes directly immersed in the scene – '[y]ou had to fix your eyes, concentrate' (63) – before the focus returns to what Enid sees and hears: quiet stillness, a boat gently rising and falling, and finally a message spoken directly to her, '*You know. You know*' (64; emphasis in orig.). The net affect of these images – a pathway, grazing cows, lushly growing weeds, mist, spots of light on the river glinting through the tangled willows, the gently rocking boat – is a growing sense of mystery.

At the very end of the story, in a sequence at dusk, these key images are reprised: the path, 'the big fleshy thistles' that the cows won't eat, the 'flash of water [that] came through the black branches', and 'the boat waiting, riding in the shadows, just the same' (78). Additional elements not mentioned in the first scene intensify the reader's sense of engagement: Rupert with his little hatchet, the 'cloud of tiny bugs . . . constantly in motion', the roots '[y]ou had to watch that you didn't trip over' (78) and the hidden oars. The contrast of the approaching night and the flashes of light from the far bank of the river, the accumulation of images of swarming insects and lush vegetable life, the intense quietness that allowed Enid to 'hear Rupert's movements in the bushes' (78) – all these heighten engagement without ruling out any possible endings that the reader may be expecting. As her boots sink into the mud at the water's edge, Enid stands held in place at a boundary line between land and water, between one kind of life and another, poised on the threshold of an unknown future. 'But if she concentrated on the motion of the boat, a slight and secretive motion, she could feel as if everything for a long way around had gone quiet' (78). As Munro told Eleanor Wachtel in an interview soon after the publication of *Friend of My Youth* (1990), she withholds the readerly satisfaction of closure because 'I want the stories to keep going on. I want the story to exist somewhere so that in a way it's still happening, or happening over and over again. I don't want it to be shut up in the book and put away – oh well, that's what happened' (Munro in Wachtel 52).

3. 'Jakarta': 'A Place of Their Own'

'The Love of a Good Woman', as we have seen, contains multiples of threes – three adolescent boys, three noontime dinners, three versions of Mrs Quinn's account of the murder and, of course, the triangle of Enid, Rupert and Mrs Quinn. 'Jakarta', by contrast, is based on doubles. This second story in the collection involves two couples, two dinner parties, two geographic settings, two plot lines and two time periods. In addition, long-time Munro readers will recognise another kind of doubling. As Tracy Ware has pointed out, 'Jakarta' is in part a redo of Munro's story 'Mischief' from *Who Do You Think You Are? / The Beggar Maid* (1978, 1979) (Ware, 'Momentous Shifts' 160). Both stories are about the break-up of a marriage, although they are very different in structure and in feeling. In contrast to 'Mischief', with its focus on Rose, 'Jakarta' is more like a string quartet. The structure of this story is unusual in Munro's oeuvre. Divided into four untitled but numbered sections, the narrative in 'Jakarta' alternates between two time periods and is focalised through two protagonists, the young mother Kath starting out in life for sections I and III and Kath's former husband Kent, now married to his third wife, for sections II and IV.

'Jakarta' is an enormously rich story – too much to discuss in its entirety. I have chosen to focus on two features often found in Munro's short stories that are particularly salient here. One is the distinctive handling of the passage of time and the second is Munro's reuse with variations of a previous story motif or situation. As is the case with many stories in this volume, key events in 'Jakarta' are spread over long periods of time, a structure that reveals how what seems like a small action or insignificant choice has long-term consequences in the lives of the characters. Section I establishes two young couples living in West Vancouver in the mid-1950s; section II jumps forward some thirty-five years to catch up with the characters in old age; and sections III and IV repeat and intensify this pattern of youth-to-old-age. The affect of this doubling is an elegiac sense of the winding down of life and the depletion of energy.

The many decades silently passed over have been condensed to a few significant details, mentioned as if incidentally. Here they are: Kath has lived for a long time in a house that she and her partner (now dead) built together beside a small lake in the Haliburton district in Ontario. After the farewell party in West Vancouver, Sonje went to Oregon to look after Cottar's blind mother Delia and together they established a dance studio with Delia playing the piano. During the silently passed over decades, Kent has been divorced, remarried, widowed, remarried again and has undergone at least two serious (heart?) operations. And Cottar, who never made it to Oregon after his 'journalistic junket to the Far East' (86), was reported to have died in Jakarta '"of some tropical bug"' (93). We, the readers, don't need to know more than we have been told about these missing years, but Munro herself knows. In a later interview made available to promote the then just-published collection *Too Much Happiness* (2009), Munro told the Knopf Doubleday interviewer, 'I always have to know my characters in a lot of depth – what clothes they'd choose, what they were like at school, etc. . . . And I know what happened before and what will happen after the part of their lives I'm dealing with. I can't see them just now, packed into the stress of the moment' (Munro in Knopf Doubleday).

The second feature of note is the way that Munro has returned in 'Jakarta', as she often does in her stories, to a significant story motif that she has used before, each time reworking it and finding in it something new.

Sabrina Francesconi speaks of how 'Munro anticipates, recovers, develops, offers variations on a theme, and invites the reader to perceive and recognize the echo of other stories in every new story' (Francesconi, 'Alice Munro' 49). Robert Thacker describes this method of Munro's, which he sees as culminating in her final three books, as 'a recursive late style all her own' (Thacker, *Late Style* 3). Three stories published over a period of almost twenty-five years – 'Mischief' and 'Jakarta' and 'Comfort' – include a central scene in which a married couple go to a party where the husband embarrasses his wife by getting into a loud argument with one or all of the other guests. A reader who has read all three stories has the opportunity to note significant differences in the portrayals of the three husbands, in the responses of the three wives and in the way events at each party affect what happens later. For example, stuffed-shirt Patrick in 'Mischief' is decidedly unpleasant as he pontificates on the need to drag so-called Indians '"[k]icking and screaming into the twentieth century"' (108). Kent in 'Jakarta' is more sympathetic, even when defending causes unlikely to be supported by the reader, because in section II an account of the party scene is given from his perspective. The case in the later story 'Comfort' is more complex. Lewis stands for a position supported by Munro herself and likely to be supported by Munro readers: strong opposition to an organised campaign by the religious right to push creationist propaganda in the schools and restrict intellectual freedom. But his uncalled-for attack on Kitty's talk on saints is a failure in kindness – an absence of empathy that is in large part what the rest of the story is about.

The two features that I have highlighted – the handling of time and the reappearance, with variation, of a previously used motif – are connected so that discussing one involves discussing the other. Let's start with the party motif. In stories by Munro, hidden information is often revealed or self-discoveries are made in the course of attendance at some ritual event such as a funeral, a wedding or a party. Heightened emotions, especially if intensified by alcohol, may lead to arguments, loss of inhibitions and risk-taking. 'Mischief' begins with the sentence, 'Rose fell in love with Clifford at a party which Clifford and Jocelyn gave and Patrick and Rose attended' (98). Leaving the reader in no doubt about the importance of the party, the narrator says proleptically at the end of the second paragraph: '[s]he had no idea that her life was going to be altered' (98). In contrast, 'Jakarta' proceeds by indirection. Section I offers intimations of Kath's readiness for change, and the introduction of the life-altering party is delayed until section II.

The opening paragraph of 'Jakarta' signals the centrality of the two young wives and their efforts to carve out for themselves some figurative space and a separate identity:

Kath and Sonje have a place of their own on the beach, behind some large logs. They have chosen this not only for shelter from the occasional sharp wind – they've got Kath's baby with them – but because they want to be out of sight of a group of women who use the beach every day. They call these women the Monicas.

The Monicas have two or three or four children apiece. (79)

The phrase 'a place of their own' (79) echoes Virginia Woolf's 'a room of her own' (Woolf, *A Room of One's Own* 2) and suggests the desire of these two young wives for connection to the creative and artistic life. Sonje 'had wanted to be a ballet dancer until she got too tall' and she continued to regret this lost dream 'until she met Cottar, who said, "Oh, another little bourgeois girl hoping she'll turn into a dying swan"' (83). Kath and Sonje knew each other when both were working in the Vancouver Public Library and they remain friends during the becalmed period of their lives presented in section I. For child-related reasons, both women have found it necessary to leave their jobs: Kath because in those days a pregnant woman could continue to work in an academic library, but not in a public library where children could see her; and Sonje because it was feared that a woman married to a left-wing writer who had visited China could be a pro-Communist influence on children visiting the library. In this 'place of their own' (79), these two friends read and discuss their reading in order to keep alive their connection to the life of the mind.

Why are Kath and Sonje so dismissive of the Monicas? '[T]he real Monica' (79), when we meet her, seems friendly, practical and helpful. But the Monicas are perceived as a threat. With 'their strung-out progeny and maternal poundage' and their absorption into a life dominated by diaper bags, picnic hampers, inflatable rafts, sun hats and lotions, the Monicas have 'reached a stage in life that Kath and Sonje dread' (80). These mothers represent the encroaching danger of losing one's independent identity and being swallowed up in child care, domestic preoccupations and the 'sludge of animal function' (80). Kath, with her nursing baby Noelle and her carry-cot, feels particularly at risk but she tries to keep the sludge factor at bay with cigarettes and books. The scene of reading in 'Jakarta' replays a parallel scene in 'Mischief' in which Rose and Jocelyn, who have met in the maternity ward of the North Vancouver General Hospital, form an alliance of serious readers against the other new mothers who can talk only about the organisation of kitchen cupboards and the proper use of vacuum-cleaner attachments (100–1). At the beach in 'Jakarta', Kath is reading stories by Katherine Mansfield and D.H. Lawrence. Because Sonje's husband Cottar has told her that if she has to read fiction, then leftist Howard Fast is the author to read, Sonje limits herself to only one of Mansfield's or Lawrence's stories before going back dutifully to Howard Fast.

The stories that Kath and Sonje are shown discussing – Mansfield's 'At the Bay' and Lawrence's 'The Fox' – are each disturbing but for different reasons. Whereas in 'Mischief' the third-person narrator signals at the outset the coming fracture in Rose's marriage to Patrick, in 'Jakarta' Kath herself becomes uncomfortably aware of her dissatisfaction with marriage to Kent while she is discussing with Sonje characters in the stories they are reading at the beach. Mansfield's 'At the Bay' presents the two contrasting male types who also appear in many of Munro's own stories including the later works 'What Is Remembered' and 'Passion': the safe, reliable, prudent choice in husband material and the exciting, dangerous, adrenaline-junkie choice. Kath and Sonje consider the unlovable Stanley Burnell, 'with his pushy love, his greed at the table, his self-satisfaction. Whereas Jonathan Trout – oh, Stanley's wife, Linda, should have married Jonathan Trout' (83). Jonathan Trout is 'full of irony ... subtle and weary' and says, '"The shortness of life, the shortness of life"' (83). 'Is Kent something like Stanley?' Kath wonders but 'can't mention it or think about it' (83).

The Love of a Good Woman (1998)   151

Reading Lawrence's 'The Fox' intensifies in Kath a feeling of something being wrong or missing in her life. In Lawrence's story, a soldier and a woman named March 'are committed to each other, but they are not truly happy. Not yet' (84). Kath and Sonje surprise themselves by their 'unexpected and disturbing argument' (84) over this story. What infuriates Kath is the soldier's insistence that they will not be truly happy or achieve a true marriage until March 'gives her life over to him', stops 'struggling against him', surrenders 'her efforts to hang on to her woman's soul, her woman's mind' – in short, 'she must stop thinking and stop wanting and let her consciousness go under, until it is submerged in his' (84). Sonje disagrees with Kath, saying, '"I think it would be beautiful, if a woman could"' and in 'another alarming conversation' has said, '"My happiness depends on Cottar"' (85). Kath is especially incensed by the imagery of reeds submerged and swaying in the water that is used in Lawrence's story 'The Fox' as a simile for how March's 'female nature must live within [the soldier's] male nature' (84).

Kath 'can't stand that part about the reeds and the water, she feels bloated and suffocated with incoherent protest. ... She herself is the very woman that Lawrence is railing about' (85). She can't talk about or think about her real reasons for being so angry 'because it might make Sonje suspect – it might make Kath herself suspect – an impoverishment in Kath's life' (85). Even before Kent has made his first appearance in the story, this imagery of suffocation helps channel readers' expectation that Kath will leave him. Kath wouldn't want it to be true to say that her happiness depends on Kent. But she can't help worrying that she is 'a woman who had missed out on love. Who had not considered, who had not been offered, the prostration of love' (86). The narrator of 'Hard-Luck Stories' in *The Moons of Jupiter* (1982) distinguishes between two kinds of love: '"There's the intelligent sort of love that makes an intelligent choice. That's the kind you're supposed to get married on. Then there's the kind that's anything but intelligent, that's like a possession. And that's the one, that's the one, everybody really values. That's the one nobody wants to have missed out on"' (195). There are risks either way. Sonje, who has chosen the second sort in marrying Cottar ('"I do love him, agonizingly"' – 97) is herself the sensible choice of the man she loves, not very sensibly. In this volume, the choice between sensible love and the love that in the words of 'Hard-Luck Stories' is 'like a possession' (195) appears in different versions in 'Jakarta', 'Cortes Island' and 'The Children Stay'.

Section II opens with a great leap forward in time. Kent and his third wife Deborah are trying to find the house in Oregon to which Sonje and Cottar – or possibly just Sonje alone – had moved at the end of that summer in West Vancouver which Kath and Sonje had spent reading on the beach. Now Kent and Deborah are on the homecoming stretch of a leisurely road trip to visit family and reconnect with Kent's old friends. Having visited Kent's daughter Noelle in Toronto, then his two sons by his second wife Pat in Montreal and Maryland, and Deborah's parents in Santa Barbara, they are heading up the West Coast and home to Vancouver, with Deborah driving and their taking it easy 'so as not to tire Kent out' (86). When they do find the house on the outskirts of town at the end of the road in the sand dunes, there is a sign: PACIFIC SCHOOL OF DANCE with Sonje's name and underneath a FOR SALE sign. The Oregon visit starts with two matched cases of mistaken identity, which serve to emphasise the passage of time and the ravages of age. Kent sees Sonje's blind mother-in-law cutting bushes with shears – but no, it is Sonje herself, her joints stiffened with age, her hair 'white and skimpy' and 'a couple of shining silver-white spots' (87) on her face where skin cancers had likely been removed. 'He had made the usual mistake, of not realizing how many years – decades – had gone by' (87). Making her own mistake, when Sonje sees Deborah with Kent she says, '"And is this Noelle?"' (87). The FOR SALE sign on the dance studio anticipates a pattern of details of life winding down and energy trickling away. Deborah, a physiotherapist who is 'a year younger than Noelle', met Kent 'after his first operation' (88). Sonje and Cottar's mother Delia started the dance school 'around 1960, soon after they heard that Cottar was dead', but when Delia went into a nursing home and then died Sonje 'saw that it was time to give up' since 'perhaps the spirit went out of it' (89). Kent finds the house 'chilly' (88). Having walked through the dance studio, through the kitchen, then 'along a hallway lined with shelves . . . crammed with books and tattered magazines, possibly even newspapers' (89) and onto a side porch, Kent is very grateful at last to be able to sit down.

The sight of books and magazines and evidently old newspapers in Sonje's hallway and 'the whole sense of discomfort, of disregard' (90), made Kent think of the house above the beach where Sonje and Cottar had lived in West Vancouver. Kent had visited that house only once – to go to the ill-fated dinner party with Kath decades earlier. In contrast with the parallel account of Patrick-baiting in 'Mischief' which is focalised by Rose, the version of the party in 'Jakarta' is presented first in section II as Kent remembers it – with himself the designated target of the other guests who saw in him everything they despised about capitalism. In Kent's version, Kath is not mentioned. He focuses entirely on his sense that his identity – everything he is and everything he stands for – had been under attack. From the outset, 'he felt the hostility, the judgment, in the room' (91) aimed at his outfit of shirt and tie, his profession as a pharmacist working for a drugstore chain, his career path '"on the management track"' (92) and his right-wing ideas. One of the guests says, '"I can't believe this guy. Can you believe this guy?"' (92), replicating a similar line in 'Mischief': '"There's this guy in the living room you wouldn't believe him. Listen"' (107). Kent 'didn't know what propelled him' to defend authority, capitalism, drug companies, the US military and the RCMP when '[h]e didn't even take these people seriously' (92). Kent's version is largely self-justifying: he thinks that 'his younger self . . . had been brash maybe, but not wrong' (93). He wonders, however, 'about the anger in that room, all the bruising energy, what had become of it' (93).

The energy that is ebbing in section II is recovered in the next section that begins with the announcement of a second party: 'Cottar and Sonje were having a farewell party, before Cottar went off to the Philippines or Indonesia or wherever he was going, and Sonje went to Oregon to stay with his mother' (94). But the account of the second party is deferred as Kath is reminded of the previous dinner party earlier that year 'when Kent got into the fight with everybody' (95). In this recapitulation of the party scene, Kath's version provides a wider panorama of dramatis personae that includes herself, Kent, Sonje, Cottar and the other dinner guests, each individualised by a brief, sharp portrait – for example, the older, 'low-slung' (91) woman appeared to be 'full of moral repugnance, as if she held

Kent personally responsible for Hiroshima, Asian girls burned to death in locked factories' (95). Pregnant with Noelle, Kath had sat silently as the other dinner guests 'tied Kent up in knots and he didn't even realize it' (95). To her it seemed as if 'Kent was asking for most of this' (95). As Tracy Ware observes, 'Kath is caught between sides, even as her sympathies shift' (Ware, 'Momentous Shifts' 167). Kath sits out the argument, but in her choice of casual clothing she has already signalled her affinity with artists and the counterculture, not with the management track.

Compared with the first party, the farewell party gathers together a much larger cross-section of social types, including Public Library staff who were co-workers with Sonje, the Monicas from the beach, and the counterculture people who had once lived with Sonje and Cottar in a communal house, where sharing was obligatory, including sexual partners. Kath considered 'the idea of those stipulated and obligatory copulations exciting as well as disgusting' (96). At the farewell party, she is intrigued by an older couple from the communal house – the 'low-slung' (91) woman and her ex-clergy husband – and the husband's 'outside mistress' (96), Amy, who has a 'very pale' face, 'almost white' lips and eyelids 'painted a purplish blue right up to her sleek black brows' (99). As the night wears on, the farewell party takes on a Saturnalian quality as the beverage of choice changes from beer to spiked punch and party-goers strip off their clothes to splash in the ocean. When Kath admires Amy's lipstick, Amy says, '"Come along. . . . // . . . We'll do the whole job on you"' (103), and gets out her jars and tubes and pencils to apply liquids, paste, powder and mascara to Kath's cheeks, eyelids, eyebrows, lashes and lips. Thus masked and transformed, Kath is pulled into a sexualised dance with an older, unknown stranger 'around Cottar's age' with 'a spoiled, bruised look around the eyes' (104). In the intoxication of the dance with the demon lover who resembles Cottar, Kath feels dizzy and says, '"I may fall overboard"' (104). She is on the threshold between one life and another when a call from the babysitter breaks the spell, '"Your baby. Your baby's awake. Can you come and feed her?"' (105). Section III ends with Kath's returning to the house to find Kent in an armchair feeding Noelle from a supplemental bottle. She thinks, '[h]e must have seen her dancing. Or else he would have said, "What have you done to your face?"' (107). The choice is clear: domesticity, duty and the sensible choice versus possession, sexual passion and the satisfaction of not having missed out on 'the prostration of love' (86).

Section IV answers the reader's question about why a story set in Vancouver and Oregon would have the exotic title, 'Jakarta'. Of the four individuals that form the two couples, Cottar is the character whose self is least revealed to the reader. The sparse details we are given do little more than establish him as the risky, unreliable, selfish, but glamorous choice of partner. The title establishes his importance, but Cottar remains an absence, a blank screen upon which other characters project their antipathies and desires. From Kent's perspective, Cottar was a key instigator at that first party of the attack on everything that he, Kent, represented. For Kath, Cottar and the other sexually generous members of the commune confirmed her worry that she had married the wrong guy. For Sonje, whose '"happiness depends on Cottar"' (85), he represents a lost happiness that might yet be recovered through a quest that will start '[i]n the streets of Jakarta' (111). Over the second gin and tonic on the side porch, Sonje announces that she has a theory: Cottar *didn't* die thirty years ago of an infectious disease but faked his own death.

During their conversation, Kent and Sonje have each been locked into their own separate thoughts as they brood about the past. Kent has been thinking about Kath. His discourse on 'the astounding, really obscene prices of real estate' (107) in West Vancouver relates to Kath and an old marital rift: whereas Kent, like Patrick in 'Mischief', wanted to trade up to a new, showplace house, Kath preferred what Kent called The Glorified Shack on the beach. Meanwhile Sonje has been thinking about Cottar and her theory that Cottar is alive and possibly living under a '"[f]alse identity he could slip into"' (109). Sonje explains to Kent her imagined scenario of how Cottar might have fabricated his own death: '"False papers. He used to hint about things like that. That was part of the glamour about him, for me"' (109). Sonje's theory involves a conspiracy and a bribed doctor from Jakarta who concocted a false report of Cottar's death and entails the plan to go herself to Jakarta 'to find Cottar, or find the truth' (109). 'Off her rocker', Kent thinks, with the jarring recognition that his whole purpose in visiting Sonje would fail: '[w]ith every visit he had made on this trip, there had come a moment of severe disappointment' when he realised that the person he had travelled to see 'was not going to give him whatever it was he had come for' (110). And what had he come for? Confirmation. Some kind of acknowledgement, perhaps, that he had been underestimated and undervalued. In visiting Sonje, he had 'the silly hope that Sonje might report to Kath how well he was looking ... and how satisfactorily he was married' (114). Kent 'waited for Sonje to speak of Kath again', but '[i]nstead it was all Cottar, and stupidity, and Jakarta' (114).

While Sonje goes into the house to search through drawers to find the papers and maps she had assembled in her research on Jakarta, Kent seizes the opportunity, unobserved by Sonje, to take 'a small pill' for 'his condition' (112). Kent is not as well as he would like others to believe. The narrator reports, 'The pill was just in time. A tide of faintness, unfriendly heat, threatened disintegration, came crawling upwards and broke out in sweat drops on his temples' (112). When Sonje returns, Kent is 'stabilized now, the pill giving him back some reliability of his inner workings, halting what had felt like the runoff of bone marrow' (113). With the late afternoon wind rocking the bushes and the light glinting off the tough shiny leaves, Kent thinks that 'once in a while came a moment when everything seemed to have something to say to you' (115). Kent's long circular journey has been undertaken in the hope of receiving some message, some affirmation. But '[j]ust when you wanted summing up, you got a speedy, goofy view, as from a fun-ride. . . . That somebody dead might be alive and in Jakarta' (115). In contrast, Kent knew that Kath was alive and they could have driven to her 'very door' but 'let the opportunity pass' (115), saying to Deborah, '"Let's not go out of our way. It wouldn't be worth it"' (114). 'Jakarta' of the title represents the dream of recovering something precious from the past that has been lost to both Kent and Sonje. Kent's summary is: '"They got away ... Both of them"' (115). The story ends with Kent stranded between past and present, his energy trickling away.

'Because of the pill his thoughts stretch out long and gauzy and lit up like vapor trails. He travels a thought that has to do with staying here, ... that has to do with not having to go on, to go home' (116).

4. 'Cortes Island': Sources and Transformations

This third story feels very different from the first two stories, but there are some linkages to note. In the discussion that follows, I focus in particular on sources and on how Munro, in returning to material that she used before, has created something entirely new in feeling and in affect. Readers often ask writers: Where do you get your ideas from? In Munro's case the answer often is that she starts with a seed, a memory, a feeling from her own experience and builds a story to house that feeling. In the case of 'Cortes Island', Munro has written a story with a double plot, with one plot line introduced immediately and the other emerging only gradually. The surface plot line uses autobiographical material from Munro's early married life in the 1950s when she first moved to the Kitsilano area of Vancouver with her new husband and tried to write a novel. Some of this material has also been used in 'Jakarta', notably Kath's aversion to the constraints of domesticity as represented by the Monicas, her lack of enthusiasm for a showplace house, her clerical work in the Vancouver Public Library, her passion for reading and her growing awareness of cracks in her marriage. In an interview with Louise France following the publication of *Runaway* (2004), Munro described the restrictive atmosphere she experienced in Canada in the early 1950s – material that she uses with variations in 'Jakarta', 'Cortes Island' and 'The Children Stay'. 'When I was married in my twenties', Munro remarks, 'I hated being regarded as "the little wife." You don't know what it was like then! I'd never even written a cheque. I had to ask my husband for money for groceries' (Munro in France). She explains that '[t]here was no interest in reading. It was almost considered disloyal to the idea of being a good housewife' (Munro in France). As for her own writing, Munro reports that while she continued to dream of producing a great novel, '[i]t would always go flat on me' (Munro in France).

The narrator of 'Cortes Island' shares with Alice Munro the split between her ambition to be a writer and her need to hide her secret life of the imagination by appearing ordinary. As the narrator put it near the end of the story after she got a real job in the Kitsilano Library, '[n]ot weird. I could pass' (141). The tension between being a not-weird person living an ordinary life versus having the special powers of the artist goes back a long way for Munro. In an unpublished 1984 interview with Thomas E. Tausky, Munro described a 'very *Wuthering Heights*y' first novel that, in her teens, she had all planned out, with the 'deathbed scenes' written. The eponymous heroine Charlotte Muir, who is reputed to be 'weird and witchlike', sets her sights on a freckle-faced farm boy who is 'not a romantic hero' at all 'and decides to make him fall in love with her. They become engaged, and this is her way of redeeming herself and getting herself into ordinary life.' But then along comes 'the dark, powerful, Puritanical, sexually attractive preacher' who breaks up the engagement to the freckle-faced boy. After putting an angry 'curse on the preacher, because she really has powers', Charlotte realises she loves the preacher, takes the curse upon herself and dies, leaving the preacher to realise 'he's in love with her after she's dead. It's *Wuthering Heights* then – it's united in death.' Munro told Tausky that in retrospect she realised why this material had attracted her: 'I can see that these were the twin choices of my life, which were marriage and motherhood or the black life of the artist. I was aware of that and I was working with it fictionally before I had any idea of it' (Munro in Ross, *Alice Munro* 17–18).

The second plot line was adapted from a historical account of adultery and murder that Munro came across in a local history book, *Evergreen Islands* (1979) by Doris Andersen. In an article about Alice Munro's source for the title story of her Giller Prize-winning *The Love of a Good Woman*, Robert Fulford provides details, based on what Munro herself said about her local history source in *Prize Writing* (2003), a collection of essays written by past Giller winners and distributed at the tenth-anniversary Giller Prize dinner. Here it is: long ago, on Cortes Island at the north end of the Strait of Georgia, there lived an adulterous wife, her fisherman husband and her lover. When the husband was away in his boat, the wife would signal to the lover by hanging a white cloth on her clothes line. One day the husband came home unexpectedly, found the two together and killed the lover, following which the wife helped her husband conceal the murder. Fulford summarises, '[w]hile he put the body into the lover's own boat, towed it out into the Strait, and left it to drift, she cleaned up the evidence. Their lives returned to normal, until a visitor, who turned out to be a detective, wormed the truth out of her' (Fulford). Well, not quite.

When I tracked down *Evergreen Islands* in Western's academic library, I discovered that Munro had already modified the historical story somewhat, even while describing what she had said was her source material. According to the ur-source in Andersen's local history, in October 1894 a skiff carrying a dead body was found adrift in Sutil Channel between Cortes Island and Read Island and was towed ashore, where the body was identified as belonging to a local farmer and logger. A neighbour, one John Smith, suggested that the dead man might have had a heart attack and fallen against the side of his boat, the fall accounting for the injuries to his face. But the coroner in Vancouver who performed the autopsy reported that the dead man had been hit repeatedly on the head and cheek with a blunt instrument. The details wormed out of Mrs Smith by the undercover detective included the cloth on the clothes line, the husband's unexpectedly early return home from a hunting trip, the enraged husband's assault on the lover with a wooden mallet and the cooperative work of Mr and Mrs Smith together carrying the body to the skiff and scrubbing blood from the floor. At John Smith's trial for murder in Vancouver, planking from the bedroom floor, scrubbed but still bloodstained, was produced in evidence. The jury, Andersen reports, found him not guilty, despite the testimony from the Smith children that they had heard 'sounds of blows and groans from the bedroom' (Andersen 105). But an interesting detail: Andersen's chapter 'Cortes Island' does not contain this account; it appears in the chapter 'Read Island'. The murder actually happened on nearby Read Island, a name and a title that would have been just too much, given the emphasis in this story on reading and writing.

This piece of local history, transformed in two very different ways, became a source for both 'The Love of a Good Woman' and 'Cortes Island'. In her section of 'Contributors' Notes' for the 1997 volume of The O. Henry Awards stories, Munro discusses the origins of the title story:

> What did I know first about this story? A man and woman disposing of her lover's body . . . off the B.C. coast – they put him in his own boat and towed him out into open water . . . The sudden switch from sex to murder to marital cooperation seemed to me one of those marvelous, unlikely, acrobatic pieces of human behavior. Then the lover got transferred into a car, and it all went on in Huron County . . . And there is the boat, still, waiting by the bank of the river. (Munro, 'Contributors' Notes' 443)

In the second story, the murder victim gets changed from lover to husband. Read Island gets changed to Cortes Island, a name with the exoticism of its association with adventurer Hernán Cortés, after whom the island was named. And the boat waiting on a shore is also there at the end of 'Cortes Island', conveying its own sense of power and mystery.

'Cortes Island' brings together these two plot lines – the choice between what Munro described to Tausky as 'marriage and motherhood or the black life of the artist' (Munro in Ross, *Alice Munro* 18) and the story of adultery and murder – and locates them in the downstairs/upstairs geography of the house on Arbutus Street. In comparison with the first two stories in this collection, 'Cortes Island' initially appears less elaborately structured. In eleven untitled sections of varying lengths, the first-person narrator looks back several decades to tell a story, in more or less chronological order, about her early married life to Chess during the year when they occupied the basement apartment below the Gorries. In the final section, which functions as an epilogue, the narrator reveals the continuing impact of Mr Gorrie on her life for many years thereafter, as he became an erotic presence in her dream life. Complexity in this story comes not from multiple subjects of focalisation or from dazzling time shifts but through the patterning of three interlocking triangles of characters. Mrs Gorrie and Mr Gorrie turn out to provide the points of articulation that connect the two plot lines and give the hidden plot its resonance. The first six sections develop the triangle formed by the narrator and her relationship with Mrs Gorrie and Mr Gorrie. Towards the end of section 6, the triangle of the adulterous wife, the lover and the murdered husband emerges when Mr Gorrie gets the narrator to read two newspaper accounts pasted into his scrapbook from 1923. The epilogue concludes with the triangle of Chess (who bears some resemblance to the freckle-faced farm boy in the Charlotte Muir story), Mr Gorrie (who has taken on some qualities of 'the dark, powerful, Puritanical, sexually attractive preacher') and the narrator.

The opening paragraph of 'Cortes Island' introduces the narrator, who resembles the young Alice Munro herself:

> Little bride. I was twenty years old, five feet seven inches tall, weighing between a hundred and thirty-five and a hundred and forty pounds, but some people – Chess's boss's wife, and the older secretary in his office, and Mrs Gorrie upstairs, referred to me as a little bride. Our little bride, sometimes. Chess and I made a joke of it, but his public reaction was a look fond and cherishing. Mine was a pouty smile – bashful, acquiescent. (117)

'Little bride' (117). The oddity of the first-person narrator's starting immediately by revealing her body mass index score shows just how indignant she is about the diminutive, despite the paragraph's ending with the misleadingly meek words 'bashful, acquiescent' (117). A lot is packed into this paragraph. There's the contrast between private feelings and 'public reaction' and, within the latter category, a further differentiation between Chess's proprietary 'cherishing' and the narrator's apparently submissive 'pouty smile' (117). Through the reference to 'Mrs Gorrie upstairs' (117), the opening paragraph also introduces the two contrasting spaces of upstairs and downstairs and the two female characters whose relationship starts badly and gets worse. From Mrs Gorrie's first appearance, with her pink eyebrows, her 'thin, rouged, vivacious' face and 'her teeth large and glistening' (119) and 'wolfish smile' (120), she is presented as a grotesque and she becomes increasingly monstrous as the story develops. No mention yet of Mr Gorrie.

Just as 'Jakarta' swallows up 'Mischief', the first-encountered plot in 'Cortes Island' is a variant of 'The Office' from *Dance of the Happy Shades* (1968). In both cases, the narrator recalls a significant event from her past when, as a young married woman, she was driven out of her rented office / rented apartment by the relentless intrusions of a landlord / quasi-landlady. In both cases, publicly identifying herself as a writer leaves the narrator feeling exposed and vulnerable. In 'The Office' the narrator says, 'here comes the disclosure which is not easy for me: I am a writer' (59). In 'Cortes Island' the narrator considers her writing to be 'secret', although known to Chess: '[n]ot entirely secret, either. Chess knew that I read a lot and that I was trying to write' (124), although his 'generous faith ... just added to the farce of my disasters' (125). In both stories, the narrator's desperate need to carve out her own time for writing is frustrated by the emotional blackmail of unwanted offerings of conversation and gifts associated with domesticity. These offerings variously include an extra chair, a potted plant, a flowery teapot, a wastebasket and a cushion from the landlord Mr Malley in 'The Office' and sawdust-flavoured cookies, gluey raisin tarts and unsolicited advice from Mrs Gorrie.

Unable to fend off cravings for intimacy that take 'no account of resistance' (119), both narrators choose to hide from their tormentors and try to conceal their writing, a strategy of evasion that elicits accusations of craziness and immorality. In 'The Office', Mr Malley says, '"That's not a normal way for a person to behave"' (70) and later connects '"literature"' with '"Obscenity laws"' (72), implying that writers are responsible for the corruption of youth. In 'Cortes Island', Mrs Gorrie, who has been letting herself into the downstairs apartment to snoop and to read the narrator's writing, says, '"She's a sneak ... And a liar. She isn't right in the head. She'd sit down there and say she's writing letters and she writes the same thing over and over again – it's not letters, it's the same thing over and over"' (142). In the end, the rented space does not provide the hoped-for 'solution to [the narrator's] life' (59) or even 'a room of her own' (Woolf, *A Room of One's Own* 2). Both narrators are driven out, but each gets away with a good story to tell. As Munro has reported in her brief essay 'On Writing "The Office"', that story was the only thing she managed to write in the office. Ailsa Cox notes that 'The Office' is the first of many of Alice Munro's stories to use the figure of the writer to investigate the process of transmuting everyday experience into the narrative patterns of fiction (Cox, '"Bizarre but Somehow Never Quite Satisfactory"' 135).

In short, the plot line signalled by the 'Little bride' (117) explores the narrator's uneasy adjustment to her new status as wife and draws on experiences very similar to Munro's own. Like Kath in 'Jakarta' and Pauline in 'The Children Stay', the newly married narrator is beginning to feel weighted down by the shackles of domesticity. The narrator of 'Cortes Island' recalls proleptically, 'I met women with baby carriages and complaining toddlers and never thought that so soon I'd be in the same shoes' (127). Marriage break-up is certainly implied near the story's end when the narrator condenses married life with Chess into a series of moves from the basement apartment to a better apartment to the first house they owned together in Vancouver to the second house in a different city, Victoria, '[u]ntil the last and by far the grandest house, which I entered with inklings of disaster and the faintest premonitions of escape' (142).

Like Munro herself, the narrator of 'Cortes Island' is an avid reader who 'had to be a writer as well as a reader' (124). Behind the green curtain that was always kept closed across the foot of the bed – an image, my co-author Tim Struthers reminds me, that evokes the title story of *A Curtain of Green* (1941), the first book by one of Munro's favourite writers, Eudora Welty (Struthers, Message to Catherine Sheldrick Ross) – was the site of two voluptuous pleasures: married sex and voracious reading. The narrator describes 'that churned-up state of astonishment that a book could bring me to, a giddiness of gulped riches' (124). Metaphors of reading as eating and reading as surrender capture the intensity of the joyous, indiscriminate reading of childhood: 'I bolted them down one after the other without establishing any preferences, surrendering to each in turn just as I'd done to the books I read in my childhood. I was still in that stage of leaping appetite, of voracity close to anguish' (124). But reading isn't enough. The narrator had, as Munro describes herself as having, 'a kind of monomania about being a writer' (Munro in Rasporich 3). The euphoria of the initial writing was followed by anguish:

> I bought a school notebook and tried to write – did write, pages that started off authoritatively and then went dry, so that I had to tear them out and twist them up in hard punishment and put them in the garbage can. I did this over and over again until I had only the notebook cover left. Then I bought another notebook and started the whole process once more. The same cycle – excitement and despair, excitement and despair. It was like having a secret pregnancy and miscarriage every week. (124)

The narrator of 'Cortes Island,' like many others in this volume, looks back at least several decades to tell a story that has consequences into the present. She begins her retrospective account soon after she and her new husband Chess have moved into the small basement apartment owned by Mrs Gorrie's son Ray. Unlike Chess and Ray, the narrator is by temperament unable to say no to Mrs Gorrie's appeals for company and friendship. Section 1 develops the narrator's sense of being weighted down by Mrs Gorrie's imposition of indigestible home baking and unwanted tips on housekeeping routines, china cabinet maintenance, proper hostess behaviour – 'never serve coffee in mugs' (121) – and obligatory sorting of whites from coloured laundry. The narrator says that the more Mrs Gorrie talked about 'the house and the future she assumed I would have, . . . the more I felt an iron weight on my limbs' (120). She envies the way Mrs Gorrie's son Ray is able to resist 'her wheedling and disappointment' with a flat no: '[h]e didn't even say, "No, Mother." Just no' (118).

Gradually we realise that 'Cortes Island' has a second, emergent plot line, which provides the title. This hidden story is hinted at, little by little, through small details that don't initially seem of importance. The first such clue is Ray's implacable rejection of his mother with a 'Just no' (118). As we discover, he has good reason. The second reference to this buried story comes couched as one of Mrs Gorrie's unwanted domestic tips, when she says, '"Even when I lived away off in the wilds, I always liked to –"' (121). Where and when was this? wonders the narrator. '"Oh, away up the coast," she said. "I was a bride, too, once upon a time. I lived up there for years. Union Bay. But that wasn't too wild. Cortes Island"' (121). This exchange is given prominence both by this first indication of the source of Munro's title and by the implication that a story is involved: 'once upon a time' (121) on Cortes Island, there was another 'Little bride' (117). The narrator and Mrs Gorrie are doubles as well as opposites.

In section 6, the hidden story of what happened on Cortes Island is revealed through the device of the inset story, in this case provided by two clipped-out articles from a newspaper. While waiting for job opportunities to open up at the public library, the narrator accepts a part-time job of 'sitting with Mr Gorrie in the afternoons' (130). He has had a stroke and is referred to by his wife as '"my husband in the wheelchair"' (121), although he spends most of his time in the bright-green recliner in the living room upstairs. Because of his stroke, the sounds that Mr Gorrie makes emerge as 'grunts, snorts, hawk-ings, barks, mumbles' (133). However, like narrators in several other Munro stories who are able to understand the speech of the mother with Parkinson's disease, this narrator translates garbled sounds into meaningful sentences. As Mr Gorrie gestures towards a pile of scrapbooks labelled by year, the narrator hears: '[l]ook at this one. 1923' (134). A newspaper clipping from the *Vancouver Sun* on 17 April 1923 reports a fire: 'CORTES ISLAND. Early Sunday morning or sometime late Saturday night the home of Anson James Wild at the south end of the island was totally destroyed by fire' (134). The newspaper account includes the following elements: the burnt body of Mr Wild found in the charred ruins along with a blackened tin can thought to have contained kerosene; the wife Mrs Wild, who left home by boat on Wednesday, returned on a friend's boat on Sunday morning, and, together with the friend, discovered the body; and the Wild's young son, who was found Sunday night in the woods less than a mile from the destroyed house, cold but unharmed, with some pieces of bread with him.

A second *Vancouver Sun* clipping dated 4 August 1923 reported that the inquest into the fire that caused Mr Wild's death considered the presence of an empty kerosene can inconclusive and 'found that suspicion of arson by the deceased man or by person or persons unknown cannot be substantiated' (136). It was reported as new information that the seven-year-old son initially 'said that his father had given him some bread and apples and told him to walk to

Manson's Landing but that he lost his way' (136), yet later he denied remembering anything. An important new detail was the identification of 'the friend' (135) who owned the boat: 'Mrs Wild was not at home at the time of the fire having gone to Vancouver Island on a boat belonging to James Thompson Gorrie of Union Bay' (136). The conclusion at the inquest: '[t]he death of Mr Wild was ruled to be an accident due to misadventure, its cause being a fire of origins unknown' (136). The supplementary information helps make sense of details from the initial account that don't add up: the house burns down in the middle of the night killing Mr Wild, but his seven-year-old son is safely away and provisioned with food.

In adapting the local history source to the requirements of her story, Munro has used fire rather than water as the means to hide the crime and she has switched the identity of the dead man from lover to husband, leaving Mrs Wild free to marry her lover and change her name. This name change delays the reader's identification of Mrs Gorrie, doyenne of conservative manners, with the wilder Mrs Wild of Cortes Island. One detail from the original local history story – the adulterous wife's signalling her lover with a white cloth on the clothes line – is retained, slyly transformed in Munro's story into the whites that Mrs Gorrie advises must be separated from the coloureds as '"the way you take care of your man"' (129). In the last sentence in section 6, the narrator interprets Mr Gorrie's last barks and mumbles as a wry comment on the whirligigs of time: '[d]*id you ever think that people's lives could be like that and end up like this? Well, they can*' (137; emphasis in orig.).

The revelation provided by the newspaper clippings is the final step in the shifting of the power balance in the triangle formed by Mrs Gorrie, Mr Gorrie and the narrator. The threat posed by Mrs Gorrie in sections 1–5 fades when the narrator starts 'working at a real job' (137) on the permanent staff of the library. For the time being, she feels satisfaction at passing as a non-weird person living an ordinary life, engaging professionally with reading 'addicts' from 'the other side of the desk' (137). 'What a simple pleasure' to be seen by library users as a competent professional 'who knew the ropes, who had a clear function in the world. To give up my lurking and wandering and dreaming' (138). In the first flush of satisfaction with her new role, the narrator recalls: '[a]t such times my immediate past could seem vaguely disgraceful. Hours behind the alcove curtain, hours at the kitchen table filling page after page with failure . . . And it seemed to be a part of myself – a sickly part – that was now going into the discard' (140). But not without misgivings, because what is at issue here is the narrator's abdication of herself as a person with powers:

> I had less time for reading now, and sometimes I would hold a book in my hand for a moment, in my work at the desk – I would hold a book in my hand as an object, not as a vessel I had to drain immediately – and I would have a flick of fear, as in a dream when you find yourself in the wrong building or have forgotten the time for the exam and understand that this is only the tip of some shadowy cataclysm or lifelong mistake. (138)

The terms associated with the narrator's turning away from reading and from writing – initial satisfaction and then 'a flick of fear, as in a dream', 'the tip of some shadowy cataclysm or lifelong mistake' (138) – anticipate, and are connected to, the description a few pages later of the narrator's misgivings about her moves with Chess to successively grander houses.

By the second half of the story (sections 6–11), Mr Gorrie has moved out of the shadows and taken centre stage. In section 1, the narrator had reported that '[a]ll I could usually see of Mr Gorrie was a trouser leg stretched out on the bright-green recliner' (122). At first, she avoids looking at his face, especially his eyes, because for her people 'crippled by strokes or disease were bad omens' (122). But by section 6, when she has the job reading to Mr Gorrie in the afternoons, she has 'got used to him' and then begins to see him in legendary terms, built 'on a grand scale, with his big noble head and wide laboring chest and his powerless right hand' (131): '[l]ike a relic, he was, an old warrior from barbarous times. Eric Blood-Axe. King Knut' (132). The narrator is reminded of the opening lines from Scottish poet Charles Mackay's 'The Sea-King's Burial': '*My strength is failing fast, said the sea king to his men. / I shall never sail the seas, like a conqueror again*' (132; emphasis in orig.). In Mackay's poem, the sea-king commands his warriors to put his 'crown upon [his] head' and his 'good sword in [his] hand' and take him to the strand where his ship lies at anchor. The sea-king in this poem is Baldur, the beloved son of Odin and the goddess Frigg, who was treacherously killed and then buried at sea, set adrift in his own burning boat. In Norse burial practices, boats were used ceremoniously because they offer safe passage to the underworld. The paragraph by Munro that follows the quoted lines from Mackay's poem begins, '[t]hat was what he was like', and goes on to describe Mr Gorrie in terms of failing, but still powerful, masculinity: 'half-wrecked hulk of a body', 'lordly excretions and animal heat', 'expression of ancient privilege', 'some mangy, still powerful beast' (132).

How to end the story? Munro's editors have described how carefully Munro works at her endings, writing them and revising them over and over until she gets them right. 'The Office' ended when the narrator moved out of the rented space and the story's arc from hopeful entry to passage through a series of setbacks to chastened exit was concluded. Had Munro repeated the pattern used in 'The Office', she could have stopped part way through section 9, which opens with the statement that 'Chess had heard of another apartment' (141), then concludes with the sentence '[u]ntil the last and by far the grandest house, which I entered with inklings of disaster and the faintest premonitions of escape' (142). In her influential work on narrative closure, Susan Lohafer introduced the term 'preclosure points' (Lohafer 132) to indicate places within stories where they could have ended before the actual ending. The concept of preclosure focuses attention on the difference it makes that the author *didn't* stop at an earlier point. Lohafer notes that stopping at preclosure points can retrieve 'putative stories' (Lohafer 132) contained in the text as it proceeds towards actual closure. That's because the ending determines in large part the reader's assessment of what type of story it is – whether a happily-ever-after story, ironic tale of failed hopes, reality-check tale, turn-in-the road story, recognition story, *künstlerroman*, or open-ended mystery. So in this case, what difference does it make that Munro *didn't* stop earlier but capped off her story with an eleventh section?

The six paragraphs of the concluding section gather together in quick succession key motifs and images from both of the double plots. First there is the reprise of the basement apartment and its connection to the 'Little bride' (117) plot: looking back retrospectively, the narrator does 'remember a few things – the alcove curtain, the china cabinet, Mr Gorrie's green recliner – so well' (144). The story of their 'crazy landlady' (144) became something amusing for the narrator and Chess to tell to other young couples, she reports, but adds, '[o]therwise, I didn't think of Mrs Gorrie' (144). What remains and stays with her for years is Mr Gorrie, who dominates the second, hidden plot. He 'showed up in [her] dreams' as an 'agile and strong' (144), though not young, lover. For years, the 'faithful, regularly satisfied' narrator has recurrent erotic dreams 'in which the attack, the response, the possibilities, went beyond anything life offered. And from which romance was banished. . . . There was a relish of what you might call ugliness' (145). Their bed 'was the gravelly beach or the rough boat deck or the punishing coils of greasy rope' (145). Sexual relish is intensified by a prickle of disgust, signalled by the reference to '[h]is pungent smell, his jelly eye, his dog's teeth' (145). Conflating different levels of reality, this final section introduces a new triangle: the husband Chess who is the partner in her daytime life sharing the quotidian experiences of young starting-out couples of the period; the dreaming narrator; and a dream version of Mr Gorrie who has taken on the legendary qualities of a Norse sea-king.

The ending of 'Cortes Island' resembles that of 'The Love of a Good Woman' in its density and suggestiveness. For readers aware of the source story from *Evergreen Islands* and the two stories derived from it, reading 'Cortes Island' involves observing some remarkable shape-shifting. The adulterous wife with the laundry line in the local history account becomes Mrs Quinn in the title story and also Mrs Gorrie. Even more notable are the transformations and exchanges involved in the evolution of the husband/lover figure in Munro's two stories. The murdering husband who towed the skiff behind his own boat and set it adrift becomes both Rupert with his rowboat on the Peregrine River and also Mr Gorrie, the Norse sea-king. And in a further conflation, the fallen beams and charred remains of the burned house on Cortes Island merge with the burning-and-set-adrift ship burial of the sea-king.

But then, unexpectedly, the narrator says: '[f]or years and years . . . Mr Gorrie operated in my nightlife this way. Until I used him up' (145). How did she use him up? His night-time use was to make it possible for the narrator to stay married for many years to Chess, the prudent choice of husband – until she escaped that showplace house and, in my reading of the story, embraced 'the black life of the artist' (Munro in Ross, *Alice Munro* 18). In Munro narratives, dreams quite often are gateways to an alternate life that runs alongside the everyday life and that represents another outcome in life, what else might have happened that didn't. Here the narrator's 'pagan dreams' (145) of voluptuous sex with Mr Gorrie keep alive the dream-possibility of the risky choice – the dark, powerful, sexually attractive lover associated with legend.

In the narrator's dream (which paradoxically is said to seem beyond anything imaginable), she is back with Mr Gorrie on Cortes Island. Mrs Gorrie is absent from the dream and the narrator has taken her place. Another boat lies waiting in another lushly described setting: '[a]nd the boat and the dock and the gravel on the shore, the trees sky-pointed or crouching, leaning out over the water, the complicated profile of surrounding islands and dim yet distinct mountains, seemed to exist in a natural confusion, more extravagant and yet more ordinary than anything I could dream or invent' (145). The heightened intensity of this description is achieved through a series of oppositions and irreconcilable contrasts: trees 'sky-pointed or crouching', mountains 'dim yet distinct', scenery 'more extravagant and yet more ordinary' (145). We are being prepared for the final contradiction, for the irreducible part of the story – the charred remains hidden under new forest growth – that the narrator leaves out of her dream but makes a crucial part of the story she tells us. The final turn is signalled by the word 'But' (145). 'But I never saw the charred beams of the house fallen down on the body of the husband. That had happened a long time before and the forest had grown up all around it' (145). These final sentences represent another elusive Munro ending, which keeps drawing readers back into the story, mulling over implications.

5. What Ordinary Readers Say about Reading *The Love of a Good Woman*

I have been making claims about 'the reader' – for example, how certain textual features are designed to shape a reader's response but also how responses are shaped by readers themselves who pay attention to textual features that resonate most powerfully with their own lives and reading histories. But how, we might ask, do ordinary readers actually read and experience the stories in *The Love of a Good Woman*? To get some empiric data about the experience of common readers who read Munro for pleasure, I have turned to accounts provided in postings for three weeks in December 1999 by participants in an online reading group (ConstantReader.com: the website for discerning readers) in which twelve people, ten women and two men, discussed the stories in *The Love of a Good Woman* over 110 posts.

The reading group participants engaged in a give-and-take exchange as they worked together to solve puzzles and fill in gaps, starting with Steve's reference in post #3 to the first question of why the three boys 'took so long to tell anyone about their discovery of the automobile with corpse in the river' and 'kept their mouths shut like that'. Canvassing the reading group, Steve introduced the story's overarching puzzle: '[n]o question in my mind that Enid and old Rupert lived happily ever after though . . . Does anybody believe that Rupert dumped her in the river?' Not Jane (post #7), who said, 'I am convinced that Enid talked herself out of confronting Rupert with the murder of Dr Willens.' As evidence, Jane pointed to the passage in the final subsection in 'IV. Lies': '[t]hrough her silence, her collaboration in a silence, what benefits could bloom. For others, and for herself' (76). Bolstering her interpretation, Jane went back to that red box: '[i]n fact, on the first page, "Also there is a red box . . ." I think Enid found the box when she was later straightening out Rupert's life and sent it to the museum.'

Unlike Jane, Tonya described herself as becoming less, rather than more, certain of her interpretations as she reread and reflected on the story. She tracked her growing uncertainty: '[a]s I read it, I believed the murder and believed Enid wanted to disbelieve the murder ... After I finished, and looked back over the story, a few doubts started sprouting in my mind' (post #20). Anne (post #22) responded, 'Munro definitely suggests it is possible the murder never occurred ... but I never doubted it. I don't think the dying woman has the imagination or the motivation to invent it from scratch.' Barbara (post #35) saw Enid as 'the stereotypical "good woman"' whose life gets turned around: 'I enjoy watching people whose lives have been plotted between bright lines, who assume all situations have simple solutions, learning that it may be more complex than all that.' By the time these readers finished their online discussion of 'The Love of a Good Woman', they had collaboratively achieved a reading of the story that took account of elements that emerged for them as keys to the meaning of the story: the red box; the three boys who keep their mouths shut; the truth status of Mrs Quinn's account of the murder; Enid's character and the choices she makes; and the benefits of expedient silence.

While puzzling over their interpretations of the eight stories in *The Love of a Good Woman*, these book club readers simultaneously reflected on their experience of reading Munro and on what was required of them as readers. Ruth (post #44) highlighted 'Munro's propensity for twitching us about in a direction we never figured the story was heading. In "The Love of a Good Woman," it turns out the story isn't about the boys at all. . . . we're twitched this way and that. Just as we think, aha, this is what this story is about, Munro forces us into what seems like a detour.' Book club readers commented in particular on the way that Munro leaves strategic gaps. Steve (post #81) speculated, 'I think Alice Munro writes out these stories at first, telling everything completely. Then she goes back and lops out big chunks of those same stories to make them this ambiguous and mysterious.' Theresa (post #86) didn't 'buy the theory that Munro chops off parts of her stories', instead arguing that '[t]here is always plenty of information there – she is just subtle – you must draw your own conclusions, just like real life'.

Whatever the writing process, readers agreed that the stories lingered in the mind when they were not reading them. Ruth (post #31) commented that in Munro's two latest books, *Open Secrets* (1994) and *The Love of a Good Woman* (1998), she seems to have 'gotten more and more inscrutable, never tying anything up in a neat little package. It leaves one pondering and mulling over her stories.' In sum, a residue of uneasiness or unresolved tension or mystery draws readers back into rereading the stories and, when we do, key scenes or phrases or details often reveal significances not noticed on first reading, thereby intensifying these works' gathering sense of mystery.

Works Consulted

1 Corinthians. *The Holy Bible*. Cambridge: Cambridge UP, n.d. Authorised King James Vers.
'Alice Liddell as "The Beggar Maid"'. The Metropolitan Museum of Art, New York. <https://www.metmuseum.org/art/collection/search/283092>.
Andersen, Doris. *Evergreen Islands: The Islands of the Inside Passage: Quadra to Malcolm*. Sidney, BC: Gray's Publishing, 1979.
Anderson, Linda. *Autobiography*. 2nd ed. Abingdon: Routledge, 2011. The New Critical Idiom.
Apel, Thomas. 'Baldur'. *Mythopedia*. <https://mythopedia.com/topics/baldur>.
Arbus, Diane. *A Family On Their Lawn One Sunday in Westchester, New York*. The Art Institute of Chicago. <https://www.artic.edu/artworks/67961/a-family-on-their-lawn-one-sunday-in-westchester-new-york>.
Aristophanes. *The Complete Plays*. Trans. Paul Roche. New York: New American Library, 2005.
Armatrading, Joan. 'Show Some Emotion'. *Show Some Emotion*. A&M, 1977.
Atwood, Margaret. 'Death by Landscape'. *Saturday Night* July 1989: 46, 48–53. Rpt. in *Wilderness Tips*. 1991. London: Virago, 1992. 107–29.
—. '*Lives of Girls and Women*: A Portrait of the Artist as a Young Woman'. *The Cambridge Companion to Alice Munro*. Ed. David Staines. Cambridge: Cambridge UP, 2016. 96–115.
Austen, Jane. *Persuasion*. 1818. Ed. James Kinsley. Introd. Deidre Shauna Lynch. Oxford: Oxford UP, 2004.
—. *Pride and Prejudice*. 1813. Ed. James Kinsley. Introd. Christina Lupton. Oxford: Oxford UP, 2019.
Bakhtin, Mikhail. 'The Banquet, the Body and the Underworld'. Introd. Pam Morris. Trans. Hélène Iswolsky. *The Bakhtin Reader: Selected Writings of Bakhtin, Medvedev and Voloshinov*. Ed. Pam Morris. London: Edward Arnold, 1994. 226–44.
—. 'Epic and Novel: Toward a Methodology for the Study of the Novel'. *The Dialogic Imagination: Four Essays*. Ed. Michael Holquist. Trans. Caryl Emerson and Michael Holquist. Austin: U of Texas P, 1982. 3–40.
Baldeshwiler, Eileen. 'The Lyric Short Story: The Sketch of a History'. *Studies in Short Fiction* 6 (1969): 443–53. Rpt. in *The New Short Story Theories*. Ed. Charles E. May. Athens, OH: Ohio UP, 1994. 231–41.
Banerjee, Sidhartha. 'Class Action Filed Against Montreal's Grey Nuns Over Alleged Abuse at Orphanage'. *CTV News* 7 July 2020. <https://montreal.

ctvnews.ca/class-action-filed-against-montreal-s-grey-nuns-over-alleged-abuse-at-orphanage-1.5014306>.

Bentley, Lucile. '"A body in which nothing was real": Taxidermy and Fiction in "Vandals" by Alice Munro'. La question animale dans les nouvelles d'Alice Munro / The Animal Question in Alice Munro's Stories. Ed. Héliane Ventura. *Caliban: French Journal of English Studies* 57 (2017): 47–56. <https://journals.openedition.org/caliban/2673>.

—. 'Extra-ordinary Bodies in Alice Munro's *Dance of the Happy Shades*'. *Caliban: French Journal of English Studies* 53 (2015): 185–94. <https://journals.openedition.org/caliban/1038>.

Beran, Carol L. 'The Luxury of Excellence: Alice Munro in the *New Yorker*'. *Alice Munro Writing On . . .* Ed. Robert Thacker. *Essays on Canadian Writing* 66 (1998): 204–31. Rpt. in *The Rest of the Story: Critical Essays on Alice Munro*. Ed. Robert Thacker. Toronto: ECW, 1999. 204–31.

—. 'The Pursuit of Happiness: A Study of Alice Munro's Fiction'. *The Social Science Journal* 37 (2000): 329–45.

Bergman, Ingmar, dir. *Through a Glass Darkly*. Perf. Harriet Andersson, Gunnar Björnstrand, Max von Sydow, Lars Passgård. Janus Films, 1962.

Bergson, Henri. *Laughter: An Essay on the Meaning of the Comic*. Trans. Cloudesley Brereton and Fred Rothwell. New York: Macmillan, 1911.

Bigot, Corinne. 'Alice Munro's "A Wilderness Station" and Anne Wheeler's *Edge of Madness*: Filling in the Blanks'. *Adaptation of Stories and Stories of Adaptation: Media, Modes and Codes*. Ed. Sabrina Francesconi and Gerardo Acerenza. Trento: Università degli Studi di Trento, 2020. 37–55.

—. 'Ghost Texts in Alice Munro's Stories'. *Short Fiction in Theory & Practice* 7 (2017): 141–52.

—. '"Locking the Door": Self-deception, Silence and Survival in Alice Munro's "Vandals"'. *Trauma Narratives and Herstory*. Ed. Sonya Andermahr and Silvia Pellicer-Ortin. New York: Palgrave Macmillan, 2013. 113–26.

Blaise, Clark. 'The Justice-Dealing Machine'. *Selected Essays*. By Clark Blaise. Ed. John Metcalf and J.R. (Tim) Struthers. Windsor, ON: Biblioasis, 2008. 191–6.

Blake, William. '33. To Thomas Butts'. 6 July 1803. *Letters*. Ed. Geoffrey Keynes. 2nd ed. London: Hart-Davis, 1968. 68–71.

—. *The Marriage of Heaven and Hell*. *The Complete Poetry and Prose of William Blake*. Ed. David V. Erdman. Commentary by Harold Bloom. Rev. ed. Garden City, NY: Anchor, 1982. 33–44.

Blanchard, Gérard. *La lettre*. Paris: Éditions du gymnase topographique, 1975.

Blodgett, E.D. *Alice Munro*. Boston: Twayne, 1988. Twayne's World Authors Ser. 800.

Bloom, Harold. 'Criticism, Canon-Formation, and Prophecy: The Sorrows of Facticity'. *Poetics of Influence: New and Selected Criticism*. Ed. and introd. John Hollander. New Haven, CT: Henry R. Schwab, 1988. 405–24.

—. *Hamlet: Poem Unlimited*. New York: Riverside, 2003.

The Book of Job. *The Holy Bible*. Cambridge: Cambridge UP, n.d. Authorised King James Vers.

The Book of Kells: Reproductions from the Manuscript in Trinity College Dublin. With a Study of the Manuscript by Françoise Henry. London: Thames & Hudson, 1974.

Botting, Fred. *Gothic*. 2nd ed. London: Routledge, 2013. The New Critical Idiom.

Boyce, Pleuke, and Ron Smith. 'A National Treasure: An Interview with Alice Munro'. *Meanjin* 54 (1995): 222–32.

Boyle, Harry. 'Alice Munro Challenges Censorship'. 1979. Item 28. of '90 Things To Know about Master Short Story Writer Alice Munro'. *CBC Books* 28 April 2017. <https://www.cbc.ca/books/90-things-to-know-about-master-short-story-writer-alice-munro-1.4088507>.

Brontë, Charlotte, Emily and Anne [*published as* Currer, Ellis and Acton Bell]. *Poems*. 1847. n.p.: Astounding Stories, 2015.

Brontë, Emily. *Wuthering Heights: The 1847 Text; Backgrounds and Context; Criticism*. 5th ed. Ed. Alexandra Lewis. New York: W.W. Norton, 2019. A Norton Critical Edition.

Brooks, Peter. *Seduced by Story: The Use and Abuse of Narrative*. New York: New York Review Books, 2022.

Butt, William. 'Killer OSPs and Style Munro in "Open Secrets"'. *Alice Munro Country: Essays on Her Works I*. Ed. J.R. (Tim) Struthers. Toronto: Guernica Editions, 2020. 255–62.

Byatt, A.S. 'Their Normal Daily Lives Punctuated by Disaster'. Rev. of *The Love of a Good Woman*, by Alice Munro. *Literary Review* December 1998. <https://literaryreview.co.uk/their-normal-daily-lives-punctuated-by-disaster>.

Carrington, Ildikó de Papp. *Controlling the Uncontrollable: The Fiction of Alice Munro*. DeKalb: Northern Illinois UP, 1989.

—. '"Don't Tell (on) Daddy": Narrative Complexity in Alice Munro's "The Love of a Good Woman"'. *Studies in Short Fiction* 34 (1997): 159–70.

—. 'Talking Dirty: Alice Munro's "Open Secrets" and John Steinbeck's *Of Mice and Men*'. *Studies in Short Fiction* 31 (1994): 595–606.

—. 'What's in a Title?: Alice Munro's "Carried Away"'. *Studies in Short Fiction* 30 (1993): 555–64.

Carroll, Lewis. *Alice's Adventures in Wonderland*. 1865. *The Annotated Alice:* Alice's Adventures in Wonderland *and* Through the Looking-Glass. Introd. and notes by Martin Gardner. Illus. John Tenniel. Rev. ed. Harmondsworth: Penguin, 1970. 17–164.

—. *Through the Looking-Glass: And What Alice Found There*. 1871. *The Annotated Alice:* Alice's Adventures in Wonderland *and* Through the Looking-Glass. Introd. and notes by Martin Gardner. Illus. John Tenniel. Rev. ed. Harmondsworth: Penguin, 1970. 166–345.

Carscallen, James. *The Other Country: Patterns in the Writing of Alice Munro*. Toronto: ECW, 1993.

Chariots of Fire. Dir. Hugh Hudson. Screenplay by Colin Welland. Prod. David Puttnam. Music by Vangelis and by Gilbert and Sullivan. Allied Stars Ltd and Enigma Productions, 1981.

Charles, Michel. *Introduction à l'étude des textes*. Paris: Éditions du Seuil, 1995. Poétique.

Cicurel, Francine. 'Le texte et ses ornementations'. *Figures d'ajout: phrase, texte, écriture*. Ed. Jacqueline Authier-Revuz and Marie-Christine Lala. Paris: Presses Sorbonne Nouvelle, 2002. 51–63.

Clark, Miriam Marty. 'Allegories of Reading in Alice Munro's "Carried Away"'. *Contemporary Literature* 37 (1996): 49–61.

Clark, Timothy. 'Not Seeing the Short Story: A Blind Phenomenology of Reading'. *The Blind Short Story*. Ed. Timothy Clark and Nicholas Royle. *The Oxford Literary Review* 26 (2004): 5–30.

Cohen, Leonard. *Beautiful Losers*. Toronto: McClelland and Stewart, 1966.
Colville, Georgiana M.M. 'Relating (to) the Spec(tac)ular Other: Alice Munro's "The Albanian Virgin"'. *Commonwealth Essays and Studies* 21.1 (1998): 83–91.
ConstantReader. Discussion of 'The Love of a Good Woman'. December 1999. <http://www.constantreader.com/discussions/loveofagoodwoman.htm>.
Courbet, Gustave. *L'Origine du Monde*. Le musée d'Orsay, Paris. <https://www.musee-orsay.fr/fr/oeuvres/lorigine-du-monde-69330>.
Cox, Ailsa. *Alice Munro*. Tavistock: Northcote, 2004. Writers and Their Work.
—. '"Bizarre but Somehow Never Quite Satisfactory": Storytelling in "The Office"'. *Stylistic Perspectives on Alice Munro's* Dance of the Happy Shades. Ed. Manuel Jobert and Michael Toolan. *Études de Stylistique Anglais* 8 (2015): 135–48.
—. *The Real Louise and Other Stories*. Wirral: Headland, 2009.
—. 'Thoughts from England: On Reading, Teaching, and Writing Back to Alice Munro's "Meneseteung"'. *Alice Munro Country: Essays on Her Works I*. Ed. J.R. (Tim) Struthers. Toronto: Guernica Editions, 2020. 281–302.
—, ed. *Short Fiction in Theory & Practice* (2011–present).
Dante Alighieri. *The Banquet of Dante Alighieri*. Trans. Elizabeth Price Sayer. Introd. Henry Morley. London: George Routledge, 1887. n.p.: Book Jungle, 2008.
—. *The Divine Comedy*. Rendered into English Verse by John Ciardi. New York: W.W. Norton, 1970. Rpt. as *The Divine Comedy: The Inferno; The Purgatorio; The Paradiso*. Trans. John Ciardi. New York: New American Library-Penguin, 2003.
Davies, Robertson. *Fifth Business*. Toronto: Macmillan of Canada, 1970.
Davis, Jessica Milner. *Farce*. 2001. Rev. ed. New Brunswick, NJ, Transaction, 2003.
Dawson, Carrie. 'Skinned: Taxidermy and Pedophilia in Alice Munro's "Vandals"'. *Canadian Literature* 184 (2005): 69–83.
Deleuze, Gilles, and Félix Guattari. *A Thousand Plateaus: Capitalism and Schizophrenia*. Trans. and fwd. Brian Massumi. Minneapolis: U of Minnesota P, 1987.
Dickens, Charles. *Hard Times*. 1854. Ed. and introd. David Craig. London: Penguin, 1969.
Dickinson, Emily. '1263 Tell all the truth but tell it slant'. *The Poems of Emily Dickinson*. Variorum Edition. Ed. R.W. Franklin. Vol. 2. Cambridge, MA: The Belknap P of Harvard UP, 1998. 1089. 3 vols.
Doerfler, Jill, Niigaanwewidam James Sinclair and Heidi Kiiwetinepinesiik Stark, eds. *Centering Anishinaabeg Studies: Understanding the World through Stories*. East Lansing and Winnipeg: Michigan State UP and U of Manitoba P, 2013. American Indian Studies Ser.
'The Dreaming: Australian Aboriginal Mythology'. *Encyclopedia Britannica*. <https://www.britannica.com/topic/the-Dreaming-Australian-Aboriginal-mythology>.
Duffy, Dennis. '"A Dark Sort of Mirror": "The Love of a Good Woman" as Pauline Poetic'. *Alice Munro Writing On . . .* Ed. Robert Thacker. *Essays on Canadian Writing* 66 (1998): 169–90. Rpt. in *The Rest of the Story: Critical Essays on Alice Munro*. Ed. Robert Thacker. Toronto: ECW, 1999. 169–90.
—. 'On Fact and Fiction in Hugh Hood's *Reservoir Ravine*'. A Visionary Tradition: Canadian Literature and Culture at the Turn of the Millennium. MacKinnon Bldg., U of Guelph, Guelph, ON. 11 Nov. 1999.
Duncan, Isla. *Alice Munro's Narrative Art*. New York: Palgrave Macmillan, 2011. Rev. ed. New York: Palgrave Macmillan, 2014.
—. Message to Catherine Sheldrick Ross. 29 May 2021. E-mail.

Duplessis, Rachel Blau. *Writing Beyond the Ending: Narrative Strategies of Twentieth-Century Women Writers*. Bloomington: Indiana UP, 1985.

Durham, M. Edith. *High Albania*. London: Edward Arnold, 1909. <https://digital.library.upenn.edu/women/durham/albania/albania.html>.

'Eddy Match Co. / Pembroke Soundscapes'. <https://pembrokesoundscapes.ca/eddy-match>.

Eliot, George. *Middlemarch*. 1871–2. Ed. David Carroll. Introd. David Russell. Oxford: Oxford UP, 2019.

Eliot, T.S. *The Waste Land*. *Collected Poems 1909–1962*. London: Faber and Faber, 1963. 61–86.

Elliott, George. 'Crotch shot'. *The bittersweet man*. Guelph, ON: Red Kite, 1994. 14–21.

Emerson, Ralph Waldo. 'Circles'. *The Annotated Emerson*. Ed. David Mikics. Fwd. Phillip Lopate. Cambridge, MA: The Belknap P of Harvard UP, 2012. 186–98.

'Euphemia'. <https://en.wikipedia.org/wiki/Euphemia>.

'Euphemia de Ross'. <https://en.wikipedia.org/wiki/Euphemia_de_Ross>.

Faulkner, William. 'Beyond'. *Collected Stories of William Faulkner*. New York, 1950. 781–98.

—. 'Red Leaves'. *Collected Stories of William Faulkner*. New York, 1950. 313–41.

Fiamengo, Janice. 'Encountering Blocks of Solid Darkness in Alice Munro's "Vandals"'. *Alice Munro Everlasting: Essays on Her Works II*. Ed. J.R. (Tim) Struthers. Toronto: Guernica Editions, 2020. 245–59.

Fitzgerald, F. Scott. *The Great Gatsby*. 1925. Ed. James L.W. West III. Introd. Jesmyn Ward. Fwd. Eleanor Lanahan. New York: Scribner, 2018.

Flaubert, Gustave. Lettre 1628. 'A Mme Tennant'. Jour de Noël 1876. *Correspondance: Nouvelle édition augmentée: Septième série (1873–1876)*. Ed. Caroline Franklin-Grout. *Oeuvres complètes de Gustave Flaubert*. Paris: Louis Conard, 1930. 377–9. <https://gallica.bnf.fr/ark:/12148/bpt6k24529f/texteBrut>.

Ford, Richard. Introduction. *The Progress of Love*. By Alice Munro. Toronto: Penguin, 2006. ix–xvi.

Foy, Nathalie. '"Darkness Collecting": Reading "Vandals" as a Coda to *Open Secrets*'. *Alice Munro Writing On . . .* Ed. Robert Thacker. *Essays on Canadian Writing* 66 (1998): 147–68. Rpt. in *The Rest of the Story: Critical Essays on Alice Munro*. Ed. Robert Thacker. Toronto: ECW, 1999. 147–68.

France, Louise. 'Mistress of All She Surveys'. *The Guardian* 6 February 2005. <https://www.theguardian.com/books/2005/feb/06/fiction.features2>.

Francesconi, Sabrina. 'Alice Munro as the Master of Storytelling'. *Alice Munro and the Anatomy of the Short Story*. Ed. Oriana Palusci. Newcastle upon Tyne: Cambridge Scholars, 2017. 45–57.

—. 'Barking (with) Dogs: The Grammar System of Transitivity in Munro's "Save the Reaper" and "Floating Bridge"'. La question animale dans les nouvelles d'Alice Munro / *The Animal Question in Alice Munro's Stories*. Ed. Héliane Ventura. *Caliban: French Journal of English Studies* 57 (2017): 69–84. <https://journals.openedition.org/caliban/2699>.

—. 'Film Adaptations as Intersemiotic Contact Zones: *Edge of Madness* by Anne Wheeler'. *Textus: English Studies in Italy* 32.2 (2019): 77–91.

Fremlin, Gerald, with Arthur H. Robinson. *Maps as Mediated Seeing: Fundamentals of Cartography*. 2nd ed. Victoria, BC: Trafford, 2006.

Fremlin, Gerald, Editor-in-Chief. *The National Atlas of Canada*. 4th ed. Rev. Pref. Gerald Fremlin. Ottawa: Department of Energy, Mines and Resources, 1974.

Freud, Sigmund. *The Interpretation of Dreams*. Trans. James Strachey. Ed. James Strachey assisted by Alan Tyson. Ed. Angela Richards. London: Penguin, 1991. Vol. 4 of *The Penguin Freud Library*. 15 vols.

—. *Jokes and Their Relation to the Unconscious*. Trans. and ed. James Strachey. Ed. Angela Richards. London: Penguin, 1991. Vol. 8 of *The Penguin Freud Library*. 15 vols.

—. 'Notes upon a Case of Obsessional Neurosis (The "Rat Man") (1909)'. *Case Histories II*. Trans. and ed. James Strachey. Ed. Angela Richards. London: Penguin, 1991. 31–128. Vol. 9 of *The Penguin Freud Library*. 15 vols.

Frye, Northrop. *Anatomy of Criticism: Four Essays*. Princeton, NJ: Princeton UP, 1957.

—. 'The Expanding World of Metaphor'. *Myth and Metaphor: Selected Essays, 1974–1988*. By Northrop Frye. Ed. Robert D. Denham. Charlottesville: UP of Virginia, 1990. 108–23.

—. *The Secular Scripture: A Study of the Structure of Romance*. Cambridge, MA: Harvard UP, 1976.

Fulford, Robert. 'The Seeds of Prize Writing: Alice Munro Reveals Inspiration for Her Giller-Winning Story.' *The National Post*. <http://www.robertfulford.com/2003-11-11-munro.html>.

Gallant, Mavis. 'My Heart Is Broken'. *My Heart Is Broken: Eight Stories and a Short Novel*. New York: Random House, 1964. 194–202.

Genesis. *The Holy Bible*. Cambridge: Cambridge UP, n.d. Authorised King James Vers.

Gerlach, John. 'To Close or Not To Close: Alice Munro's "The Love of a Good Woman"'. *Journal of Narrative Theory* 37 (2007): 146–58.

Gibson, Douglas. Comment on 'The Only Voice: A Tribute to Alice Munro' by J.R. (Tim) Struthers. The Alice Munro Symposium. University of Ottawa, Ottawa. 11 May 2014.

Gilman, Charlotte Perkins. 'The Yellow Wallpaper'. *The Art of the Short Story*. By Dana Gioia and R.S. Gwynn. New York: Pearson Longman, 2006. 297–308.

Glover, Douglas. 'The Style of Alice Munro'. *The Cambridge Companion to Alice Munro*. Ed. David Staines. Cambridge: Cambridge UP, 2016. 45–59.

Goldman, Marlene. 'Alice Munro's Dramatic Fictions: Challenging (Dis)Ability by Playing with *Oedipus the King* and Embracing the Queer Art of Failure'. *Ethics and Affects in the Fiction of Alice Munro*. Ed. Amelia DeFalco and Lorraine York. Cham: Palgrave Macmillan, 2018. 79–108.

Gregory, Lady. *A Book of Saints and Wonders*. London: John Murray, 1907.

Grimm, Jacob and Wilhelm. 'Volume I: 50 Briar Rose'. *The Original Folk & Fairy Tales of the Brothers Grimm: The Complete First Edition*. Trans. and ed. Jack Zipes. Illus. Andrea Dezsö. Princeton, NJ: Princeton UP, 2014. 162–4. <https://img.4plebs.org/boards/tg/image/1416/91/1416918759518.pdf>.

—. 'Volume I: 62 Bluebeard'. *The Original Folk & Fairy Tales of the Brothers Grimm: The Complete First Edition*. Trans. and ed. Jack Zipes. Illus. Andrea Dezsö. Princeton, NJ: Princeton UP, 2014. 202–4. <https://img.4plebs.org/boards/tg/image/1416/91/1416918759518.pdf>.

Guignery, Vanessa. '"Where Is the Voice Coming From?": A Question of Origins in Alice Munro's *Dance of the Happy Shades*'. *"With a Roar from Underground":*

Alice Munro's Dance of the Happy Shades. Ed. Corinne Bigot and Catherine Lanone. Nanterre: Presses Universitaires de Paris Ouest, 2015. 19–33.

Gzowski, Peter. Interview with Alice Munro. Part 1. *Morningside*. CBC Radio. 30 September 1994. CBC Archives.

—. Interview with Alice Munro. *Morningside*. CBC Radio. 9 October 1996. CBC Archives. Rebroadcast on *Rewind*. CBC Radio. 14 August 2014. <https://www.cbc.ca/radio/rewind/alice-munro-on-morningside-1.2801197>.

Hadley, Tessa. 'The Book That Had the Greatest Influence on My Writing'. *The Guardian* 17 November 2017. <https://www.theguardian.com/books/2017/nov/17/tessa-hadley-books-that-made-me>.

—. 'Tessa Hadley on Alice Munro Reading "Differently": "A Little More Abrasive, Buoyant ... Defiant?"' *Literary Hub* 10 July 2017. <https://lithub.com/tessa-hadley-on-alice-munro-reading-differently/>.

Hancock, Geoff. 'Alice Munro'. *Canadian Writers at Work: Interviews with Geoff Hancock*. Toronto: Oxford UP, 1987. 187–224.

Hardy, Thomas. *Tess of the d'Urbervilles*. 3rd ed. Ed. Scott Elledge. New York: W.W. Norton, 1991. A Norton Critical Edition.

Hay, Elizabeth. 'The Mother as Material'. *The Cambridge Companion to Alice Munro*. Ed. David Staines. Cambridge: Cambridge UP, 2016. 178–92.

Heller, Deborah. 'Getting Loose: Women and Narration in Alice Munro's *Friend of My Youth*'. *Alice Munro Writing On . . .* Ed. Robert Thacker. *Essays on Canadian Writing* 66 (1998): 60–80. Rpt. in *The Rest of the Story: Critical Essays on Alice Munro*. Ed. Robert Thacker. Toronto: ECW, 1999. 60–80. Rpt. in *Literary Sisterhoods: Imagining Women Artists*. By Deborah Heller. Montreal, QC and Kingston, ON: McGill-Queen's UP, 2005. 69–87, 157–9.

Herman, Judith Lewis. *Trauma and Recovery*. New York: Basic Books, 1992.

Hood, Hugh. 'The End of It'. *Flying a Red Kite*. Toronto: Ryerson, 1962. 218–39. Introd. Hugh Hood. Erin, ON: The Porcupine's Quill, 1987. 223–42. Vol. 1 of *The Collected Stories*. 5 vols. 1987–2003.

—. *The New Age / Le nouveau siècle*. Ottawa: Oberon, 1975–79; Toronto: ECW, 1982; Toronto: Stoddart, 1984–2000.

—. *The Scenic Art*. Toronto: Stoddart, 1984.

Howells, Coral Ann. *Alice Munro*. Manchester: Manchester UP, 1998. Contemporary World Writers.

Hunter, Adrian. *The Cambridge Introduction to the Short Story in English*. Cambridge: Cambridge UP, 2007. Cambridge Introductions to Literature.

—. 'Taking Possession: Alice Munro's "A Wilderness Station" and James Hogg's *Justified Sinner*'. *Studies in Canadian Literature / Études en littérature canadienne* 35.2 (2010): 114–28.

Iser, Wolfgang. 'The Reading Process: A Phenomenological Approach'. *New Literary History* 3 (1971–2): 279–99.

James, Henry. 'Preface to "Roderick Hudson"'. *The Art of the Novel: Critical Prefaces*. Introd. Richard P. Blackmur. New York: Charles Scribner's Sons, 1934. 3–19.

—. *The Scenic Art: Notes on Acting and the Drama 1872–1901*. Ed. and introd. Allan Wade. Fwd. Leon Edel. London: Rupert Hart-Davis, 1949.

—. 'The Turn of the Screw'. *The Turn of the Screw and Other Ghost Stories*. Ed. and introd. Susie Boyt. London: Penguin, 2017. 148–257.

Jenny, Laurent. *La parole singulière*. Paris: Belin, 1990. L'extrême contemporain.

Jeremiah. *The Holy Bible*. Cambridge: Cambridge UP, n.d. Authorised King James Vers.

Jernigan, Kim. 'Narrative Haunting in Alice Munro's "Meneseteung"'. *Alice Munro and the Souwesto Story*. Ed. J.R. (Tim) Struthers. *Short Story* 21.1 (2013): 44–69.

Jobes, Gertrude. *Dictionary of Mythology Folklore and Symbols*. 3 vols. New York: Scarecrow, 1962.

Johnston, Basil H. 'Is That All There Is? Tribal Literature'. *New Contexts of Canadian Criticism*. Ed. Ajay Heble, Donna Palmateer Pennee and J.R. (Tim) Struthers. Peterborough, ON: Broadview, 1997. 346–54.

Jouve, Vincent. 'La quête du silence comme projet littéraire, autour de Beckett'. *Limites du langage: indicible ou silence*. Ed. Aline Mura-Brunel and Karl Cogard. Paris: L'Harmattan, 2002. 283–90.

Joyce, James. 'The Dead'. *Dubliners: Authoritative Text; Contexts; Criticism*. Ed. Margot Norris. Text ed. Hans Walter Gabler with Walter Hettche. New York: W.W. Norton, 2006. 151–94. A Norton Critical Edition.

—. 'Grace'. *Dubliners: Authoritative Text; Contexts; Criticism*. Ed. Margot Norris. Text ed. Hans Walter Gabler with Walter Hettche. New York: W.W. Norton, 2006. 128–51. A Norton Critical Edition.

—. *A Portrait of the Artist as a Young Man: Authoritative Text; Backgrounds and Contexts; Criticism*. Ed. John Paul Riquelme. Text ed. Hans Walter Gabler with Walter Hettche. New York: W.W. Norton, 2007. A Norton Critical Edition.

—. *Ulysses: The Corrected Text*. Ed. Hans Walter Gabler, Wolfhard Steppe and Claus Melchior. Harmondsworth: Penguin, 1986.

King, Thomas. *The Truth about Stories: A Native Narrative*. Toronto: House of Anansi, 2003. The Massey Lectures Ser.

Knopf Doubleday Publishing Group. 'A Conversation with Alice Munro'. *Reading Group Center*. 8 January 2010. <https://knopfdoubleday.com/2010/01/08/alice-munro-interview/>.

Kristeva, Julia. *Powers of Horror: An Essay on Abjection*. Trans. Louis S. Roudiez. New York: Columbia UP, 1982.

Landor, Walter Savage. 'Rose Aylmer'. *Poems*. Selected and introd. Geoffrey Grigson. London: Centaur, 1964. 3. <https://www.poetryfoundation.org/poems/44567/rose-aylmer>.

LaPierre, Megan. '"The Music Itself": Musical Representation and Musicality in the Short Stories of Alice Munro'. *Alice Munro Everlasting: Essays on Her Works II*. Ed. J.R. (Tim) Struthers. Toronto: Guernica Editions, 2020. 103–22.

Laurence, Margaret. *The Diviners*. Toronto: McClelland and Stewart, 1974.

Lawrence, D.H. 'The Fox'. *Three Novellas: The Ladybird; The Fox; The Captain's Doll*. Harmondsworth: Penguin, 1960. 83–158.

Lecercle, Jean-Jacques. *Interpretation as Pragmatics*. London: Macmillan, 1999. Language, Discourse, Society.

Lecker, Robert. 'Machines, Readers, Gardens: Alice Munro's "Carried Away"'. *Alice Munro Writing On . . .* Ed. Robert Thacker. *Essays on Canadian Writing* 66 (1998): 103–27. Rpt. in *The Rest of the Story: Critical Essays on Alice Munro*. Ed. Robert Thacker. Toronto: ECW, 1999. 103–27.

Lee, Monika. 'An Eerie and Numinous Place of Quiet Unknowing: Alice Munro's "The Love of a Good Woman" in Context'. *Alice Munro: A Souwesto Celebration*. Ed. J.R. (Tim) Struthers and John B. Lee. *The Windsor Review* 47.2 (2014): 102–23.

Levene, Mark. 'Alice Munro's *The Progress of Love*: Free (and) Radical'. *Critical Insights: Alice Munro*. Ed. Charles E. May. Ipswich, MA: Salem-EBSCO, 2013. 142–59.
—. '"It was about vanishing": A Glimpse of Alice Munro's Stories'. *University of Toronto Quarterly* 68 (1999): 841–60.
Lewis, C.S. *The Allegory of Love: A Study in Medieval Tradition*. 1936. New York: Oxford UP, 1958.
Lohafer, Susan. *Reading for Storyness: Preclosure Theory, Empirical Poetics, and Culture in the Short Story*. Baltimore, MD: The Johns Hopkins UP, 2003.
Löschnigg, Maria. 'Carried Away by Letters: Alice Munro and the Epistolary Mode'. *Alice Munro's Miraculous Art: Critical Essays*. Ed. Janice Fiamengo and Gerald Lynch. Ottawa: U of Ottawa P, 2017. 97–113. Reappraisals: Canadian Writers 38.
Lundén, Rolf. *The United Stories of America: Studies in the Short Story Composite*. Amsterdam-Atlanta, GA: Rodopi, 1999.
Macfarlane, David. 'Writer in Residence'. *Saturday Night* December 1986: 51–2, 54, 56.
Mackay, Charles. 'The Sea-King's Burial'. *PoetryArchive*. <https://www.poetry-archive.com/m/the_sea_kings_burial/>.
MacKendrick, Louis K. 'Giving Tongue: Scorings of Voice, Verse, and Flesh in Alice Munro's "Meneseteung"'. *Alice Munro Country: Essays on Her Works I*. Ed. J.R. (Tim) Struthers. Toronto: Guernica Editions, 2020. 303–22.
—, ed. *Probable Fictions: Alice Munro's Narrative Acts*. Downsview, ON: ECW, 1983.
Mahony, Patrick J. *Freud and the Rat Man*. Fwd. Otto F. Kernberg. New Haven, CT: Yale UP, 1986.
Manet, Édouard. *Deux Chapeaux*. 1880. Le musée des Beaux-Arts de Dijon. Dijon. <https://fr.m.wikipedia.org/wiki/Fichier:%C3%89douard_Manet_-_Deux_Chapeux.jpg>.
Mansfield, Katherine. 'At the Bay'. *The Collected Fiction of Katherine Mansfield, 1916–1922*. Ed. Gerri Kimber and Vincent O'Sullivan. Edinburgh: Edinburgh UP, 2012. 342–72. Vol. 2 of The Edinburgh Edition of the Collected Works of Katherine Mansfield. 4 vols.
—. 'The Garden Party'. *The Collected Fiction of Katherine Mansfield, 1916–1922*. Ed. Gerri Kimber and Vincent O'Sullivan. Edinburgh: Edinburgh UP, 2012. 401–14. Vol. 2 of The Edinburgh Edition of the Collected Works of Katherine Mansfield. 4 vols.
—. 'Prelude'. *The Collected Fiction of Katherine Mansfield, 1916–1922*. Ed. Gerri Kimber and Vincent O'Sullivan. Edinburgh: Edinburgh UP, 2012. 56–93. Vol. 2 of The Edinburgh Edition of the Collected Works of Katherine Mansfield. 4 vols.
Marlatt, Daphne. '"Perform[ing] on the Stage of Her Text"'. *Readings from the Labyrinth*. Edmonton: NeWest, 1998. 200–12. The Writer as Critic 6.
Martin, W.R. *Alice Munro: Paradox and Parallel*. Edmonton: U of Alberta P, 1987.
Martin, W.R., and Warren U. Ober. 'Alice Munro as Small-Town Historian: "Spaceships Have Landed"'. *Alice Munro Writing On . . .* Ed. Robert Thacker. *Essays on Canadian Writing* 66 (1998): 128–46. Rpt. in *The Rest of the Story: Critical Essays on Alice Munro*. Ed. Robert Thacker. Toronto: ECW, 1999. 128–46. Rpt. (abridged) in *Alice Munro Country: Essays on Her Works I*. Ed. J.R. (Tim) Struthers. Toronto: Guernica Editions, 2020. 237–54.

—. 'The Comic Spirit in Alice Munro's *Open Secrets*: "A Real Life" and "The Jack Randa Hotel"'. *Studies in Short Fiction* 35 (1998–99): 41–7.
Marzano-Lesnevich, Alexandria. *The Fact of a Body: A Murder and a Memoir*. New York: Flatiron, 2017.
May, Charles E. *"I Am Your Brother": Short Story Studies*. Garden Grove, CA: Amayzing Editions, 2013.
—. 'The Nature of Knowledge in Short Fiction'. *Studies in Short Fiction* 21 (1984): 327–38. Rpt. in *The New Short Story Theories*. Ed. Charles E. May. Athens, OH: Ohio UP, 1994. 131–43.
McCombs, Judith. 'Searching Bluebeard's Chambers: Grimm, Gothic, and Bible Mysteries in Alice Munro's "The Love of a Good Woman"'. *The American Review of Canadian Studies* 30 (2000): 327–48. Rpt. in *Alice Munro*. Ed. and introd. Harold Bloom. New York: Bloom's Literary Criticism-Infobase, 2009. 123–43. Bloom's Modern Critical Views.
McCulloch, Jeanne, and Mona Simpson. 'Alice Munro: The Art of Fiction CXXXVII'. *The Paris Review* 131 (1994): 226–64. <https://www.theparisreview.org/interviews/1791/the-art-of-fiction-no-137-alice-munro>.
McGill, Robert. 'Where Do You Think You Are?: Alice Munro's Open Houses'. *Mosaic: A Journal for the Interdisciplinary Study of Literature* 35.4 (2002): 103–19. Rpt. (rev.) in *Space and Place in Alice Munro's Fiction: "A Book with Maps in It"*. Ed. Christine Lorre-Johnston and Eleonora Rao. Rochester, NY: Camden House, 2018. 27–40.
McLuhan, Herbert Marshall. 'The Mechanical Bride'. *The Mechanical Bride: Folklore of Industrial Man*. New York: Vanguard, 1951. 98–101.
Mendez, Eva. *"And Write She Did": Prerequisites for Women's Writing in the Writer Narratives of Virginia Woolf and Alice Munro*. Würzburg: Königshausen & Neumann, 2022.
Metcalf, John. 'Editing the Best'. *Kicking Against the Pricks*. 1982. Rev. ed. Guelph, ON: Red Kite, 1986. 143–73. Rpt. in *How Stories Mean*. Ed. John Metcalf and J.R. (Tim) Struthers. Erin, ON: The Porcupine's Quill, 1993. 39–68. Critical Directions 3.
Michelangelo. *David*. Accademia Gallery, Florence. <https://www.accademia.org/explore-museum/artworks/michelangelos-david/>.
Micros, Marianne. 'Et in Ontario Ego: The Pastoral Ideal and the Blazon Tradition in Alice Munro's "Lichen"'. *Alice Munro Writing On . . .* Ed. Robert Thacker. *Essays on Canadian Writing* 66 (1998): 44–59. Rpt. in *The Rest of the Story: Critical Essays on Alice Munro*. Ed. Robert Thacker. Toronto: ECW, 1999. 44–59.
—. '"Pearl Street . . . is another story": Poetry and Reality in Alice Munro's "Meneseteung"'. *Alice Munro Country: Essays on Her Works I*. Ed. J.R. (Tim) Struthers. Toronto: Guernica Editions, 2020. 323–44.
—. '"Ryse Up Elisa" – Woman Trapped in a Lay: Spenser's "Aprill"'. *Renaissance and Reformation / Renaissance et Réforme* new ser. 17.2 (1993): 63–73.
Miller, Judith Maclean. 'Deconstructing Silence: The Mystery of Alice Munro'. *The Antigonish Review* 129 (2002): 43–52.
Milton, John. *Paradise Lost*. *Complete Poems and Major Prose*. Ed. Merritt Y. Hughes. New York: Odyssey, 1957. 207–469.
Mitchell, W.J.T. 'Representation'. *Critical Terms for Literary Study*. Ed. Frank Lentricchia and Thomas McLaughlin. 2nd ed. Chicago: U of Chicago P, 1995. 11–22.

Moore, Lorrie. 'Artship'. Rev. of *Hateship, Friendship, Courtship, Loveship, Marriage*. By Alice Munro. *The New York Review of Books* 17 January 2002: 41–2. Rpt. as 'Alice Munro's *Hateship, Friendship, Courtship, Loveship, Marriage*'. *See What Can Be Done: Essays, Criticism, and Commentary*. New York: Alfred A. Knopf, 2018. 132–8.

—. Introduction. *The Moons of Jupiter*. By Alice Munro. Toronto: Penguin. 2006. ix–xii. Rpt. as 'Alice Munro's *The Moons of Jupiter*'. *See What Can Be Done: Essays, Criticism, and Commentary*. New York: Alfred A. Knopf, 2018. 212–15.

—. 'Leave Them and Love Them: In Alice Munro's Fiction, Memory and Passion Reorder Life'. Rev. of *Runaway*. By Alice Munro. *The Atlantic Monthly* December 2004: 125–8. Rpt. as 'Alice Munro's *Runaway*'. *See What Can Be Done: Essays, Criticism, and Commentary*. New York: Alfred A. Knopf, 2018. 184–9.

Munro, Alice. 'Accident'. *Toronto Life* November 1977: 60–1, 87–8, 90–5, 149–50, 153–6, 159–60, 162–5, 167, 169–73. Rpt. in *The Moons of Jupiter*. Toronto: Macmillan of Canada, 1982. 77–109.

—. Afterword. *Emily of New Moon*. By L.M. Montgomery. Toronto: McClelland & Stewart, 1989. 357–61. The New Canadian Library.

—. 'The Albanian Virgin'. *The New Yorker* 27 June and 4 July 1994: 118–21, 123–7, 129–34, 136–8. Rpt. in *Open Secrets*. Toronto: McClelland & Stewart, 1994. 81–128.

—. 'Before the Change'. *The Love of a Good Woman*. Toronto: McClelland & Stewart, 1998. 254–92.

—. *The Beggar Maid: Stories of Flo and Rose*. New York: Alfred A. Knopf, 1979. London: Allen Lane, 1980. Harmondsworth: Penguin, 1980. [Originally published in Canada as *Who Do You Think You Are?* Toronto: Macmillan of Canada, 1978.]

—. 'The Beggar Maid'. *The New Yorker* 27 June 1977: 31, 35–41, 44–7. Rpt. in *Who Do You Think You Are?* Toronto: Macmillan of Canada, 1978. 65–97. Rpt. in *The Beggar Maid: Stories of Flo and Rose*. New York: Alfred A. Knopf, 1979. 68–100. London: Allen Lane, 1980. 68–100. Harmondsworth: Penguin, 1980. 68–100.

—. 'Carried Away'. *The New Yorker* 21 October 1991: 34–46, 48–51, 54–8, 60–1. Rpt. in *Open Secrets*. Toronto: McClelland & Stewart, 1994. 3–51.

—. 'Chaddeleys and Flemings'. *The Moons of Jupiter*. Toronto: Macmillan of Canada, 1982. 1–35.

—. 'Chance'. *Runaway*. Toronto: McClelland & Stewart, 2004. 48–86.

—. 'The Children Stay'. *The Love of a Good Woman*. Toronto: McClelland & Stewart, 1998. 181–214.

—. 'Circle of Prayer'. *The Progress of Love*. Toronto: McClelland and Stewart, 1986. 254–74.

—. 'The Colonel's Hash Resettled'. *The Narrative Voice: Short Stories and Reflections by Canadian Authors*. Ed. and introd. John Metcalf. Toronto: McGraw-Hill Ryerson, 1972. 181–3.

—. 'Comfort'. *Hateship, Friendship, Courtship, Loveship, Marriage*. Toronto: McClelland & Stewart, 2001. 118–53.

—. 'Contributors' Notes' on 'The Love of a Good Woman'. *Prize Stories 1997: The O. Henry Awards*. Ed. and introd. Larry Dark. New York: Doubleday, 1997. 442–3.

—. 'Cortes Island'. *The Love of a Good Woman*. Toronto: McClelland & Stewart, 1998. 117–45.

—. *Dance of the Happy Shades*. Fwd. Hugh Garner. Toronto: Ryerson, 1968.

—. 'Dance of the Happy Shades'. *Dance of the Happy Shades*. Fwd. Hugh Garner. Toronto: Ryerson, 1968. 211–24.

—. *Dear Life*. Toronto: McClelland & Stewart, 2012.

—. 'Dear Life'. *Dear Life*. Toronto: McClelland & Stewart, 2012. 299–319.

—. 'Differently'. *Friend of My Youth*. Toronto: McClelland & Stewart, 1990. 216–43.

—. 'Dimensions'. *Too Much Happiness*. Toronto: McClelland & Stewart, 2009. 1–31.

—. 'Dulse'. *The New Yorker* 21 July 1980: 30–9. Rpt. in *The Moons of Jupiter*. Toronto: Macmillan of Canada, 1982. 36–59.

—. 'Epilogue: Messenger'. *The View from Castle Rock*. Toronto: McClelland & Stewart, 2006. 341–9.

—. 'Epilogue: The Photographer'. *Lives of Girls and Women*. Toronto: McGraw-Hill Ryerson, 1971. 243–54. Harmondsworth: Penguin, 1982. 239–50.

—. 'Family Furnishings'. *Hateship, Friendship, Courtship, Loveship, Marriage*. Toronto: McClelland & Stewart, 2001. 84–117.

—. 'Fathers'. *The New Yorker* 5 August 2002: 64–71. Rpt. in *The View from Castle Rock*. Toronto: McClelland & Stewart, 2006. 173–96.

—. 'The Ferguson Girls Must Never Marry'. *Grand Street* 1.3 (Spring 1982): 27–64.

—. 'Finale'. *Dear Life*. Toronto: McClelland & Stewart, 2012. 255–319.

—. 'Fits'. *The Progress of Love*. Toronto: McClelland and Stewart, 1986. 106–31.

—. 'Five Points'. *Friend of My Youth*. Toronto: McClelland & Stewart, 1990. 27–49.

—. 'Floating Bridge'. *Hateship, Friendship, Courtship, Loveship, Marriage*. Toronto: McClelland & Stewart, 2001. 53–83.

—. *Friend of My Youth*. Toronto: McClelland & Stewart, 1990.

—. 'Friend of My Youth'. *The New Yorker* 22 January 1990: 36–48. Rpt. in *Friend of My Youth*. Toronto: McClelland & Stewart, 1990. 3–26.

—. 'Goodness and Mercy'. *Friend of My Youth*. Toronto: McClelland & Stewart, 1990. 156–79.

—. 'Hard-Luck Stories'. *The Moons of Jupiter*. Toronto: Macmillan of Canada, 1982. 181–97.

—. *Hateship, Friendship, Courtship, Loveship, Marriage*. Toronto: McClelland & Stewart, 2001.

—. 'Hateship, Friendship, Courtship, Loveship, Marriage'. *Hateship, Friendship, Courtship, Loveship, Marriage*. Toronto: McClelland & Stewart, 2001. 1–52.

—. 'Hold Me Fast, Don't Let Me Pass'. *Friend of My Youth*. Toronto: McClelland & Stewart, 1990. 74–105.

—. 'Home'. *74: New Canadian Stories*. Ed. David Helwig and Joan Harcourt. Ottawa: Oberon, 1974. 133–53. Rpt. (rev.) in *The View from Castle Rock*. Toronto: McClelland & Stewart, 2006. 285–315.

—. 'Images'. *Dance of the Happy Shades*. Fwd. Hugh Garner. Toronto: Ryerson, 1968. 30–43.

—. Introduction. *Selected Stories*. Toronto: Penguin, 1996. ix–xvii. Rpt. in *A Wilderness Station: Selected Stories 1968–1994*. Toronto: Penguin, 2015. xiii–xxi.

—. Introduction. *The Moons of Jupiter*. Harmondsworth: Penguin, 1986. xiii–xvi.

—. 'The Jack Randa Hotel'. *Open Secrets*. Toronto: McClelland & Stewart, 1994. 161–89.

—. 'Jakarta'. *The Love of a Good Woman*. Toronto: McClelland and Stewart, 1998. 79–116.

—. 'Jesse and Meribeth'. *The Progress of Love*. Toronto: McClelland & Stewart, 1986. 162–88.

—. 'Labor Day Dinner'. *The New Yorker* 28 September 1981: 47–56, 59–60, 65–6, 70, 75–6. Rpt. in *The Moons of Jupiter*. Toronto: Macmillan of Canada, 1982. 134–59.

—. 'Lichen'. *The Progress of Love*. Toronto: McClelland and Stewart, 1986. 32–55.

—. *Lives of Girls and Women*. Toronto: McGraw-Hill Ryerson, 1971. Harmondsworth: Penguin, 1982.

—. *The Love of a Good Woman*. Toronto: McClelland & Stewart, 1998.

—. 'The Love of a Good Woman: A Murder, a Mystery, a Romance'. *The New Yorker* 23 and 30 December 1996: 102–5, 107–8, 110–14, 116–22, 124–32, 134–8, 140–1. Rpt. as 'The Love of a Good Woman'. *The Love of a Good Woman*. Toronto: McClelland & Stewart, 1998. 3–78.

—. 'Lying Under the Apple Tree'. *The New Yorker* 17 and 24 June 2002: 88–90, 92, 105–8, 110–14. Rpt. in *The View from Castle Rock*. Toronto: McClelland & Stewart, 2006. 197–226.

—. 'Meneseteung'. *The New Yorker* 11 January 1988: 28–38. Rpt. (rev.) in *Friend of My Youth*. Toronto: McClelland & Stewart, 1990. 50–73.

—. 'Miles City, Montana'. *The New Yorker* 14 January 1985: 30–40. Rpt. in *The Progress of Love*. Toronto: McClelland and Stewart, 1986. 84–105.

—. 'Mischief'. *Who Do You Think You Are?* Toronto: Macmillan of Canada, 1978. 98–132. Rpt. in *The Beggar Maid: Stories of Flo and Rose*. New York: Alfred A. Knopf, 1979. 101–36. London: Allen Lane, 1980. 101–36. Harmondsworth: Penguin, 1980. 101–36.

—. 'Monsieur les Deux Chapeaux'. *The Progress of Love*. Toronto: McClelland and Stewart, 1986. 56–83.

—. 'The Moon in the Orange Street Skating Rink'. *The Progress of Love*. Toronto: McClelland and Stewart, 1986. 132–61.

—. *The Moons of Jupiter*. Toronto: Macmillan of Canada, 1982.

—. 'The Moons of Jupiter'. *The New Yorker* 22 May 1978: 32–9. Rpt. (rev.) in *The Moons of Jupiter*. Toronto: Macmillan of Canada, 1982. 217–33.

—. 'My Mother's Dream'. *The Love of a Good Woman*. Toronto: McClelland & Stewart, 1998. 293–340.

—. 'No Advantages'. *The View from Castle Rock*. Toronto: McClelland & Stewart, 2006. 3–26.

—. 'The Office'. *Dance of the Happy Shades*. Fwd. Hugh Garner. Toronto: Ryerson, 1968. 59–74.

—. 'Oh, What Avails'. *Friend of My Youth*. Toronto: McClelland & Stewart, 1990. 180–215.

—. 'On Writing "The Office"'. *How Stories Mean*. Ed. John Metcalf and J.R. (Tim) Struthers. Erin, ON: The Porcupine's Quill, 1993. 192–4. Critical Directions 3.

—. *Open Secrets*. Toronto: McClelland & Stewart, 1994.

—. 'Open Secrets'. *Open Secrets*. Toronto: McClelland & Stewart, 1994. 129–60.

—. 'Oranges and Apples'. *Friend of My Youth*. Toronto: McClelland & Stewart, 1990. 106–36.

—. 'The Ottawa Valley'. *Something I've Been Meaning To Tell You*. Toronto: McGraw-Hill Ryerson, 1974. 227–46. Harmondsworth: Penguin, 1985. 218–35.

—. 'Passion'. *Runaway*. Toronto: McClelland & Stewart, 2004. 159–96.
—. 'The Peace of Utrecht'. *Dance of the Happy Shades*. Fwd. Hugh Garner. Toronto: Ryerson, 1968. 190–210. London: Vintage, 2000. 190–210.
—. 'Pictures of the Ice'. *Friend of My Youth*. Toronto: McClelland & Stewart, 1990. 137–55.
—. 'Places at Home'. Alice Munro Fonds. Special Collections Division. University of Calgary Libraries. MsC 37.13.10.
—. *The Progress of Love*. Toronto: McClelland and Stewart, 1986.
—. 'The Progress of Love'. *The New Yorker* 7 October 1985: 35–46, 49–50, 53–4, 57–8. Rpt. in *The Progress of Love*. Toronto: McClelland and Stewart, 1986. 3–31.
—. 'Prue'. *The New Yorker* 30 March 1981: 34–5. Rpt. in *The Moons of Jupiter*. Toronto: Macmillan of Canada, 1982. 129–33.
—. 'A Queer Streak'. *The Progress of Love*. Toronto: McClelland and Stewart, 1986. 208–53.
—. 'A Real Life'. *Open Secrets*. Toronto: McClelland & Stewart, 1994. 52–80.
—. 'Rich as Stink'. *The Love of a Good Woman*. Toronto: McClelland & Stewart, 1998. 215–53.
— 'Royal Beatings'. *The New Yorker* 14 March 1977: 36–44. Rpt. in *Who Do You Think You Are?* Toronto: Macmillan of Canada, 1978. 1–22. Rpt. in *The Beggar Maid: Stories of Flo and Rose*. New York: Alfred A. Knopf, 1979. 3–24. London: Allen Lane, 1980. 3–24. Harmondsworth: Penguin, 1980. 3–24.
—. *Runaway*. Toronto: McClelland & Stewart, 2004.
—. 'Save the Reaper'. *The Love of a Good Woman*. Toronto: McClelland & Stewart, 1998. 146–80.
—. 'Silence'. *Runaway*. Toronto: McClelland & Stewart, 2004. 126–58.
—. *Something I've Been Meaning To Tell You*. Toronto: McGraw-Hill Ryerson, 1974.
—. 'Soon'. *Runaway*. Toronto: McClelland & Stewart, 2004. 87–125.
—. 'Spaceships Have Landed'. *The Paris Review* 131 (1994): 265–94. Rpt. (rev.) in *Open Secrets*. Toronto: McClelland & Stewart, 1994. 226–60.
—. 'Spelling'. *Who Do You Think You Are?* Toronto: Macmillan of Canada, 1978. 174–88. Rpt. in *The Beggar Maid: Stories of Flo and Rose*. New York: Alfred A. Knopf, 1979. 178–92. London: Allen Lane, 1980. 178–92. Harmondsworth: Penguin, 1980. 178–92.
—. 'The Stone in the Field'. *The Moons of Jupiter*. Toronto: Macmillan of Canada, 1982. 10–35.
—. 'Tell Me Yes or No'. *Something I've Been Meaning To Tell You*. Toronto: McGraw-Hill Ryerson, 1974. 106–24.
—. 'The Time of Death'. *Dance of the Happy Shades*. Fwd. Hugh Garner. Toronto: Ryerson, 1968. 89–99.
—. 'To Reach Japan'. *Dear Life*. Toronto: McClelland & Stewart, 2012. 3–30.
—. *Too Much Happiness*. Toronto: McClelland & Stewart, 2009.
—. 'The Turkey Season'. *The New Yorker* 19 December 1980: 36–44. Rpt. in *The Moons of Jupiter*. Toronto: Macmillan of Canada, 1982. 60–76.
—. 'Vandals'. *Open Secrets*. Toronto: McClelland & Stewart, 1994. 261–94.
—. *The View from Castle Rock*. Toronto: McClelland & Stewart, 2006.
—. 'Walker Brothers Cowboy'. *Dance of the Happy Shades*. Fwd. Hugh Garner. Toronto: Ryerson, 1968. 1–18.

—. 'What Do You Want To Know For?' *The View from Castle Rock*. Toronto: McClelland & Stewart, 2006. 316–40.

—. 'What Is Real?' *Making It New: Contemporary Canadian Stories*. Ed. John Metcalf. Toronto: Methuen, 1982. 223–6. Rpt. in *How Stories Mean*. Ed. John Metcalf and J.R. (Tim) Struthers. Erin, ON: The Porcupine's Quill, 1993. 331–4. Critical Directions 3. Rpt. in *The Art of Short Fiction: An International Anthology*. Ed. Gary Geddes. Toronto: HarperCollins, 1993. 824–7.

—. 'What Is Remembered'. *Hateship, Friendship, Courtship, Loveship, Marriage*. Toronto: McClelland & Stewart, 2001. 217–41.

—. 'White Dump'. *The Progress of Love*. Toronto: McClelland and Stewart, 1986. 275–309.

—. *Who Do You Think You Are?* Toronto: Macmillan of Canada, 1978. Rpt. (rev.) as *The Beggar Maid: Stories of Flo and Rose*. New York: Alfred A. Knopf, 1979. London: Allen Lane, 1980. Harmondsworth: Penguin, 1980.

—. 'Who Do You Think You Are?' *Who Do You Think You Are?* Toronto: Macmillan of Canada, 1978. 189–206. Rpt. in *The Beggar Maid: Stories of Flo and Rose*. New York: Alfred A. Knopf, 1979. 193–210. London: Allen Lane, 1980. 193–210. Harmondsworth: Penguin, 1980. 193–210.

—. 'Wigtime'. *Friend of My Youth*. Toronto: McClelland & Stewart, 1990. 244–73.

—. 'A Wilderness Station'. *Open Secrets*. Toronto: McClelland & Stewart, 1994. 190–225.

—. 'Winter Wind'. *Something I've Been Meaning To Tell You*. Toronto: McGraw-Hill Ryerson, 1974. 192–206.

—. 'Working for a Living'. *Grand Street* 1.1 (Autumn 1981): 9–37. Rpt. (rev.) in *The View from Castle Rock*. Toronto: McClelland & Stewart, 2006. 127–70.

Munro, Sheila. *Lives of Mothers & Daughters: Growing Up with Alice Munro*. Toronto: McClelland & Stewart, 2001.

New, W.H. 'Re-reading *The Moons of Jupiter*'. *The Cambridge Companion to Alice Munro*. Ed. David Staines. Cambridge: Cambridge UP, 2016. 116–35.

O'Brien, Edna. *Saints and Sinners*. London: Faber and Faber, 2011.

O'Connor, Frank. *The Lonely Voice: A Study of the Short Story*. London: Macmillan, 1963.

Ong, Walter J. *Orality and Literacy: The Technologizing of the Word*. 1982. London: Routledge, 1988.

Ovid. *Metamorphoses*. Trans. Anthony S. Kline. Charlottesville: U of Virginia Library, 2000. The Ovid Collection. <https://ovid.lib.virginia.edu/trans/Ovhome.htm>.

Ovid. *The Metamorphoses of Ovid*. Trans. and introd. Mary M. Innes. Harmondsworth: Penguin, 1955.

Palusci, Oriana. 'Breathing and the Power of Evil in "Dimensions"'. *Alice Munro and the Anatomy of the Short Story*. Ed. Oriana Palusci. Newcastle upon Tyne: Cambridge Scholars, 2017. 111–25.

Pangman, Jennifer. Conversation on Zoom. Alice Munro Reading Group. 21 September 2022.

—. Message to J.R. (Tim) Struthers. 10 October 2022. E-mail.

Pearl, Nancy, and Jeff Schwager. 'Amor Towles'. *The Writer's Library: The Authors You Love on the Books That Changed Their Lives*. Ed. Nancy Pearl and Jeff Schwager. Fwd. Susan Orlean. Introd. Nancy Pearl and Jeff Schwager. New York: HarperOne, 2020. 170–86.

Poe, Edgar Allan. 'The Purloined Letter'. *The Murders in the Rue Morgue: The Dupin Tales*. Ed. and introd. Matthew Pearl. New York: The Modern Library, 2006. 83–100.

The Poetic Edda. Trans. with an Introd. and Explanatory Notes by Lee M. Hollander. 2nd ed., rev. Austin: U of Texas P, 1990.

Poliner, Elizabeth. 'How Mapping Alice Munro's Stories Helped Me As a Writer: Elizabeth Poliner on the Shapes That Fiction Can Take'. *Literary Hub* 27 April 2016. <https://lithub.com/how-mapping-alice-munros-stories-helped-me-as-a-writer/>.

Prose, Francine. *Reading Like a Writer: A Guide for People Who Love Books and for Those Who Want To Write Them*. 2006. New York: Harper Perennial, 2007.

Proust, Marcel. *Swann's Way*. Trans. and introd. Lydia Davis. Gen. ed. Christopher Prendergast. New York: Viking, 2003.

Rasporich, Beverly J. *Dance of the Sexes: Art and Gender in the Fiction of Alice Munro*. Edmonton: U of Alberta P, 1990.

Redekop, Magdalene. *Mothers and Other Clowns: The Stories of Alice Munro*. London: Routledge, 1992.

—. 'On Sitting Down To Read "Lichen" Once Again'. *Alice Munro's Miraculous Art: Critical Essays*. Ed. Janice Fiamengo and Gerald Lynch. Ottawa: U of Ottawa P, 2017. 289–305. Reappraisals: Canadian Writers 38.

The Revelation of St. John the Divine. *The Holy Bible*. Cambridge: Cambridge UP, n.d. Authorised King James Vers.

Ross, Catherine Sheldrick. *Alice Munro: A Double Life*. Toronto: ECW, 1992. Canadian Biography Ser. 1.

—. '"At the End of a Long Road": Alice Munro's "Dear Life"'. *Alice Munro Everlasting: Essays on Her Works II*. Ed. J.R. (Tim) Struthers. Toronto: Guernica Editions, 2020. 31–77.

—. *Circles: Fun Ideas for Getting A-Round in Math*. Illus. Bill Slavin. Boston: Addison-Wesley, 1993. [Originally published as *Circles: Shapes in Math, Science and Nature*. Illus. Bill Slavin. Toronto: Kids Can, 1992.]

—. 'An Interview with Alice Munro'. *Canadian Children's Literature* 53 (1989): 14–24.

—. *The Pleasures of Reading: A Booklover's Alphabet*. Santa Barbara, CA: Libraries Unlimited, 2014.

—. '"Too Many Things": Reading Alice Munro's "The Love of a Good Woman"'. *University of Toronto Quarterly* 71 (2002): 786–810.

Royle, Nicholas. 'Spooking Forms'. *The Blind Short Story*. Ed. Timothy Clark and Nicholas Royle. *The Oxford Literary Review* 26 (2004): 155–72.

Sartre, Jean-Paul. *L'être et le néant: essai d'ontologie phénoménologique*. Paris: Gallimard, 1943. Trans. as *Being and Nothingness: An Essay on Phenomenological Ontology*. Trans. and introd. Hazel E. Barnes. New York: Philosophical Library, 1956.

Scholes, Robert. *Fabulation and Metafiction*. Urbana: U of Illinois P, 1979.

Scott, Sir Walter. *Minstrelsy of the Scottish Border: Historical and Romantic Ballads*. 1802. Ed. Thomas Henderson. London: George G. Harrap, 1931.

Shakespeare, William. *King Lear*. Ed. R.A. Foakes. *The Arden Shakespeare: Third Series: Complete Works*. Ed. Richard Proudfoot, Ann Thompson, David Scott Kastan and H.R. Woudhuysen. London: The Arden Shakespeare, 2021. 751–87.

—. *Macbeth*. Ed. Sandra Clark and Pamela Mason. *The Arden Shakespeare:*

Third Series: Complete Works. Ed. Richard Proudfoot, Ann Thompson, David Scott Kastan and H.R. Woudhuysen. London: The Arden Shakespeare, 2021. 893–918.

—. *Romeo and Juliet*. Ed. René Weis. *The Arden Shakespeare: Third Series: Complete Works*. Ed. Richard Proudfoot, Ann Thompson, David Scott Kastan and H.R. Woudhuysen. London: The Arden Shakespeare, 2021. 1125–58.

—. *The Tragedy of Hamlet, Prince of Denmark: The First Folio (1623)*. Ed. Ann Thompson and Neil Taylor. *The Arden Shakespeare: Third Series: Complete Works*. Ed. Richard Proudfoot, Ann Thompson, David Scott Kastan and H.R. Woudhuysen. London: The Arden Shakespeare, 2021. 383–421.

—. *Twelfth Night*. Ed. Keir Elam. *The Arden Shakespeare: Third Series: Complete Works*. Ed. Richard Proudfoot, Ann Thompson, David Scott Kastan and H.R. Woudhuysen. London: The Arden Shakespeare, 2021. 1337–63.

Shaw, Bernard. *Saint Joan: A Chronicle Play in Six Scenes and an Epilogue*. Harmondsworth: Penguin, 1946.

Sidney, Sir Philip. *Astrophil and Stella*. *Sir Philip Sidney: The Major Works*. Ed. and introd. Katherine Duncan-Jones. Oxford: Oxford UP, 2002. 153–211.

Skagert, Ulrica. *Possibility-Space and Its Imaginative Variations in Alice Munro's Short Stories*. Stockholm: Stockholm U, 2008.

Smith, Stephen. 'Layers of Life: No More "Single Paths" for Alice Munro'. *Quill & Quire* August 1994: 1, 24.

Somacarrera, Pilar. 'A Spanish Passion for the Canadian Short Story: Reader Responses to Alice Munro's Fiction in Web 2.0'. *Made in Canada, Read in Spain: Essays on the Translation and Circulation of English-Canadian Literature*. Ed. Pilar Somacarrera. London: Versita, 2013. 129–44.

Sophocles. *Sophocles*. Vol. 2 of *The Complete Greek Tragedies*. Ed. David Grene and Richmond Lattimore. Chicago: U of Chicago P, 1959.

Spenser, Edmund. 'Colin Clouts Come Home Againe'. 1595. *Poetical Works*. Ed. J.C. Smith and E. de Selincourt. Introd. E. de Selincourt. Oxford: Oxford UP, 1970. 535–45.

—. 'The Shepheardes Calender'. 1579. *Poetical Works*. Ed. J.C. Smith and E. de Selincourt. Introd. E. de Selincourt. Oxford: Oxford UP, 1970. 415–67.

Stainsby, Mari. 'Alice Munro Talks with Mari Stainsby'. *British Columbia Library Quarterly* 35.1 (1971): 27–31.

Steinbeck, John. *Of Mice and Men*. Introd. Susan Shillinglaw. London: Penguin, 1994.

Stich, Klaus P. 'Letting Go with the Mind: Dionysus and Medusa in Alice Munro's "Meneseteung"'. *Canadian Literature* 169 (2001): 106–25.

Struthers, J.R. (Tim). 'Alice Munro and the American South'. 1975. Rpt. (rev. and expanded) in *Short Story Criticism: Criticism of the Works of Short Fiction Writers*. Vol. 208. Ed. Lawrence J. Trudeau. Farmington Hills, MI: Gale Cengage Learning, 99–117.

—. 'Imagining Alice Munro's "Meneseteung": The Dynamics of Co-Creation'. *Alice Munro: A Souwesto Celebration*. Ed. J.R. (Tim) Struthers and John B. Lee. *The Windsor Review* 47.2 (2014): 68–91.

—. 'In Search of the Perfect Metaphor: The Language of the Short Story and Alice Munro's "Meneseteung"'. *Critical Insights: Alice Munro*. Ed. Charles E. May. Ipswich, MA: Salem, 2013. 175–94.

—. Message to Ailsa Cox. 31 January 2023. E-mail.

—. Message to Ailsa Cox. 20 April 2023. E-mail.

—. Message to Catherine Sheldrick Ross. 25 July 2021. E-mail.
—. Message to Corinne Bigot. 12 September 2020. E-mail.
—. Personal Conversation with Hugh Hood. Montreal, Quebec. 26 February 1978.
—. 'The Real Material: An Interview with Alice Munro'. *Probable Fictions: Alice Munro's Narrative Acts*. Ed. Louis K. MacKendrick. Downsview, ON: ECW, 1983. 5–36.
— 'Reality and Ordering: The Growth of a Young Artist in *Lives of Girls and Women*'. *Essays on Canadian Writing* 3 (1975): 32–46.
—. 'Remembrance Day 1988: An Interview with Alice Munro'. *Alice Munro Country: Essays on Her Works I*. Ed. J.R. (Tim) Struthers. Toronto: Guernica Editions: 2020. 65–86.
—. Telephone Conversation with John Metcalf. 24 January 2022.
—. Telephone Conversation with Robert Thacker. 23 January 2022.
—. 'Traveling with Munro: Reading "To Reach Japan"'. *Alice Munro: Hateship, Friendship, Courtship, Loveship, Marriage; Runaway; Dear Life*. Ed. Robert Thacker. London: Bloomsbury Academic, 2016. 163–83, 231–44 passim.
Swift, Jonathan. 'Phyllis; or, The Progress of Love'. *Jonathan Swift: The Complete Poems*. Ed. Pat Rogers. Harmondsworth: Penguin, 1983. 189–92.
Szabó, Andrea F. 'Alice Munro's Australian Mirror Stories'. *Brno Studies in English* 41.2 (2015): 109–19.
Tambling, Jeremy. *Allegory*. Abingdon: Routledge, 2010. The New Critical Idiom.
Tausky, Thomas E. Unpublished interview with Alice Munro. 20 July 1984.
Tennyson, Alfred, Lord. 'Morte d'Arthur'. *Poetical Works: Including the Plays*. London: Oxford UP, 1953. 64–8. <https://www.poetryfoundation.org/poems/45370/morte-darthur>.
Thacker, Robert. *Alice Munro: Writing Her Lives: A Biography*. Toronto: McClelland & Stewart, 2005. Updated ed. Toronto: Emblem-McClelland & Stewart, 2011.
—. 'Alice Munro Country'. *Dalhousie Review* 98 (2018): 412–18.
—. *Alice Munro's Late Style: "Writing is the Final Thing"*. London: Bloomsbury Academic, 2023.
—. Interviews with Alice Munro. 21–2 August 2001. Clinton, ON.
—. Interviews with Alice Munro. 23–4 April 2004. Comox, BC.
—. 'Munro's Progress: A Review of *The Progress of Love*'. *Reading Alice Munro: 1973–2013*. Calgary, AB: U of Calgary P, 2016. 73–7.
—. *Reading Alice Munro: 1973–2013*. Calgary, AB: U of Calgary P, 2016.
—. '"This Is Not a Story, Only Life": Wondering with Alice Munro'. *Alice Munro's Miraculous Art: Critical Essays*. Ed. Janice Fiamengo and Gerald Lynch. Ottawa: U of Ottawa P, 2017. 15–40. Reappraisals: Canadian Writers 38.
—. 'What's "Material"?: The Progress of Munro Criticism, Part 2 (1998)'. *Reading Alice Munro: 1973–2013*. Calgary, AB: U of Calgary P, 2016. 167–88.
Thompson, Kent. 'Academy Stuff'. *How Stories Mean*. Ed. John Metcalf and J.R. (Tim) Struthers. Erin, ON: The Porcupine's Quill, 1993. 69–75. Critical Directions 3.
Thompson, Reg. Message to J.R. (Tim) Struthers. 30 June 2023. E-mail.
Thompson, Stith. *Motif-Index of Folk-Literature: A Classification of Narrative Elements in Folktales, Ballads, Myths, Fables, Mediaeval Romances, Exempla, Fabliaux, Jest-Books, and Local Legends*. Rev. ed. 6 vols. Bloomington: Indiana UP, 1955–8. <https://ia800408.us.archive.org/30/items/Thompson2016MotifIndex/Thompson_2016_Motif-Index.pdf>.

'Three O'Clock in the Morning'. By Julián Robledo. Lyrics by Theodora Morse using the pseudonym Dorothy Terriss. <https://en.wikipedia.org/wiki/Three_O%27 Clock_in_the_Morning>.

Todd, Paula. 'Person 2 Person: Alice Munro'. *Person 2 Person*. TVO Today Docs 5 April 2006. <https://www.youtube.com/watch?v=TlXjN6rnGb4>.

Tolstoy, Leo. *Anna Karenina*. 1878. Trans. Constance Garnett. Introd. Henri Troyat. New York: The Modern Library, 1950.

Toolan, Michael. 'Engagement via Emotional Heightening in "Passion": On the Grammatical Texture of Emotionally-Immersive Passages in Short Fiction'. [*Theoretical Approaches to Alice Munro's "Passion."* Ed. Susan Lohafer.] *Narrative* 20 (2012): 210–25.

—. 'Narrative Progression in the Short Story: First Steps in a Corpus Stylistic Approach'. *Narrative* 16 (2008): 105–20.

Treisman, Deborah. 'On "Dear Life": An Interview with Alice Munro'. *The New Yorker* 20 November 2012. <https://www.newyorker.com/books/page-turner/on-dear-life-an-interview-with-alice-munro>.

Trussler, Michael. 'Uncanny Tracks in the Snow; or, Alice Munro as Assemblage Artist'. *Alice Munro Everlasting: Essays on Her Works II*. Ed. J.R. (Tim) Struthers. Toronto: Guernica Editions, 2020. 79–102.

'Vedrai Carino'. *Don Giovanni*. By Wolfgang Amadeus Mozart. Libretto by Lorenzo Da Ponte. Perf. Cecilia Bartoli. 2 September 2009. *operalover9001*. <https://www.youtube.com/watch?v=IZM1WEm9nKw>.

Ventura, Héliane. 'Aesthetic Traces of the Ephemeral: Alice Munro's Logograms in "Vandals"'. *Tropes and Territories: Short Fiction, Postcolonial Readings, Canadian Writing in Context*. Ed. Marta Dvořák and W.H. New. Montreal, QC and Kingston, ON: McGill-Queen's UP, 2007. 309–22.

—. 'The Female Bard: Retrieving Greek Myths, Celtic Ballads, Norse Sagas, and Popular Songs'. *The Cambridge Companion to Alice Munro*. Ed. David Staines. Cambridge: Cambridge UP, 2016. 154–77.

—. Introduction. La question animale dans les nouvelles d'Alice Munro / *The Animal Question in Alice Munro's Stories*. Ed. Héliane Ventura. *Caliban: French Journal of English Studies* 57 (2017): 5–10. <https://journals.openedition.org/caliban/2594>.

—. 'The Question of Sources: Teaching Texts Versus Hypotexts'. *Alice Munro: Understanding, Adapting and Teaching*. Ed. Mirosława Buchholtz. Cham: Springer, 2016. 117–22.

—. 'Le tracé de l'écart ou "L'Origine du Monde" réinventée dans "Lichen" d'Alice Munro'. *Texte/Image: nouveaux problèmes*. Ed. Lilianne Louvel and Henri Scepi. Rennes: Presses Universitaires de Rennes, 2005. 269–81.

Vickroy, Laurie. *Trauma and Survival in Contemporary Fiction*. Charlottesville: U of Virginia P, 2002.

Virgil. *The Aeneid of Virgil*. Trans. C. Day-Lewis. 1952. New York: Doubleday Anchor, 1953.

Wachtel, Eleanor. 'Alice Munro on Writers & Company (1990)'. *Writers & Company*. CBC Radio 8 July 2016. <https://www.cbc.ca/radio/writersandcompany/eleanor-wachtel-on-her-first-interview-with-alice-munro-1.3665320>. Printed as 'An Interview with Alice Munro'. *Brick* 40 (1991): 48–53. Rpt. as 'Alice Munro' in *Writers & Company*. By Eleanor Wachtel. Toronto: Alfred A. Knopf Canada, 1993. 101–12.

Ware, Tracy. 'A Comic Streak: The Two "Fairly Happy" Heroines of Alice Munro's

"Wigtime"'. *Alice Munro Everlasting: Essays on Her Works II*. Ed. J.R. (Tim) Struthers. Toronto: Guernica Editions, 2020. 229–43.

—. 'Momentous Shifts and Unimagined Changes in "Jakarta"'. *Alice Munro's Miraculous Art: Critical Essays*. Ed. Janice Fiamengo and Gerald Lynch. Ottawa: U of Ottawa P, 2017. 159–75. Reappraisals: Canadian Writers 38.

Weaver, John. 'Society and Culture in Rural and Small-Town Ontario: Alice Munro's Testimony on the Forty Years from 1945 to 1985'. *Alice Munro Country: Essays on Her Works I*. Ed. J.R. (Tim) Struthers. Toronto: Guernica Editions, 2020. 155–80.

Weiss, Allan. *The Mini-Cycle*. New York: Routledge, 2021. Routledge New Textual Studies in Literature.

Welty, Eudora. 'A Curtain of Green'. *A Curtain of Green and Other Stories*. 1941. San Diego, CA: Harcourt Brace Jovanovich, 1991. 165–73.

—. 'How I Write'. *The Virginia Quarterly Review* 31 (1955): 240–51. Rpt. (rev.) as 'Writing and Analyzing a Story'. *The Eye of the Story: Selected Essays and Reviews*. New York: Random House, 1978. 107–15.

Wheeler, Anne, dir. *Edge of Madness*. Montreal, QC: CinéGroupe / Credo Entertainment / Gregorian Films, 2002.

Williams, Tennessee. *A Streetcar Named Desire*. 1947. Introd. Arthur Miller. New York: New Directions, 2004.

Woolf, Virginia. *A Room of One's Own*. London: Penguin, 2014.

—. *To the Lighthouse*. Ed. Stella McNichol. Introd. Hermione Lee. London: Penguin, 2019.

—. *The Waves*. Introd. Kate Flint. London: Penguin, 2019.

—. 'The Wrong Way of Reading'. *The Essays of Virginia Woolf: Volume III: 1919–1924*. Ed. Andrew McNeillie. London: Hogarth, 1988. 218–23.

'Writers on Munro'. *The New Yorker* 10 October 2013. <https://www.newyorker.com/books/page-turner/writers-on-munro>.

Yeats, W.B. *Mythologies*. London: Macmillan, 1959.

York, Lorraine M. *"The Other Side of Dailiness": Photography in the Works of Alice Munro, Timothy Findley, Michael Ondaatje and Margaret Laurence*. Toronto: ECW, 1988.

Index of Stories and Story Collections

1. By Alice Munro

'Accident', 2
'The Albanian Virgin', 4, 9, 71, 88–9, 91–2, 103, 107–13, 118–19, 121–2, 125n

'The Beggar Maid', 3, 72
The Beggar Maid: Stories of Flo and Rose, 3, 4–5, 7, 40–1, 81, 148

'Carried Away', 4, 45, 89–93, 99–103, 113, 118, 119, 124–5, 131
'Chaddeleys and Flemings', 3
'Chance', 81
'The Children Stay', 151, 155, 159
'Circle of Prayer', 39, 40–1, 46, 47–8
'Comfort', 128, 149
'Cortes Island', 9, 33, 128, 151, 155–64

Dance of the Happy Shades, 6, 8, 29, 61–2, 106, 125n, 141, 142–3, 158–9
'Dance of the Happy Shades', 8, 29
Dear Life, 6, 7, 29, 71, 132
'Dear Life', 6, 7, 61, 132–3, 144
'Differently', 7, 51, 55–61, 69, 77, 79–80, 129
'Dimensions', 8
'Dulse', 3

'Epilogue: Messenger', 70
'Epilogue: The Photographer', 66–7

'Family Furnishings', 2
'Fathers', 1

'The Ferguson Girls Must Never Marry', 2–3
'Finale', 29
'Fits', 8, 13
'Five Points', 67–71, 80, 81, 85, 86
'Floating Bridge', 120
Friend of My Youth, 3, 4, 6–7, 8, 25, 51–87, 94, 129, 142–3, 147
'Friend of My Youth', 4, 11, 51, 53, 55–6, 59, 61–7, 70–1, 75–6, 77, 80, 81–2, 84, 86, 142–3

'Goodness and Mercy', 55, 83, 87

'Hard-Luck Stories', 151
Hateship, Friendship, Courtship, Loveship, Marriage, 1–2, 5
'Hateship, Friendship, Courtship, Loveship, Marriage', 1
'Hold Me Fast, Don't Let Me Pass', 75–6, 81, 85, 87
'Home', 1, 4

'Images', 46, 106, 142–3, 144

'The Jack Randa Hotel', 89, 90, 93–4, 103, 107, 118–19, 124–5
'Jakarta', 57, 127, 128–9, 133, 147–55, 158, 159
'Jesse and Meribeth', 10

'Labor Day Dinner', 3
'Lichen', 13, 23–33, 118, 130

Lives of Girls and Women, 18, 56, 65, 66, 81, 128, 138
The Love of a Good Woman, 3, 4, 6–7, 8, 29, 36, 57, 91, 113, 118, 127–65
'The Love of a Good Woman', 3, 4, 118, 126n, 127, 129, 132–48, 156–7, 163, 165
'The Love of a Good Woman: A Murder, a Mystery, a Romance', 133
'Lying Under the Apple Tree', 1

'Meneseteung', 4, 9, 25, 51, 52, 63, 67, 71–7, 81, 85, 86, 87
'Miles City, Montana', 4, 13, 28
'Mischief', 148, 149, 150, 152, 154, 158
'Monsieur les Deux Chapeaux', 9, 13, 34–45
'The Moon in the Orange Street Skating Rink', 27
The Moons of Jupiter, 1–5, 53, 151
'The Moons of Jupiter', 3
'My Mother's Dream', 29, 36, 127, 129

'No Advantages', 28

'The Office', 158–9, 162
'Oh, What Avails', 55, 57, 81, 83, 85–7
Open Secrets, 3, 4, 6–7, 8, 20–1, 25, 44–5, 71, 80, 88–126, 129, 131, 135, 165
'Open Secrets', 25, 80, 89, 90–1, 92, 93, 95–9, 119, 120, 122–4, 125
'Oranges and Apples', 52–3, 57, 82, 86–7, 94
'The Ottawa Valley', 4, 62

'Passion', 132, 150
'The Peace of Utrecht', 61–2
'Pictures of the Ice', 52, 81, 84–5, 86
'Places at Home', 4
The Progress of Love, 3, 4, 5, 6–50, 118, 129
'The Progress of Love', 4, 9–23, 26, 27, 33, 36, 38, 39, 46, 56
'Prue', 3

'A Queer Streak', 11, 16–17, 46, 47

'A Real Life', 89, 93, 103–7, 119–20, 125n
'Rich as Stink', 113, 127, 129
'Royal Beatings', 3, 6–7
Runaway, 2, 55, 81, 155

'Save the Reaper', 120, 127, 129
'Silence', 81
Something I've Been Meaning To Tell You, 22, 62
'Soon', 81
'Spaceships Have Landed', 89–91, 94–5, 103, 113, 119–20, 125n
'Spelling', 33
'The Stone in the Field', 143

'Tell Me Yes or No', 22
'The Time of Death', 141
'To Reach Japan', 71
Too Much Happiness, 8, 148
'The Turkey Season', 3

'Vandals', 20–1, 88, 90–1, 93, 95, 113–18, 119–21, 123, 125
The View from Castle Rock, 1, 28, 70, 106, 125

'Walker Brothers Cowboy', 8, 125n
'What Do You Want To Know For?', 125n
'What Is Remembered', 150
'White Dump', 9, 13, 26, 32–3, 34, 46, 48–9
Who Do You Think You Are?, 3, 4–5, 6–7, 40–1, 81, 148
'Who Do You Think You Are?', 40–1
'Wigtime', 57, 69, 77–80, 83–4, 85, 87
'A Wilderness Station', 89, 90–2, 118, 121, 122, 124–5, 126n
'Winter Wind', 4
'Working for a Living', 1, 106

2. By Other Writers

'At the Bay' (Katherine Mansfield), 10, 150

'Beyond' (William Faulkner), 49
'Bluebeard' (Jacob and Wilhelm Grimm), 134, 143
'Briar Rose' (Jacob and Wilhelm Grimm), 142

'Crotch shot' (George Elliott), 30
'A Curtain of Green' (Eudora Welty), 159

'The Dead' (James Joyce), 20–1, 22, 36, 37, 130
'Death by Landscape' (Margaret Atwood), 97–8
Dubliners (James Joyce), 22, 130

'The End of It' (Hugh Hood), 19–20

'The Fox' (D.H. Lawrence), 150–1

'The Garden Party' (Katherine Mansfield), 31
'Grace' (James Joyce), 22

'My Heart Is Broken' (Mavis Gallant), 19–20

'Prelude' (Katherine Mansfield), 10
'The Purloined Letter' (Edgar Allan Poe), 112

'Red Leaves' (William Faulkner), 44–5

Saints and Sinners (Edna O'Brien), 41
'Sleeping Beauty' (Jacob and Wilhelm Grimm), 142, 144

'The Turn of the Screw' (Henry James), 59–60

'The Yellow Wallpaper' (Charlotte Perkins Gilman), 18

General Index

1 Corinthians, 30

'Academy Stuff' (Kent Thompson), 11
The Aeneid of Virgil (Virgil), 123
Afterword to *Emily of New Moon* (Alice Munro), 60
Alice Liddell as 'The Beggar Maid' (Lewis Carroll), 72–3
Alice Munro (Ailsa Cox), 10, 33, 133
Alice Munro (Coral Ann Howells), 23, 54, 74, 75, 89, 93, 94, 133
Alice Munro (E.D. Blodgett), 9, 43
Alice Munro: A Double Life (Catherine Sheldrick Ross), 9, 25, 48, 156, 157, 163
Alice Munro: Paradox and Parallel (W.R. Martin), 11, 27
Alice Munro: Writing Her Lives: A Biography (Robert Thacker), 2, 4, 5, 10, 53, 62, 67, 81, 90, 93, 96–7, 107, 125n, 126n
Alice Munro's Late Style: "Writing is the Final Thing" (Robert Thacker), 1, 3, 5, 149
Alice Munro's Narrative Art (Isla Duncan), 31, 33, 65, 134, 137, 145
Alice's Adventures in Wonderland (Lewis Carroll), 72–3
The Allegory of Love: A Study in Medieval Tradition (C.S. Lewis), 21
Anatomy of Criticism: Four Essays (Northrop Frye), 20, 23, 35
"And Write She Did": Prerequisites for Women's Writing in the Writer Narratives of Virginia Woolf and Alice Munro (Eva Mendez), 24

Andersen, Doris, 156–7, 163
Anna Karenina (Leo Tolstoy), 37, 132
Arbus, Diane, 31
Aristophanes, 20
Armatrading, Joan, 36
Astrophil and Stella (Sir Philip Sidney), 26
Atwood, Margaret, 18, 22, 97–8
Austen, Jane, 104, 106

Bakhtin, Mikhail, 63, 67, 84
Banerjee, Sidhartha, 141–2
The Banquet of Dante Alighieri (Dante Alighieri), 15
Beautiful Losers (Leonard Cohen), 26
Being and Nothingness: An Essay on Phenomenological Ontology (Jean-Paul Sartre), 45
Bentley, Lucile, 90
Beran, Carol L., 60, 77, 134
Bergman, Ingmar, 30
Bergson, Henri, 75
Bigot, Corinne, 8, 20–1, 27, 35, 54, 88–126
Blaise, Clark, 12
Blake, William, 21
Blanchard, Gérard, 122
Blodgett, E.D., 9, 43
Bloom, Harold, 17, 35
The Book of Job, 21, 24
The Book of Kells: Reproductions from the Manuscript in Trinity College Dublin, 26, 130
The Book of Psalms, 83
A Book of Saints and Wonders (Lady Gregory), 26

Boyce, Pleuke, 135
Boyle, Harry, 128
Brontë, Charlotte, Emily and Ann, 25, 53
Brontë, Emily, 25, 37, 53, 155–6
Brooks, Peter, 54
Butt, William, 98–9
Byatt, A.S., 131

The Cambridge Introduction to the Short Story in English (Adrian Hunter), 55
Carrington, Ildikó de Papp, 43, 92, 98, 100, 102, 126n, 137
Carroll, Lewis, 72–3
Carscallen, James, 27, 45
Chariots of Fire (Hugh Hudson, dir.), 42
Charles, Michel, 123–4
Cicurel, Francine, 123
'Circles' (Ralph Waldo Emerson), 6, 34
Circles: Fun Ideas for Getting A-Round in Math (Catherine Sheldrick Ross), 7
Clark, Miriam Marty, 118
Clark, Timothy, 55, 63
Cohen, Leonard, 26
'The Colonel's Hash Resettled' (Alice Munro), 46
Colville, Georgiana M.M., 88, 108, 109, 110
'Contributors' Notes' to *Prize Stories 1997: The O. Henry Awards* on 'The Love of a Good Woman' (Alice Munro), 156–7
Controlling the Uncontrollable: The Fiction of Alice Munro (Ildikó de Papp Carrington), 43
Courbet, Gustave, 30–1
Cox, Ailsa, 8, 10, 11, 31, 33, 51–87, 71–2, 133, 158–9

Da Ponte, Lorenzo, 83
Dance of the Sexes: Art and Gender in the Fiction of Alice Munro (Beverly J. Rasporich), 23, 27, 39, 159
Dante Alighieri, 11, 15–16
David (Michelangelo), 26
Davies, Robertson, 40–1
Dawson, Carrie, 115, 120
Deleuze, Gilles, and Félix Guattari, 89

Deux Chapeaux (Édouard Manet), 34
Dickens, Charles, 100
Dickinson, Emily, 13
Dictionary of Mythology Folklore and Symbols (Gertrude Jobes), 26
The Divine Comedy (Dante Alighieri), 15–16
The Diviners (Margaret Laurence), 128
Don Giovanni (Wolfgang Amadeus Mozart), 83
Duffy, Dennis, 28, 45, 133–4, 143
Duncan, Isla, 31, 33, 65, 134, 137, 145, 146
Duplessis, Rachel Blau, 45
Durham, M. Edith, 112–13, 126n

Edge of Madness (Anne Wheeler, dir.), 122, 126n
'Editing the Best' (John Metcalf), 28
Eliot, George, 103, 140
Eliot, T.S., 44
Elliott, George, 30
Emerson, Ralph Waldo, 6, 34
Emily of New Moon (L.M. Montgomery), 60
L'être et le néant: Essai d'ontologie phénoménologique (Jean-Paul Sartre), 45
Evergreen Islands: The Islands of the Inside Passage: Quadra to Malcolm (Doris Andersen), 156–7, 163

The Fact of a Body: A Murder and a Memoir (Alexandria Marzano-Lesnevich), 91, 126n
A Family On Their Lawn One Sunday in Westchester, New York (Diane Arbus), 31
Faulkner, William, 44–5, 49
Fifth Business (Robertson Davies), 40–1
Fitzgerald, F. Scott, 48
Flaubert, Gustave, 88
Ford, Richard, 23
Foy, Nathalie, 88, 113
France, Louise, 128, 155
Francesconi, Sabrina, 120, 149
Fremlin, Gerald, 24, 130
Fremlin, Gerald, with Arthur H. Robinson, 24

General Index

Freud, Sigmund, 16, 22, 23, 31, 32, 37, 39, 40, 43
Freud and the Rat Man (Patrick J. Mahony), 31
Frye, Northrop, 20, 23, 35
Fulford, Robert, 156

Gallant, Mavis, 19–20
Genesis, 24, 42
Gerlach, John, 132–3
Gibson, Douglas, 1, 5, 96–7
Gilman, Charlotte Perkins, 18
Glover, Douglas, 55–6, 138, 141
Goldman, Marlene, 117
The Great Gatsby (F. Scott Fitzgerald), 48
Gregory, Lady, 26
Guignery, Vanessa, 118
Gzowski, Peter, 88, 111

Hadley, Tessa, 4, 56, 58
Hamlet: Poem Unlimited (Harold Bloom), 35
Hancock, Geoff, 60
Hard Times (Charles Dickens), 100
Hardy, Thomas, 49, 100
Hay, Elizabeth, 53–4
Heller, Deborah, 51, 74, 94
Herman, Judith Lewis, 116
High Albania (M. Edith Durham), 112–13, 126n
Hood, Hugh, 19–20, 22, 28, 46–7
'How I Write' (Eudora Welty), 6, 21, 49–50
Howells, Coral Ann, 23, 54, 74, 75, 89, 93, 94, 133
Hunter, Adrian, 55

"I Am Your Brother": Short Story Studies (Charles E. May), 34, 42–3
Interpretation as Pragmatics (Jean-Jacques Lecercle), 124
The Interpretation of Dreams (Sigmund Freud), 16, 22, 23, 37, 39, 40, 43
Introduction à l'étude des textes (Michel Charles), 123–4
Introduction to *Selected Stories* (Alice Munro), 8

Introduction to *The Moons of Jupiter* (Alice Munro), 53
Iser, Wolfgang, 122

James, Henry, 28, 46–7, 59–60
Jenny, Laurent, 102
Jeremiah, 28
Jernigan, Kim, 72, 75
Jobes, Gertrude, 26
Johnston, Basil H., 45
Jouve, Vincent, 122
Joyce, James, 11, 16, 18, 20–1, 22, 33, 36, 37, 53, 130
'The Justice-Dealing Machine' (Clark Blaise), 12

King, Thomas, 10
King Lear (William Shakespeare), 44
Kristeva, Julia, 73, 74

Landor, Walter Savage, 83, 85
LaPierre, Megan, 29
Laughter: An Essay on the Meaning of the Comic (Henri Bergson), 75
Laurence, Margaret, 128
Lawrence, D.H., 150–1
Lecercle, Jean-Jacques, 124
Lecker, Robert, 90, 92, 100
Lee, Monika, 137
La lettre (Gérard Blanchard), 122
Levene, Mark, 19, 91, 111, 117
Lewis, C.S., 21
Lives of Mothers & Daughters: Growing Up with Alice Munro (Sheila Munro), 52–3
Lohafer, Susan, 14, 48, 162
The Lonely Voice: A Study of the Short Story (Frank O'Connor), 42–3, 65–6
Löschnigg, Maria, 103
Lundén, Rolf, 81

Macbeth (William Shakespeare), 66
Macfarlane, David, 129
Mackay, Charles, 162
MacKendrick, Louis K., 46, 72
Mahony, Patrick J., 31
Manet, Édouard, 34
Mansfield, Katherine, 10, 31, 33, 150

Maps as Mediated Seeing: Fundamentals of Cartography (Gerald Fremlin with Arthur H. Robinson), 24
Marlatt, Daphne, 17
The Marriage of Heaven and Hell (William Blake), 21
Martin, W.R., 11, 27
Martin, W.R., and Warren U. Ober, 52, 89, 103
Marzano-Lesnevich, Alexandria, 91, 126n
May, Charles E., 34, 42–3
McCombs, Judith, 133–4
McCulloch, Jeanne, and Mona Simpson, 24, 61
McGill, Robert, 88–9
McLuhan, Herbert Marshall, 39
Mendez, Eva, 24
Metamorphoses (Ovid), 27, 111, 118–21, 123, 125
Metcalf, John, 28
Michelangelo, 26
Micros, Marianne, 26, 27, 29, 72
Middlemarch (George Eliot), 103, 140
Miller, Judith Maclean, 141, 143
Milton, John, 29, 37
The Mini-Cycle (Allan Weiss), 81
Mitchell, W.J.T., 7
Montgomery, L.M., 60
Moore, Lorrie, 2, 5
Mothers and Other Clowns: The Stories of Alice Munro (Magdalene Redekop), 9–10, 12, 15, 23, 26, 31, 61, 118
Motif-Index of Folk-Literature: A Classification of Narrative Elements in Folktales, Ballads, Myths, Fables, Mediaeval Romances, Exempla, Fabliaux, Jest-Books, and Local Legends (Stith Thompson), 140
Mozart, Wolfgang Amadeus, 83
Munro, Alice, 6, 8, 23–4, 46, 53, 55, 60, 156–7, 158
Munro, Sheila, 52–3
Mythologies (W.B. Yeats), 26

The National Atlas of Canada, 4th ed. (Gerald Fremlin, Editor-in-Chief), 24
New, W.H., 5

The New Age / Le nouveau siècle (Hugh Hood), 46–7

O'Brien, Edna, 41
O'Connor, Frank, 42–3, 65–6
Oedipus Rex (Sophocles), 23
Of Mice and Men (John Steinbeck), 126n
'On Writing "The Office"' (Alice Munro), 158
Ong, Walter J., 29
Orality and Literacy: The Technologizing of the Word (Walter J. Ong), 29
L'Origine du Monde (Gustave Courbet), 30–1
The Other Country: Patterns in the Writing of Alice Munro (James Carscallen), 27, 45
"The Other Side of Dailiness": Photography in the Works of Alice Munro, Timothy Findley, Michael Ondaatje and Margaret Laurence (Lorraine M. York), 44
Ovid, 27, 111, 118–21, 123, 125

Palusci, Oriana, 8
Pangman, Jennifer, 16
Paradise Lost (John Milton), 29, 37
La parole singulière (Laurent Jenny), 102
'Perform[ing] on the Stage of Her Text' (Daphne Marlatt), 17
Persuasion (Jane Austen), 106
The Pleasures of Reading: A Booklover's Alphabet (Catherine Sheldrick Ross), 134
Poems (Charlotte, Emily and Anne Brontë), 25
The Poetic Edda (Lee M. Hollander, trans.), 9, 49
Poliner, Elizabeth, 130
A Portrait of the Artist as a Young Man (James Joyce), 18
Possibility-Space and Its Imaginative Variations in Alice Munro's Short Stories (Ulrica Skagert), 110–11
Powers of Horror: An Essay on Abjection (Julia Kristeva), 73, 74

Pride and Prejudice (Jane Austen), 104
Probable Fictions: Alice Munro's Narrative Acts (MacKendrick, Louis K., ed.), 46
Prose, Francine, 9
Proust, Marcel, 58

Rasporich, Beverly J., 23, 27, 39, 159
Reading Alice Munro: 1973–2013 (Robert Thacker), 12, 21, 23, 46
Reading for Storyness: Preclosure Theory, Empirical Poetics, and Culture in the Short Story (Susan Lohafer), 14, 48, 162
Reading Like a Writer: A Guide for People Who Love Books and for Those Who Want To Write Them (Francine Prose), 9
Redekop, Magdalene, 9–10, 12, 15, 23, 25, 26, 31, 61, 118, 130
The Revelation of St. John the Divine, 32
Romeo and Juliet (William Shakespeare), 27
A Room of One's Own (Virginia Woolf), 149–50, 158
Ross, Catherine Sheldrick, 6, 7, 8, 9, 25, 33, 45, 48, 127–65, 127, 131, 132, 134, 137, 144, 156, 157, 163
Royle, Nicholas, 55, 63

Saint Joan: A Chronicle Play in Six Scenes and an Epilogue (Bernard Shaw), 23
Sartre, Jean-Paul, 45
The Scenic Art (Hugh Hood), 46–7
The Scenic Art: Notes on Acting and the Drama 1872–1901 (Henry James), 46–7
The Secular Scripture: A Study of the Structure of Romance (Northrop Frye), 23
Seduced by Story: The Use and Abuse of Narrative (Peter Brooks), 54
Shakespeare, William, 18, 23, 26, 27, 29–30, 35, 44, 47, 57, 66, 130
Shaw, Bernard, 23
Short Fiction in Theory & Practice (Ailsa Cox), 8

'Show Some Emotion' (Joan Armatrading), 36
Sidney, Sir Philip, 26, 27
Skagert, Ulrica, 110–11
Smith, Ron, 135
Smith, Stephen, 129
Somacarrera, Pilar, 132
Sophocles, 20, 23
Spenser, Edmund, 23, 34, 44
Stainsby, Mari, 4–5
Steinbeck, John, 126n
Stich, Klaus P., 74
A Streetcar Named Desire (Tennessee Williams), 26
Struthers, J.R. (Tim), 6–50, 6, 14, 18, 60, 67, 70, 123, 127, 129, 159
Swann's Way (Marcel Proust), 58
Swift, Jonathan, 23, 27, 34
Szabó, Andrea F., 93–4, 107

Tausky, Thomas E., 155–6, 157
Tennyson, Alfred, Lord, 53, 86
Thacker, Robert, 1–5, 10, 12, 21, 23, 25, 46, 53, 62, 67, 81, 90, 93, 96–7, 107, 125n, 126n, 149
Thompson, Kent, 11
Thompson, Reg, 10
Thompson, Stith, 140
A Thousand Plateaus: Capitalism and Schizophrenia (Gilles Deleuze and Félix Guattari), 89
'Three O'Clock in the Morning' (Julián Robledo), 48
Through a Glass Darkly (Ingmar Bergman, dir.), 30
Through the Looking-Glass: And What Alice Found There (Lewis Carroll), 72–3
To the Lighthouse (Virginia Woolf), 25, 32, 130
Todd, Paula, 61
Tolstoy, Leo, 37, 53, 132
Toolan, Michael, 135, 147
Towles, Amor, 131
The Tragedy of Hamlet, Prince of Denmark: The First Folio (1623) (William Shakespeare), 18, 23, 35, 47
Trauma and Recovery (Judith Lewis Herman), 116

Trauma and Survival in Contemporary Fiction (Laurie Vickroy), 116
Treisman, Deborah, 132
Trussler, Michael, 90
The Truth about Stories: A Native Narrative (Thomas King), 10
Twelfth Night (William Shakespeare), 26, 29–30

Ulysses: The Corrected Text (James Joyce), 16, 18
The United Stories of America: Studies in the Short Story Composite (Rolf Lundén), 81

'Vedrai, carino' (Cecilia Bartoli, perf.), 83
Ventura, Héliane, 30–1, 49, 90, 109, 115, 117, 118
Vickroy, Laurie, 116
Virgil, 122, 123

Wachtel, Eleanor, 51, 61–2, 66–7, 147

Ware, Tracy, 80, 148, 153
The Waste Land (T.S. Eliot), 44
The Waves (Virginia Woolf), 24–5
Weaver, John, 4–5, 52
Weiss, Allan, 81
Welty, Eudora, 6, 21, 49–50, 53, 159
'What Is Real?' (Alice Munro), 6, 8, 23–4, 55
Wheeler, Anne, 122, 126n
Williams, Tennessee, 26
Woolf, Virginia, 24–5, 32, 33, 122, 130, 149–50, 158
Writing Beyond the Ending: Narrative Strategies of Twentieth-Century Women Writers (Rachel Blau Duplessis), 45
'The Wrong Way of Reading' (Virginia Woolf), 122
Wuthering Heights (Emily Brontë), 25, 37, 155–6

Yeats, W.B., 26
York, Lorraine M., 44